PAUL AND HIS
OPPONENTS

PAULINE STUDIES

SERIES EDITOR
Stanley E. Porter
MCMASTER DIVINITY COLLEGE
HAMILTON, ONTARIO, CANADA

VOLUME 2

PAUL AND HIS
OPPONENTS

PAUL AND HIS OPPONENTS

Edited by
Stanley E. Porter

Society of Biblical Literature
Atlanta

Copyright © 2005 by Koninklijke Brill NV, Leiden,
The Netherlands

This edition published under license from Koninklijke Brill NV,
Leiden, The Netherlands by the Society of Biblical Literature.

All rights reserved. No part of this work may be reproduced or transmitted in any form or by any means, electronic or mechanical, including photocopying and recording, or by any means of any information storage or retrieval system, except as may be expressly permitted by the 1976 Copyright Act or in writing from the Publisher. Requests for permission should be addressed in writing to the Rights and Permissions Department, Koninklijke Brill NV, Leiden, The Netherlands.

Authorization to photocopy items for internal or personal use is granted by Brill provided that the appropriate fees are paid directly to The Copyright Clearance Center, 222 Rosewood Drive, Suite 910, Danvers, MA 01923, USA. Fees are subject to change.

Library of Congress Cataloging-in-Publication Data

Paul and his opponents / [edited by] by Stanley E. Porter.
      p. cm. – (Pauline studies ; v. 2)
      Originally published: Leiden ; Boston : Brill, 2005.
      Includes bibliographical references and index.
      ISBN 978-1-58983-430-9 (paper binding : alk. paper)
  1. Paul, the Apostle, Saint–Adversaries. 2. Bible. N.T. Epistles of Paul–Criticism, interpretation, etc. I. Porter, Stanley E., 1956–
    BS2506.3.P375 2009
    225.9'2–dc22

2009011936

Printed in the United States of America
on acid-free paper

CONTENTS

Preface	vii
Abbreviations	ix
Introduction to the Study of Paul's Opponents *Stanley E. Porter*	1
Studying Paul's Opponents: Advances and Challenges *Jerry L. Sumney*	7
Intruding "Spies" and "Pseudo-brethren": The Jewish Intra-Group Politics of Paul's Jerusalem Meeting (Gal 2:1–10) *Mark D. Nanos*	59
Apostolic Identity and the Conflicts in Corinth and Galatia *N. H. Taylor*	99
Reflections Concerning Paul's "Opponents" in Galatia *John C. Hurd*	129
Did Paul Have Opponents in Rome and What Were They Opposing? *Stanley E. Porter*	149
The Opponents at Colossae *Christian Stettler*	169
Paul and "Works of Law" Language in Late Antiquity *Craig A. Evans*	201
Paul and the Imperial Cult *Ross Saunders*	227
Index of Ancient Sources	239
Index of Modern Authors	251

PREFACE

This volume on Paul and his opponents follows on from the previous volume, *The Pauline Canon*, ed. Stanley E. Porter (PAST 1; Leiden: Brill, 2004), as the second in the Pauline Studies series published by Brill Publishers of Leiden. The reception to the first volume of this projected five (or more) volume series has been very encouraging, and I wish to thank those who have used the book for their comments regarding that volume, as well as the larger project. Like its predecessor, this volume brings together a number of different papers by leading scholars in recent discussion of the topic of Paul and his opponents. The balance of this volume is reflective of the general tenor of current discussion of the topic of Paul and his opponents. Subsequent volumes currently scheduled to appear are as follows:

Volume 3: Paul the Theologian
Volume 4: Paul's World
Volume 5: Paul: Jew, Greek and Roman

As I mentioned in the first volume, I would like to invite any scholars interested in making contributions to one or more of these volumes to be in contact with me regarding submission. Contact information is provided below. The topics of the volumes are being defined and interpreted broadly, so that papers that deal, for example, with clearly related subjects, such as the Paul of the Letters and of Acts, we hope will be able to find a home in these collections of papers. Papers for the third and fourth volumes are already being gathered for publication, in anticipation of the appearance of these volumes in a timely manner to keep the series moving forward with one volume appearing each year. We are also beginning to assess topics for future volumes, should the series be extended due to scholarly and readerly interest in it and its contribution to the wider field of Pauline studies. Suggestions for such volumes are always welcome.

I would again like to thank all of the individual authors for their worthy contribution to this second volume of essays in the PAST series. There is little overlap in the contributors from the first to the second volume (the present editor excepted), but this is not intentional. Multiple submissions by scholars with wide-ranging interests are welcome. This volume brings a number of important voices into conversation in this one volume on this important topic. Many, if not most, scholars would not be able to do their work if it were not for their institutions that support them. I wish, on the authors' behalf, to thank their institutions for such tangible efforts, as well as the intangible encouragement and environments that enable such scholarship to take place. I would also like to thank the several people at Brill, including Louise Schouten, Hans van der Meij, and Mattie Kuiper, who have continued to be an encouragement as this project not only took shape but has continued to develop and come to timely fruition. My sincere hope is that this volume will make a significant contribution to the topic of Paul's opponents.

Stanley E. Porter

McMaster Divinity College
1280 Main St. W.
Hamilton, ON, Canada L8S 4K1
princpl@mcmaster.ca

ABBREVIATIONS

AB	Anchor Bible
ABRL	Anchor Bible Reference Library
ACNT	Augsburg Commentaries on the New Testament
AGJU	Arbeiten zur Geschichte des antiken Judentums und des Urchristentums
AnBib	Analecta biblica
ANRW	*Aufstieg und Niedergang der römischen Welt*
ANTC	Abingdon New Testament Commentaries
APOT	R. H. Charles (ed.), *Apocrypha and Pseudepigrapha of the Old Testament* (2 vols.; Oxford: Clarendon Press, 1913)
ArBib	Aramaic Bible
AUSS	*Andrews University Seminary Studies*
BAFCS	Book of Acts in its First Century Setting
BAGD	W. Bauer, W. F. Arndt, F. W. Gingrich and F. W. Danker, *Greek–English Lexicon of the New Testament and Other Early Christian Literature* (second edition; Chicago: University of Chicago Press, 1979)
BETL	Bibliotheca ephemeridum theologicarum lovaniensium
BFCT	Beiträge zur Förderung christlicher Theologie
Bib	*Biblica*
BibLeb	*Bibel und Leben*
BibSac	*Bibliotheca Sacra*
BIS	Biblical Interpretation Series
BNTC	Black's New Testament Commentaries
BZNW	Beihefte zur Zeitschrift für die neutestamentliche Wissenschaft
CBQ	*Catholic Biblical Quarterly*
CBQMS	Catholic Biblical Quarterly Monograph Series
CJT	*Canadian Journal of Theology*
ConBNT	Conectanea neotestamentica
EB	Etudes bibliques
EKKNT	Evangelisch-katholischer Kommentar zum Neuen Testament
ETL	*Ephemerides theologicarum lovaniensium*
ETS	Erfurter theologische Studien

FRLANT	Forschungen zur Religion und Literatur des Alten und Neuen Testaments
HNT	Handbuch zum Neuen Testament
HNTC	Harper's New Testament Commentaries
HO	Handbuch der Orientalistik
HSS	Harvard Semitic Studies
HTKNT	Herders theologischer Kommentar zum Neuen Testament
HTR	*Harvard Theological Review*
HTS	Harvard Theological Studies
IBC	Interpretation: A Biblical Commentary for Teaching and Preaching
ICC	International Critical Commentary
Int	*Interpretation*
JBL	*Journal of Biblical Literature*
JCPS	Jewish and Christian Perspectives Series
JR	*Journal of Religion*
JRS	*Journal of Religious Studies*
JSNT	*Journal for the Study of the New Testament*
JSNTSup	Journal for the Study of the New Testament Supplement Series
JSOTSup	Journal for the Study of the Old Testament Supplement Series
JTS	*Journal of Theological Studies*
KNT	Kommentar zum Neuen Testament
LTQ	*Lexington Theological Quarterly*
MeyerK	H. A. W. Meyer (ed.), Kritisch-exegetischer Kommentar über das Neue Testament
MNTC	Moffatt New Testament Commentary
MTS	Marburger theologische Studien
NCB	New Century Bible
NEchtB	Neue Echter Bibel
Neot	*Neotestamentica*
NHS	Nag Hammadi Codices
NIBCNT	New International Biblical Commentary on the New Testament
NICNT	New International Commentary, New Testament
NIGTC	New International Greek Testament Commentary
NovT	*Novum Testamentum*
NovTSup	Novum Testamentum Supplements
NTD	Das Neue Testament Deutsch
NTS	*New Testament Studies*

NTTS	New Testament Tools and Studies
ÖTK	Ökumenischer Taschenbuch-Kommentar
OTL	Old Testament Library
OTP	J. H. Charlesworth (ed.), *Old Testament Pseudepigrapha* (2 vols.; New York: Doubleday, 1983)
RB	*Revue Biblique*
RevQ	*Revue de Qumran*
RNT	Regensburger Neues Testament
SBLDS	Society of Biblical Literature Dissertation Series
SBLSBS	Society of Biblical Literature Sources for Biblical Study
SBLSCS	Society of Biblical Literature Septuagint and Cognate Studies
SBM	Stuttgarter biblische Monographien
SBT	Studies in Biblical Theology
SD	Studies and Documents
SE	*Studia Evangelica*
SHVL	Skrifter Utgivna Av Kungl. Humanistika Vetenskapssamfundet i Lund
SJ	Studia judaica
SJT	*Scottish Journal of Theology*
SNT	Studien zum Neuen Testament
SNTSMS	Society for New Testament Studies Monograph Series
SP	Sacra Pagina
ST	*Studia theologica*
SUNT	Studien zur Umwelt des Neuen Testaments
TDNT	G. Kittel and G. Friedrich (eds.), *Theological Dictionary of the New Testament* (10 vols.; trans. G. W. Bromiley; Grand Rapids: Eerdmans, 1964–76)
ThSt	Theologische Studiën
TNTC	Tyndale New Testament Commentaries
WBC	Word Biblical Commentary
WD	*Wort und Dienst*
WJT	*Westminster Journal of Theology*
WMANT	Wissenschaftliche Monographien zum Alten und Neuen Testament
WUNT	Wissenschaftliche Untersuchungen zum Neuen Testament
ZBK	Zürcher Bibelkommentare
ZNW	*Zeitschrift für die neutestamentliche Wissenschaft*

INTRODUCTION TO THE STUDY OF PAUL'S OPPONENTS

STANLEY E. PORTER
McMaster Divinity College
Hamilton, ON, Canada

There are three major questions that readily emerge in discussion of Paul and his opponents: defining what one means by Paul's opponents; determining the best method for discussing such opponents; and differentiating and describing the opponents. Each of these questions is treated in various ways in this volume—without exhausting the topic and often by suggesting areas for further and continued study and research.

The first question is how one defines the notion of opponents. It has long been recognized in critical scholarship that Paul was faced with situations in which there was some opposition to his work.[1] This opposition has come to be characterized in terms of his opponents. As a result, an accepted axiom of Pauline studies is that Paul was frequently faced with opposition in various places during his missionary work, and this opposition has provided a means of accounting for the content of Paul's letters. Various commentaries and other critical exegetical works on Paul's letters often assume the presence of Pauline opponents, and treatments continue to be written that attempt to define these opponents. However, it is surprising how few of these critical works actually attempt to define what one means by an opponent. No doubt this is at least in part due to the difficulty of definition itself, especially when one has a relatively limited and constricted form and amount of evidence. The evidence is limited for the most part to Paul's response to a situation. The resultant reconstructive readings have often been criticized because they lack the desired controls. The problem is compounded by the fact that opposition, if and when present, can involve a variety of factors, such as personal or

---

[1] This particular discussion is often traced back to F. C. Baur. One of his earliest treatments is his "Die Christuspartie in der korinthischen Gemeinde, der Gegensatz des petrischen und paulinischen Christentum in der ältesten Kirche, der Apostel Petrus in Rom," *Tübingen Zeitschrift für Theologie* 4 (1931): 61–206; repr. in Ferdinand Christian Baur, *Historisch-kritische Untersuchungen zum Neuen Testament* (ed. K. Scholder; intro. E. Käsemann; Stuttgart-Bad Cannstatt: Frommann, 1963) 1–146.

corporate opposition, theological conflict, inter- or intra-group social dynamics, and the like. Nicholas Taylor in his essay in this volume[2] attempts to define Paul's opponents in Corinth and Galatia in terms of their agendas, including what he calls theological, missiological and ecclesiastical features. As a result of such discussion, some wish to assume a fairly narrow definition of opposition, such that this opposition is a definable and coherent group, while others are content to see any expressed or implied opposition as designating an opponent. In this collection of essays, Mark Nanos is probably the most deliberate in attempting to define the nature of opposition.[3] Treating Paul's letter to the Galatians, he is arguing for a minority position, in which the opponents are not Jewish Christians (an intra-group dispute) but from outside the Christian community (an inter-group dispute). In aid of his analysis, he invokes recent work in social theory.

The second question is how one goes about discussing the opponents, in other words, the question of method in defining the opponents of Paul. The question of method is another question that has often been ignored or side-stepped in discussion of Paul and his opponents. Assuming that one can recognize an opponent when one sees one, the further question is how one goes about seeing whether there are such opponents in any or all of Paul's letters. This typically includes examining the individual letters, but also a variety of surrounding factors, such as inter-Jewish disputes and the relation of Paul's mission to the larger Graeco-Roman religious and philosophical world. The book of Colossians in particular has been the source of much recent methodological dispute. Scholars continue to define a wide-ranging number and type of opponents to Paul in the Colossian church. This oppositional industry comes about even though over thirty years ago Morna Hooker published a trenchant essay in which she called into question whether there even were any false teachers at Colossae.[4] Though acknowledged, she has been rigorously followed by few, N. T. Wright being an exception.[5] Most of the time her

---

[2] "Apostolic Identity and the the Conflicts in Corinth and Galatia."

[3] "Intruding 'Spies' and 'Pseudo-brethren': The Jewish Intra-Group Politics of Paul's Jerusalem Meeting (Gal 2:1–10)."

[4] M. D. Hooker, "Were there False Teachers in Colossae?" in B. Lindars and S. S. Smalley (eds.), *Christ and Spirit in the New Testament: Studies in Honour of Charles Francis Digby Moule* (Cambridge: Cambridge University Press, 1973) 315–32.

[5] N. T. Wright, *Colossians and Philemon* (TNTC; Grand Rapids: Eerdmans, 1986) 23–30.

essay is conveniently ignored.⁶ In this collection of essays, Christian Stettler does a commendable job of surveying and analyzing the various proposals regarding the opponents at Colossae.⁷ He is sensitive to the questions that Hooker has raised and attempts to address them by differentiating false teachers or heretics within the community and opposition from without. Another dimension to this question of method is how it is that Paul's letters relate to the book of Acts. Most scholars treat the letters and Acts as inextricably intertwined. In his essay in this volume, John Hurd addresses the relation of Paul to his letters and to Acts in discussing the opponents in Galatia.⁸ Rather than Acts, he looks to the Corinthian letters in an attempt to establish relative levels of probability regarding the opponents.

Jerry Sumney has probably done more than any other recent scholar to develop an explicit and consistent method for determining the nature of Paul's opponents. In his first two volumes, he developed a method by which he differentiates explicit statements, allusions and affirmations, and whether these statements are found within polemical, apologetic and didactic contexts, and within the main sections of the letter (what he calls the epistolary periods). On the basis of this evidence, Sumney attempts to establish the certainty and reliability of the references to the opponents.⁹ As one might expect from such a scheme, explicit statements have a greater reliability than other types of statements, and didactic contexts more so than polemical and hortatory ones. In this volume, Sumney returns to his analysis of the Pauline letters and analyzes recent work in the light of the method that he has developed in his major volumes on this topic.¹⁰ As a result, he provides an excellent introduction to most of the discussion of Paul's opponents in recent scholarship. However, as rigorous as his method appears to be, not all are entirely convinced by it. For example, in this volume, Christian Stettler does not wish to distinguish between allusions and affirmations, since he contends that they can

---

⁶ This is not to say that it is not cited, but only that the responses to it have often effectively sidelined its significance.

⁷ "The Opponents at Colossae."

⁸ "Reflections Concerning Paul's 'Opponents' in Galatia."

⁹ J. L. Sumney, *Identifying Paul's Opponents: The Question of Method in 2 Corinthians* (JSNTSup 40; Sheffield: JSOT Press, 1990); *'Servants of Satan', 'False Brothers' and Other Opponents of Paul* (JSNTSup 188; Sheffield: Sheffield Academic Press, 1999).

¹⁰ "Studying Paul's Opponents: Advances and Challenges."

only be used in relation to the explicit statements. One of the books that has not been examined as often as others in terms of opposition is Paul's letter to the Romans. One of the reasons is that Paul is writing to a church that he had not founded or visited previously. There is very little direct evidence but only indirect or inferential evidence by which to reconstruct a possible opposition. In this volume, Porter examines statements in the thanksgiving and closing of Romans that seem to imply some reservations or hesitation regarding Paul.[11]

The third question is who the opponents are, and whether they are a single anti-Pauline group, or whether they vary letter to letter or place to place. Modern critical discussion of Paul's opponents in many ways began with the overarching analysis of F. C. Baur, who defined the Pauline opposition in terms of what has come to be variously characterized as the Paulinist/Hellenist/libertine versus Petrine/Jacobean/legalist opposition.[12] Baur has had a number of significant followers through the years, most recently including Gerd Lüdemann and Michael Goulder.[13] Also arguing for a single opposition, though a different one, is Walther Schmithals,[14] who posits that Paul's opponents were Gnostics. Most discussion of Paul's opponents, however, has been content to discuss the opposition particular to a single place. Scrutiny of such works as Sumney's and the earlier work by Gunther shows the range of proposals that has been developed.[15] The letters to the Corinthians, the Galatians and, more recently, the Colossians have been the major recipients of such discussion, and the number of theories does not show signs of abating. These have ranged from one extreme to the other, and have included Jewish and Gentile, Hellenistic and legalist, elitist and commonplace, and exclusivist and syncretistic proposals. Included in this collection are two essays that represent some of the range of discussion. Ross Saunders

---

[11] "Did Paul Have Opponents in Rome and What Were They Opposing?"

[12] F. C. Baur, *Paul the Apostle of Jesus Christ: His Life and Works, his Epistles and Teachings* (two volumes in one; Peabody, MA: Hendrickson, 2003; repr. of 1873–75 English trans. of 1845 German edn). His sustained treatment of Paul was preceded by a number of often extensive articles on various related topics.

[13] G. Lüdemann, *Opposition to Paul in Jewish Christianity* (trans. M. E. Boring; Minneapolis: Fortress, 1989); M. Goulder, *A Tale of Two Missions* (London: SCM Press, 1994); cf. idem, *Paul and the Competing Mission in Corinth* (Library of Pauline Studies; Peabody, MA: Hendrickson, 2001).

[14] W. Schmithals, *Paul and the Gnostics* (trans. J. E. Steely; Nashville: Abindon, 1972).

[15] J. J. Gunther, *St. Paul's Opponents and their Background: A Study of Apocalyptic and Jewish Sectarian Teachings* (NovTSup 35; Leiden: E. J. Brill, 1973).

examines Paul in terms of the Imperial cult,[16] while Craig Evans examines the significance of language regarding "works of law" from Jewish sources and its relationship to Paul's letters, especially Galatians.[17] Most are familiar by now with the Qumran document 4QMMT, and Evans brings the use of its language into dialogue with other Jewish references regarding "works of law" to inform understanding of Paul's treatment of this topic. Evans sees those who were promoting "works of law" to be in opposition to Paul's theology. Saunders contends, by contrast, that Paul's greatest opponent, especially at Corinth, was the Imperial cult, although its influence is to be found elsewhere in Paul's letters and the New Testament. He also argues that the cult had a significant impact on the subsequent development of Christianity.

This volume in many ways mirrors the range and proportion of discussion of Paul and his opponents that is currently being undertaken. As a result, there are treatments of various letters, but most of the discussion focuses upon Galatians, the Corinthian letters and Colossians. These letters will no doubt continue to generate the most interest, since the evidence available within the individual letters seems to be the most abundant and in need of explanation. With the refinement of methods, however, there may be the possibility of extending discussion to some of the less well-studied letters. There are also a range of approaches currently being utilized, most of them concentrating on particular letters, but some of them introducing other factors, such as socio-historical data. In any case, the discussion of Paul and his opponents—whether they be one or many, in one place or several—is bound to continue.

---

[16] "Paul and the Imperial Cult."
[17] "Paul and 'Works of Law' Language in Late Antiquity."

STUDYING PAUL'S OPPONENTS: ADVANCES AND CHALLENGES

Jerry L. Sumney
Lexington Theological Seminary
Lexington, KY, USA

F. C. Baur's *Paul the Apostle of Jesus Christ*, published in 1845, has been among the most influential works in New Testament critical scholarship.[1] It has become the touchstone from which others have worked as they envision the earliest Church and its internal struggles. Baur has been particularly important in the search for the identity of those opposed in the Pauline letters. Baur put this topic into the center of New Testament scholarship with his proposal of a significant and permanent rift between Paul and Peter. His emphasis on Paul's opponents and their importance for reconstructing the early Church finds support in the number of Paul's letters that clearly oppose other teachers or teachings. Baur's understanding of the opposition to Paul serves as the basis for his construct of the first-century Church. Since so many of Paul's letters do oppose others, interpreters must be as clear as possible about those he opposes, if they are to understand those letters or the history of the churches they address. Baur's work shows clearly the power such investigations have to shape our understanding of that period.

Baur's understanding of Paul's opponents and the shape of the early Church has, of course, not gone unchallenged.[2] Subsequent interpreters

---

[1] *Paul, The Apostle of Jesus Christ—His Life and Work, His Epistles and Doctrine* (2 vols.; 2nd ed.; trans. Eduard Zeller; London: Williams and Norgate, 1876; reprinted Peabody, MA: Hendrickson, 2003). The argument, outline, and direction of this larger work was evident in his earlier "Die Christuspartei in der korinthischen Gemeinde, der Gegensatz des petrischen und paulinischen Christentum in der ältesten Kirche, der Apostel Petrus in Rom," *Tübingen Zeitschrift für Theologie* 4 (1831): 61–206. For an account of thought about Paul's opponents from the Reformation to Baur see E. Earle Ellis, "Paul and His Opponents: Trends in the Research," in *Christianity, Judaism, and Other Graeco-Roman Cults; Part 1* (ed. J. Neusner; Leiden: E. J. Brill, 1975) 264–73.

[2] J. B. Lightfoot responded directly in his 1865 commentary on Galatians. See the excursus on "Paul and the Three," *Saint Paul's Epistle to the Galatians* (London: Macmillan, 1865).

have questioned nearly every aspect of his work, yet it has set much of the agenda for subsequent investigations into the development of the early Church. Since identifying Paul's opponents has such far-reaching consequences for interpreting Paul's letters and for understanding the earliest Church, interpreters have rightly turned to this question with great frequency. Given its importance, it is no surprise that scholars have produced scores of hypotheses about Paul's opponents, with no letter being exempt from the imposition of multiple theories. While these proposals about those opposed in any given Pauline letter are often influenced, indeed determined, by a presupposed reconstruction of the early Church, they have also contributed significantly to various proposals about the shape of the earliest Church.

Before turning to more recent discussions of opponents, some accounting of Baur's hypothesis and its legacy may help us understand why discussions of this topic have proceeded as they have. After a glance at this legacy and a survey of hypotheses about the opponents of various Pauline letters, we will turn to questions of appropriate methods for identifying opponents. Finally, we will discuss two recent proposals about those opposed in Colossians.

Baur's identification of Paul's opponents and reconstruction of the earliest Church assumed Hegel's philosophy of history. Baur identified Petrine or Jewish Christianity as the thesis and Pauline or Gentile Christianity as the antithesis. These merged into early catholic Christianity in the second century and the cycle began again. In fact, the Pseudo-Clementine Homilies seem to be the real starting point for his reconstruction of Paul's opponents.[3] How much Hegelian philosophy shaped Baur's historical findings is evident in his treatment of 1 Corinthians. Baur admits there is no evidence in this letter that Paul is opposing members of "Petrine Christianity," and yet he insists that representatives of this branch of the Church must be present and must be causing the problems the letter addresses.[4] Since his historical schema allows only two possible types of Christians, if Paul opposes someone, it has to be a member of that one other possible type.

One legacy of Baur has been an understanding of the early Christian movement that presupposes this sort of simple opposition of two, and

---

[3] See "Die Christuspartei," 116–20.
[4] See "Die Christuspartei," 77 and *Paul*, 259–60.

only (or primarily) two, types of Christianity. While Baur's hypothesis was supported by his Hegelian presuppositions, subsequent studies that accepted this scheme have not held that philosophical presupposition.[5] In the wake of the *religionsgeschichtliche Schule*'s synchronic investigations into the Iranian parallels with Gnosticism and of the finding of the Nag Hammadi library, Walter Schmithals proposed that the opponents of Paul were all Gnostics.[6] 1 Corinthians, with its extensive attention to knowledge and wisdom, is the foundation of this hypothesis. Schmithals presupposed the sort of two-party scheme Baur had proposed, even though he changed the particulars of the opponents' identity. So, like Baur, Schmithals's reconstruction of the early Church left no room for any alternative types of opponents. And again, a lack of evidence in the letters themselves was no deterrent to adherence to the two-party presupposition. Schmithals argued that when a particular letter does not seem to oppose Gnostics, it is because Paul misunderstood his opposition. Once Paul understood them more clearly (that is, as clearly as Schmithals himself), then he opposed the Gnostic teaching that was surely present. Schmithals had to rely on overly speculative hypotheses about the redaction history of several Pauline letters to make the two-party scheme work. Only by proposing that various sections of nearly every letter came from a time before Paul clearly understood his opponents could Schmithals show that Paul's understanding of the situation grew to the place where he recognized that his opponents were Gnostics.

Schmithals and Baur develop different understandings of Paul's opponents largely because of their different starting points. Baur begins with Acts and Galatians (and the Pseudo-Clementine Homilies), where he finds opposition from Jewish Christians and makes all the letters fit this

---

[5] Even those who do not formally accept the presupposition have been significantly influenced by it. For example, without explicitly accepting this presupposition, Derek Oostendorp interprets 2 Corinthians through parallels in other Pauline texts and so finds Judaizers there, as well as in Galatians, Philippians, and Romans (*Another Jesus: A Gospel of Jewish-Christian Superiority in II Corinthians* [Kampen: J. H. Kok, 1967] 83). Ellis vigorously rejects Baur's hypothesis about the identity of the opponents, but explicitly accepts the presupposition that there is one type of Pauline opponent ("Paul and His Opponents," 291 n. 92).

[6] *Gnosticism in Corinth* (Nashville: Abingdon, 1971); *Paul and the Gnostics*, (Nashville: Abingdon, 1972); "Judaisten in Galatien?" *ZNW* 74 (1983): 27–58; "The *Corpus Paulinum* and Gnosis," in *The New Testament and Gnosis: Essays in Honor of Robert McL. Wilson* (ed. A. H. B. Logan and A. J. M. Wedderburn; Edinburgh: T. & T. Clark, 1983) 107–24.

problem. Schmithals begins with 1 Corinthians, with its emphasis on knowledge, and conforms all that he finds in other letters to this issue. This is in part a difference stemming from which letter of Paul they began with, and in part from the cultural environment each sees as the primary backdrop for the emergence of second-century Christianity: Baur emphasizes his vision of Jewish Christianity, Schmithals his vision of first-century Gnosticism.[7]

Beyond such adoptions of Baur's two-party oppositional scheme, even his identification of Paul's opposition as Jewish or Petrine Christianity has continued to find supporters among New Testament scholars. Gerd Lüdemann argued for a modification of Baur's hypothesis in his 1983 study of Paul's opponents.[8] Lüdemann uses Acts and Galatians 2 to posit an anti-Pauline party in Jerusalem which counts James among its supporters.[9] Lüdemann does, however, recognize that Paul's Corinthian opponents do not hold the same views as those opposed in Galatians. So he proposes that the Corinthian opponents are a middle position between Paul and the Galatian group. This change to a three-party scheme is not as great a shift as it might appear, because both anti-Pauline movements are based in Jerusalem and related to "Jewish Christianity."[10]

Michael Goulder is a recent advocate of Baur's reconstruction of the early Church. He argues for this reconstruction at length in two books: *St. Paul versus St. Peter: A Tale of Two Missions* and *Paul and the Competing Mission in Corinth*.[11] For Goulder, the opposition between Pauline and Petrine Christianity provides the reasons Paul must address a wide array of issues, including Christology, pneumatology, and the place of wisdom in Christian theology, to say nothing of the importance of the debate about the Law. C. K. Barrett is also among those who agree

---

[7] Of course, both of these reconstructions are themselves quite questionable, as subsequent scholarship has made abundantly evident.

[8] Gerd Lüdemann, *Paulus, der Heidenapostel, vol. 2: Antipaulinismus im frühen Christentum* (FRLANT 130; Göttingen: Vandenhoeck & Ruprecht, 1983), ET: *Opposition to Paul in Jewish Christianity* (trans. M. Eugene Boring; Minneapolis: Fortress, 1989); see also his *Paulus, der Heidenapostel, vol. 1* (FRLANT 123; Göttingen: Vandenhoeck & Ruprecht, 1980), ET: *Paul, Apostle to the Gentiles: Studies in Chronology* (Philadelphia: Fortress, 1984).

[9] *Paulus, der Heidenapostel, vol. 2*, 69, 59–66, 84 (ET: 35–63).

[10] *Paulus, der Heidenapostel, vol. 2*, 141–43 (ET: 197–99).

[11] *St. Paul versus St. Peter: A Tale of Two Missions* (Louisville: Westminster, 1994); *Paul and the Competing Mission in Corinth* (Library of Pauline Studies; Peabody, MA: Hendrickson, 2001).

with Goulder's reaffirmation of the structure and substance of Baur's two-party conflict in the first-century Church.[12]

Thus, Baur's two-party scheme and his specific identification of Paul's constant opponents as Judaizers continues to exert enormous influence on reconstructions of the early church. Even Walter Bauer's powerful critique of such a simple understanding of the earliest Church has not kept interpreters from adopting a two-party scheme. While W. Bauer's 1934 *Orthodoxy and Heresy in Earliest Christianity*[13] has its own faults, it clearly demonstrates that the early Church included a significantly wider range of diversity than two parties.

The tendency to follow F. C. Baur is more pronounced in studies that investigate the broader shape of Paul's opposition than it is in studies that investigate the opponents of particular letters. But even these works often rely unintentionally on elements of Baur's work. Minimally, most interpreters presuppose that those opposed in a Pauline letter are members of an anti-Pauline movement. Many identify Jerusalem as its headquarters, with James as a supporter or as its leader. My own reading of the Pauline letters finds insufficient support for either the constant connection to Jerusalem, or the limitation of Paul's opponents to a single group. There are anti-Pauline movements by the mid-50s, but there is no good evidence that links them to the leaders of the Jerusalem church.

Important early works that refused the imposition of this paradigm include those of J. B. Lightfoot and Wilhelm Lütgert. Lightfoot argued for two groups among "Judaizers," one with a pharisaic tendency (seen in Galatians) and the other with a gnosticizing tendency (seen in 1 Corinthians). Lightfoot yields to the idea that all Paul's opponents come from within a "Judaizing" perspective, but refuses to see them as a single unified movement.[14] Lightfoot's modification of Baur exercised sufficient influence to limit the sway Baur's thesis held over British scholarship. Lütgert offered powerful arguments against Baur's hypothesis and identified the Corinthian opponents as Gnostics. He, thus,

---

[12] "Deuteropauline Ethics: Some Observations," in *Theology and Ethics in Paul and His Interpreters: Essays in Honor of Victor Paul Furnish* (ed. Eugene Lovering and J. L. Sumney; Nashville: Abingdon, 1996) 172.

[13] *Orthodoxy and Heresy in Earliest Christianity* (ed. Robert A. Kraft and Gerhard Krodel; Philadelphia: Fortress, 1971).

[14] *Saint Paul's Epistle to the Galatians*, 292–374. Lightfoot's position shares a great deal with the much later proposal of Lüdemann (see above).

advanced a view that rejected Baur's scheme and particular thesis.[15] Similarly, Dieter Georgi's study of the opponents of 2 Corinthians was not constrained by the single-front presupposition.[16] Interpreters of the disputed Paulines have also been less tied to Baur's proposal. Thus, many identify the opponents of the Pastorals as some sort of Gnostics, or a form of incipient Gnosticism that did not yet exist when Paul wrote his letters.

SURVEY OF HYPOTHESES ABOUT THE OPPONENTS OF INDIVIDUAL LETTERS

Being less constrained by Baur's scheme, interpreters of individual letters have produced a broad range of hypotheses for each letter. Our review of these hypotheses will move through the letters in their canonical order, but will not include Philemon, a letter clearly not concerned with opponents.

Romans

Romans has provoked fewer hypotheses about opponents of Paul than most other letters. While Baur finds advocates of Gentile observance of circumcision and Mosaic purity regulations,[17] and Schmithals discovers Gnostics in chapter 16,[18] most interpreters reject the idea that Paul composes Romans to combat opponents of his teaching or apostleship. The occasion of Romans remains a matter of debate, but it seems that three factors contribute to the form of its composition: Paul's desire to include the Roman church among those he represents as he delivers the collection for the saints in Jerusalem (and so claim them as a church under his apostolic authority); his desire to prepare them for his arrival and request for help with his mission to Spain; and his attempt to address questions about the relationship between Jewish and Gentile believers in Christ,

---

[15] *Freiheitspredigt und Schwarmgeister in Korinth: Ein Beitrag zur Charakteristik der Christuspartei* (BFCT 12/3; Gütersloh: Bertelsmann, 1908).

[16] Dieter Georgi, *Die Gegner des Paulus im 2. Korintherbrief: Studien zur religiösen Propaganda in der Spätantike* (WMANT; Neukirchen-Vluyn: Neukirchener Verlag, 1964). ET: *The Opponents of Paul in Second Corinthians* (Philadelphia: Fortress, 1986).

[17] *Paul* 1, 321–81.

[18] *Paul and the Gnostics*, 219–38.

particularly in the wake of the return of Jewish believers following their expulsion under Claudius.[19]

Moo speculates that Paul may have given extended attention to this last issue because false rumors about his teaching had probably found their way to Rome. Thus he needs to clarify what he does teach.[20] What distinguishes the occasion of Romans from other letters, Moo argues, is that its readers raise questions about Paul from opposing viewpoints: some favor observance of elements of Torah that designate believers as specifically Jewish, while others are inclined to reject the Torah in ways Paul finds objectionable.[21] While some in Rome may have questions about Paul's teaching, there is no good evidence that he faces opponents who reject his teaching in some organized fashion, even if some are skeptical about him because of what they had heard of his teaching.

1 Corinthians

1 Corinthians is the foundation of Schmithals's argument that Paul's opponents everywhere are Gnostics. While a number of interpreters agree that the teaching Paul rejects has elements of Gnosticism, most reject the idea that a roving band of Gnostics has invaded the house churches of Corinth. Barrett asserts that Cephas himself, or representatives of the Jerusalem church, have come to Corinth and have begun to question Paul's apostolic authority and to advocate that the Gentiles begin to observe the food laws of Judaism.[22] This understanding of the Corinthian situation relies heavily on Baur's scheme (which Barrett affirmed recently, see above note 9), but it also draws on Paul's characterization of the Corinthian factions as groups that all claim some authority (Cephas, Apollos, Paul, or Christ) in their disputes with one another (1:12). Lüdemann also thinks the Cephas party was founded by Jerusalem-based missionaries who had come to Corinth. However, he asserts that they had left before the time of 1 Corinthians.[23]

---

[19] See the essays in *The Romans Debate* (ed. Karl P. Donfried; Minneapolis: Augsburg, 1977) and L. Ann Jervis, *The Purpose of Romans: A Comparative Letter Structure Investigation* (JSNTSup 55; Sheffield: Sheffield Academic Press, 1991).

[20] Douglas Moo, *The Epistle to the Romans* (NICNT; Grand Rapids: Eerdmans, 1996) 21.

[21] Moo, *Epistle to the Romans*, 20.

[22] C. K. Barrett, *A Commentary on the First Epistle to the Corinthians* (HNTC; San Francisco: Harper & Row, 1968) 44–45.

[23] Lüdemann, *Opposition to Paul in Jewish Christianity* 69–71 (where he makes the connection with Jerusalem), 79–80.

Most interpreters find no opponents in the sense of teachers who have come from outside to oppose Paul's teaching or apostleship. Still, Fee discerns a turn against Paul that is being led by local Corinthian leaders.[24] There are clearly questions about and challenges to Paul's authority at the time of 1 Corinthians. Pearson, Horsley, and Sellin argue that Paul opposes growing understandings of wisdom that have been influenced by Hellenistic Judaism's wisdom tradition.[25] Dahl, Pogoloff, Kuck, and Mitchell all contend that what Paul opposes in 1 Corinthians is less some particular group or theological position, and more the posture of competitiveness.[26] My analysis agrees that there are no intruding teachers, even while the Corinthians challenge Paul's authority. Neither do I find good evidence for the presence of a Sophia theology or soteriology. And while Paul rejects the Corinthians' understanding of the presence and manifestation of the Spirit, that difference in understanding has not led to an overt challenge to his status or authority.[27]

2 Corinthians

The task of identifying the opponents of 2 Corinthians is complicated by questions about the document's literary integrity. However, interpreters uniformly see a continuity of opposition to Paul in however many letters they find. Hypotheses about the identity of these opponents fall into four groups: advocates of Gentiles adopting circumcision, Sabbath, and food laws from the Torah, Gnostics, "divine men," and Pneumatics.[28]

---

[24] Gordon D. Fee, *The First Epistle to the Corinthians* (NICNT; Grand Rapids: Eerdmans, 1987) 6–15.

[25] Birger A. Pearson, *The Pneumatikos-Psychikos Terminology in 1 Corinthians* (SBLDS 12; Missoula: SBL, 1973); Richard A. Horsley, "Gnosis in Corinth: 1 Cor. 8.1–6," *NTS* 27 (1979): 32–51; Gerhard Sellin, "Das 'Geheimnis' der Weisheit und das Rätsel der 'Christuspartei' (zu 1 Kor 1–4)," *ZNW* 73 (1982): 70–71.

[26] Nils Dahl, "Paul and the Church at Corinth According to 1 Corinthians 1:10–4:21," in *Christian History and Interpretation* (ed. W. R. Farmer, C. F. D. Moule, R. Niebuhr; Cambridge: Cambridge University Press, 1967) 313–35; Stephen M. Pogoloff, *Logos and Sophia: The Rhetorical Situation of 1 Corinthians* (SBLDS 134; Atlanta: Scholars Press, 1992) 189; David W. Kuck, *Judgment and Community Conflict: Paul's Use of Apocalyptic Judgment Language in 1 Corinthians 3:5–4:5* (NovTSup 66; Leiden: E. J. Brill, 1992) 155; Margaret M. Mitchell, *Paul and the Rhetoric of Reconciliation: An Exegetical Investigation of the Language and Composition of 1 Corinthians* (Louisville: Westminster/John Knox, 1991) 297–302.

[27] Jerry L. Sumney, *'Servants of Satan', 'False Brothers', and Other Opponents of Paul* (JSNTSup 188; Sheffield: Sheffield Academic Press, 1999) 34–78, esp. 76–78.

[28] For a more extended survey of views of the opponents of 2 Corinthians see my

Baur, Oostendorp, Gunther, Lüdemann, and Hafemann (among many others) identify these traveling apostles as teachers who require Gentile Christians to be circumcised and to take up observance of Jewish food laws and the Sabbath.[29] Those who do not rely on a presupposed single type of opponent cite 2 Corinthians 3 as the primary evidence for their view. In ch. 3, Paul compares his ministry with that of Moses. Some furthermore identify the pejorative label "super-apostles" (11:5; 12:11) as a veiled reference to the Jerusalem apostles. This, in turn, indicates that the opponents are from Jerusalem, and so must hold this view of Gentile Torah observance.[30]

Lütgert and Schlatter have been among those who argue that the opponents of 2 Corinthians are some type of Gnostics.[31] Following them, Schmithals is the central proponent of this thesis. Schmithals's treatment of these opponents is completely dependent on his prior decision that Gnostics are Paul's opponents everywhere. Schmithals, Lütgert, and Schlatter all presuppose a well-developed, pre-Christian Gnosticism.[32]

Identifying Paul's Opponents; The Question of Method in 2 Corinthians (JSNTSup 40; Sheffield: JSOT, 1990) 15–67.

[29] Baur, *Paul* 1, 268–320; Oostendorp, *Another Jesus*; C. K. Barrett, "Paul's Opponents in 2 Corinthians," *NTS* 17 (1971): 233–54; idem, *The Second Epistle to the Corinthians* (HNTC; New York: Harper & Row, 1973) 28–36; J. J. Gunther, *St. Paul's Opponents and their Background: A Study of Apocalyptic and Jewish Sectarian Teachings* (NovTSup 35; Leiden, E. J. Brill, 1973); Lüdemann, *Opposition to Paul*; Scott Hafemann, *Suffering and the Spirit: An Exegetical Study of II Cor. 2:14–3:3 within the Context of the Corinthian Correspondence* (WUNT; Tübingen: J. C. B. Mohr, 1986); idem, *Suffering and Ministry in the Spirit: Paul's Defense of his Ministry in II Corinthians 2:14–3:3* (Carlisle, Cumbria: Paternoster, 2000); idem, "Corinthians, Letters to the," in *Dictionary of Paul and His Letters* (ed. G. F. Hawthorne and R. P. Martin; Downers Grove: IVP, 1993) 177–78. Also John M. Court, "The Controversy with Adversaries of Paul's Apostolate in the Context of His Relations to the Corinthian Congregation (2 Corinthians 12,14–13,13)," in *Verteidigung und Begründung des Apostolischen Amtes (2 Kor 10–13)* (ed. E. Lohse; Rome: Abtei St. Paul vor den Mauern, 1992) 107–28.

[30] E.g., Gunther, *Paul's Opponents*, 301; Georg Strecker, "Die Legitimität des Paulinischen Apostolates nach 2 Korinther 10–13," *NTS* 38 (1992): 112; Court, "The Controversy with Adversaries of Paul's Apostolate in the Context of His Relations to the Corinthian Congregation," 96–97.

[31] Lütgert, *Freiheitspredigt und Schwarmgeister in Korinth*; Adolf Schlatter, *Paulus, der Bote Jesu: Eine Deutung seiner Briefe an die Korinther* (Stuttgart: Calwer Vereinsbuchhandlung, 1934).

[32] Schmithals, *Gnosticism in Corinth*, 30–79. Schlatter held that these opponents were Jewish-Christian Gnostics before Schmithals developed the case in this extended way.

Schmithals asserts that the verbal similarities he finds between 2 Corinthians and Gnostic texts indicate that the ideas expressed are the same (or closely related). These parallels then serve as his evidence that 2 Corinthians opposes Gnostics. Few current interpreters argue that 2 Corinthians opposes a fully-formed Gnosticism.

A number of interpreters, led by Georgi, argue that the opponents of 2 Corinthians are "divine men." These traveling Hellenistic-Jewish propagandists demonstrate the presence of God's Spirit in their lives with displays of ecstatic experiences and their interpretation of Scripture.[33] Georgi develops his understanding of the opponents of 2 Corinthians from the image of the "divine man" that he reconstructs from Hellenistic Judaism. Much of Georgi's treatment of the texts of 2 Corinthians is controlled by the assumption that they have adopted the theology of the "divine men." He contends that they see competition as the essence of preaching and so look for displays of power from Paul and comparisons between him and them.[34] These opponents also argue that refusal to engage in such testing and comparison shows that he is not a genuine "divine man." Georgi relies most heavily on his reconstruction of the "divine man" when he interprets ch. 3, the place that shows they have an aberrant Christology in which they identify Jesus as a "divine man" in the same sense Moses and they are "divine men."[35] Georgi sees clearly that these opponents and those Jewish propagandists he reconstructs both make claims about the abundant presence and power of God in their lives and ministry. However, such connections with a reconstruction are an insufficient basis for importing the "divine man" theological scheme into the theology of the Corinthian opponents.[36]

Finally, Käsemann argues that the opponents of 2 Corinthians are traveling preachers who have a different understanding of apostleship than Paul does. These teachers claim "marks of an apostle" that only a special measure of the Spirit imparts. They say that their connection with the Jerusalem apostles, their working of the requisite wonders, and their receiving of financial support all show that they are genuine apos-

---

[33] Georgi, *Die Gegner*, 87–96 (ET: 84–91).
[34] Georgi, *Die Gegner*, 225–29 (ET: 234–36).
[35] Georgi, *Die Gegner*, 265–300, esp. 283 (ET: 254–83).
[36] See the critique of Georgi's portrait of the "divine man" in Carl Holladay, *Theios Aner in Hellenistic-Judaism: A Critique of This Category in New Testament Christology* (SBLDS 40; Missoula: Scholars Press, 1977).

tles. Paul, however, fails each of these tests and so is not a legitimate apostle.[37] Käsemann rightly identifies the central issue of the letters of 2 Corinthians to be the way the Spirit manifests itself in apostles. The opponents contend that it makes them powerful speakers, and personalities who must be obeyed by the congregation. Accepting financial support is one way they exercise this spiritual power. However, there is far too little justification for Käsemann's claim that they are related to the Jerusalem church. These opponents do reject Paul's claim to be an apostle because of his refusal to adopt a demeanor of power and dominance.[38] The only theological point about which Paul finds it necessary to argue with them is that of the image of the apostle/minister. In contrast to them, he contends that ministry must be conducted in a way that reflects the crucified (and raised) Christ. Thus, whatever other theological, soteriological or christological differences there may be between Paul and these teachers, those issues are not what require Paul to oppose them.

Galatians

The opponents of Galatians have become a significant locus of attention among New Testament scholars engaged in rethinking the relationship between the Church and the synagogue. The majority of interpreters throughout the twentieth century identified the opponents of Galatians as emissaries of the Jerusalem church who reject Paul's apostleship and require Gentile believers to observe those elements of Torah Paul says they are not required, or even allowed, to adopt. While most have argued that these teachers claim that such observance is necessary for salvation,[39] other interpreters contend that they say it is only necessary for the Galatians to achieve perfection.[40]

---

[37] E. Käsemann, "Die Legitimität des Apostels," *ZNW* 41 (1942): 33–71.

[38] Sumney, *Identifying Paul's Opponents*, 127–91; *Servants of Satan*, 79–133.

[39] E.g., Ernest De Witt Burton, *A Critical and Exegetical Commentary on the Epistle to the Galatians* (ICC; Edinburgh: T. & T. Clark, 1921) liv–lv; M.-J. Lagrange, *Saint Paul Epitre aux Galates* (2nd ed.; EB; Paris: Gabalda, 1925); George S. Duncan, *The Epistle of Paul to the Galatians* (MNTC; New York: Harper, 1934) xxxii–xxxiv; Pierre Bonnard, "L'Épitre de Saint Paul aux Philippiens," *Commentaire du Nouveau Testament, 10* (Paris: Delachaux & Niestlé, 1950) 12–14; Franz Mussner (who thinks the text does not indicate that these opponents are connected with Jerusalem), *Der Galaterbrief* (HTKNT 9; Freiburg: Herder, 1974) 12–26.

[40] So, e.g., John Bligh, *A Discussion of St. Paul's Epistle* (Householder Commentaries; London: St. Paul Publ., 1969) 26–29; Karl Kertelge, "Gesetz und Freiheit im Galaterbrief," *NTS* 30 (1984): 382–94.

Most interpreters connect these opponents with the Jerusalem church, assuming that they are ethnically Jewish. Ropes and Harvey, however, argue that the advocates of circumcision are Gentiles who had adopted this type of Torah observance at an earlier time.[41] Munck accepts that they are Gentiles, and denies that they are connected to the Jerusalem church.[42] Throughout the nineteenth and early twentieth century, interpreters also often derided the motives of these intruding teachers. For example, Ellicott spoke of them as "unprincipled and self-seeking."[43]

Many interpreters also believe that Paul's apostleship is under attack. The letter's extended greeting and the stories Paul relates about his conversion and interactions with the Jerusalem apostles are the primary evidence for this view.[44] However, recent studies of the argument and rhetorical structure of the letter render this reading unlikely.[45]

The exceptions to the trend to identify these opponents as legalists, who require Gentiles to adopt Jewish identity, have been those who find Pneumatics or Gnostics.[46] Lütgert argued that Paul faced two types of opponents when he wrote Galatians, one demanding that Gentiles observe those commands that bring them into Judaism, and one composed of pneumatic libertines.[47] Jewett also finds a libertine group. He contends that, under threat from fellow Jews in Judea, some in Galatia

---

[41] James H. Ropes, *The Singular Problem of the Epistle to the Galatians* (Cambridge: Harvard University Press, 1929); A. E. Harvey, "The Opposition to Paul," *SE* 4: 319–32.

[42] Johannes Munck, *Paul and the Salvation of Mankind* (Richmond: John Knox Press, 1959).

[43] Charles J. Ellicott, *St. Paul's Epistle to the Galatians* (3rd ed.; London: Longman, Green, Longman, Roberts, and Green, 1863) xxix.

[44] H. D. Betz is a prime example of this view. His understanding even of the genre and rhetorical arrangement of Galatians is based on this understanding (*Galatians: A Commentary on Paul's Letter to the Churches in Galatia* [Hermeneia; Philadelphia: Fortress, 1979] 5–25).

[45] E.g., Beverly R. Gaventa, "Galatians 1 & 2: Autobiography as Paradigm," *NovT* 28 (1986): 309–26; B. C. Lategan, "Is Paul Defending His Apostleship in Galatians? The Function of Galatians 1.11–12 and 2.19–20 in the Development of Paul's Argument," *NTS* 34 (1988): 411–30; Robert G. Hall, "The Rhetorical Outline for Galatians: A Reconsideration," *JBL* 106 (1987): 277–87; Joop Smit, "The Letter of Paul to the Galatians: A Deliberative Speech," *NTS* 35 (1989): 1–26.

[46] Schmithals, *Paul and the Gnostics*, 13–64.

[47] Wilhelm Lütgert, *Gesetz und Geist: Eine Untersuchung zur Vorgeschichte des Galaterbriefes* (Gütersloh: C. Bertelsmann, 1919). Followed by Raymond T. Stamm, "The Epistle to the Galatians," in *The Interpreter's Bible* (ed. G. A. Buttrick; Nashville: Abingdon, 1953) 10:430.

advocate that the church be more observant. But the situation involves more melding of Judaism and Hellenistic religions than is normally thought. This combination leads them to interpret their possession of the Spirit as proof that they had attained self-sufficiency and immortality. This self-understanding, combined with the belief that they would not face a final judgment, produced some antinomianism.[48] In a similar vein, Ellis sees them combine Torah observance and attention to angelic powers, which may show they have an Essene background.[49] Others have identified the main issue as the Spirit and find only one front of opposition, as we will see below.[50]

Since E. P. Sanders's thorough questioning of the construction of first-century Judaism as a legalistic religion,[51] hypotheses about the opponents of Galatians have become more diverse, more cautious, and more nuanced. Once interpreters reject the assumption that all Judaism is legalistic, new avenues of understandings of Galatians open. Sanders himself argues that the dispute with the opponents of Galatians is about the conditions of membership in the people of God.[52]

Many interpreters continue to hold that the opponents of Galatians demand that Gentile believers accept circumcision and mirror the Torah observance of Jews in order to be Christians, though readers less often attribute legalism or disreputable motives to them.[53] Such interpreters often acknowledge that the issue was not whether Gentile Christ-believers should keep the Law, an issue on which Paul and these opponents would agree (with both saying they should observe it), but *how* they

---

[48] Robert Jewett, "The Agitators and the Galatian Congregation," *NTS* 17 (1971): 198–212. Jewett was preceded in seeing syncretism by Frederic R. Crownfield, "The Singular Problem of the Dual Galatians," *JBL* 64 (1945): 491–500.

[49] Ellis, "Paul and His Opponents: Trends in the Research," 293–95.

[50] E.g., David Lull, *The Spirit in Galatians* (SBLDS 49; Chico: Scholars Press, 1980).

[51] *Paul and Palestinian Judaism: A Comparison of Patterns of Religions* (Philadelphia: Fortress, 1977).

[52] E. P. Sanders, *Paul, the Law, and the Jewish People* (Philadelphia: Fortress, 1983) 18–19.

[53] E.g., Brendan Byrne, *'Sons of God'—'Seed of Abraham': A Study of the Idea of the Sonship of God of All Christians in Paul against the Jewish Background* (AnBib 83; Rome: Biblical Institute Press, 1979) 141–43; H. D. Betz (who seems to see the opponents as legalists), *Galatians*, 6; Daniel King (who identifies them with early Ebionites), "Paul and the Tannaim: A Study in Galatians," *WJT* 45 (1983): 340–70; Frank Thielman, *From Plight to Solution: A Jewish Framework for Understanding Paul's View of the Law in Galatians and Romans* (NovTSup 61; Leiden: E. J. Brill, 1989) 50–58.

should observe it. Räisänen rejects the idea that these opponents are legalists, arguing that the law/grace opposition is Paul's polemical construction of the issue. Thus, they are not legalists, but "Biblicists," who say Gentiles must submit to circumcision because the demand is in Scripture.[54]

Dunn represents a significant group of newer interpreters when he finds the argument between Paul and these intruders to be about what accepting Jesus as Messiah means for Gentiles. The opponents say they must proselytize to sustain their identity as God's people. Thus these opponents call for the Gentile believers to adopt the central identity markers of Jews: circumcision and the observance of food laws and the Sabbath.[55] Dunn identifies these opponents as covenantal nomists.[56]

Barclay maintains that the opponents argue that, without circumcision, the Christ-believing Gentiles are only half way to joining the people of God, and they must accept circumcision to join fully.[57] What separates Paul and these teachers is that Paul thinks living by the Spirit is a suitable alternative to living by the Law.[58] Watson likewise maintains the traditional view that the issue at stake in Galatians is whether Gentiles must convert to Judaism to be fully Christian. Furthermore, he argues that the problem comes to Galatia through people sent from Jerusalem. His position is, however, more nuanced than that of earlier interpreters. He, like Ebeling,[59] sees the basic question to be whether Christianity is to be "a reform-movement within Judaism or a sect outside it."[60]

---

[54] Heikki Räisänen, *Paul and the Law* (Tübingen: J. C. B. Mohr [Siebeck], 1983) 183–87, 256–62.

[55] James D. G. Dunn, "Works of the Law and the Curse of the Law (Gal 3:10–14)," *NTS* 31 (1985): 523–42. See also *idem, A Commentary on the Epistle to the Galatians* (BNTC; London: A. & C. Black, 1993).

[56] James D. G. Dunn, "The Theology of Galatians: The Issue of Covenantal Nomism," in *Pauline Theology; Volume 1* (ed. J. M. Bassler; Minneapolis: Fortress, 1991) 128–31.

[57] John M. G. Barclay, *Obeying the Truth: A Study of Paul's Ethics in Galatians* (Studies of the New Testament and its World; Edinburgh: T. & T. Clark, 1988) 54–60. Olaf Linton argues that the opponents contend that Paul preaches circumcision after the Jerusalem Conference agreement ("The Third Aspect: A Neglected Point of View," *ST* 3 [1949]: 79–95).

[58] John M. G. Barclay, "Mirror-Reading a Polemical Letter: Galatians as a Test Case," *JSNT* 31 (1987): 73–93, esp 87. See the earlier thesis of David Lull (*The Spirit in Galatians* [Chico: Scholars Press, 1980]) who argued that the dispute was over the meaning of the presence of the Spirit in the lives of Christians.

[59] Gerhard Ebeling, *The Truth of the Gospel: An Exposition of Galatians* (Philadelphia: Fortress, 1985) 51–54.

[60] Francis Watson, *Paul, Judaism, and the Gentiles: A Sociological Approach*

Martyn attributes the difference over what elements of the Law Gentiles must literally obey to the different eschatologies that Paul and his opponents hold.[61] Paul's more radical eschatology includes Gentiles within the end-time people of God without their conversion to Judaism, while the opponents call the Gentiles to accept God's Law as the way to receive the Spirit and join the people of God.[62]

Howard also thinks that the differences between Paul and these teachers stem from their different eschatologies. Furthermore, he argues, they insist that they preach the same gospel Paul preaches. They do not see Paul as an enemy, but as an ally. Their assertions that Paul is dependent on Jerusalem and that he preaches circumcision are not accusations, but compliments. Paul rejects them so vehemently because he wants to make the distinctions between him and these teachers as clear as possible.[63] Borgen also argues that these opponents claim that their position on circumcision is the same as Paul's. That is, they say Paul thinks that physical circumcision must follow ethical circumcision to complete their conversion and identification with the people of God.[64] Howard and Borgen take seriously statements in Galatians that many interpreters must gloss over in order to maintain their understanding of the opponents as teachers who intentionally oppose Paul's teaching.

Segal also locates the problem's core in eschatology. He argues that the

---

(SNTSMS 56; Cambridge: Cambridge University Press, 1986) 49, 49–61. Similarly, J. Christiaan Beker, *Paul the Apostle: The Triumph of God in Life and Thought* (Philadelphia: Fortress, 1980) 42, though Beker thinks Paul's apostleship is under attack. See also the connections to social identity in Roman Heiligenthal, "Soziologische Implikation der Paulinischen Rechtfertigungslehre im Galaterbrief am Beispiel der 'Werke des Gesetzes'," *Kairos* 26 (1984): 38–51.

[61] J. Louis Martyn, "Apocalyptic Antinomies in Paul's Letter to the Galatians," *NTS* 31 (1985): 410–24; "A Law-Observant Mission to Gentiles: The Background of Galatians," *SJT* 38 (1985): 307–24; "Events in Galatia: Modified Covenantal Nomism versus God's Invasion of the Cosmos in the Singular Gospel: A Response to J. D. G. Dunn and B. R. Gaventa," in *Pauline Theology; Volume 1* (ed. Bassler) 160–70, esp. 162–64, 175–76. Others who look to eschatology as the reason for the difference include Beverley R. Gaventa, "The Singularity of the Gospel: A Reading of Galatians," in *Pauline Theology; Volume 1* (ed. Bassler) 147–50.

[62] J. Louis Martyn, *Galatians* (AB; New York: Doubleday, 1997) 117–26.

[63] George Howard, *Crisis in Galatia* (SNTSMS 35; 2nd ed.; Cambridge: Cambridge University Press, 1990). The first edition of this work was published in 1975 and so was among the first to advocate the distinctive positions found here.

[64] Peder Borgen, "Paul Preaches Circumcision and Pleases Men," in *Paul and Paulinism* (ed. M. D. Hooker and S. G. Wilson; London: SPCK, 1982) 37–46.

issue is not salvation, but association with Gentiles. Paul has adopted the God-fearer model, but has added connection with Christ as the central requirement for inclusion within the people of God in the new time inaugurated by Christ. Paul thinks this means believing that Jews and Gentiles now form a single community. It is this complete merging of communities, without the Gentiles adopting fully the signs of Jewish self-identity, that the opponents repudiate.[65]

Cosgrove rejects the idea that the dispute at Galatia is about attaining salvation. He contends that the central issue concerns the Spirit. According to Cosgrove, the opponents claim that adopting the Law promotes the believers' ongoing experience of the Spirit. Paul raises questions about justification and sonship only to make points about the grounds of life in the Spirit.[66] So the question is not about entrance into the community of God's people, but rather about maintaining one's place in that group.

Lategan does not assume that some great theological issue lies behind Paul's rejection of these opponents. He suggests that the Law is attractive to the Galatian Gentiles because they are uncertain about how to live their new lives. The opponents offer the Law as the guide to life that is appropriate for those who have come to believe in Christ. Furthermore, it offers them acceptance in a known social group with a long history. This offers them a more fixed self-identity and sense of security.[67] The insight that some fierce debates spring from practical rather than theoretical matters is an important one.

Walter reorients the discussion of these opponents by arguing that they are not from within the Christian community. The "different gospel" they preach is not Christian. In fact, they only use the term "gospel" as a trick to lure Paul's converts away from the affirmations about Christ upon which their Christian existence was founded. They say that Paul's teaching has a human rather than a divine source, because God would not lead a person to deny the universal validity of the Law or to affirm that any human could be the Son of God. So they are trying to move these Gentile

---

[65] Alan F. Segal, *Paul the Convert: The Apostolate and Apostasy of Saul the Pharisee* (New Haven: Yale, 1990) 194–210.

[66] Charles H. Cosgrove, *The Cross and the Spirit: A Study in the Argument and Theology of Galatians* (Macon: Mercer, 1988) 2–13.

[67] B. C. Lategan, "The Argumentative Situation of Galatians," in *The Galatians Debate: Contemporary Issues in Rhetorical and Historical Interpretation* (ed. Mark D. Nanos; Peabody, MA: Hendrickson, 2002) 383–95.

Christ-believers out of the Christian community and into the Jewish community.[68] Walter's thesis returns to viewing those who urge circumcision for the Galatian Gentiles as disingenuous, and therefore, morally defective. Still, locating these teachers outside the Christ-believing community prepared the way for Nanos's understanding of them.

Nanos argues that the Jewish community accepted the claim that the Christ-believing Gentiles have turned to God, but not that they are "full and equal members of the communities of the righteous."[69] The Jewish community viewed Paul's Gentile congregants as *candidates* for full proselyte conversion, but not as already fully within the community. This highlights the liminal status Paul's converts already experienced, as those who were not quite Jewish but were no longer pagan. Since they were not fully Jewish, they would have been pressured to participate in the civil and imperial cults. Thus the non-Christ-believing Jewish community offers them a way (i.e., full proselytism) to attain the status they seek inside that community and in relation to the outside community. This path would have been all the more attractive as they witnessed the acceptance and protection afforded proselytes within the community. It is these proselytes who urge the Galatians to accept this clear and advantageous status.[70] This position shares much with that of Barclay. However, Barclay identifies those Paul opposes as Christ-believers rather than as non-Christ-believing Jews.

It seems most probable that these teachers are Christ-believers who will be surprised at Paul's response to them. They claim their teaching is the same as Paul's (as Paul's denial that he preaches circumcision shows, 5:11), and we have no good reasons to doubt their honesty when making this claim, even though they are mistaken. These teachers urge the Galatian Gentiles to receive circumcision, but Paul does not reveal what they think is gained by it. Nanos may be correct that it is clearer status in relation to the outside world, and perhaps also within the Jewish

---

[68] Nikolaus Walter, "Paulus und die Gegner des Christus-evangeliums in Galatien," in *L'Apôtre Paul: Personnalité, style, et conception du ministère* (ed. A. Vanhoye; Leuven: Leuven University Press, 1986) 351–56.

[69] Mark Nanos, "The Inter- and Intra-Jewish Political Context of Paul's Letter to the Galatians," in *The Galatians Debate* (ed. Nanos) 396.

[70] Nanos, "Inter- and Intra-Jewish Political Context," 396–98, 404–405. Pheme Perkins, *Abraham's Divided Children: Galatians and the Politics of Faith* (Harrisburg: Trinity, 2001) 15–17 also holds that the problem involved interaction with the local Jewish community.

community. But the text of Galatians gives insufficient evidence to argue that they attach great theological significance to the circumcision they advocate. Indeed, they seem to play down its significance, since the letter's recipients do not know that accepting circumcision entails committing oneself to the kind of Torah observance found in the synagogue. It is Paul, not the other teachers, who invests circumcision with the theological significance it has in Galatians. Neither do the episodes Paul relates in chs. 1–2 indicate that Paul's apostleship is under attack. It is also Paul who identifies those urging circumcision as opponents. While Paul's previous battles involving circumcision and table fellowship may make his vitriol here explicable, it may also have made those he opposes into enemies he would have to face elsewhere.[71]

Ephesians

Heinrich Schlier is a foundational interpreter among those who argue that Ephesians opposes Gnostics.[72] This has been the most common theory about opponents for Ephesians. This identification rests on loose vocabulary and imagery parallels with some Gnostic texts. But Ephesians does not engage specifically Gnostic ideas.[73] Goulder differs from this interpretive tradition when he argues that Ephesians opposes Jewish visionaries who claim to have ascended to heaven and been granted a place in God's presence.[74] While this identification fits the argument of Colossians, Ephesians does not seem to reflect that problem beyond its adoption of material from Colossians.[75]

Other interpreters posit an ongoing debate between Jewish and Gentile believers about superiority.[76] But Ephesians seems to address a time

---

[71] See my argument for this understanding of the opponents in *Servants of Satan*, 134–59.

[72] Heinrich Schlier, *Der Briefe an die Epheser* (Dusseldorf: Patmos, 1957). Others who find Gnostics opposed include Petr Pokorný, *Der Epheserbrief und die Gnosis* (Berlin: Evangelische Verlagsanstalt, 1965). Cf. Ralph P. Martin who sees Ephesians combat a turn to astrology and magic in the wake of the readers' acceptance of Gnostic dualism (*Ephesians, Colossians and Philemon* [IBC; Atlanta: John Knox, 1991]).

[73] Margaret Y. MacDonald, *Colossians, Ephesians* (SP; Collegeville, MN: Glazier, 2000) 20.

[74] Michael D. Goulder, "The Visionaries of Laodicea," *JSNT* 43 (1991): 15–39.

[75] See MacDonald, *Colossians, Ephesians*, 223–25. See also the problems with Goulder's proposal raised by Ernest Best, *Ephesians* (ICC; Edinburgh: T. & T. Clark, 1998) 67–68.

[76] E.g. D. C. Smith's proposal that Gentile converts to Judaism who later converted to

when the initial severe conflicts between Christ-believing Jews and Gentiles have passed because the author claims the place of Israel for the Church without expecting that he needs a lengthy argument in support of that proposition.

There is insufficient evidence to argue that opponents are a significant part of the occasion of Ephesians.[77] Not only is there little polemic in this letter, but there is only a single direct reference to false teaching (4:14).

Philippians

The picture of the situation at Philippi is complicated by the possibility that it is a composite of as many as three letters. While three letters could address three different situations, finding it to be a composite has not expanded the range of identifications of the opponents at Philippi. Interpreters have usually argued that Philippians, particularly ch. 3, opposes teachers who want to impose circumcision, Jewish food laws, and the Sabbath on Gentiles, as conditions for full membership in the church.[78]

Some interpreters, however, find the primary issue to be the opponents' over-realized eschatology. Koester argues that they urge Gentiles to fulfill the Law to claim the fuller possession of the Spirit that includes attaining the resurrection and freedom from suffering.[79] Similarly,

---

Christianity are claiming superiority over Jewish believers ("The Ephesian Heresy," *SBL Seminar Papers, 1974* [Missoula: Scholars Press, 1974]).

[77] So also Pheme Perkins, *Ephesians* (ANTC; Nashville: Abingdon, 1997) 29.

[78] E.g., J. Ernst, *Die Briefe an die Philipper, an Philemon, an die Kolosser, an die Epheser* (RNT; Regensburg: Friedrich Pustet, 1974) 25; Peter T. O'Brien, *The Epistle to the Philippians: A Commentary on the Greek Text* (NIGTC; Grand Rapids: Eerdmans, 1991) 14. Others who identify these opponents in this way include Chris L. Mearns, "The Identity of Paul's Opponents at Philippi," *NTS* 33 (1987): 194–204, esp. 198; P. Benoit, *Épitres de saint Paul aux Philippiens, à Philémon, aux Colossiens, aux Éphésiens* (La sainte bible de Jérusalem; 4th ed.; Paris: Les Éditions du Cerf, 1969) 33; J. L. Houlden, *Paul's Letters from Prison* (Philadelphia: Westminster, 1970) 103; Wilhelm Egger (though he thinks they may also claim to have attained perfection), *Galaterbrief, Philipperbrief, Philemonbrief* (NEchtB; Würzburg: Echterverlag, 1985) 48; Robert T. Fortna, "Philippians: Paul's Most Egocentric Letter," in *The Conversation Continues: Studies in Paul and John in Honor of J. Louis Martyn* (ed. R. T. Fortna and B. R. Gaventa; Nashville: Abingdon, 1990) 223.

[79] Helmut Koester, "The Purpose of the Polemic of a Pauline Fragment (Philippians III)," *NTS* 8 (1961/2): 317–32. Others who find a realized eschatology include: Joachim Gnilka, *Der Philipperbrief* (HTKNT; Freiburg: Herder, 1968) 197; John Reumann, "Philippians 3:20–21—A Hymnic Fragment?" *NTS* 30 (1984): 593–609.

Collange finds teachers who claim to have achieved perfection and to experience visions. This cluster of characteristics leads him to associate these opponents with those Paul combats in 2 Corinthians.[80] Minear likewise argues that they contend that Paul's sufferings are a disgrace and an impediment to the gospel. He identifies them in this way because he connects them with those spoken of in ch. 1.[81] Klijn rejects such hypotheses, arguing that they rely too heavily on supposed parallels with the Corinthian correspondence.[82]

Lohmeyer and Holden contend that Paul would not call fellow believers "dogs," because this would imply that they were unclean. Since Paul considers all within the church, even his enemies, clean, these opponents must be non-Christian Jews who are rivals of the Christian missionary movement.[83] Schenk also concludes that these opponents are non-Christian teachers. He thinks they represent a Jewish-dualistic Wisdom tradition.[84] However, Baumbach notes that "dogs" is used as an insult in arguments about various things in the Old Testament, New Testament, and Mishnah, and so does not necessarily designate outsiders.[85]

Other interpreters find Paul's derogatory characterizations of these teachers in 3:18–19 evidence that they do not urge observance of the Mosaic code, but a completely different outlook. Michael takes literally Paul's accusations that they are enemies of the cross whose god is their belly and whose glory is shame, rather than seeing them as polemical characterization or caricature. Thus he identifies these teachers as

---

[80] Jean-François Collange, *The Epistle of St. Paul to the Philippians* (London: Epworth, 1979) 123–39.

[81] Paul S. Minear, "Singing and Suffering in Philippi," in *The Conversation Continues* (ed. Fortna and Gaventa) 208–17.

[82] A. F. J. Klijn, "Paul's Opponents in Philippians III," *NovT* 7 (1964/65): 278–84. However, Klijn himself relies heavily on mirror reading.

[83] Ernst Lohmeyer, *Die Briefe an die Philipper, an die Kolosser und an Philemon* (MeyerK 9; 13th ed.; Göttingen: Vandenhoeck & Ruprecht, 1964) 125–26; Houlden, *Paul's Letters from Prison*, 103. Others who identify them as non-Christ-believing Jews include Benoit, *Les Épitres de Saint Paul aux Philippiens, a Philémon, aux Colossiens, aux Éphésiens*, 31–33.

[84] Wolfgang Schenk, *Die Philipperbriefe des Paulus* (Stuttgart: W. Kohlhammer, 1984) 250–91.

[85] Günther Baumbach, "Die von Paulus im Philipperbrief bekämpften Irrlehrer," in *Gnosis und Neues Testament* (ed. K. W. Tröger; Berlin: Gütersloher Mohn, 1973) 299.

antinomians.[86] Based on much the same evidence, Schmithals and R. Martin find Gnostic libertines.[87]

A number of interpreters find two types of opponents in Philippians 3. Lohmeyer finds in 3:12–21 a group for whom Paul expresses sympathy, an emotion he never expresses for Judaizers. Such concern indicates that they were once members of the community, but have capitulated in the face of persecution.[88] Jewett, on the other hand, says Paul's claim in 3:18 that they are "enemies of the cross" shows they are Gnostics who refuse the cross a place in their soteriology. They also advocate a libertine outlook.[89] Since this does not fit with Paul's comments about the Law in 3:2–7, they are a second type of opponent.[90] Ernst also distinguishes between Judaizers in the first part of ch. 3, and libertines in the final part.[91] Calling them "enemies of the cross" also contributes to Ulonska's proposal that these opponents are Cybele-Attis cult eunuchs.[92] All these kinds of readings of 3:18–19 rely too heavily on unsupported mirror reading to be convincing.[93]

Baumbach, instead, finds Judaizers throughout. These teachers claim to have attained perfection, but are not libertines. Rather, the exaggerated statements about them simply reflect Paul's usual manner of writing rather than the actual presence of libertines.[94]

---

[86] Hugh Michael, *The Epistle of Paul to the Philippians* (MNTC; New York: Harper, 1927) 172–73.

[87] Schmithals, *Paul and the Gnostics*, 106; Ralph P. Martin, *Philippians* (NCB; London: Oliphants, 1976) 143–44.

[88] *Die Briefe an die Philipper, an die Kolosser und an Philemon*, 153–55. Houlden, who agrees that these opponents are non-Christian, thinks Paul is addressing the same group that demands circumcision and makes other commands throughout ch. 3 (*Paul's Letters from Prison*, 103).

[89] Robert Jewett, "The Epistolary Thanksgiving and the Integrity of Philippians," *NovT* 12 (1970): 45–46; "Conflicting Movements in the Early Church as Reflected in Philippians," *NovT* 12 (1970): 378–80. This same characterization of the opponents leads Joseph Tyson to assert that they are docetists ("Paul's Opponents at Philippi," *Perspectives* 3 [1976]: 95).

[90] Robert Jewett, "The Epistolary Thanksgiving and the Integrity of Philippians," *NovT* 12 (1970): 45–51.

[91] Ernst, *Die Briefe an die Philipper, an Philemon, an die Kolosser, an die Epheser*, 25.

[92] H. Ulonska, "Gesetz und Beschneidung: Überlegungen zu einem paulinischen Ablösungskonflikt," in *Jesu Rede von Gott* (ed. D. Koch; Gütersloh: Gütersloher Verlag Mohn, 1989) 314–31, esp. 320ff.

[93] See Baumbach, "Die von Paulus im Philipperbrief bekämpften Irrlehrer," 305 and Pheme Perkins, "Philippians: Theology for the Heavenly Politeuma," in *Pauline Theology; Volume 1* (ed. Bassler) 91 n. 10 for comments on such accusations as typical of polemical exchanges.

[94] Baumbach, "Die von Paulus im Philipperbrief bekämpften Irrlehrer," 303–10.

Chapter 3 provides sufficient evidence to be certain that it opposes teachers who require circumcision and base their authority on their Jewish identity (3:4–6). Paul does not explicitly say that they want Gentiles to observe the Sabbath or *kashrut*. Paul's use of ἐργάτης (3:2) to describe these opponents probably indicates that they are part of a group involved in mission efforts that include Paul's churches. They probably define circumcision as necessary for salvation or membership in the people of God. While Paul sees these traveling teachers as a threat, they do not seem to have a foothold in Philippi. Paul tells the Philippians to be cognizant of them (3:2), expounding the consequences of accepting them.[95] Calling them "enemies of the cross" is inflammatory language used to make them unattractive to the readers, not a straightforward description of them.

Beyond the teachers Paul warns against in ch. 3, Paul mentions people who preach to bring him grief (1:15–18). But he designates no differences in the substance of their teaching that leads him to reject them. Rather, they seem to be personal enemies of Paul, and to be where Paul is rather than in Philippi.[96] Paul says only that they preach from bad motives. Yet, he is happy for them to go on preaching because they are spreading the gospel. So they do not oppose Paul's teaching, even though they dislike him enough to cause him pain deliberately.

Paul mentions a third group of "opponents" in 1:28, those who oppose the Philippians' living of the gospel. Some identify these adversaries as people who deny the cross or reject suffering as part of the life of a believer.[97] Jewett is even more specific, identifying them as "divine men."[98] But these adversaries are better understood as non-Christians who persecute the church in Philippi. So while Paul calls them "opponents" (ἀντικειμένων) of the Philippians, they are not a group that specifically targets the Pauline mission in support of a different under-

---

Perkins also asserts that 3:19 is typical of Pauline rhetoric and so does not indicate that Gnostics are troubling the Philippians ("Philippians: Theology for the Heavenly Politeuma," 90–91).

[95] Sumney, *Servants of Satan*, 160–87. For the understanding of βλέπετε assumed here see George D. Kilpatrick, "*Blepete*, Phil 3,2," in *In Memoriam Paul Kahle* (ed. M. Black and G. Fohrer; Berlin: Töpelmann, 1968) 146–48; G. B. Caird, *Paul's Letters from Prison* (New Clarendon Bible; Oxford: Oxford University Press, 1976) 132–33.

[96] Sumney, *Servants of Satan*, 166–70.

[97] Collange, *The Epistle of St. Paul to the Philippians*, 11.

[98] Jewett, "Conflicting Movements," 366–69.

standing of believing in Christ. Rather, they are persecutors of the church at Philippi.[99]

There are, then, three different groups Paul refers to in Philippians: those who persecute the Philippians, those who dislike Paul but seem to preach a compatible gospel, and those who advocate circumcision for Gentile believers.[100] Only the last of these fits into the category of "opponent" which we have been using here.

Colossians

A few interpreters have argued that Colossians has no opponents in view,[101] but most see rejecting some sort of teaching as the primary purpose of the letter. Hypotheses about the opponents of Colossians may be divided into three types: advocates of the worship of angels as part of Christian piety, visionaries who worship with angels, and non-Christians who are influencing the Colossian church. As with other letters, there are significant differences within these categories.

According to most interpreters, these opponents encourage the Colossians to worship angels as a supplement to, or completion of, their practice of Christianity. Furthermore, they call on the Colossians to adopt some ascetic practices as a part of their veneration of these beings.[102] Lightfoot argues that these opponents adhere to a form of

---

[99] So also O'Brien, *The Epistle to the Philippians*, 34–35; Ernst, *Die Briefe an die Philipper*, 60–61; Schenk, *Die Philipperbriefe*, 129 (who remarks that this need not refer to sudden persecution, but the more general opposition of society that Christians faced); Houlden, *Paul's Letters from Prison*, 65; Gnilka, *Der Philipperbrief*, 99–100; Caird, *Paul's Letters from Prison*, 116; Fortna, "Philippians: Paul's Most Egocentric Letter," 227; Raymond Brewer, "The Meaning of *POLITEUESTHE* in Phil 1:27," *JBL* 73 (1954): 81–83 (who argues that these persecutors coerce them to participate in the imperial cult).

[100] See my fuller argument for this understanding of these opponents in *Servants of Satan*, 160–87.

[101] Most notably Morna D. Hooker, "Were there False Teachers in Colossae?" in *Christ and the Spirit in the New Testament* (ed. B. Lindars and S. S. Smalley; Cambridge: Cambridge University Press, 1973) 315–31. Though not denying the presence of some rejected teaching, Thomas Olbricht argues that defeat of that teaching is not the primary intent of Colossians ("The Stoicheia and the Rhetoric of Colossians: Then and Now," in *Rhetoric, Scripture and Theology: Essays from the 1994 Pretoria Conference* [ed. Stanley E. Porter and Thomas H. Olbricht; JSNTSup 131; Sheffield: Sheffield Academic Press, 1996] 310–12).

[102] E.g., Eduard Lohse, *A Commentary on the Epistle to the Colossians and to Philemon* (Hermeneia; Philadelphia: Fortress, 1971) 2–3.

incipient Gnosticism that grew out of adding aspects of philosophical speculation and oriental mysticism to Judaism. This combination produced something akin to the Essenes.[103] Bruce holds a similar view, though without the emphasis on Essenism.[104] Lewis finds an incipient Gnosticism influenced by Essenes, but also by mystery religions.[105] Also finding a Jewish basis for their teaching, Gewiess thinks they remain monotheists, even though veneration of astral deities stands at the center of their cult. Veneration of these beings is necessary because they are close enough to God to influence God. In fact, the influence they wield is such that salvation is dependent upon them.[106] Lohse rejects the idea that Judaism forms the basis for the opponents' teaching. He argues that the demands for circumcision and the observance of the Sabbath do not show that the teaching was based in Judaism, only that it included elements from Judaism.[107]

Dibelius identified these opponents as syncretists. He argued that they bring into Christianity features of an "elements" cult and mystery religion rituals.[108] His view rests in no small part on his understanding of ἐμβατεύω as a technical term for initiation into mystery cults. Similarly, Scott argues that these syncretists import pagan elements into the church. They worship angels to supplement the work of Christ because, for them, the work of Christ only provides forgiveness of sins, and so addresses only one aspect of the human situation. The angels they worship exercise power within the material realm, and so are needed to

---

[103] Joseph B. Lightfoot, "The Colossian Heresy," in *Conflict at Colossae: A Problem in the Interpretation of Early Christianity Illustrated by Selected Modern Studies* (ed. F. O. Francis and W. A. Meeks; SBLSBS 4; Missoula: SBL, 1973) 13–38. Lightfoot connects the Essenes with such an outlook because he views Essenism, with its angelology and its dualism, as "Gnostic Judaism" (24). A similar view is held by T. K. Abbott, *A Critical and Exegetical Commentary on the Epistles to the Ephesians and to the Colossians* (ICC; Edinburgh: T. & T. Clark, 1897) xlviii–xlix.

[104] F. F. Bruce, "Colossian Problems Part 3: The Colossian Heresy," *BibSac* 141 (1984): 195–208.

[105] Edwin Lewis, "Paul and the Perverters of Christianity," *Int* 2 (1948): 143–57.

[106] Josef Gewiess, "Die apologetische Methode des Apostels Paulus im Kampf gegen die Irrlehre in Kolossä," *BibLeb* 3 (1962): 258–66.

[107] Eduard Lohse, "Pauline Theology in the Letter to the Colossians," *NTS* 15 (1968): 211–20, esp. 212.

[108] Martin Dibelius, "The Isis Initiation in Apuleius and Related Initiatory Rites," in *Conflict at Colossae: A Problem in the Interpretation of Early Christianity Illustrated by Selected Modern Studies* (ed. Francis and Meeks) 61–122.

attain a higher spiritual life.[109] Arnold (whose work I will discuss at length below) returns to a view quite close to that of Dibelius. He argues that the opponents of Colossians have been initiated into mystery cults and bring the veneration of beings involved in those cults into the church.[110]

Several interpreters look to Hellenistic popular philosophy as the source of the opponents' teaching. Schweizer sees an influence of Jewish practices, but finds the teachings of Platonists and Pythagoreans more important as sources of the opponents' beliefs. He contends that they urge the Colossians to add ascetic practices to their belief in Christ. These practices are designed to enable the soul to ascend through the "elements" to the upper world.[111] Caird detects an amalgam of Stoic and Jewish ideas and practices, but finds the focus of the teaching to be on conduct of life rather than on speculation about spiritual powers.[112] DeMaris also argues that these teachers draw on Middle Platonism along with Jewish and Christian beliefs. He contends that their combination of beliefs and practices from these sources provides a way for the Colossians to pursue wisdom.[113] Troy Martin follows this general line of interpretation when he identifies the opponents of Colossians as non-Christian Cynic philosophers.[114] (I will also discuss Martin's proposal at length below.) According to Percy, the opponents' ascetic practices draw on Neo-Pythagorean and Neo-Platonic thought that they combine with Jewish

---

[109] E. F. Scott, *The Epistles of Paul to the Colossians, to Philemon, and to the Ephesians* (MNTC; New York: Harper and Bros., 1930) 7–12. Similarly Ralph P. Martin, *Colossians and Philemon* (NCB; London: Oliphants, 1974) 5–20.

[110] Clinton E. Arnold, *The Colossian Syncretism: The Interface between Christianity and Folk Belief at Colossae* (Grand Rapids: Baker, 1996).

[111] Eduard Schweizer, "Die 'Elemente der Welt' Gal 4,3. 9; Kol 2,8. 20," in *Verborum Veritas* (ed. O. Böcher and K. Haacker; Wuppertal: Theologischer Verlag Rolf Brockhaus, 1970) 245–59; "Christianity of the Circumcised and Judaism of the Uncircumcised: The Background of Matthew and Colossians," in *Jews, Greeks and Christians: Religious Cultures in Late Antiquity* (ed. R. Hamerton-Kelly and R. Scroggs; Leiden: E. J. Brill, 1976) 245–60 (where he argues that their teaching was quite close to that of some Pythagoreans, though they had added observance of the Sabbath and perhaps circumcision from Judaism, p. 257); "Slaves of the Elements and Worshipers of Angels: Gal 4:3, 9 and Col 2:8, 18, 20," *JBL* 107 (1988): 455–68; *The Letter to the Colossians: A Commentary* (Minneapolis: Augsburg, 1982) 126–36, 157.

[112] Caird, *Paul's Letters from Prison*, 160–64.

[113] Richard E. DeMaris, *The Colossian Controversy: Wisdom in Dispute at Colossae* (JSNTSup 96; Sheffield: Sheffield Academic Press, 1994).

[114] Troy Martin, *By Philosophy and Vain Deceit: Colossians as a Response to a Cynic Critique* (JSNTSup 118; Sheffield: Sheffield Academic Press, 1996).

thought and law, in a manner similar to that seen among the Ebionites and Philo's Therapeutae. However, Percy argues, they do not worship angels. Rather, the author of Colossians constructs this polemical exaggeration from the combination of their keeping of the Law (which by tradition was delivered by angels) and their asceticism.[115]

The primary early proponent of the view that the opponents worship with angels, rather than engage in angel veneration, is Fred Francis. He argued that these opponents participate in worship with angels during their visions of the heavenly realms. He draws on Jewish sources where ἐμβατεύω refers to the experience of entering the heavenly sphere in visions.[116] Sappington also thinks these opponents have a strong orientation "toward the ascetic-mystical piety of Jewish apocalypticism."[117] He adds that they teach the Colossians to take up their regulations because of the coming judgment, which is based on the Law, and in which angels serve as witnesses about them.[118] Bandstra agrees that these opponents engage in worship with the angels while in their mystic flights. But he also asserts that they claim not to need a mediator, not even Christ, to attain those experiences, and so to receive knowledge of the divine mysteries. In the face of this teaching, Colossians asserts that Christ is a divine intermediary.[119]

The views of Francis and Sappington better suit the evidence of Colossians. While the opponents of this letter draw on various sources, they are Christians who argue that all must attain visionary experiences through the exercise of their mildly ascetic practices (some of which are

---

[115] Ernst Percy, *Die Probleme der Kolosser- und Epheserbriefe* (Lund: Gleerup, 1946) 137–70.

[116] Fred O. Francis, "Humility and Angelic Worship in Col 2:18," *ST* 16 (1962): 109–34; "Visionary Discipline and Scriptural Tradition at Colossae," *LTQ* 2 (1967): 71–78; "Humility and Angelic Worship in Col 2:18," in *Conflict at Colossae: A Problem in the Interpretation of Early Christianity Illustrated by Selected Modern Studies* (ed. Francis and Meeks) 163–96. On the use of ἐμβατεύω in apocalyptic Judaism without identifying it as a technical term for visionary experiences, see Christopher Rowland, "Apocalyptic Visions and the Exaltation of Christ in the Letter to the Colossians," *JSNT* 19 (1983): 73–83 and Thomas J. Sappington, *Revelation and Redemption at Colossae* (JSNTSup 53; Sheffield: JSOT Press, 1991) 154–60.

[117] Sappington, *Revelation and Redemption at Colossae*, 225.

[118] Sappington, *Revelation and Redemption at Colossae*, 208–28.

[119] Andrew J. Bandstra, "Did the Colossian Errorists Need a Mediator?" in *New Dimensions in New Testament Study* (ed. R. N. Longenecker and M. C. Tenney; Grand Rapids: Eerdmans, 1974) 329–43.

derived from Judaism). They further argue that those without such experiences have not received God's full forgiveness, and so are not fully a part of God's people. The primary thing Colossians rejects about these visionaries is their passing of judgment against those without visions. Colossians maintains that all forgiveness and relationship with God is attained through Christ at baptism, so that no other experiences are required for one's place with God.[120]

1 Thessalonians

Since at least 1912, interpreters have argued that Paul's opponents in 1 Thessalonians are not members of the Christian community.[121] Many interpreters perceive them as Thessalonian Jews who find Paul too disruptive of their synagogue(s).[122] Others argue that 1 Thessalonians rebukes some Thessalonian Christians who have quit their jobs in anticipation of the parousia, without assuming that they form any opposition to Paul or his teaching.[123]

Still, several interpreters discern opposition within the Thessalonian church. Harnisch, Friedrich, and Jewett contend that these opponents are Pneumatics who have quit their jobs, advocate a licentious sexual ethic, and raise questions about the legitimacy of Paul's leadership, as well as that of the local church leaders.[124] Harnisch and Jewett add that

---

[120] See my fuller argument for this view in *Servants of Satan*, 188–213.

[121] James E. Frame, *A Critical and Exegetical Commentary on the Epistles of St. Paul to the Thessalonians* (ICC; Edinburgh: T. & T. Clark, 1912) 9–10.

[122] E.g., Frame, *Epistles of St. Paul to the Thessalonians*, 9–14; William Neil, *The Epistle of Paul to the Thessalonians* (MNTC; New York: Harper, 1950) xv–xvi; D. E. H. Whiteley, *Thessalonians* (New Clarendon Bible; London: Oxford University Press, 1969) 40; A. L. Moore, *1 and 2 Thessalonians* (Century Bible; Camden: Nelson, 1969) 5, 32; I. Howard Marshall, *1 and 2 Thessalonians* (NCB; Grand Rapids: Eerdmans, 1983) 17, 20; William Horbury, "1 Thessalonians 2:3 As Rebutting the Charge of False Prophecy," *JTS* 33 (1982): 507.

[123] E.g., Calvin Roetzel, "Theodidactoi and Handwork in Philo and 1 Thessalonians," in *L'Apôtre Paul: Personnalité, style, et conception du ministère* (ed. Vanhoye) 324–31.

[124] Gerhard Friedrich, "Der Zweite Brief an die Thessalonicher," in *Die Briefe an die Galater, Epheser, Philipper, Kolosser, Thessalonicher und Philemon* (NTD 8; 14th ed.; Göttingen: Vandenhoeck & Ruprecht, 1976) 205, 225; Wolfgang Harnisch, *Eschatologische Existenz: Ein exegetischer Beitrag zum Sachanliegen von 1 Thessalonicher 4:13–5:11* (FRLANT 110; Göttingen: Vandenhoeck & Ruprecht, 1973), 27–37; Robert Jewett, *The Thessalonian Correspondence: Pauline Rhetoric and Millenarian Piety* (Philadelphia: Fortress, 1986) 94–106.

over-realized eschatology is the basis for the various elements of opposition to Paul.[125] But there is no evidence of a connection between the Thessalonians' questions about eschatology and claims about measures of possession of the Spirit.[126] Seeing the opposition in a different light, Donfried and Lambrecht propose that Paul faces some personal attacks, but that these are not related to doctrinal differences between Paul and those who attack him.[127] Gillman, following Donfried, suggests that Paul must present an apology for his integrity and sincerity in 2:1–12, perhaps because he is being blamed for the persecution the Thessalonians are enduring, particularly since he left town because of persecution.[128]

Many interpreters conclude that 1 Thessalonians has no opponents in view.[129] The absence of any direct mention of opponents within the church lends initial support to this position. Moreover, nothing in the letter suggests this church faces or countenances opposition to Paul, only that there is a need for additional and corrective instruction. In fact, Timothy's good report about them suggests that Paul has no opponents within this church.[130] Furthermore, analyses of the rhetorical function of 2:1–10[131] and its similarities with philosophers' descriptions of their

---

[125] Harnisch, *Eschatologische Existenz*, 27–37; Jewett, *The Thessalonian Correspondence*, 169–70.

[126] So Charles A. Wanamaker, *The Epistles to the Thessalonians: A Commentary on the Greek Text* (NIGTC; Grand Rapids: Eerdmans, 1990) 55.

[127] Karl P. Donfried, "The Cults of Thessalonica and the Thessalonian Correspondence," *NTS* 31 (1985): 350–51; Jan Lambrecht, "Thanksgivings in 1 Thessalonians 1–3," in *The Thessalonian Correspondence* (ed. R. F. Collins; BETL 87; Leuven: Leuven University Press, 1990) 200.

[128] J. Gillman, "Paul's ΕΙΣΟΔΟΣ: The Proclaimed and the Proclaimer (1 Thess 2, 8)," in *The Thessalonian Correspondence* (ed. Collins) 62–70; Donfried, "The Cults of Thessalonica and the Thessalonian Correspondence," 350–51.

[129] Beda Rigaux, *Saint Paul: Les épitres aux Thessaloniciens* (EB; Paris: Gabalda, 1956) 59; Charles Masson, *Les deux épitre de Saint Paul aux Thessaloniciens* (Neuchatel: Delachaux & Niestlé, 1957) 32; Abraham Malherbe, "'Gentle as a Nurse': The Cynic Background to 1 Thessalonians 2," *NovT* 12 (1970): 203–17; Raymond F. Collins, "Paul as Seen Through His Own Eyes," in *Studies on the First Epistle to the Thessalonians* (BETL 66; Leuven: Leuven University Press, 1984) 184; Sumney, *Servants of Satan*, 214–28.

[130] So, Rigaux, *Saint Paul: Les épitres aux Thessaloniciens*, 59.

[131] So Hans D. Betz, "The Problem of Rhetoric and Theology According to the Apostle Paul," in *L'Apôtre Paul: Personalité, style, et conception du ministère* (ed. Vanhoye) 23; Frank W. Hughes, "The Rhetoric of 1 Thessalonians," in *The Thessalonian Correspondence* (ed. Collins) 98–102; Wilhelm Wuellner, "The Argumentative Structure of

work,¹³² suggest that 2:1–13 is not providing an apology in the face of opposition but establishing Paul's ethos.¹³³ Munck acknowledges Paul's use of this literary topos, but asserts that Paul would probably not use it unless the situation required him to clarify this distinction.¹³⁴ Schlier finds it probable that the Thessalonians had heard echoes of the charges made against Paul by opponents in other churches.¹³⁵ But little beyond opposition from outsiders would be necessary to move Paul to employ this topos. Indeed, Horbury concludes that the language Paul uses in this pericope would respond very well to charges brought by non-Christ-believing Jews that he is a false prophet.¹³⁶

2 Thessalonians

The majority of twentieth-century interpreters identified the opponents of 2 Thessalonians as teachers who proclaimed that the Day of the Lord was imminent.¹³⁷ Reicke, among many, maintains this view by arguing that,

---

1 Thessalonians as Paradoxical Encomium," in *The Thessalonian Correspondence* (ed. Collins) 131–33.

¹³² Helmut Koester, "1 Thessalonians—Experiment in Christian Writing," in *Continuity and Discontinuity in Church History* (ed. F. F. Church and T. George; Leiden: E. J. Brill, 1979) 41–42; Malherbe, "'Gentle as a Nurse': The Cynic Background to 1 Thessalonians ii," 203–17; Ronald Hock, *The Social Context of Paul's Ministry* (Philadelphia: Fortress, 1980) 48–49.

¹³³ So Rigaux, *Saint Paul: Les épitres aux Thessaloniciens*, 61; Masson, *Les deux épitres de Saint Paul aux Thessaloniciens*, 26–32; Ernest Best, *A Commentary on the First and Second Epistles to the Thessalonians* (BNTC; London: A. & C. Black, 1972) 21–22.

¹³⁴ Johannes Munck, "1 Thess. I.9–10 and the Missionary Preaching of Paul," *NTS* 9 (1963): 96. Cf. I. Howard Marshall who asserts that Paul thinks there are actual or possible accusations about him (*1 and 2 Thessalonians* [NCB; Grand Rapids: Eerdmans, 1983] 61). Similarly, Bruce C. Johanson finds no open distrust of Paul but asserts that Paul sees the potential for it (*To All the Brethren: A Text-Linguistic and Rhetorical Approach to 1 Thessalonians* [ConBNT; Stockholm: Almquist and Wiksell, 1987] 53–54).

¹³⁵ Heinrich Schlier, "Auslegung des 1. Thessalonicherbriefes," *BibLeb* 3 (1962): 91.

¹³⁶ William Horbury, "1 Thessalonians ii.3 as Rebutting the Charge of False Prophecy," *JTS* 33 (1982): 492–508. Cf. Raymond F. Collins, who compares Paul's comments with confessions of Jeremiah and notes, following Hock, that they serve as a paradigm for the later hortatory material ("Paul as Seen Through His Own Eyes," 184–87). For further comparison with Jeremiah and with Isaiah see Albert-Marie Denis, "L'Apôtre Paul, Prophète 'Messianique' des Gentils: Étude Thématique de 1 Thess II, 1–6," *ETL* 33 (1957): 245–318.

¹³⁷ E.g., George Milligan, *St. Paul's Epistles to the Thessalonians* (London: Macmillan, 1908) xxxviii; Ernst von Dobschütz, *Die Thessalonicher Briefe* (Göttingen: Vandenhoeck & Ruprecht, 1909) 21–22; Rigaux, *Saint Paul: Les épitres aux Thessaloniciens*,

since the issue of people quitting their jobs is present in both letters, the same eschatological outlook must be present in both.¹³⁸ Of course, this view assumes that the "disorderliness" (the more correct translation of ἀτάκτως) of the two letters is the same. But that is far from certain, especially if 2 Thessalonians is pseudonymous.¹³⁹

The direct evidence this understanding of the opponents must overcome is the explicit characterization of the opponents' position on the parousia in 2:2 ("the Day of the Lord has come," using the perfect tense of ἐνίστημι). Trilling recognizes this problem, and so argues that they have an over-realized eschatology.¹⁴⁰ Frame argued earlier that the "idle" of the two letters remain the same group, but that the problem with eschatology has changed. Though the eschatology he attributes to the opponents is not as over-realized as later interpreters recognize, he rejects interpretations of 2:2 that posit an imminent expectation of the parousia. He contends that they say the Day of the Lord has dawned and its completion is imminent. While this does not do full justice to the perfect tense of ἐνίστημι, it is a step toward recognizing its sense, and toward allowing the text of 2 Thessalonians to determine the setting it addressed.

653; Albrecht Oepke, "Die Briefe an die Thessalonicher," in *Die kleineren Briefe des Apostels Paulus* (NTD 8; 9th ed.; Göttingen: Vandenhoeck & Ruprecht, 1962) 156; Wolfgang Trilling, *Untersuchungen zum zweiten Thessalonicherbrief* (ETS 27; Leipzig: St. Benno, 1972) 91; Friedrich, "Der zweite Brief an die Thessalonicher," 257; Gören Argell, *Word, Toil, and Sustenance* (trans. S. Westerholm; Lund: Ohlssons, 1976) 123; Gerhard Krodel, "2 Thessalonians," in *Ephesians, Colossians, 2 Thessalonians, The Pastoral Epistles* (Philadelphia: Fortress, 1978) 87–88; C. H. Giblin, *The Threat to Faith: An Exegetical and Theological Re-Examination of 2 Thessalonians 2* (AB 31; Rome: Pontifical Biblical Institute, 1967) 243; Roger Aus, "2 Thessalonians," in *1–2 Timothy, Titus, 2 Thessalonians* (ACNT; Minneapolis: Augsburg, 1984) 192–94. See the common type of argument for this view in Robert Gundry, "The Hellenization of the Dominical Tradition and Christianization of Jewish Tradition in the Eschatology of 1–2 Thessalonians," *NTS* 33 (1987): 161–78.

¹³⁸ Bo Reicke, *Diakonie, Festfreude und Zelos in Verbindung mit der altchristlichen Agapenfeier* (Uppsala: Lundequistska, 1951) 244–45. Those who see such continuity between the two letters include F. F. Bruce, *1 & 2 Thessalonians* (WBC; Waco: Word, 1982) 205.

¹³⁹ One of the reasons Trilling judges 2 Thessalonians to be pseudonymous is that its eschatology is so different from that of 1 Thessalonians, *Der zweite Brief an die Thessalonicher* (EKKNT; Neukirchen-Vluyn: Neukirchener, 1980) 22. Marxsen also contends that 2 Thessalonians has given its own meaning to this term that it shares with 1 Thessalonians, *Der zweite Thessalonicherbrief* (ZBK; Zürich: Theologischer Verlag, 1982) 26, 29.

¹⁴⁰ Trilling, *Der zweite Brief an die Thessalonicher*, 26. See the comments of Abraham Malherbe on ἐνίστημι (*The Letters to the Thessalonians* [AB; New York: Doubleday, 2000] 417, 428–31).

Frame also is among the first not to attribute bad motives to this group (or any group a Pauline letter opposes). He argues that their eschatology comes from a misunderstanding of Paul; they "innocently attributed to Paul" the view that the Day of the Lord was already present.[141] Whiteley supports Frame's view by noting that those rejected here might see miracles and possession of the Spirit as evidence that the Day of the Lord had come, just as some within Jewish circles saw such phenomena as evidence of that day's arrival. Thus the Day has come, even though it may come more fully in the immediate future.[142] In a twist on this view, Menken argues that they believe Christ has returned to earth and has begun his work, or is about to begin it. Thus it is the sort of view the Synoptic Gospels warn against.[143]

Those who argue that ἐνίστημι must point to the future, because the following argument does not directly refute a spiritualized understanding of the parousia (e.g., von Dobschütz and Dibelius),[144] impose too narrow a limit on the type of argument an author may employ. Writers sometimes choose lines of argument that assume the denial of the claim they are refuting. This may be the way the author of 2 Thessalonians chooses to counter the opponents' understanding of the parousia.

Jewett and Hughes argue that the opponents' over-realized eschatology leads them to claim special pneumatic endowments.[145] Their fuller participation in the new age also leads them to reject the authority of Paul, and of traditional morality.[146] Giblin agrees that the problem is with pneumatics who argue the Day of the Lord has either begun, or is very imminent. Furthermore, the problem with them is so serious that Paul identifies their leader as the "Restrainer" who must be taken out of the way before the parousia may come.[147] Schmithals and Marxsen identify

---

[141] Frame, *Epistles of St. Paul to the Thessalonians*, 18.

[142] Whiteley, *Thessalonians*, 98.

[143] M. J. J. Menken, "Paradise Regained or Still Lost? Eschatology and Disorderly Behavior in 2 Thessalonians," *NTS* 38 (1992): 271–89, esp. 284–85.

[144] Ernst von Dobschütz, *Die Thessalonicher Briefe* (Göttingen: Vandenhoeck & Ruprecht, 1909) 267–68; Martin Dibelius, *An die Thessalonicher I, II und die Philipper* (HNT; 12th ed.; Tübingen: J. C. B. Mohr [Siebeck], 1925) 37. Others who hold this view include: Best, *First and Second Epistles to the Thessalonians*, 276–78; Bruce, *1 & 2 Thessalonians*, 166.

[145] Jewett, *The Thessalonian Correspondence*; Frank W. Hughes, *Early Christian Rhetoric and 2 Thessalonians* (JSNTSup 30; Sheffield: JSOT Press, 1989) 85–93.

[146] B. N. Kaye argues that Paul's discussion of ethics in 2 Thessalonians gives no indication that the readers are abandoning ethical expectations ("Eschatology and Ethics in 1 and 2 Thessalonians," *NovT* 17 [1975]: 47–57, esp. 53).

[147] Giblin, *The Threat to Faith*, 150–51, 243.

these opponents as Gnostics, at least in part because of their over-realized eschatology.[148] Alternatively, Hughes connects these opponents with those of Colossians and Ephesians, to whom he also attributes an over-realized eschatology.[149]

Rigaux, Wanamaker, and Russell, among others, contend that 2 Thessalonians has no opponents or formal opposition in view.[150] According to Wanamaker, the author is correcting serious misunderstandings (an over-realized eschatology that has spiritualized the resurrection) rather than refuting opposition, even in 2:1–2.[151] Holland argues for the nuanced position that those 2 Thessalonians opposes do not intend to oppose Paul or his teachings. Rather, they have misunderstood him. At least, this is the perspective of the letter's author. Thus, they are opponents only in the sense that the letter opposes them, even as they think they correctly represent Paul's teaching. My reading also finds that those rejected in this letter do not think they oppose Paul or his teaching.[152] Still, the writer of 2 Thessalonians argues that its readers must reject their over-realized eschatology. It is their individualized sense of participating in the Day of the Lord that leads those opposed, because of their superior spirituality and experiences of God, to quit their jobs and dedicate themselves to ministry within the church. Though some interpreters see the ἀτάκτοι and those who hold the over-realized eschatology as two distinct and unrelated factions,[153] this seems unlikely.[154] The ἄτακτοι see their experiences as qualifications for ministry and support, as well as evidence of their authority.[155] But 2 Thessalonians asserts that such views are unacceptable to Paul.

---

[148] Marxsen, *Der zweite Thessalonicherbrief*, 42, 54; Schmithals, *Paul and the Gnostics*, 123–218.

[149] Hughes, *Early Christian Rhetoric*, 85–93.

[150] Rigaux, *Saint Paul: Les épitres aux Thessaloniciens*, 72; Wanamaker, *The Epistles to the Thessalonians*, 51; R. Russell, "The Idle in 2 Thessalonians 3:6–12: An Eschatological or Social Problem?" *NTS* 34 (1988): 105–19.

[151] Wanamaker, *The Epistles to the Thessalonians*, 51.

[152] See the discussion in *Servants of Satan*, 229–52.

[153] Kaye, "Eschatology and Ethics in 1 and 2 Thessalonians," 47–57; Russell, "The Idle in 2 Thessalonians 3.6–12," 105–19; Best, *First and Second Epistles to the Thessalonians*, 278. Best admits it is possible they are related in his treatment of 3:6–10, but adds that 2 Thessalonians does not make this connection (ibid. 334).

[154] See the arguments of Menken, "Paradise Regained or Still Lost? Eschatology and Disorderly Behavior in 2 Thessalonians," 271–89.

[155] Though Friedrich thought they held an immanentist eschatology, his instinct that they sought authority in the community was on target ("Der zweite Brief an die Thessalonicher," 205).

Pastoral Epistles

Interpreters throughout the modern period have usually studied the Pastoral Epistles as a group, rather than as individual letters. As a result, interpreters commonly assume they address a common situation.[156] Those who read the Pastorals as separate letters also often assume, and then find, a single type of opponent for all three.[157] Such presuppositions impose settings that distort our readings of these letters. Even if the Pastorals were written as a corpus and by the same author, each letter within the corpus may address different situations, outlooks, or opponents.[158]

The opponents of the Pastorals are usually identified as Gnostics or proto-Gnostics with some inclination toward requiring Gentile believers

---

[156] So, e.g., Günter Haufe, "Gnostische Irrlehre und ihre Abwehr in den Pastoralbriefen," in *Gnosis und Neues Testament: Studien aus Religionswissenschaft und Theologie* (ed. K.-W. Tröger; Gutersloh: Gerd Mohn, 1973) 325–39; Peter Trummer, "Corpus Paulinum—Corpus Pastorale: Zur Erörterung der Paulustradition in den Pastoralbriefen," in *Paulus in den neutestamentlichen Spätschriften* (ed. K. Kertelge; Freiburg: Herder, 1981) 122–45; Jürgen Roloff, *Der erste Brief an Timotheus* (EKKNT 15; Neukirchen: Neukirchener, 1988) 43; Norbert Brox argues that several things indicate that they are a group, including their: focus on community concerns and order, address to pastors rather than congregations, style, theological thought, church organization, opposition to the same heresy (*Die Pastoralbriefe* [RNT 7; Regensburg: Pustet, 1969] 11–12). Lorenz Oberlinner sees these documents as a group to such an extent that he does not allow that they are letters. When referring to them, he puts *Briefe* in quotation marks (*Die Pastoralbriefe* [HTKNT 11/2; vol. 1; Freiburg: Herder, 1994] xxvi). Philip Towner makes the somewhat unusual move of finding the Pastorals to be written by Paul and yet interpreting the three letters as a group (*The Goal of Our Instruction: The Structure of Theology and Ethics in the Pastoral Epistles* [JSNTSup 34; Sheffield: JSOT Press, 1989]).

[157] Wolfgang Schenk is one of the few who offers a justification for viewing the opponents of the Pastorals as a single group. He asserts that the overlapping ways they are described supports this understanding of them. But earlier on the same page he asserts that the polemic against them is so stylized that we can tell little about them ("Die Pastoralbriefe in der neueren Forschung," in *ANRW* II: Principat, 25: 3427). Given both these assertions, it seems that the overlap may exist because of the stylized polemic rather than similarities in the views the letters oppose.

[158] So also Luke T. Johnson, "2 Timothy and the Polemic Against False Teachers: A Re-examination," *JRS* 6–7 (1978–79): 1–26; Peter G. Bush, "A Note on the Structure of 1 Timothy," *NTS* 36 (1990): 152; Jerome Murphy-O'Connor, "2 Timothy Contrasted with 1 Timothy and Titus," *RB* 98 (1991): 403–18. J. N. D. Kelly sees a "broad pattern" that combines Jewish and Gnostic elements (even though they are not full fledged Gnostics) common to all the Pastorals, but acknowledges some differences among those opposed in Ephesus and Crete (*A Commentary on the Pastoral Epistles* [BNTC; London: A. & C. Black, 1963] 10–11). Anthony T. Hanson maintains that it is difficult to be specific about the opponents' identity because the Pastorals' description of them remains so general. He surmises that this is the case because these letters function as a handbook and so want to reject all sorts of heresy, not just one type (*The Pastoral Epistles* [NCB; Grand Rapids: Eerdmans, 1982] 15–16).

to adopt additional practices of Judaism.[159] But within this broad identification, interpreters differ on some points. Gritz finds "a gnosticizing form of Jewish Christianity" in which women played a leading role and that has both an ascetic wing and a libertine wing.[160] Similarly, Haufe argues that the Gnosticism of these opponents includes a licentious element, while they are ascetics and advocates of Gentiles taking up the Law.[161] But they do not advocate an aberrant Christology.[162] In this same vein, Roloff argues that, while they have Gnostic tendencies, they are not docetists.[163] After all, not all Gnostics are docetists.

Some interpreters clarify their image of these opponents with material from other writings. Finding Gnostic elements in their teaching, Knight sees them as similar to the opponents of Colossians.[164] Drawing on parallels in Colossians and 1 Corinthians, Towner finds an over-realized eschatology that is not a direct ancestor of Gnosticism. This over-realized eschatology is the source of both their prohibition against marriage and their emancipatory trend with respect to women.[165] Verner is also among those who argue that the opponents' sexual asceticism included tendencies toward female emancipation. He compares it to the outlook of the *Acts of Paul and Thecla*.[166]

Spicq identifies a single opponent for the three Pastoral letters, but rejects the Gnostic hypothesis. He argues that these opponents are Christ-believing Jews who use both rabbinic and Hellenistic interpretive techniques to give prominence to the Torah.[167] Their ascetic regulations, including their prohibition of marriage, have an Essene origin and are a

---

[159] So, e.g., Haufe, "Gnostische Irrlehre und ihre Abwehr in den Pastoralbriefen," 325–39; E. F. Scott, *The Pastoral Epistles* (MNTC; New York: Harper, 1937) xxix–xxx; Martin Dibelius/Hans Conzelmann, *The Pastoral Epistles* (Hermeneia; Philadelphia: Fortress, 1972) 65; Roloff, *Der erste Briefe an Timotheus*, 46; Oberlinner, *Die Pastoralbriefe*, xxxvii; Brox, *Die Pastoralbriefe*, 32–33.

[160] Sharon Hodgin Gritz, *Paul, Women Teachers, and the Mother Goddess at Ephesus* (New York: University Press of America, 1991) 115–16, 110–11.

[161] Haufe, "Gnostische Irrlehre und ihre Abwehr in den Pastoralbriefen," 326–27.

[162] Haufe, "Gnostische Irrlehre und ihre Abwehr in den Pastoralbriefen," 330.

[163] Roloff, *Der erste Briefe an Timotheus*, 46.

[164] George W. Knight III, *The Pastoral Epistles: A Commentary on the Greek Text* (NIGTC; Grand Rapids: Eerdmans, 1992) 12. Scott also connects these opponents to those of Colossians, but says they represent a combination of Jewish and pagan elements (*The Pastoral Epistles*, xxix–xxx).

[165] Towner, *The Goal of Our Instruction*, 22, 37–41.

[166] David C. Verner, *The Household of God: The Social World of the Pastoral Epistles* (SBLDS 71; Chico: Scholars Press, 1983) 178.

[167] Ceslas Spicq, *Saint Paul: Les Épîtres Pastorales* (EB; Paris: Lecoffre, 1947) lxiv–lxx, 22.

reaction to the moral laxity of the surrounding culture. Though the opponents of each letter emphasize different things, they all participate in magic, are ascetic, engage in extensive debates about the Law, and teach legends about the Jewish Patriarchs.[168] However, he doubts that they are even a heresy; they are only a mentality.[169]

Müller perhaps represents the polar opposite of those who assume a single front. He asserts that the opponents of 1 Timothy and Titus represent a group that stands in sharp opposition to those opposed in 2 Timothy.[170]

1 Timothy

Interpreters who reject the assumption that all three Pastorals address the same situation still often allow evidence from another of the other Pastorals to determine the nature of those 1 Timothy opposes. Thus, Murphy-O'Connor uses Titus to identify the opponents of 1 Timothy as Jewish Christ-believers who keep the food laws of Judaism and engage in speculative, though non-Gnostic, interpretations of Scripture, particularly its genealogies.[171] Similarly, Müller, who criticizes other interpreters for assuming a single type of opponent, uses Titus to identify the opponents of 1 Timothy as Law observant Jewish Christ-believers whose practices also include asceticism. He further speculates that this group includes the author of Revelation.[172] On the other hand, MacDonald finds Gnostics in 1 and 2 Timothy, but distinguishes them from the Jewish Christians of Titus. MacDonald connects concerns about food regulations, sexual asceticism, and the prominence of women, with the image of Paul found in later legendary materials.[173] Fee draws on 1 and 2 Timothy to identify these opponents as rogue elders of churches in Ephesus. These elders advocate ascetic practices, possess an over-realized eschatology, and relate to the Law in an unacceptable manner.[174]

Some interpreters do, however, work with the evidence of 1 Timothy alone. With this evidence, McEleney proposes that these opponents are

---

[168] Spicq, *Saint Paul: Les Épîtres Pastorales*, lv–lxx, 21, 137–38.
[169] Spicq, *Saint Paul: Les Épîtres Pastorales*, lxx.
[170] Ulrich Müller, *Zur frühchristlichen Theologiegeschichte* (Gütersloh: Gerd Mohn, 1976) 75–77.
[171] Murphy-O'Connor, "2 Timothy Contrasted with 1 Timothy and Titus," 415–16.
[172] Müller, *Zur frühchristlichen Theologiegeschichte*, 56–57, 61–64.
[173] Dennis R. MacDonald, *The Legend and the Apostle: The Battle for Paul in Story and Canon* (Philadelphia: Fortress, 1983) 56–66.
[174] Gordon Fee, *1 and 2 Timothy, Titus* (rev. ed.; NIBCNT; Peabody, MA: Hendrickson, 1988) 7–8.

libertines who disparage the Law.[175] Oden is still able to find proto-Gnostics who judge the material world to be evil.[176] But Lane argues that their rejection of marriage stems from their over-realized eschatology: they note that there will be no marriage in the age to come, and since that age has come, they eschew marriage.[177] Johnson, on the other hand, finds simply local elitists who have characteristics common to esoteric groups throughout the Hellenistic world. They present themselves as teachers of esoteric knowledge, and advocate an asceticism that opposes marriage and includes dietary regulations.[178]

The central issue that causes the author to reject these opponents is their interpretation of the Law, an interpretation that requires Gentile Christians to adopt the Torah's dietary laws. They impose stricter regulations about marriage than 1 Timothy thinks is proper, but this does not necessarily mean they think the material world is evil, as Stoic and Cynic discussions about marriage demonstrate.[179] Recognizing that these teachers may have other reasons for imposing marriage regulations leaves no substantial evidence that they advocate a general asceticism. Neither is there evidence that they are libertines or that they possess an over-realized eschatology.[180]

2 Timothy

Few interpreters distinguish between opponents of 2 Timothy and those of the rest of the Pastorals. This is the case in part because it devotes the least attention to those it opposes.[181] So little is said about opponents in

---

[175] Neil J. McEleney, "Vice Lists of the Pastoral Epistles," *CBQ* 36 (1974): 205–10.

[176] Thomas C. Oden, *First and Second Timothy and Titus* (IBC; Louisville: John Knox, 1989) 59. Similarly, Walter Lock thinks that the marriage regulations point to eastern tendencies that developed into Gnosticism (*A Critical and Exegetical Commentary on the Pastoral Epistles* [ICC; New York: Scribners, 1924] 47).

[177] William L. Lane, "1 Tim IV.1–3. An Early Instance of Over-realized Eschatology?" *NTS* 11 (1965): 164–67.

[178] Luke T. Johnson, *The Writings of the New Testament* (rev. ed.; Philadelphia: Fortress, 1999) 439–40.

[179] For treatment of those discussions see Will Deming, *Paul on Marriage and Celibacy: The Hellenistic Background of 1 Corinthians 7* (Cambridge: Cambridge University Press, 1995).

[180] See my argument for this view in *Servants of Satan*, 254–78.

[181] Robert J. Karris asserts that the only passage in 2 Timothy that is polemic is 3:1–9, and it contains many stock charges. Karris finds four polemical passages in 1 Timothy (1:3–11; 4:1–7; 6:3–5, 20–21) and two in Titus (1:10–16; 3:8–9; "The Background and Significance of the Polemic of the Pastoral Epistles," *JBL* 92 [1973]: 559–60).

2 Timothy that Johnson suggests they are used "entirely as contrast" to clarify the letter's portrait of the ideal minister.[182]

Others, however, do find opponents. Spicq argues that because they adopt Greek ideas about the evil nature of the material world, they misunderstand the resurrection, confusing the resurrection of the body with the moral resurrection accomplished at baptism. Still, their preoccupation with speculative debates is the main reason 2 Timothy rejects them.[183] Müller identifies them as Hellenistic Gentile Christians who possess an over-realized eschatology and propose the emancipation of women. Thus, they are significantly different from the Jewish Christ-believing teachers of the Law in 1 Timothy and Titus.[184]

Even though the primary purpose of 2 Timothy is hortatory rather than repudiation of other teachers, the author does oppose a group that has an over-realized eschatology (2:18). While what they claim to possess remains unclear, the author's polemical tone suggests that they have enjoyed some success in the churches this letter addresses.

Titus

While most interpreters simply identify the opponents of Titus as Gnostics, because they assume that for all the Pastorals, some note significant differences in the ways they are described. Titus's opponents clearly advocate that Gentiles take up more of the Law than Titus allows. Those who find Gnostics in all three letters turn to Titus for evidence that this Gnosticism is related to Judaism. Fee, without the assumption of a single front for the Pastorals, rejects identifying these opponents as Gnostics. Rather, he says they teach that Gentile Christians must adopt more observances of Judaism than the author thinks appropriate.[185] Lock also finds Christ-believing Jews who emphasize the Law and Jewish myths, and view Judaism as a "higher philosophy." They live immoral lives, but require observance of the purity laws, including food laws (though not circumcision).[186] Rather than being converted Jews, Johnson

---

[182] Johnson, "2 Timothy and the Polemic Against False Teachers: A Re-examination," 12.

[183] Spicq, *Saint Paul: Les Épîtres Pastorales*, 354–55, 360. Similarly, Lock thinks they teach from well-known stories from Jewish Haggadah and have an over-realized eschatology, but adds that some of them are magicians (*Commentary on the Pastoral Epistles*, 78). Murphy-O'Connor finds futile debates their main fault ("2 Timothy Contrasted with 1 Timothy and Titus," 415).

[184] Müller, *Zur frühchristlichen Theologiegeschichte*, 167–75.

[185] Fee, *1 and 2 Timothy, Titus*, 171.

[186] Lock, *Commentary on the Pastoral Epistles*, 121, 132–33.

sees them as non-Christ-believing opponents who are winning converts from among recent converts to the Church.[187]

My reading of Titus finds these opponents to be Christ-believing Jews who promote interpretations and observances of the Torah for Gentiles that the author rejects. They give attention to purity regulations, but the letter does not indicate which ones. Notably, Titus presents these opponents as a local phenomenon, not as part of a movement that has now arrived in Crete.

Increased Attention to Method

One reason for the many and contradictory hypotheses about Paul's opponents is that interpreters have paid too little attention to the methods they use to identify them. Nils Dahl called attention to this issue in an important essay on 1 Corinthians, in which he asserted that no progress could be made toward identifying that letter's opponents until interpreters adopted "a strict method."[188] He then set out "principles" for pursuing the task of identifying opponents. His principles are: (1) that readers bear in mind that Paul writes the letter in the midst of a controversy and describes the situation from his own perspective; (2) that interpreters must base a reconstruction of the letter's occasion primarily on information in the letter, and evaluate types of statements within a letter so that relatively objective statements serve as the basis for our understanding, with evaluations and polemical allusions filling in the picture, while using Paul's teachings sparingly; (3) that interpreters use information from other Pauline letters and from contemporary materials only after the situation is described as much as possible on the basis of the primary text; and (4) that the hypothesis gains credibility as it accounts for more of the letter's argument and fits into our understanding of the first-century Church.[189] These principles set important directions for more controlled investigations of Paul's opponents and point the way to achieving more probable conclusions.

Others also began to give attention to method, particularly rejecting some methods previous interpreters had employed. J. Tyson, C. J. A. Hickling, K. Berger, and J. L. Martyn critiqued the ways interpreters

---

[187] Johnson, *The Writings of the New Testament*, 446.
[188] Dahl, "Paul and the Church," 317.
[189] Dahl, "Paul and the Church," 317–18.

often use texts in a rather flat manner, particularly for not distinguishing types of contexts, and so not permitting Paul to teach his readers without opposing a specific statement from the opponents.[190] R. McL. Wilson pointed out the problems involved in allowing reconstructions of later times to influence our readings of texts.[191]

Cosgrove takes up the issue of method in his study of Galatians. He points to formal analysis of epistolary transitions as an aid to identifying the primary exigency of a letter. He rejects autobiographical sections as a starting point, because such narratives can be used to argue many different points.[192] Similarly, he excludes hortatory sections as primary sources of information, because we cannot determine with certainty whether the exhortations are of the general sort often found in such sections, or whether they address a specific and problematic circumstance. Furthermore, a single exhortation may be applicable to any number of situations.[193] He does, however, allow epistolary greetings and thanksgivings to yield information about the opponents.[194] Still, according to Cosgrove, the best clues about opponents appear in the central argumentative section of the letter's body. But even here problems emerge. Not only do many parts of the argument build on former parts, but as Paul assumes the readers' knowledge of the situation, he can use general language to make a point the initial readers will apply to the matter at hand. So his point may be clear to those first readers, but not to later readers. Similarly, an allegory is such a multivalent literary type that it will not clarify the nature of the problem the letter addresses. Cosgrove concludes that the appropriate place to begin to identify the letter's exigency is with the first section that addresses the problem specifically and directly.[195] Only by starting here do interpreters respect the letter's argumentative integrity.

---

[190] Joseph B. Tyson, "Paul's Opponents in Galatia," *NovT* 10 (1968): 241–54; C. J. A. Hickling, "Is the Second Epistle to the Corinthians a Source for Early Church History?" *ZNW* 66 (1975): 284–87; Klaus Berger, "Die impliziten Gegner: Zur Methode des Erschliessens von 'Gegner' in neutestamentlichen Texten," in *Kirche* (ed. D. Lührmann and G. Strecker; Tübingen: J. C. B. Mohr [Siebeck], 1980) 372–400; Martyn, "A Law-Observant Mission to Gentiles: The Background of Galatians," 313.

[191] "How Gnostic Were the Corinthians?" *NTS* 19 (1972): 65–74; "Gnosis at Corinth," in *Paul and Paulinism* (ed. Hooker and Wilson) 102–14.

[192] Cosgrove, *The Cross and the Spirit*, 31–32.

[193] Cosgrove, *The Cross and the Spirit*, 32–33.

[194] Cosgrove, *The Cross and the Spirit*, 34–35.

[195] Cosgrove, *The Cross and the Spirit*, 38.

Cosgrove delineates clearly the problems with reading every section and type of statement in a letter in ways that allow them to supply straightforward information about the opponents. But in the end his complete exclusion of some sections is problematic. Direct statements about the opposition may appear in any sort of context, and so must not be completely excluded because they appear in a type of section that seldom supplies such information. Furthermore, his selection of the "first unit" that provides specific and direct information about the opponents as the foundation for identifying them assumes that Paul will state the problem clearly at first and then argue against it. It may rather be that Paul exaggerates the opponents' position at the beginning to make them more unacceptable. Should this first reference appear in the greeting or thanksgiving, that literary convention could also affect the reliability of Paul's statement about them. So Cosgrove's starting point is too limited to serve as a general rule. On the other hand, Cosgrove has shown the importance of looking to direct statements about the opponents as our starting point for understanding them.

Mark Nanos also gives significant attention to method in his study of Galatians. But rather than looking to the first place Paul speaks of his opposition as the most important, Nanos asserts that "situational discourse units" contain the most important information about those Paul opposes. He defines these units as sections that are written directly to the recipients, as opposed to those sections that support Paul's argument. Situational discourses are passages in which Paul uses "I-you" or "I-you-they" contrasts.[196] Nanos finds sections that express ironic rebuke as the most informative. He does not completely exclude information that appears about those opposed in other types of sections, but he does classify it as less direct.[197]

Requiring a whole section to address the letter's situation directly may well exclude from our initial gathering of data some direct and straightforward statements. It seems unwise to exclude fairly direct statements about opponents merely because they may appear in unexpected places. The need to have statements about those opposed appear in the "situational discourses" led Nanos to apply this designation to some sections that one would not expect to find classified as such. For example, Nanos identifies the hortatory material in Gal 5:2–18 as a situational

---

[196] Mark D. Nanos, *The Irony of Galatians: Paul's Letter in First-Century Context* (Minneapolis: Fortress, 2002) 62–72.

[197] Nanos, *The Irony of Galatians*, 68.

discourse, but not the vice and virtue lists in 5:19–23. But then 5:24–6:10, which continues the exhortations of 5:19–23, is again a situational discourse.[198] Such shuffling within a fairly smooth-flowing section seems to indicate that the categories are not sufficient for the task they have been given. Moreover, many interpreters see a very different relationship between the kinds of exhortations that appear in these sections and the immediate situation a letter addresses. Still, Nanos has rightly emphasized the need to begin with direct statements about the situation. He has not made the case that the whole section must be a direct statement to the readers of a point at issue.

It is rather surprising that Nanos designates a statement of ironic rebuke as the most informative about the other teaching. He is correct that this is a common tone in Galatians, but this only complicates the task of understanding those Paul opposes. An ironic remark may set itself against any of several different positions, so we need some less rhetorically-charged types of statements to help us locate the target of the irony.

The most detailed proposal for a method for identifying opponents comes from my own work. This method includes guidelines for the use of reconstructions, the use of parallels in other texts, and the use of materials within the primary text.[199] I argue that interpreters must not allow prior reconstructions of the early Church to determine the identity of a letter's opponents. Reconstructions can present possibilities, but not probabilities. Thus, interpreters must not begin with the presupposition that there is only one sort of opposition to Paul in the early Church. We may reach that conclusion at the end of a comprehensive study, but we must not start with that as a presupposition. A broad reconstruction of the early Church may also help us test a hypothesis about those opposed in a given letter. If interpreters are able to connect those opposed with known groups in the Church or culture, this adds support for the hypothesis.[200]

This method also sharply curtails use of parallels, whether from within or outside the Pauline corpus. Since language is so multivalent, it must be clear that the parallel operates within the same conceptual framework and does, in fact, use the term in the same way before we identify it as a true parallel. Then, even true parallels cannot serve as primary information about a letter's opponents, because similarities in uses of words or

---

[198] Nanos, *The Irony of Galatians*, 72.
[199] This method is argued for in most detail in my *Identifying Paul's Opponents*, 75–120 and is restated with some response to critiques in *Servants of Satan*, 13–32.
[200] *Identifying Paul's Opponents*, 77–86.

ideas do not necessarily indicate that other things about the two situations are the same.[201]

Finally, this method evaluates how certain we can be that a statement actually refers to those opposed (i.e., is it an explicit statement about them, an allusion, or an affirmation that possibly speaks of them?) and how reliable that statement is, given the type of context in which it appears.[202] In this method, explicit statements in non-polemical contexts carry more weight than similar statements in polemical contexts. Conversely, interpreters must not assume that topics addressed in a didactic section directly refute some opposition. Interpreters must demonstrate that statements in such contexts relate to things the opponents do or teach before using them to clarify our understanding of them. Weighing certainty of reference and reliability is preferable to excluding some fairly direct statements about those opposed because they appear too late in the argument (contra Cosgrove), or in the wrong sort of section (contra Nanos). Where in the letter a statement about opponents appears and in what type of context, make significant differences in how reliable it may be. But these factors should not exclude from consideration evidence that appears in problematic types of contexts, particularly if it contains an explicit statement about those opposed.

The increasing attention interpreters have given to method has not led to complete agreement about methods or the identity of those Paul opposes. Differences in interpretation of the texts will probably mean that general agreement remains elusive. Still, this attention to method gives a better starting point for discussions about those differences and some directions for resolving some of them.

ANTI-PAULINE MOVEMENTS

Our survey of hypotheses about the opponents and our discussion of method indicate that interpreters should not assume a single type of opponent for all of Paul's letters. Some Pauline letters oppose teachers or

---

[201] *Identifying Paul's Opponents*, 87–94. D. H. Fischer (*Historians' Fallacies: Toward a Logic of Historical Thought* [New York: Harper & Row, 1970] 247) calls the use of parallels that assumes that the two situations are identical "the fallacy of the perfect analogy." See also the important articles by S. Sandmel, "Parallelomania," *JBL* 81 (1962): 1–13 and John M. G. Barclay, "Mirror-Reading a Polemical Letter: Galatians as a Test Case," *JSNT* 31 (1987): 73–93 on the limits of the use of parallels.

[202] See Sumney, *Identifying Paul's Opponents*, 95–113 for a fuller discussion.

teachings that do not belong to an anti-Pauline movement. 1 Corinthians treats problems that arise from within the congregation rather than with intruders. Colossians and 2 Thessalonians oppose teachings whose advocates do not see themselves as Paul's opponents. So when Paul (or the Pauline writer) rejects another teaching or teacher, it is not always because that teacher intentionally opposed Paul. On the other hand, we cannot assume that there were no anti-Pauline movements or connections among those the letters oppose. The letters also show that some believers did intentionally oppose Paul's apostolic status or teaching. Among these intentional opponents, we can identify two organized movements that raised rather different kinds of issues.[203]

Paul's opponents in 2 Corinthians argue for an understanding of apostleship that differs significantly from Paul's. The letters of recommendation they bring to Corinth indicate that they are part of a movement that sponsors their mission in the Pauline churches. They claim to be apostles and reject Paul's claim to that position. They argue that a strong and impressive personal appearance and demeanor are evidence that God's Spirit lives in them in the measure required to qualify them for apostleship. They insist that genuine apostles engage in comparisons with others and so show themselves to be superior. By their standards, Paul falls short. They see their superiority as a demonstration that the Spirit of God dwells in them in a measure fuller than it dwells in non-apostles.

Paul and this mission movement disagree about appropriate expressions of leadership and about the structure of authority within the Church. Those teachers who came to Corinth after Paul adopt models of leadership from the Hellenistic and Roman worlds that Paul rejects, because he patterns leadership after the crucified Christ. So Paul and his following legitimated and exercised authority in ways that were significantly different from the other movement. This disagreement about structures of authority, rather than any other issues of doctrine or practice, led this movement to oppose Paul and his mission actively.

The second anti-Pauline movement differs from Paul about how to draw the boundaries of membership within the movement. Traditionally, New Testament scholars have called those within this movement Judaizers. But that label has often been denigrating and is historically inaccurate. These teachers were not trying to draw Christianity into Judaism, they wanted to keep the Christ-believing community from leaving the

---

[203] See the more detailed discussion in *Servants of Satan*, 303–22.

bounds of Israel. From their point of view, they were trying to keep Christ-believers from leaving the ways God's people had maintained their identity as, and lived as, God's people. Israel had always been called to live out their identity as God's people by keeping the Law, and since the Maccabean revolt, that had been done most obviously through circumcision, the food laws, and Sabbath observance. The Gentile Christ-believers were not conforming to this model.

Paul argues that membership within the people of God is determined by turning to the God of Israel and trusting in Christ as savior, i.e., as the one through whom one has a covenant relationship with God. A necessary part of turning to God is that one lives as God demands, but for Gentiles that does not entail becoming a proselyte to Judaism. In this way, Paul has redefined the boundaries of the people of God. Within the people of God there are still Torah observant Jews, but now there are also Christ-believing non-Jews.

Some Christ-believers rejected this reshaping of the identity of God's people and so opposed Paul's mission. Paul warns against these opponents in Philippians 3. The level of opposition between Paul and this movement is such that he is willing to call them "dogs." Discussion of this movement in Acts indicates that it was well known in the early years of the church. This group intentionally opposes Paul because they disagree with him about how Gentiles are to live as members of the people of God. The question about how to keep the Law was a matter of group identity, not legalism.

The two anti-Pauline movements we have discussed do not seem to be related. They have very different agendas and arguments for their views. Each addresses an important issue in the development of emerging movements: one is concerned with authority structures, the other with group boundaries. Their opposition to Paul and his mission is not sufficient reason to force them into a single movement or to force all those opposed in the Pauline letters into one of these groups.

Revisiting the Relationship between Historical Context (i.e., Reconstructions) and Letter

As we have seen above, the past decade has witnessed an increase in the care many interpreters exercise in evaluating statements about opponents in Pauline texts. Interpreters have become increasingly aware that the type of context in which a statement appears affects its usefulness for identifying opponents. For example, statements about the practices of others in polemical contexts that appear to be descriptions are actually exaggerations or accusations, particularly about the opposition's moral character.[204] Moreover, descriptions of the opponents' views in such contexts may be presented in ways that make them less acceptable or easier to defeat in argumentation. So when Paul says in Gal 6:12 that the only reason those he is opposing advocate circumcision is so they can avoid persecution, he impugns their character and makes them suspect in the eyes of the readers. But it seems unlikely that this is the *only* reason they urge circumcision on the Christian Gentiles. A similar exaggeration and skewing of what the opponents do occurs throughout 2 Corinthians, when Paul accuses them of illegitimate boasting. Those teachers certainly did not understand their recounting of their qualifications as expressions of hubris. But Paul's polemical description of the situation is calculated to turn the readers back to him and his understanding of the gospel's implications.

While interpreters have exercised more caution with respect to use of polemical and apologetic statements within letters, thought about how to draw on the material and intellectual culture of the context has not advanced at the same pace. The monographs on the opponents of Colossians by Troy Martin[205] and Clinton Arnold[206] will serve as illustrations of the ways interpreters continue to draw on reconstructions without sufficient limitations. These two studies make similar moves methodologically, but come to very different understandings of those opposed in Colossians. Both allow reconstructions of movements they find in the culture to determine prematurely their understandings of the language of Colossians. Both do this by means of vocabulary parallels between Colossians and the group they use to identify the opponents.

Troy Martin's study has much to commend it. Martin wrestles with the grammar and syntax of difficult passages with a rigor and openness that is rare in New Testament studies. Such careful and open examinations of

---

[204] See the treatments of this issue in Frederick Wisse, "The Use of Early Christian Literature as Evidence for Inner Diversity and Conflict," in *Nag Hammadi, Gnosticism, and Early Christianity* (ed. C. Hedrick and R. Hodgson, Jr.; Peabody, MA: Hendrickson, 1986) 177–90; idem, "The Epistle of Jude in the History of Heresiology," in *Essays on the Nag Hammadi Texts in Honor of Alexander Böhlig* (ed. M. Krause; NHS 3; Leiden: E. J. Brill, 1972) 133–43; Johnson, "2 Timothy and the Polemic Against False Teachers: A Re-examination," 1–26.

[205] Martin, *By Philosophy and Empty Deceit*.

[206] Arnold, *The Colossian Syncretism*.

the text demand the attention and consideration of all readers. Many of his proposals for readings of difficult passages have received too little attention, even though he argues on solid grounds.

Martin identifies the opponents of Colossians as Cynic philosophers who have come into the church's worship and community and, as a result, critique its beliefs and practices. These non-Christian philosophers enjoy enough success that Colossians must respond at length. Martin follows the basic structure of my own method in his initial treatment of the texts of Colossians. However, he argues that reconstructions should be used more extensively and earlier than that method allows.[207] Martin first draws elements of the opponents' beliefs and practices from Colossians. He then presents a reconstruction of Cynic beliefs and practices, arguing that Colossians opposes important, even unique, elements of their teaching. Particularly, Martin contends that the Cynics' "prohibitions against perishable consumer goods and understanding of humility as severity to the body" are unique in the contemporary culture. Colossians' opposition to these things (2:21–22, 23), he reasons, constitutes sufficient evidence to demonstrate that the opponents are Cynics.[208] He finds other corroborating evidence for this hypothesis, but these are the decisive elements.

While these elements may not appear elsewhere combined as they are in Cynic thought, the various elements that Martin identifies as Cynic are, in fact, found elsewhere. For example, Jewish apocalyptic texts recognize limited ascetic practice as a way to attain mystical experiences. In these texts, prayer and fasting are ways of preparing for such experiences (e.g., *4 Ezra* 5:13; 6:31, 35; 9:23–28; *2 Bar.* 54:6–7; *3 Bar.* 4:13–15).[209] So humility before God and moderate asceticism are found together and related in other movements. Still, there are distinctive things about the Cynic combination of these elements.

More important methodologically, Martin allows the terminology parallels he finds to exercise more influence than is sound. His level of use of both parallels and the reconstruction of Cynic thought is an intentional methodological decision. But this decision means that Cynic language and teaching determine the meaning of the text of Colossians at a very early stage. Once Martin connects Colossians and Cynic thought, he interprets all of Colossians through the lens of opposition to Cynics. The

---

[207] Martin, *By Philosophy and Empty Deceit*, 23–25.
[208] Martin, *By Philosophy and Empty Deceit*, 205; 65–78.
[209] See these and other texts in Sappington, *Revelation and Redemption at Colossae*, 65–69.

assumption of this connection allows Martin to use purely terminological parallels to confirm this identity of the opponents. Thus, the phrase "human tradition" becomes a reference to the Cynics' claim to be rooted in a tradition (hardly a unique claim among philosophers) rather than a polemical accusation that denigrates the other teaching.[210] With the same lens, the Cynic characteristic of being blunt in their critiques of the lives of others explains the opponents' practice of passing judgment on the readers.[211] Finally, it is through Cynic discussions of the structure of the cosmos that Martin understands the reference to the στοιχεῖα in Col 2:8 and 20.

The basic methodological problem is that the reconstruction of the Cynics determines the meaning of the texts of Colossians. This is the same method that Georgi used to identify the opponents of 2 Corinthians as divine men.[212] Georgi first gleaned obvious features of the opponents from the text of 2 Corinthians. He then constructed the image of the "divine man" from a rigorous investigation of Hellenistic Jewish texts. Once he had completed his reconstruction of this ideology, he returned to 2 Corinthians. He made the initial connections between the letter and the *theios aner* on the basis of some parallels in terminology and outlook. He then fitted the remaining texts of that letter into the framework he had constructed, so that 2 Corinthians addressed opponents who possessed that theology. His interpretations of crucial passages relies more on the reconstruction than on the passage's literary context.[213] Such uses of reconstructions prematurely constrict the meaning of a text in its own context. The problems with such an approach become clear when we think about the broad semantic range of many words. This problem is particularly acute when we cross from the use of a word in philosophic writings to its use in the New Testament. Neo-Platonists and Cynics often use a word in ways that are significantly different from its New Testament usages. Thus, these kinds of parallels must not determine the meaning of the primary text.

Clinton Arnold makes the same methodological moves as Martin, but comes to a very different conclusion about the opponents of Colossians,

---

[210] Martin, *By Philosophy and Empty Deceit*, 86–87.
[211] Martin, *By Philosophy and Empty Deceit*, 78–80.
[212] Georgi, *Die Gegner*.
[213] This is clearly the case with his treatment of 2 Cor 3. See the more detailed discussion of Georgi's use of his reconstruction in Sumney, *Identifying Paul's Opponents*, 49–55.

because his reconstruction of the background draws on different material. Arnold holds that Colossians opposes a mixing of the folk religion of western Asia Minor with Christian beliefs. He constructs the substance of that folk religion largely from evidence that involves magic, particularly when such appears in Jewish contexts. Arnold compiles extensive information about ways angels and various beings are invoked in the magical papyri, inscriptions, and amulets. He also draws on Jewish literature (e.g., Tobit) and other sources from western Asia Minor. From this material he argues that angels were important in the religious life of both Jewish and non-Jewish residents of that region. According to Arnold, residents of this area called upon angels to protect them from various kinds of evil, whether the source was the human or spirit world.

Arnold connects Colossians with the folk religion he reconstructs through broad parallels. For example, since both the magic tradition (especially revelatory magic) and the opponents of Colossians associate visions with purity regulations and knowledge, Arnold seems to assume that connection whenever one of these elements is mentioned. This is particularly the case when the element is combined with a term that appears in both contexts (ἄγγελος and στοιχεῖα among the most important).[214] He then infers that since angel veneration was prominent in the region, the mention of θρησκεία τῶν ἀγγέλων must mean that the opponents also venerate angels—and this even though the noun θρησκεία does not appear in the local materials he cites. Once he makes this inference, he explicitly bases his understanding of the opponents' teaching on the way angels were venerated in western Asia Minor.[215]

Arnold employs the same methodological procedure when developing his understanding of the difficult word ἐμβατεύω.[216] He notes that the second phase of initiation into mystery cults, particularly those known in western Asia Minor, involved entering a particular sacred place and having ecstatic visions. Following Ramsay and Dibelius, he identifies ἐμβατεύω as a technical term for this initiatory event. After this discussion of mystery religion initiations, Arnold simply assumes that because Colossians mentions "entering into" in association with visions, that it has such initiations in view. He supports this assumption by citing the local fear of evil spiritual powers, Apuleius's mention of the "elements," and the ascetic practices mystery cults often employed in their initiations

---

[214] Arnold, *The Colossian Syncretism*, 30–31.
[215] Arnold, *The Colossian Syncretism*, 90.
[216] Arnold, *The Colossian Syncretism*, 104–57.

as preparation for visionary experiences. According to Arnold, these common features show that the opponents of Colossians have been initiated into mystery cults and were urging others to follow this course.[217] But fear of evil spiritual powers and seeking protection from them were common phenomena throughout the ancient world. And it is not only in mystery religions that some ascetic practices were used to elicit a visionary experience.

A connection between the teaching of the Colossian opponents and local mystery cults is certainly possible. But such terminological parallels do not render that connection probable. Different communities use the same language to mean very different things (as we noted above in connection with Martin's parallels in philosophic literature). Not only can language function differently in different contexts, but the use of a word across time also changes. This significantly weakens Arnold's case for the first-century existence of the outlook he reconstructs because he draws on evidence that is as much as 200 years later than Colossians. Moreover, he seems to assume that geographic proximity to the purported recipients of Colossians is almost evidence enough that a connection exists between the letter's opponents and the region's folk religion.

The connection between the region's "folk religion" and the problem Colossians addresses is rendered yet more difficult when Arnold includes the mystery cults within the category of folk religion. While folk religion seems to refer to the religion of the common people or the majority in the area, initiation into the mystery cults would usually have been a possibility only for the more wealthy. Initiation into these cults would have been dependent on financial ability and the leisure to devote that much time to such pursuits. A sign that such rites usually involved only those of wealth is the participation of the Roman emperors in them. Given the ways that Graeco-Roman culture, including its practices of religion, was segregated by social class, it is unlikely that emperors would have been initiated into cults that were known to have large numbers of lower-class initiates. Unless Arnold understands the Colossian church to be composed primarily of the relatively wealthy, the opponents' urging of its members to be initiated into a mystery cult could not be successful. The opponents could perhaps have claimed some superiority based on their experiences in such initiations, but the experience itself would have been out of the reach of most Christians in the region.

---

[217] Arnold, *The Colossian Syncretism*, 155–57.

Beyond these philological and sociological problems with Arnold's hypothesis, he also engages in circular reasoning at crucial points. His treatment of θρησκεία is an example. As we noted above, he argues that since angel veneration was prominent in the region, the reference to "worship of angels" must indicate that the opponents engage in a sort of angel veneration. He also asserts that θρησκεία must be a critique of the opponents' practice rather than a quotation from them because the term θρησκεία does not appear in magical texts.[218] This understanding of θρησκεία assumes that the magical texts are an important source for the opponents' teaching. At this point he assumes the correctness of his connection between those texts and the problems at Colossae, and uses that assumption as a proof for that connection. There is too much circularity in reasoning if we start with a presupposition from outside a text and then confirm that presupposition by reading texts in light of it. As the history of scholarship shows, one can fit the text into many different understandings of the problem using this method.

As a further historical question, we might ask why interpreters think veneration of angels would have troubled a first-century Christian writer. It seems that Jews of this period were able to distinguish between the worship they accorded to God alone and praying to other beings for various sorts of help. Arnold's own evidence shows that this was practiced in Asia Minor. Analyses of other Jewish materials, including some which seem to speak of practices among Palestinian Jews (including religious leaders), show that Jews of this period prayed to various intermediaries without seeing it as a violation of their commitment to God.[219] If Jews made this distinction, perhaps Christians did also. The point is that it may be later presumptions about the meaning of praying to angels and its inappropriateness that leads interpreters to see "worship of angels" as the problem Colossians addresses. Still, there are clear indications that some Christians found certain kinds of veneration of other beings problematic,[220] but many continued to read apocalyptic works in which beings of various sorts aided those who experienced heavenly journeys. But such questions about the accuracy of Arnold's assessment of the historical set-

---

[218] Arnold, *The Colossian Syncretism*, 95.

[219] See Meir Bar-Ilan, "Prayers of Jews to Angels and Other Mediators in the First Centuries C.E.," in *Saints and Role Models in Judaism and Christianity* (ed. M. Poorthuis and J. Schwartz ; JCPS 7; Leiden: Brill, 2004) 79–95 and the works he cites.

[220] E.g., Rev 19:10 and 22:9 where John is told not to worship the angel who is before him.

ting of Asia Minor and of Christians in that region are secondary in comparison with the methodological issues.

Martin and Arnold highlight important information about first-century Asia Minor. Furthermore, there is no doubt that the surrounding culture and even the subcultures of various regions influenced the various ways early Christians expressed their new-found faith. But this does not mean that they imported whole systems into their practice of the faith, so that we can assume particular elements or outlooks. Interpreters must demonstrate more significant connections with this environment, not assume them on the basis of a few common words or ideas. This environment was so diverse that interpreters can use various elements of it to construct nearly any understanding of a letter's opponents. Martin and Arnold employ the same methodology that Georgi used to identify the opponents of 2 Corinthians as "divine men," and Schmithals used to identify those same opponents as Gnostics.

Like Georgi and Schmithals, Martin and Arnold begin with the text of the letter. After identifying a few key ideas or phrases, they reconstruct a religious environment or school of thought or expression of religion from some aspect of relatively contemporary culture: for Georgi, Jewish propagandists; for Schmithals, Gnostics; for Martin, Cynic philosophers; for Arnold, practitioners of regional popular religions. When these interpreters return to the text, they assume that the segment of religious or philosophical culture they have described is the source of the problem the letter addresses, because each has found some characteristics that seem to relate the opponents to the movement he has described. Then that reconstructed movement determines the meaning of various expressions in the primary text. That is, Martin and Arnold interpret Colossians according to the scheme of the reconstruction rather than first in the context of the letter itself. Thus the reconstruction dominates the exegesis.

Part of the problem with such a method is evident in the radically different proposals that it produces. Martin and Arnold each find vocabulary similarities and other apparent points of contact with the movement they identify as the trouble. Since each can establish points of contact, each reads the whole letter through greatly differing reconstructions. Using this method, an interpreter can identify the problem Colossians addresses with a vast number of movements. Methodologically, a reconstruction of a movement external to the letter in question should not determine the meaning of particular texts, especially when that text is being used to identify the opponents. That sort of circularity provides no real basis for identifying the opponents of a letter. Furthermore, contacts between groups must not be based solely on the appearance of particular features in both. We must also look to how those features function and are related to other elements of the belief system. Only then might such common elements indicate, with some probability, participation in the same movement or outlook. Still, any argument that relies heavily on a reconstruction of a different movement is in danger of falling into the fallacy of the perfect analogy, in which one assumes that because two phenomena are alike in some ways, they are alike in all or other ways.[221]

The most certain characteristics of the teachers Colossians opposes (e.g., mild asceticism and attaining visions) could be related to many religious and philosophical movements of the time. But no cluster of beliefs or practices is sufficient to affirm a definite connection with any of them. Even if we could securely locate these teachers within a particular movement, many first-century movements were so diverse that such an identification would provide little substantial information about them. To attribute beliefs or practices to those Colossians opposes on the basis of things we find in a different context moves us into a level of speculation that cannot serve as a good basis for interpretation.

The works of Martin and Arnold, for all their merits in uncovering information about the first-century religious and philosophical context of the early Church, demonstrate the need to abide by stricter limits on how we use such materials and reconstructions from them to identify opponents.[222] By refusing to allow reconstructions to function in the ways Martin, Arnold, and many others use them, we can arrive at a more secure understanding of the letter's opposition, and so a better basis from which to interpret the letter. The conversation between Christians and other religious movements of the time should be assumed, but we cannot assume that Christians simply import the view of another group whole cloth. By exercising more caution in this aspect of our method, we may be able to achieve more certainty (though perhaps less specificity) about the situations particular letters address, and more clarity about the shape of the early Christian movement.

---

[221] See Fischer, *Historians' Fallacies*, 247. See also *Identifying Paul's Opponents*, 93–94.

[222] Martin is careful and explicit about his methodology, but his decision about the use of reconstructions makes his method unreliable.

INTRUDING "SPIES" AND "PSEUDO-BRETHREN": THE JEWISH INTRA-GROUP POLITICS OF PAUL'S JERUSALEM MEETING (GAL 2:1–10)

MARK D. NANOS
Rockhurst University, Kansas City, MO, USA

Interpretation of Paul's sketchy description of his meeting in Jerusalem, retold for the benefit of the Galatian addressees, has proven to be decisive for the interpretation of the Galatian situation, as well as for constructions of early Christian history. The historical emphasis has naturally increased since the influential work of F. C. Baur, especially with the refinement of modern methodologies. This passage has even become important for investigations of the historical Jesus, if by default; for example, an important recent work on the historical Jesus explicitly appeals to the silence of the available data for any opposition of the Jerusalem priestly establishment to Paul's mission when framing the minimal historical "facts" from which to work.[1]

Any interpretation of this passage will revolve around the identity and role attributed to those whom Paul challenges for advocating the circumcision of Titus. The prevailing interpretative constructions have taken these people to be "Jewish Christians" who oppose Paul's ostensible effort to sever faith in Christ from observance of Torah, neatly framing the prevailing construction of "Paulinism."[2] By understanding the nature of the political engagement to be intra- or inter-Christian, the issue turns on the level of Jewish identity and behavior to be retained within these groups of believers in Christ. It should also be noted that for many interpreters these so-called "pseudo-brethren" represent the real—albeit momentarily repressed—beliefs and interests of the Jerusalem apostles,

---

[1] Paula Fredriksen observes that, "the earliest Christian evidence, Paul's letters, written midcentury, depict the disciples as ensconced comfortably in Jerusalem, directing a Mediterranean-wide mission without the slightest hint of constraint from Rome—or, for that matter, from Jerusalem's priestly hierarchy. Clearly, nobody in power was much worried about this movement" (*Jesus of Nazareth, King of the Jews: A Jewish Life and the Emergence of Christianity* [New York: Alfred A. Knopf, 1999] 9).

[2] See, e.g., Francis Watson, *Paul, Judaism and the Gentiles: A Sociological Approach* (Cambridge: Cambridge University Press, 1989 [1986]) esp. 19–22, 97–98.

and they are imagined to eventually prevail upon these apostles to initiate the programmatic anti-Pauline mission these interpreters find mirrored in the polemical concerns of Galatians, as well as in Paul's other letters.[3] These intruders are viewed as representatives of a "conservative" wing of so-called Jewish-Christianity, bearing within its very core the seeds of heresy which came to fruition in second- and third-century Ebionism.[4] As a result of these conclusions, from the very beginning of Paul's ministry, an unbridgeable gap is imagined to separate Pauline (i.e., so-called "Law-free") communities of Christ-believers from those expressing Jewish (i.e., Law-observant) lifestyles along with their new-found faith in Jesus as Christ.[5]

Yet such an approach interprets this narrative and its rhetorical purpose for the Galatians within the constraints of an arguably anachronistic framework. It proceeds as if Paul was only addressing inter-group political realities that are expected to characterize later institutional concerns of "Christianity," as if religious sensibilities and sectarian politics have already placed these rival "Christian" factions outside the scope of religious or political interests that might otherwise be expected to arise

---

[3] E.g., Gerd Lüdemann, *Opposition to Paul in Jewish Christianity* (trans. M. Eugene Boring; Minneapolis: Fortress Press, 1989) 35–39, 112–15; *idem, Heretics: The Other Side of Early Christianity* (Louisville: Westminster John Knox Press, 1996 [1995]) 40–43, 93–94; James D. G. Dunn, *Unity and Diversity in the New Testament: An Inquiry into the Character of Earliest Christianity* (2nd ed.; London: SCM Press and Valley Forge: Trinity Press International, 1990) 252–57; C. K. Barrett, "Paul: Councils and Controversies," in *Conflicts and Challenges in Early Christianity* (ed. Donald A. Hagner; Harrisburg, PA: Trinity Press International, 1999) 45. It is in this vein that Harnack maintained the ultimate place of Marcion as the champion of the Pauline tradition. Gager, drawing from Gaston's statement that Paul "has provided the theoretical structure for Christian anti-Judaism, from Marcion through Luther and F. C. Baur down to Bultmann," has argued that Paul's letters were canonized *for* their anti-Jewish perspective (John G. Gager, *The Origins of Anti-Semitism: Attitudes toward Judaism in Pagan and Christian Antiquity* [New York and Oxford: Oxford University Press, 1985 (1983)] 191).

[4] E.g., Dunn, *Unity*, 242–44, 252–55: "*A Jewish Christianity which had aligned itself so firmly with its Jewish heritage and which had set its face so firmly against Paul and the law-free Gentile mission was well on the way to Ebionism*" (275, emphasis his). See also Lüdemann, *Heretics*, 59–60; Raymond E. Brown and John P. Meier, *Antioch & Rome: New Testament Cradles of Catholic Christianity* (New York: Paulist Press, 1983).

[5] Dunn, *Unity*, 252–57: "it is quite clear, from Gal. 2 and Acts 15 at least, that they (e.g., the "false-brethren") were Jewish Christians—that is to say, a force *within* the Jerusalem community who could with justice claim to speak for Jewish believers in Judea. Moreover, they obviously saw it as their task to undo the evil which they thought Paul was doing with his law-free gospel; for evidently they set themselves deliberately against Paul and what he stood for" (253, emphasis his).

when a Jewish group proposes new halakic practices within the context of other Jewish groups, creating unavoidable implications for them and their political leaders, especially in Jerusalem during the Roman occupation. What has not been undertaken to date is an evaluation of Paul's language here as evidence of religious and political realities that may have arisen for the nascent Christ-believer coalition[6] within (*intra-*) and between (*inter-*) Jewish interest groups in a Judean context of the mid-first century, and thus with matters Jewish and Roman as well as Greek where social identity is concerned.

SETTING THE SCENE

In Gal 2:1–10 Paul describes an ultimate and unanimous agreement arrived at among the leaders of this group, yet in the telling a sharp disagreement is revealed as well. This important detail arises in Paul's narrative when describing some "others" who manage to gain entrance to a meeting to which they were, in Paul's opinion, unwelcome, since their attendance was intended to undermine the "truth of the gospel." In 2:4–5, as commonly translated, Paul describes them as "false-brethren [ψευδαδέλφους] secretly brought in, who slipped in to spy out our freedom which we have in Christ Jesus, that they might bring us into bondage," to whom "we did not yield submission even for a moment" (RSV).[7] Paul makes this statement in the midst of explaining how he and Barnabas had travelled to Jerusalem "by revelation" for the express purpose of yielding (ἀνεθέμην)[8] "the gospel which I preach among the Gentiles" to the

---

[6] Coalition as defined by Jeremy Boissevain (*Friends of Friends: Networks, Manipulators and Coalitions* [Oxford: Basil Blackwell, 1974] esp. 170–205) is helpful for labeling the Christ-believing group (or perhaps even groups) under discussion. A coalition is "a temporary alliance of distinct parties for a limited purpose" (171). Moreover, "coalitions may comprise individuals, other coalitions, and even corporate groups; and most show a concentric form of organization, with core and peripheral members" (173). While such groups seek to achieve a limited purpose, they nevertheless accumulate more tasks as time passes in that pursuit (171).

[7] Translations of this passage after this introduction are mine unless otherwise indicated.

[8] Bauer, *BAGD*: to lay something before someone for their consideration or opinion. See also discussions of James D. G. Dunn (*Jesus, Paul and the Law: Studies in Mark and Galatians* [Louisville: Westminster/John Knox Press, 1990] 113–16). While it may be that the relative status of the parties involved is not necessarily indicated by the use of this verb (Dunn, 114), the following phrase, "lest somehow I should be running or had run in vain," carries the sense of subordination (*contra* Dieter Georgi, *Remembering the Poor: The History of Paul's Collection for Jerusalem* [Nashville: Abingdon Press, 1992 (1965)] 25–31).

review of the apostles ("before those who were of repute" [v. 2]) having brought along Titus also (συμπαραλαβὼν καὶ Τίτον; v. 1). Paul's intention had been, however, to do so "privately [ἰδίαν]," that is, in concert with his own coalition's leaders and independent of the aims of these so-called "false-" or "pseudo-brethren." Nevertheless, they gained entrance and made their interests known.

Paul's description of the scene invites confusion, for he refers variously to two different interest groups in Jerusalem in similar subversive terms, as those who "seem to be" or are "reputed to be something." Paul notes the continued noncircumcision of Titus, a Gentile believer in Christ, as the confirmation of an agreement with some of those "of repute" (v. 3; cf. "James, Cephas, and John"; v. 9), since Titus, although a Greek, "was not being compelled to be circumcised." He clearly refers in this way to the other apostles of this coalition. However, Paul made this comment in v. 3 before interjecting a passing remark about others "of repute" in attendance. These he refers to derisively as "pseudo-brethren" who are in disagreement with both Paul and the apostles. In other words, within an intentionally private meeting (or series of meetings?), representatives of other interest groups with some right to exercise social control ("that they might bring us into bondage") were present, and unwelcome, at least by Paul. The point of retelling this incident is clear enough: even as these intruders did not have any final voice in controlling the "good news" then, so "that the truth of the gospel might be preserved for you," in the same way his readers must make it their responsibility to see that the influencers in Galatia fail to win the day now.

I propose that those Paul polemically referred to here as "pseudo-brethren" were representatives of non-Christ believing groups and interests, and Paul's description of them and this meeting bear witness to the *intra-* and *inter-*Jewish nature of the politics within which the nascent Christ-believing coalition was forged. I thus seek to reopen the historical question of precisely who they were and whom they represented, as well as how and why. Some prevailing views will be discussed, three new hypotheses for the identity of the pseudo-brethren will be sketched, a new translation of Paul's identifying terms will be proposed, and exegesis of the narrative of Gal 2:1–10 will be undertaken.

The Identity of the Pseudo-brethren Reconsidered

Gerd Lüdemann represents the views of many interpreters when he argues:

> we *must* assume that the "false brethren" had considerable support within the Jerusalem congregation for their demand that Titus be circumcised and at the beginning probably had the 'pillars' on their side. "How could they, in Jerusalem, under the very eyes of the most respected apostles, have possibly thought that they could *compel* the circumcision of Titus, unless the original apostles and the Jerusalem church already supported this view?" At least a majority of the congregation *must* have supported the "false brethren," for otherwise they could never have made the demand for circumcision so effectively.[9]

Lüdemann further maintains that, in spite of their failure against Paul, the "(indirect) influence" of the "false brethren" at the conference and later was significant; while at the same time he questions whether Paul's apostleship was even so much as recognized by the Jerusalem apostles.[10] Yet Lüdemann fails to explain why, if they had such successful influence with the apostles and the majority (in effect actually representing their true opinion), and Paul so little respect, they had to sneak in (the meeting was, after all, in Jerusalem, not Antioch), or why they lost. How does this demonstrate that they made their demand "so effectively," or that they had any "support," much less "considerable support," least of all necessarily that of the "original apostles" or "a majority of the congregation"? This observation only "must" show that the apostles supported or permitted, on the basis of their authority, the right to intrude and seek to exercise some level of social control, or at least the right to seek information, yet that the apostles (and the majority?) refused in the end to support compliance on the matter at hand, regardless of the legitimation that the pseudo-brethren may have appealed to from authorities outside or inside of this coalition.

The observations of some other scholars suggest uncertainty about whether these so-called pseudo-brethren were in any way representatives from another in-Christ Judaism; moreover, if they were even fellow-believers in Jesus. Helpful for clarifying my point are these observations, beginning with Ernest Burton:

---

[9] Lüdemann, *Opposition*, 36 (emphasis: "must" added; "compel" his).
[10] Lüdemann, *Opposition*, 37.

> the circumcision of Titus originated with spies *from without*, men who had *no proper place in the church at all*. . . .[11]

> The whole phraseology descriptive of these "false brethren" implies . . . that they were *distinct and different* from the original constituents of the church, *a foreign element*, introduced at a relatively late date, distinguished not only from the apostles but from the primitive church in general, and this not only personally but in their spirit and aims.[12]

Similarly, Richard Longenecker notes:

> Here the sinister nuance [of κατασκοπέω] applies: these intruders were as spies in the Jerusalem church working on behalf of *other interests* and *not those of Christ and the gospel*.[13]

And likewise, James D. G. Dunn concludes:

> In calling them "false *brothers*" Paul treats them as he treated the "other *Gospel*" of i.6.[14]

> If "smuggled in" may refer to their earlier entry into the Jesus movement itself, "sneaked in" is best taken as referring to their part in the Jerusalem consultation.[15]

Such language might imply that the identity of these "pseudo-brothers," unlike the leaders and other participants of this coalition, was not *essentially* derived or bounded by a shared faith in Christ. However, if the pseudo-brethren did not naturally belong within the confines of "the Jesus movement," or if they were engaged in interests at variance with "those of Christ and the gospel," and if "a foreign element," different in "their spirit and aims" "who had no proper place in the church at all," is it likely that they were believers in Jesus or proclaiming any kind of Christian gospel? Why are they regarded, for example, as "baptized" and "members of the Jerusalem (or Judean) church"?[16]

---

[11] Ernest DeWitt Burton, *A Critical and Exegetical Commentary on the Epistle to the Galatians* (ICC; Edinburgh: T. & T. Clark, 1921) 81 (emphasis added).

[12] Burton, *Galatians*, 83 (emphasis added).

[13] Richard N. Longenecker, *Galatians* (WBC 41; Dallas, TX: Word Books, 1990) 51 (emphasis added); see also Herman N. Ridderbos, *The Epistle of Paul to the Churches of Galatia* (NICNT; Grand Rapids: Eerdmans, 1953) 84: "In designating those persons *the false brethren*, Paul challenges their right to belong to the church" (emphasis his).

[14] Dunn, *The Epistle to the Galatians* (BNTC; Peabody, MA: Hendrickson Publishers, 1993) 97 (emphasis his).

[15] Dunn, *Galatians*, 99.

[16] Dunn, *Galatians*, 98.

Similar logical inconsistencies are evident in the many positions which seek to identify the pseudo-brethren as "Christians" operating within "Christian" churches with the support of the "Christian" apostles, their Jewishness being the problem, instead of recognizing that during this period the rhetoric more likely arose from intra- and inter-Jewish sociopolitical tensions. Is it not probable that a new Jewish group maintaining what this group did would run into some serious political trouble? Indeed, that is what the sources describe (e.g., Luke-Acts; Josephus, *Ant.* 20.197–203). Might not then Paul's polemic reveal that the agenda for this coalition's meeting, which he saw as a private matter of coordinating policies within this coalition on the topic of how to incorporate Gentiles, was frustrated by the constraints on this coalition within its Jerusalem—and thus inter-politically charged—context where other Jewish as well as Roman interest groups and their leaders were concerned?

Must "Brethren" Refer to Fellow Christ-believers?

One classic conclusion about these "brethren" which seems to confine interpreters to identifying them in "Christian" terms alone follows from the belief that Paul would use such fictive kinship language only for fellow believers in Christ. For example, Jerome Murphy-O'Connor put this succinctly in his objection to Burton's above mentioned suggestion that the "opponents were Jews, who had feigned to become Christians in Jerusalem precisely in order to subvert the Jesus movement":

> This hypothesis is excluded by Gal 2:4b. They were anti-Paul, not anti-Christian. Though "false" they were none the less "brethren."[17]

I will take up his first objection in due time, but the last, that the label "brethren" itself indicates necessarily that their bond is in Christian faith, is far from certain. Such a break with Jewish kinship identification bespeaks a much later view of social reality. Paul does not write of or to "Christians," but Jews and Gentiles. Some are in-Christ and some are not, though even in this case the lines are not yet sharply drawn, as witnessed in his respectful and hopeful recognition of the "stumbling" state of those fellow-Jews whom he speaks of as "my *brethren*, my *kinsmen* according to the flesh" (Rom 9:3; 11:1; note also 11:14: lit., Paul writes

---

[17] Jerome Murphy-O'Connor, *Paul: A Critical Life* (Oxford: Clarendon Press, 1996) 133 n. 15.

of "my own flesh" whom he seeks to restore by provoking their jealousy).[18] Paul says this regardless of the current lack of faith in Christ of "some" of them, which present mysterious process Paul regards in terms of a temporary vicarious suffering on behalf of the Gentiles (11:11–16, 25–26, 28–29). This indicates a wavering "measure of faith" (12:3), to be sure, that can be paralleled in the choices that had been open to Abraham in response to the "gospel" (4:16–21; Gal 3:8), but Paul refers not yet to a final decisive break among the people of God, to an "unfaith."[19]

In order to draw the conclusion that Paul reserved this fictive kinship language exclusively for Christ-believers one must maintain that Paul no longer considered himself Jewish, which would go against Paul's explicit autobiographical comments (e.g., Rom 9:3; 11:1, 13; 2 Cor 11:21–22; Gal 2:15; Phil 3:4–6), not to mention his implied social location often evident in his correspondence, as well as the biographical portrait of Luke.[20] My point is highlighted by the logic of Murphy-O'Connor's own immediate references to such kinship elsewhere, first, to this passage in Rom 9:3 to make a different point: "If Paul can use such intimate language of fellow-Jews with whom he has no blood relationship . . .";[21] and second, in a passing comment a mere eight pages after the above conclusion, when discussing the perspective of Christian Jews toward their Jewish brethren thus:

> The dilemma in which this placed politically conscious Jewish Christians is obvious. They were first and foremost Jews. All that separated them from their *brethren* was their acceptance of Jesus of Nazareth as the Messiah.[22]

In other words, if Murphy-O'Connor incorporates this recognition of brotherhood in his own descriptive kinship language now, looking back,

---

[18] For significant implications of the jealousy motif for the Jewish identity of himself and the communal context of the concerns expressed among those addressed in Romans, see the discussions in Mark D. Nanos, *The Mystery of Romans: The Jewish Context of Paul's Letter* (Minneapolis: Fortress Press, 1996) 247–55; idem, "The Jewish Context of the Gentile Audience Addressed in Paul's Letter to the Romans," *CBQ* 61 (1999): 300–303.

[19] See Nanos, *Mystery*, 110–13, 119–24, 139–43.

[20] For example Acts 23:6; 24:14–21; 26:4–23, wherein Luke reports Paul's autobiographical witness to his continued identity within Pharisaism, much less Judaism. For the point at hand, it matters not whether some other Jewish people considered Paul a deviant or even apostate, but what he considers himself. Although his punishment within the boundaries of the Jewish community suggests that the former is common (2 Cor 11:24), it also implies that he is still regarded as a Jewish person subject to such social control by the leaders of those Jewish communities.

[21] Murphy-O'Connor, *Paul*, 46.

[22] Murphy-O'Connor, *Paul*, 141 (emphasis added).

to communicate the intricacies of the period, is it not likely that Paul and other Jews of *that* period could and would have done so then? It is obvious then, as now, that such social bonds and kinship labeling continue not only for Jews who come to faith in Christ among themselves, which is natural enough, but dependent upon the social context of comparison that is salient, along many other lines of identity as well.[23] That is simply how fictive kinship works. It is a dynamic of social location which changes with the context of the meaningful comparison at any given time and place, so that one's identity and view of their relationship to the "other" changes as circumstances and group identities change, as, for example, they do for any person, who is a member of many social groups simultaneously, so that one may remain at the same time a brother, a father, a son, a friend, a teacher, a player, a fan, and so on, although the particular relationship in view will give cause to emphasize the salience of one at any given time, perhaps at the—at least ostensible—expense of the many others. A stranger easily considered insignificant on the streets of one's own home town may become instead a cherished friend in a distant place, becoming thereafter a fictive brother or sister forever, although initially perhaps sharing nothing more binding than that past geographical proximity.

The other interest group was still regarded as fictive family by Paul, but its members were qualified, in this case, for some particular reason, as "pseudo." Whether this labeling indicates in any way that they were believers in Christ, or (mis)represented themselves to be such, is far from certain. This aspect of their identity (at least now from Paul's hindsight perspective as he writes to the Galatians) as "false," though fellow Jews with some "right" to "meddle" in the affairs of the coalitions of Jewish believers in Jesus, is certainly central to the core meaning of ψευδής, but may not suggest that they "lied" about themselves, that is, about their relationship with Christ, or to other believers in Jesus that they were "Christians" too. The label pseudo-brethren could certainly apply to such a misrepresentation of faith in Christ; yet this would mean that they were in fact *not* believers in Jesus, but pretenders. But it is difficult to understand why they would have represented themselves as such if they had the authority to be present on other grounds, for example, as agents

---

[23] Nanos, *Mystery*, 110–13, for extensive evidence in Romans of Paul's indiscriminate use of kinship language for both believers in Jesus and Jews who did not share this faith in Jesus, including their assumed link to each other (see also Wayne A. Meeks, *The First Urban Christians* [New Haven and London: Yale University Press, 1983] 86–89).

of social control (that which Paul refers to as seeking to bring into "bondage"). Or whom they would have fooled by pretending to be "in Christ," given the setting in Jerusalem in the presence of the apostles and Paul.[24] Or even why their position would have been associated with faith in Jesus, if it was opposed to all of these higher authorities for such faith. Such an identification fails to make sense of their authority to be present and seek social control against the wishes of the highest authorities of this coalition.

THE SOCIO-POLITICAL SETTING OF THE JERUSALEM CHRIST-BELIEVING COALITION

In what way are they "pseudo" brethren? I have questioned whether this label is derived from their pretensions to be believers in Christ, "falsely" so from Paul's perspective. I propose that it is more likely an accusation of bearing false witness, misrepresenting the beliefs and practices of the coalition of believers in Jesus to their Jewish brethren; in this case, to those leaders of other Jewish groups to whom these "spies" report: they are thus "pseudo." Their interests in this coalition are not as they wish to make them appear to be. They should not be trusted.

I propose that Paul's labeling of the pseudo-brethren in this dishonoring way when later relating this story to the Galatian addressees is better explained by each of the following hypotheses, or some combination of them.

(1) The pseudo-brethren may have represented a Jewish interest group seeking to take matters into their own hands without the authority to do so, in other words, they "misrepresented" their *authority*, or the *intentions* of other authorities *they professed to represent*. In this case they were in some fashion *vigilantes* who were seeking to step into a gap created by the tolerance of the various other Jewish authorities/groups toward the Jewish coalition of Christ-believers, a failure to exercise proper social control of this "deviance" which these ones felt must not be allowed to continue unchecked.[25] (Fear of Roman reprisals may or may not be

---

[24] *Contra* John Muddiman, "The Anatomy of Galatians," in *Crossing the Boundaries: Essays in Biblical Interpretation in Honour of Michael Goulder* (ed. Stanley E. Porter, Paul Joyce, and David E. Orton; Leiden: E. J. Brill, 1994) 263.

[25] H. Jon Rosenbaum and Peter C. Sederberg, "Vigilantism: An Analysis of Establishment Violence," in *Vigilante Politics* (ed. Rosenbaum and Sederberg; Philadelphia:

implied.) In this zealot-like role they need not have been entirely unauthorized; they may have been more like Paul in his earlier "advanced" and "extremely zealous" pursuit of members of this coalition (Gal 1:13–14), with the (perhaps extracted or implored) authority to so act on behalf of the high priests (Acts 9:1–2; 26:9–11). In Paul's account here there is no indication that they took any violent or coercive action in this case, but rather that they sought to intimidate and collect incriminating data.[26] If vigilantes, they would have likely been seeking to gain information to present to the legitimate authorities that would cast the in-Christ coalitions in a negative light. They would seek to stir the authorities to the action desired, to wake them from their indifference or policies of tolerance.[27]

(2) Paul's point may have been to disclose that the *intentions* of the pseudo-brethren toward this particular Jewish coalition were suspect, that

---

University of Pennsylvania Press, 1976) 4: "It consists of acts or threats of coercion in violation of the formal boundaries of an established sociopolitical order which, however, are intended by the violators to defend that order from some form of subversion." This particularly applies in the sphere of social-group-control vigilantism with regard to, for example, suspected heresy (14); especially when a zero-sum or limited good culture is assumed, there would be great concern to keep other groups in "their place": "illegal coercion is often the response of those who feel threatened by upwardly mobile segments of society or by those who appear to advocate significant change in the distribution of values" (12). Torrey Seland, *Establishment Violence in Philo and Luke: A Study of Non-Conformity to the Torah and Jewish Vigilante Reactions* (Leiden: E. J. Brill, 1995) explores this dynamic of conflict management as it applies to Philo and Luke, drawing especially from the work of Peter C. Sederberg (*Terrorist Myths: Illusion, Rhetoric, and Reality* [Englewood Cliffs, NJ: Prentice Hall, 1989]; and Rosenbaum and Sederberg, "Vigilantism"). Vigilantism is developed as a model by which to understand the kind of social frontier situations which applied for Jews in Judaea as well as the Diaspora. The vigilantes seek to protect social boundaries (established values and institutions) from violation or subversion, either when the formal authorities are expected to support such actions, or if these authorities have been ineffective in such efforts against the non-conformists against which the vigilantes are concerned to provide protection (Seland, *Establishment Violence*, esp. 1–16, 83–85).

[26] Rosenbaum and Sederberg, "Vigilantism," 27–28: "The principal goal of vigilantes is deterrence; their tactics consist of threats and sanctions.... The range of vigilante activities seems to extend from subtle and restrained use of force to acts of brutal compulsion and retribution. Violent force may not be used on all occasions, but its future utilization is always implied."

[27] This suggestion resonates with Robert Jewett's thesis ("The Agitators and the Galatian Congregation," in *The Galatians Debate: Contemporary Issues in Rhetorical and Historical Interpretation* [ed. Mark D. Nanos; Peabody, MA: Hendrickson Publishers, 2002] 334–47), although Jewett's proposed application to the Galatians' situation has been extensively challenged (Mark D. Nanos, *The Irony of Galatians* [Minneapolis: Fortress Press, 2002] esp. 166–69, 207–15).

is, they *misrepresented* themselves to the Christ-believing leaders, for example, by stating that their purpose was not to bring them into conformity ("bondage") but only to *investigate* so as to understand.[28] In this case, they misrepresented the concerns and positions of the in-Christ coalition to others in authority *to whom they reported*, though their presence as informants was well within their legitimate function as inspectors. This suggestion provides cause for the thick negative coloring Paul is able to achieve by labeling them "spies who slipped in," undermining without entirely negating the legitimacy of their right to be present, to intrude where they are unwelcome—a nuanced position towards this always suspect profession which he would most likely not take toward coercive vigilantes or illegitimate spies who gained access by forced entry. This proposal respects that at this time there was, as yet, no reason to assume that legitimate authorities of other Jewish or even Roman interest groups were unavailable or unconcerned with questionable beliefs or actions among newly formed Jewish groups.

Some combinations of these first two explanations for their identity are surely possible as well. The pseudo-brethren do appear to be exercising a more zealous role than the ultimate authorities of the overall Jewish community(s) in that the pseudo-brethren can be defeated by this coalition, yet without these Jewish believers in Jesus being thereby cut off from their continuing (though perhaps disadvantaged) role within the larger Jewish body to which they answer.

This kind of complex of motives and actions is present in Luke's accounts of Paul's earliest presence at and involvement in the vigilante actions taken against Stephen and others, versus his later validation of such actions by seeking and obtaining the sanction of the high priest to so continue (Acts 7:54–8:3; 9:1–2). This initially vigilante and then later legitimated but still "extremely zealous" action may reflect the perceived failure of the highest Jewish authorities, such as Gamaliel and the council, to carry out the interests of the more zealous members of the community (5:27–42).

If this was the case for Paul and those who worked with him when he opposed this coalition, it is not difficult to imagine such varied and difficult to strictly define approaches continued with regard to this movement in the period Paul sought to herein describe, albeit from the other

---

[28] See, e.g., Hans Dieter Betz, *Galatians: A Commentary on Paul's Letter to the Churches in Galatia* (Philadelphia: Fortress Press, 1977) 90.

side.²⁹ Luke certainly understood this intra-Jewish context, filled with many competing groups and agendas, to have continued to still be the case upon Paul's later arrival in Jerusalem, and throughout his trials there.³⁰ This, of course, corresponds with Paul's stated fears about possible negative interaction with authorities from other Jewish groups upon his imminent arrival in Jerusalem (Rom 15:31).

In addition, the possible affiliation of these "spies" with the various roles of the Pharisees or priests is also worth consideration. Of value here may be the suggestion that the Pharisees may have had the authority to exercise control in some religious matters without the involvement of the chief priests; however, in matters of official action such as arrest, trial, conviction and sentencing to death, where the interests of Roman officials would be expected to govern, interaction with the chief priests would have been necessary.³¹ In such cases the Pharisees' exercise of power was limited to the role of influence, while the chief priests were responsible for the actual decisions. In Josephus, for example,

> the Pharisees are presented as an influential group, but at the same time the limits of their power and influence continue to be represented in the texts. They are presented as a group which exercise [sic] power through influence on the priests but not because of any political power of their own.³²

---

[29] Ernst Bammel, "Jewish Activity Against Christians in Palestine According to Acts," in *The Book of Acts in Its Palestinian Setting* (BAFCS 4; ed. Richard Bauckham; Grand Rapids: Eerdmans and Carlisle: The Paternoster Press, 1995) 361 n. 17, makes the interesting observation that Paul "was accompanied by fellow-investigators on his way to Damascus (9:7ff.; 26:14). None of them is mentioned as having joined Paul later on. Did they carry on with what they had been engaged in before?" See also Simon Légasse, "Paul's Pre-Christian Career According to Acts," in *Palestinian Setting*, 385, who notes: "What is conceivable is that Paul contributed to bringing Christians before the Rabbinic courts: a role of *spy and informer* which had to bring about the dispensing of the statutory punishments in the context of the synagogue, such as Paul himself later boasts of having received (2 Cor 11:24) and such as other Christians had to undergo (Mk 13:9)" (emphasis added).

[30] The deeper the differences run between and within the ruling coalitions the more difficult it is to apply such models, which was, of course, the case in this period in Jerusalem. It must also be remembered that members of vigilante groups may participate in this more extreme action in addition to holding legitimate positions in the ruling coalitions (establishment) which they see as failing to act sufficiently; moreover, they may in some way represent the deeper wishes of the ruling coalition which is otherwise obliged not to act outside the legal channels as they may wish (see Rosenbaum and Sederberg, "Vigilantism," 17–18).

[31] Urban C. von Wahlde, "The Relationships between Pharisees and Chief Priests: Some Observations on the Texts in Matthew, John and Josephus," *NTS* 42 (1996): 516 n. 32, 515.

[32] von Wahlde, "Relationships," 513.

Similarly in John,

> the chief priests are brought into combination with the Pharisees precisely at the point where some official action (which the Pharisees do not have the power to enact unilaterally) is called for.[33]

With respect to the pseudo-brethren of our passage, then, it is possible that these are Pharisees who report to the priests on this matter, thus Paul's sense of betrayal by members of his own Pharisaic affiliation. In this case it could be Paul's continuing identification with the Pharisees, even if not with regard to faith in Jesus as the basis for such identity, that is behind the resentment that surfaces in the label pseudo-brethren. Or it may indicate the unwelcome presence of members of suspect priestly coalitions, the ruling class of Judaea, that is, for a Pharisee who would likely continue to resent such representatives as intruders or charlatans or mere puppets of a despised regime, an observation which leads to the next point.

(3) The crux of Paul's critique may not be of their present legislated right to function as representatives in Jerusalem, but of the inherent *illegitimacy* of the present *ruling class* they *represent*, and thus of their authority to represent a legitimate (from God) challenge to this coalition's interpretation of the revelation of God in Christ on the matter at hand. In this case their authority was based on the machinations of the Roman regime and not on Israel's, that is, on God's provision for the government of his people in the land.

Martin Goodman provides an insightful study of the prevailing discontent toward the ruling class of Judaea of this period. They were appointed by the Romans according to their methods of occupation; however, this process was incompatible with those respected by the Jewish people.[34] These rulers were not accorded the prestige generally

---

[33] von Wahlde, "Relationships," 515.

[34] Martin Goodman, *The Ruling Class of Judaea: The Origins of the Jewish Revolt against Rome A.D. 66–70* (Cambridge: Cambridge University Press, 1987) 46ff., *passim*, for the various Roman policies that led to the elevation of the ruling class that would have been in power during the time of Paul's visit and writing of this letter (in the late forties or early fifties), and the reasons for such in Roman, Greek, and Jewish terms. On 109–33, Goodman explains how the ruling class failed, in essence, because their power did not derive in the ways that Jews respected but from the occupying Romans and their systems of such selections. These included, for example, possession of property (117) and wealth (125ff.); descendancy from Herod (122): "It was thus useful for members of the Judaean ruling class to emphasize such Herodian or high-priestly connections as they could

granted such office holders, and the eventual outcome of this unacceptable situation was the disastrous revolt which led to the destruction of Jerusalem and the Temple:

> If all the ruling class did indeed manage, as did Josephus, to delude themselves that they were the natural Jewish elite, they were the only section of Jewish society to have this delusion. Other Jews felt no such confidence in the right of the ruling class to rule. The rulers of Judaea were thus in a sense marginal within their own society.[35]

Thus Goodman concludes that "they were not capable of controlling the increasing expressions of social discontent, fueled by economic disparities, that afflicted the population over which they tried to rule."[36] The methods of rule were incompatible with Jewish expectations and values: they were regarded as puppets of the enemy government and thus their presence bore witness to Israel's anguished state of exile. Moreover, not only did this ruling class fail to gain authority and prestige among the Jewish people over whom they ruled, but they also operated without the ultimate respect and confidence of Rome, although the Roman rulers did not seem to recognize the depth of this problem.[37]

This resentment toward the ruling class ran extremely deep and would make perfect sense of Paul's ambivalent admission of some right to intrude on this coalition's meeting on formal grounds, yet with suspicion and resentment on the operative scriptural and interpretative grounds shared by most of his fellow Jews. Note also that this coalition already represented, at some level, a persecuted minority Jewish group (by Paul himself, no less!; cf. 1:13–14, 22–24). When Paul's probable Pharisaic sensitivities to the ruling priestly class are factored in, the political nature of his subversive description is further intensified.

Simply put, whoever these Jewish "brethren" are, Paul calls them "pseudo" because he does not trust them: it is an expression of political

---

boast, but in no case could they expect to win unthinking obedience from the populace just because of their birth. Their prestige was in neither case reckoned by other Jews to have been a divine gift, and anyway, much though ancestry mattered in Jewish society, it was only one factor among others in the allotment of status: power was never based on caste" (123). Even when they appealed to normative Jewish terms such as the possession of wisdom, they failed to impress other Jews that they had any special dispensation (this was especially a problem with the response of Pharisees!; 123ff.).

[35] Goodman, *Ruling Class*, 46.
[36] Goodman, *Ruling Class*, 133.
[37] Goodman, *Ruling Class*, 125.

discontent and alienation.[38] This is not a religious charge *per se*, but a political one. It is not their particular kind of Christianity or its practice that is suspect: they are not believers in Christ or members of an in-Christ Judaism, nor do they claim to be. Rather, it is a challenge by Paul on the grounds of "reputational authority," which "derives from the successful criticism and dislocation of the higher-order norms which legitimate the authority prevailing in a given society,"[39] in this case, toward their representation of themselves as authorities serving the interests of the larger Jewish community(s), on the matter at hand, at a (what should have been) private (i.e., without them) meeting of the leaders of this coalition.

It is precisely this kind of "meddling" in one's affairs considered internal, even if by indisputable authorities whom one otherwise appreciates when their enforcement of social control is directed at "others" who may violate one's concerns, which quickly excites a burning resentment (who do they think they are?). This paradoxical response is perhaps best seen in the example of the extremely mixed but seldom ambivalent attitudes toward the work of the traffic officer or tax agent. And this is especially the case if the interfering authorities are not as highly regarded by one's self or group as they are by the others with whom one must cooperate, as is the case in Jerusalem for Paul when seeking the agreement of the other leaders of this group, who apparently regard the legitimacy or concerns of these authorities with more deference than does Paul. In such a situation, as for name-calling, untrustworthy, intruding *pseudo*-brethren, translated as "so-called," "false," or even "lying," represent polemical labeling that is not difficult to comprehend. Paul believes that their inter-

---

[38] William A. Gamson, *Power and Discontent* (Homewood, IL: The Dorsey Press, and Georgetown, ON: Irwin-Dorsey Limited, 1968) for development of the socio-political dynamics evident in such reactions and labeling. On 125, he discusses the labels used for persuasion by the authorities: "The choice of words is merely a reflection of the speaker's attitude toward the social system and its agents. If one believes the authorities are faithful agents of a social system which is accorded legitimacy, then they are 'socializing' potential partisans when they exercise social control. If one sides with the potential partisans and identifies with their grievances against the authorities, then this latter group is using 'manipulation' as a form of control."

[39] Bruce J. Malina, *The Social World of Jesus and the Gospels* (London and New York: Routledge, 1996) 129, drawing from the work of B. Schwartz, further describes reputational authority dynamics thus: "This authority emerges from a person's effective ability to convince members of a given society to recognize no longer some higher-order norm as binding. For example, if in a given society, office holders occupy their position because of divine will, a reputational authority will successfully demonstrate to the collectivity that divine will is not at issue at all, but force, chicanery, collusion, conspiracy, or some other principle."

ests are not as they might otherwise appear to be, that at this meeting they proved themselves to be "untrustworthy" as representatives of the true ("revealed") interests of this coalition on the matter at hand.

Similarly, this perspective on the social context for defining the label "pseudo" is evident in Luke's telling of the intra-Jewish nature of the politico-religious situation in Jerusalem. For example, Luke notes that when Stephen was brought before the council, those responsible for doing so "set up false [pseudo] witnesses [ἔστησάν τε μάρτυρας ψευδεῖς]" who misrepresented what Stephen had said (Acts 6:12–14). Luke's point is not that they are not really witnesses although they represent themselves to be, but that they are witnesses who now "lied" about ("misrepresented") what they heard, bringing forth a false charge.[40] They are thus not true witnesses as it might otherwise appear, and they ought not to be trusted. Yet is it not likely that they would have twisted this accusation around some grain of truth in order for it to be convincing? Or that at least some of them may have actually believed this to be the case?

Luke also reports that upon Paul's arrival in Jerusalem he was informed of false charges against himself by James and "all the elders," following their recognition of his work among the gentiles, for which they "glorified God" (Acts 21:18–25, 26ff.). These are not represented as charges that the Jerusalem elders were making or believed, but rather that some others were making to believers in Jesus who "zealously" observed and protected the Torah. James and these elders now suggested how Paul could personally demonstrate these charges were unfounded. In other words, Luke reports that the other leaders of these groups of Jewish believers in Jesus are "all" standing on behalf of Paul, not against him.[41]

---

[40] Craig C. Hill, *Hellenists and Hebrews: Reappraising Division within the Earliest Church* (Minneapolis: Fortress Press, 1992) 57, points out that commentators miss the point that "would have been obvious to Luke and to his readers, living after A.D. 70, that the charges were precisely contrary to fact. The temple had in truth been destroyed—but not by Jesus." Commentators instead assume that these accusations are true and the falsehood is rather that, as Wilfred Knox put it: "any witness who gives evidence against a martyr must be a 'false' witness since his is against the truth."

[41] Cf. Richard Bauckham, "James and the Jerusalem Church" in *Palestinian Setting*, 478. *Contra* Dunn, *Unity*, 256–57. Seland, *Establishment Violence*, 273, argues similarly on the point of James supporting Paul, however, he understands the ones bringing the charges to be "zealotic Nazarenes," and thus James may be a mediator of a divided Nazarene coalition which he is trying to hold together. Such an identification is not necessary, and, I would suggest, is not warranted. The zealotic Nazarenes have been told such things about Paul; they are merely rumors among them, regardless of how many may be convinced by them. But this does not suggest that the rumors were begun by them. In fact,

However, Luke also observes that some members of other Jewish interest groups do oppose Paul's work, and they also have access to and influence among these Jewish believers in Jesus. The *pseudo* charges were that Paul taught "all the Jews who are among the Gentiles to forsake Moses, telling them not to circumcise their children or observe the customs," in which he then participated at some level in a Nazarite vow to dispel as unfounded, upon the recommendation of James (Acts 21:21–26). But when he was in the Temple for this purpose, some particular Jews of Asia stirred up others present with the false charge that: "This is the man who is teaching men everywhere against the people and the law and this place; moreover he also brought Greeks into the temple, and he has defiled this holy place." The latter accusation Luke says was a result of some of these Asian Jews having "previously seen Trophimus the Ephesian with him in the city, and they *supposed* [ἐνόμιζον] that Paul had brought him into the temple," a charge that Luke clearly portrays as untrue (21:27–29; cf. 24:11–20). The next few chapters of Luke's account are concerned with Paul's defense against these *pseudo* charges (22–27). Interestingly enough, Luke's Paul sympathizes with their intentions as having formerly been his own against Jewish groups of believers in Jesus (22:3–5; 26:9–12; cf. Gal 1:13–14).

These various suggestions for the identity of the pseudo-brethren, in addition to impacting our investigation of the degree to which the Jerusalem coalition of Christ-believers was still operating within the context of other Jewish movements, not as isolated or sectarian groups at the time of Paul's visit, also impact the implied situation of the later Galatian addressees for whom this narrative was rhetorically constructed. They suggest a social setting for the Galatians that is likewise within the context of the Jewish community(s).[42] Such intra- and inter-communal action would be dynamic, and could be cast in the language of political

---

James's concern that they will "certainly hear" that Paul has come to Jerusalem means most likely that they were not represented by James and the elders present (cf. Rom 15:31). Furthermore, the Jews from Asia who then accuse Paul are not identified as Nazarenes. Nevertheless, on 299, Seland again recognizes the thoroughly intra-Jewish nature of the situation in this passage for which I am arguing, including the observation that the zealous Jewish Nazarenes whom "James feared would take action against Paul because of the prevalent rumors" "probably were under pressure from conservative, zealous non-Nazarenes," and thus concludes: "the Nazarenes were still considered a part of the Jewish people thus making them liable to social measures" (see also 302).

[42] See Nanos, *Irony of Galatians*; idem, "The Inter- and Intra-Jewish Political Context of Paul's Letter to the Galatians," in *Galatians Debate* (ed. Nanos) 396–407.

demagoguery, as it is here.[43] The presence of representatives of one or more (non-Jesus believing) Jewish interest groups at gatherings of Christ-believers, even at important meetings among those with influential roles, was still perhaps commonplace at the point of Paul's letter to the Galatians, so that Paul could speak of this kind of interaction rather categorically.[44]

Exegesis of the Roles of the Pseudo-Brethren

With these hypothetical constructions in hand, let us turn to exegesis of Paul's narrative. Are the "pseudo-brethren" of Gal 2:1–10 in some way representatives of non-Christ-believing Jewish interest groups or authorities who are "looking" into the affairs of this new coalition? Walther Schmithals appeals to the context of the problems with the "Hellenists" of Acts 6:8–8:4 to make a suggestion along this line, although it has been generally dismissed.[45] Yet without conflating these two narratives as does Schmithals, even the prevailing translations of Gal 2:1–10 may be taken to indicate this kind of construction. An investigative role on behalf of powerful Jewish non-Christ-believing interest groups would make perfect sense of the pseudo-brethren's ability to gain such access and apply such pressure,[46] *unwanted* ("but because of false brethren secretly

---

[43] Betz, *Galatians*, 90, observes that Paul here uses "military language turned into political metaphors."

[44] Nanos, *Irony of Galatians*.

[45] Walther Schmithals, *Paul and James* (trans. Dorothea M. Barton; Naperville, IL: Alec R. Allenson, 1965 [1963]) 107–108. Note Acts 5:17–42; Adolf Schlatter, *Die Briefe an die Galater, Epheser, Kolosser und Philemon* (Schlatters Erläuterungen zum Neuen Testament 7; Stuttgart: Calwer Verlag, 1948) 32, suggests that these are non-Christian Jews. See too Dom Gregory Dix, *Jew and Greek: A Study in the Primitive Church* (London: Dacre Press Westminster, 1953) 36; W. Foerster, "Die δοκοῦντες in Gal. 2," *ZNW* 36 (1937) 286ff.; Peter Richardson, *Israel in the Apostolic Church* (Cambridge: Cambridge University Press, 1969) 91–94, who comments on 94 n. 4, after his discussion of the "rest of the Jews" as likely to be non-Christian Jews: "The *pseudadelphoi* may also be unconverted Jews trying to embarrass Christians."

Due to space, reconsideration of the identity of the individuals opposed unanimously by Paul and the other apostles in Jerusalem will be investigated free of the thicket of complications which result from trying to coordinate this account with that of Luke in Acts 15, since the language of Luke fails to conform naturally with that of Paul, and there are at least five major constructs for such reconciliation (cf. Fred O. Francis and J. Paul Sampley, *Pauline Parallels* [2nd ed.; Philadelphia: Fortress Press, 1984 (1975)] 67, 141, 175, 207, 223).

[46] Paul's concerns, with the response of both believers and non-believers in Jesus upon

brought in [διὰ δὲ τοὺς παρεισάκτους ψευδαδέλφους], who slipped in [οἵτινες παρεισῆλθον] to spy out [κατασκοπῆσαι] our freedom which we have in Christ Jesus"), and *unaccepted* by Paul and the other apostles present ("to them we did not yield submission even for a moment"). Let us attend to the translation decisions that are available to the interpreter to see if the probability of meaningful results in this direction is enhanced.

To begin with, Burton's discussion of παρείσακτος ("secretly") is helpful for developing the nuances present for identifying these pseudo-brethren as "inspectors" rather than "spies" on linguistic grounds:

> it is doubtful whether the passive sense can be insisted upon, as if these false brethren had been brought in by others. The relative clause, οἵτινες etc., distinctly makes the men themselves active in their entrance into the church, which though by no means excluding the thought that some within were interested in bringing them in, throws the emphasis upon their own activity in the matter. Nor is the idea of surreptitiousness, secrecy, at all clearly emphasised. That they are alien to the body into which they have come is what the term both etymologically and by usage suggests.[47]

This observation allows the technical possibilities latent in Paul's choice of κατασκοπῆσαι ("to spy out" or "to examine/inspect") to be magnified, for it "carries the nuance of distrust"[48] as well as "inquiry with a claim to the right of supervision," which picks up the bureaucratic implications present in the wordplay on ἐπισκοπῆσαι ("to supervise").[49] This is perhaps the position or responsibility of those Paul calls pseudo-brethren.

---

his arrival in Jerusalem with the collection as expressed in Rom 15:25–32, bear witness to such continued interaction well into the late 50's. And it was certainly Luke's understanding that the subgroup of believers in Jesus functioned within the authority of the larger Jewish community(s) before, during, and after the account of Stephen. He even cites "some" members of specific synagogues who engaged Stephen and brought him before the council (Acts 6:9–12), and the authority of Saul to enter houses of believers to arrest them (8:3). This interaction continues in the accounts of Paul (cf. ch. 21). See also Dunn, *Jesus, Paul*, 133–36.

[47] Burton, *Galatians*, 78. W. Michaelis, *TDNT* 5.824, notes that the verb παρεισάγω from which this verbal adjective is derived is rare, yet in the common usage of Polybius it has a neutral sense of bringing forward, presenting or introducing, yet with the suggestion of "at least the unexpected." Paul does not expect them to be present in this meeting he intends to be in private, they are thus παρείσακτος.

[48] E. Fuchs, *TDNT* 7.417, who also notes that such spying "includes an element of suspicion."

[49] E. Fuchs, *TDNT* 7.417 n. 1; Ronald Y. K. Fung, *The Epistle to the Galatians* (NICNT; Grand Rapids: Eerdmans, 1953) 93; Betz, *Galatians*, 91 n. 307, notes Schlier's suggestion that "the opponents may claim a right to 'inspection.'"

Their role is to "*inspect*" in the sense of to "*investigate*" Jerusalem communal affairs, to seek to prohibit any questionable or dangerous tendencies developing among these (or other) Jewish groups (as had Paul formerly!). Thus Paul's slighting of their "intrusive intentions" for being present as "stealthily to destroy"[50] reveals his misgivings about their ability to gain access in order, ostensibly, to inspect.

Support for this approach to translation is suggested by the multiple usages of κατάσκοπος and κατασκόπεω employed by the second-century BCE Greek historian Polybius. For example, the soldiers who were to "polish up, repair, and examine [κατασκοπεῖν] their arms," were not spying or informing but inspecting them. Moreover, they were not doing so in any covert sense, but they were rather to make this inspection of their weapons purposely "in full view" (*Hist.* 10.20.2; Loeb). So too it is as "inspectors" rather than as "spies" that "Tiberius Gracchus and the other legates arrived" and were received so courteously by Antiochus at the end of his ostentatious games (*Hist.* 30.27.1–2).[51] Another Greek historian, Appian (2nd cent. CE), writes of those whom the Romans send as "ambassadors [πρέσβεις]," but whom an Illyrian tribe chains, charging them with being κατασκόπους instead (*Hist. rom.*, "The Illyrian Wars," 9), which ought to remind interpreters that declarations of identity are subjective and negotiable: they express points of view![52]

While the intrusive and harmful political intentions of the pseudo-brethren may be of a piece with the intentions and activities of spies or scouts to gather information for a hostile party, it is not the clandestine nature of their identity but the intrusiveness ("alien to the body into which they have come")[53] on false pretenses that Paul resents. They are "the intruding pseudo-brethren" who were seeking to "*inspect*," as in conduct an investigation—from Paul's perspective with a negative twist, to "*inform*"—on "our freedom." The threat is to the maintenance of Jewish honor and conformist behavior within the (occupied Jerusalem or minority Diaspora) Jewish communities represented by such disputable positions as, for example, the admission of Gentiles as *equals* (not just

---

[50] Burton, *Galatians*, 83: "κατασκοπέω, 'to spy out,' with the associated idea of hostile intent, purpose to destroy... is here nearly equivalent to 'stealthily to destroy.'"

[51] In some cases Polybius does have the sense of scouts, informants, or spies in view (e.g., *Hist.* 2.24.10; 3.95.8; 13.5.7; 14.3.7; 15.5.4–5), and note also the nuanced usage in 4.3.7, where informants/spies profess themselves to be instead guards.

[52] Cf. Richard Jenkins, *Social Identity* (London and New York: Routledge, 1996).

[53] Burton, *Galatians*, 78.

righteous Gentile associates) into the Jesus community(s) without proselytizing[54] (i.e., Titus), and concomitant *indiscriminate* table-fellowship with them (i.e., Antioch incident: Gal 2:11–21).[55] These were arguably the very reasons for Paul's former opposition to the movement, and that which he now calls "our freedom which we have in Christ Jesus."

Perhaps the Jerusalem apostles had no choice about the presence of such *"inspectors"* (even if to some degree *"informants"*), that is, as long as the leaders (and members) regarded this as a Jewish coalition seeking a good reputation (honor) and legitimacy within the larger Jewish communities, they recognized their accountability to such authorities (guardians of honor and order).

It is possible, indeed likely, that the Jerusalem apostles did not really desire the presence of such inspectors or their investigations, yet they found it necessary to tolerate their intrusions in order to demonstrate good standing. This in itself would seem to be a noble intention (even if debatable on any given point or at any particular time by others, such as Paul), as would be the concerns of these inspectors to ensure the compliance of these communities with prevailing norms in seeking the protection of the rest of those under their social control, for a host of socio-economic, political, and religious reasons. This might, for example, be not only to avoid compromising Jewish religious interests in the face of suspected Hellenistic encroachments (failure to circumcise members), but perhaps also to preempt any rumors of developments that might be perceived as threats to Roman interests and policies (breaking with prevailing conventions on the basis of a claim to a rival king [of both Israel and the world!]).[56]

The Pseudo-brethren and the Arrival of Titus

The context of Paul's concern has suggested to many interpreters that the Jerusalem apostles were initially leaning toward compliance with the demands of these intruders.[57] Yet Paul says *in this case* "to them *we* did

---

[54] Similarly E. P. Sanders, *Paul, the Law, and the Jewish People* (Philadelphia: Fortress Press, 1985 [1983]) 290–92.

[55] See Mark D. Nanos, "What was at Stake in Peter's 'Eating with Gentiles' at Antioch?" in *Galatians Debate* (ed. Nanos) 282–318.

[56] See Paula Fredriksen, *From Jesus to Christ: The Origins of the New Testament Images of Jesus* (New Haven and London: Yale University Press, 1988) 154–56.

[57] Dunn, *Jesus, Paul*, 120, notes that 2:4–5 "strongly suggest that the Jerusalem apostles *advised* Paul to conform or concede the point on account of, or for the sake of the

not yield by way of subjection even for a moment [οἷς οὐδὲ πρὸς ὥραν εἴξαμεν τῇ ὑποταγῇ],[58] that the truth of the gospel might be preserved for you."[59] The passive use of ἠναγκάσθη in v. 3 with regard to Titus "not *being compelled* to be circumcised" suggests that the apostles not only did not bring such pressure to bear,[60] but that they would not have on their own terms, any more than would have Paul; "but because of [the pressure brought on by] pseudo-brethren" who have arrived, unwelcome, yet not without the authority to be present (because they have learned of the arrival of a Greek?), the leaders are experiencing social anxiety.[61] In other words, the purpose of Paul's visit and the laying out of his gospel to those of repute could have been private, as he intended. This would not have necessarily come to the attention of the inspectors, or triggered their arrival on the scene—but they have learned of the presence of Titus.

Paul indicates that he did not specifically bring along Titus to provoke this confrontation.[62] If that was his motive, Paul constructed this aspect

---

'false brothers', but evidently they did not insist" (emphasis his). So also Burton, *Galatians*, 81; J. B. Lightfoot, *St. Paul's Epistle to the Galatians* (Lynn, MA: Hendrickson Publishers, 1981 [1865]) 105–106. This view turns on the assumption that it is Paul's independence from the Jerusalem apostles that is being emphasized here.

[58] See Kirsopp Lake, "Galatians II.3–5," *The Expositor* (7th Series) 1 (1906) 236–45; Burton, *Galatians*, 75–82; Betz, *Galatians*, 88–91; Longenecker, *Galatians*, 49–50; Philip F. Esler, "Making and Breaking an Agreement Mediterranean Style: A New Reading of Galatians 2:1–14," in *Galatians Debate* (ed. Nanos) 269–70, for discussions of variant textual readings which omit οἷς οὐδέ as secondary and illogical (*contra* F. C. Burkitt, *Christian Beginnings* [London: University of London Press, 1924] 118).

[59] It is not clear whether "we" refers to Paul, Barnabas and Titus, or to all of those representing the interests of this coalition, and thus, the other apostles present. This latter inference is probable, since it is Paul and Barnabas who bring along Titus to subordinate their view on this matter to the Jerusalem apostles, and they together resist the intentions of the investigators from outside of this coalition who intrude. And this is confirmed in the following verses of the agreement of Paul and the Jerusalem apostles on the nature of the good news Paul will continue to proclaim to Gentiles apart from proselyte conversion.

[60] Burton, *Galatians*, 75–82, for discussion of the various interpretative possibilities for ἠναγκάσθη.

[61] Paul J. Achtemeier, *The Quest for Unity in the New Testament Church* (Philadelphia: Fortress Press, 1987) 5, notes in a similar vein, though not about this specific passage, that Paul and the Jerusalem leaders were preoccupied with different aspects of their relation: "The preoccupation of the leadership of the Jerusalem church may well have been with one aspect of that problem: remaining in contact with the non-Christian Jews."

[62] *Contra* Esler, "Making," 264–76, who argues from an honor challenge and response model that Paul was challenging the apostles by taking Titus, who was publicly known to be present, as well as why he was in this closed session so that Paul could press his point ("this visit represented a clear challenge, a claim to enter the social space of the Jerusalem church"; 267), though Esler otherwise argues that Paul sought a private meeting "so as

of his otherwise strident narrative poorly, missing the opportunity to make this challenge emphatic. One would expect him to thus state his principled intention of bringing Titus for the purpose of confrontation, to show them how it is or must be: to shame them into compliance as he does Peter in the retelling of the Antioch incident which follows in vv. 11ff. Yet Paul, in contrast with most interpreters and the account in Acts 15 with which this passage is often conflated, does not give his reason for the trip as the response to some provocations in his ministry, whether from Jerusalem, or in Antioch, or somewhere else, which he now aims to set aright. Instead, he describes the presence of Titus as incidental: "taking along *also* Titus [συμπαραλαβὼν καὶ Τίτον]" (v. 1);[63] his intention as largely acquiescent ("put before them," v. 2); and the primary cause not as the result of compelling circumstances or the request of the other apostles, but as a result of "revelation."[64]

Such action is not difficult to understand in dyadic terms: group confirmation of his revelation and interpretation are to be expected, especially from his fellow apostles, so too are the contractual ties necessary for implementation.[65] This also provides insight into the "private" nature of his plans, that is, Paul did not intend to initiate an honor challenge, which is by nature a public confrontation.[66] And it respects the fragile

---

not to embarrass them in public" (268). Yet Paul in seeking a private meeting was not making an honor challenge, which is an action seeking public judgment, a point which is further strengthened when the dyadic nature of the personalities is considered (so too Esler, 264–67). Rather, the pseudo-brethren challenge the apostles and Paul (seek to bring them into bondage), and the united apostles respond and win the day, that is, maintain their honor on the point of Titus's non-circumcision status within this coalition according to the revealed truth of the gospel: they did not yield to the challenge of the pseudo-brethren. Also *contra* Georgi, *Remembering*, 24–25.

[63] This may account for the often noted awkward sentence construction here. Paul includes the digression from the main line of the argument in vv. 3–6, because it serves to illustrate a concrete case which captures the essence of the larger narrative concerns.

[64] These features appear to set this incident apart from that as reported by Luke in Acts 15, where, for example, there is no Titus present and specific disputes rather than revelation are the cause, both points that would seem to fit Luke's generally assumed agenda for Paul, but which Luke fails to report.

[65] Bruce J. Malina, *The New Testament World: Insights from Cultural Anthropology* (rev. ed.; Atlanta: John Knox Press, 1993) 63–89, 99–103; Malina and Jerome H. Neyrey, "First-Century Personality: Dyadic, Not Individualistic," in *The Social World of Luke-Acts: Models for Interpretation* (ed. J. H. Neyrey; Peabody, MA: Hendrickson Publishers, 1991) 67–96.

[66] Malina, *New Testament World*, 28–62; for classical Greek culture, see Alvin W. Gouldner, *Enter Plato: Classical Greece and the Origins of Social Theory* (New York and London: Basic Books, 1965) 48–49, 79–132; for modern Mediterranean culture see Julian Pitt-Rivers, "Honour and Social Status," in *Honour and Shame: The Values of*

political climate for this suspicious coalition on matters considered subversive, or otherwise dangerous, by some in authority in Jerusalem; good cause for lying low.

No. Paul did not seek to make this coalition's "private" meeting "public," that is, to bring an issue of concern *within* this Jewish coalition to the attention of other interest groups, especially those in power who did not share their convictions about Jesus. But upon the arrival of Paul, Barnabas and Titus, and the commencement of their meeting/s, the issue became somehow known. Thus the pseudo-brethren came to investigate what was taking place.

Paul's actions are consistent with the humble and subordinate nature of the gospel message Paul champions in this letter and elsewhere, not to mention of the person he proclaims (so, e.g., Luke 22:24–30): Paul is humbly concerned with ascertaining and implementing God's will, and to do so involves confirmation of his revelation and its interpretation in concert with the other apostles of this coalition.[67] But the informants have learned of the presence of Titus, they thus "slipped [came] in alongside [παρεισῆλθον]"[68] to bring their opinion on this matter (the need to circumcise such Gentiles if they are to be present as full members)—which they regard within their proper jurisdiction—to bear. This suggests not opposition to this coalition per se, but the right to come into this meeting to inquire, as well as some limitation of the rights of these informants to censorship and manipulative appeal (e.g., argument, accusation, shaming, censure), yet perhaps not physical coercion.[69] The pseudo-brethren

---

Mediterranean Society (ed. J. G. Peristiany; Chicago: University of Chicago Press, 1966) 21–38.

[67] In addition to the dyadic and socially derived nature of honor for Paul as a person of the Mediterranean culture of the time, as noted above (see also Malina and Neyrey, *Portraits of Paul: An Archaeology of Ancient Personality* [Louisville, KY: Westminster John Knox, 1996] 198–201), this is suggested also by the sociological perspective of role theory: "identity is socially bestowed, socially sustained and socially transformed" (Peter L. Berger, *Invitation to Sociology: A Humanistic Perspective* [New York: Doubleday, 1963] 98, cf. 37: "Human role-playing is always dependent upon the recognition of others. The individual can identify himself with a role only insofar as others have identified him with it"). Paul seeks group confirmation. The apostles would have played a part in Paul's self-definition even as he would have played a part in their own. This social dynamic is also supported by modern social identity theory (cf. Michael A. Hogg and Dominic Abrams, *Social Identifications: A Social Psychology of Intergroup Relations and Group Processes* [London and New York: Routledge, 1988]; Jenkins, *Social Identity*).

[68] Bauer, *BAGD*, 424–25; Burton, *Galatians*, 83.

[69] Paul accuses them of attempting in their role as informants of doing so in order "that they might bring us into bondage," which suggests more than just a reporting role, but

are the ones who throw down the challenge on the matter of Titus, and they do so toward Paul and the other apostles as one. Paul *and* the apostles *together* then respond to this challenge: "to them [the pseudo-brethren] we did not yield submission even for a moment, that the truth of the gospel might be preserved for you [Galatians]" (v. 5).

That is not to say that Paul was naive. One who had both persecuted and been punished, as had Paul, was well aware of the areas of dispute, especially with regard to the danger a change of policy toward Gentiles could represent. As one who regarded his zeal for the Law unmatched, he would certainly understand how the presence of a Gentile in an inappropriate "place" would be cause for considerable suspicion, or more. It is clear in the retelling that Paul understood the symbolic function of Titus. But the point here is that he intended to have a private meeting with others of the coalition of believers in Jesus. Among this group ("in this place"), presumably, Paul did not consider the presence of Titus at all inappropriate.

It should also be noted that the construction of Paul's almost redundant phrasing of their refusal to "yield [εἴξαμεν]"—on the matter in question—"by way of subjection [τῇ ὑποταγῇ]," supports the sense that their refusal was not a general resistance to the authority of the inspectors. It was instead related to "a particular subjection that was being demanded,"[70] the circumcision of Titus, a righteous Gentile believer in Christ, who, presumably, in such an environment, observed the halakhot deemed appropriate for fellowship, but who was not being regarded (by Paul and the apostles) as a candidate for proselytizing, although he was being perceived otherwise by the pseudo-brethren, that is, if he was to be regarded as more than a welcome guest.[71]

---

some authority to exercise social control, though it may be limited to censorship and manipulation. That is not to say that those to whom the informants reported did not have such power, and Acts 4:1–31; 5:17–42; 6:12; 8:1–3, for example, indicate such authorities to be operative concerning this Jewish coalition. Marc J. Swartz, Victor W. Turner, and Arthur Tuden (eds.), *Political Anthropology* (Chicago: Aldine Publishing Company, 1966) 1–41, discusses the various means of social control short of coercive or violent force. See also Jesse R. Pitts and Amitai Etzioni, "Social Control," in *International Encyclopedia of the Social Sciences* (New York: Macmillan, 1968) 381–402.

[70] Longenecker, *Galatians*, 52. Betz, *Galatians*, 91 n. 320, states, "[t]he article raises the question whether a formal demand was in fact made."

[71] That the issue of Titus was confined to his status as proselyte candidate or not, not in an academic environment, but one of intense social pressure to demonstrate conformity to prevailing notions for the inclusion of Gentiles, certainly implies that he was living as a righteous Gentile and not a pagan when among these Jews. I suggest that the idea of not eating according to Jewish food laws was simply beyond their imagination at this time,

The Thorny Problem of Identifying "Those of Repute"

The emphasis within Paul's argument of his unified stance with the Jerusalem apostles indicates that the resistance to the pressure of the pseudo-brethren on this issue was not reported so as to emphasize his unique role or influence, his independence, but the united decision to resist such circumcising of Gentiles in-Christ by all those "of repute [τοῖς δοκοῦσιν]" present, except the pseudo-brethren.[72] The context resonates with the language of honor and shame: pleasing people of influence or God. But the contrast is not between Paul and the Jerusalem apostles; it is with the pseudo-brethren, against whom, on this issue (the [non]circumcision of Gentiles in Christ), the apostles and Paul are one.[73] In this context, the pseudo-brethren, in their authoritative capacity, could also be regarded as "of repute," and thus the ironic or sarcastic play on words. In other words, it is possible that Paul's use of the label "those of repute" (2:2, τοῖς δοκοῦσιν), and its variations (2:6a, "the ones reputing to be something" [τῶν δοκούντων εἶναί τι]"; 6c, "the ones of repute [οἱ δοκοῦντες]"; 9, "the ones reputing to be pillars [οἱ δοκοῦντες στῦλοι εἶναι]"), was broadly applied to all of those authorities with which he had to deal in Jerusalem, though in different ways, so as to refer in some cases to the apostles, and in others to the "pseudo-brethren."[74]

Such an understanding of the ironic edge to δοκεῖν was in the air, being a common theme in philosophical argument between what "really is" versus what "seemed" or "appeared to be," which was brought out in the antithesis of δοκεῖν/εἶναι.[75] So too was the recognition that the Lord did

---

thus it is not even discussed in the context as a point of tension. Jews in Christ ate halakhically, including Paul, and Gentiles among these Jews ate appropriately for righteous Gentiles (cf. e.g., the apostolic decree of Acts 15; 21; see discussion in Nanos, *Mystery*, esp. 337–71, entitled, "Peter's Hypocrisy [Gal. 2:11–21] in the Light of Paul's Anxiety [Rom 7]").

[72] Paul E. Koptak, "Rhetorical Identification in Paul's Autobiographical Narrative: Galatians 1.13–2.14," in *Galatians Debate* (ed. Nanos) 157–68, for discussion of the rhetoric of consubstantial unity with the apostles versus the pseudo-brethren (esp. 163–66).

[73] The implication is that Paul and the apostles are all in agreement similarly with regard to the Galatians: they must resist any pressure from authorities of other Judaisms on this particular issue.

[74] See also David M. Hay, "Paul's Indifference to Authority," *JBL* 88 (1969): 38; C. K. Barrett, "Paul and the 'Pillar' Apostles," in *Studia Paulina in Honorem Johannis de Zwaan Septuagenarii* (Haarlem: De Erven F. Bohn, 1953) 1–2.

[75] Cf. Plato, *Rep.* 2.361b–362a; G. Kittel, *TDNT* 2.232–37, esp. 233; Hay, "Indifference," 39–42; Burton, *Galatians*, 72; Barrett, "'Pillars,'" 2–4.

not judge by the same outward appearance so readily seen by men (i.e., the flesh), but by the heart (1 Sam 16:7).[76] If Paul used the label in this way, then it may be that the seemingly disparaging remark in v. 6, which is made in the midst of the digression in vv. 4–6, is toward the inspectors/informants, and follows from the sudden comment of v. 3 on the unanimity of the apostles against the (proposed) circumcision of Titus. In this same sense Paul writes later for the Galatians to resist those seeking to influence them: "if anyone thinks he is something, when he is nothing, he deceives himself [εἰ γὰρ δοκεῖν τις εἶναί τι μηδὲν ὤν, φρεναπατᾷ ἑαυτόν]" (6:3), which is in keeping with Paul's habitual use of δοκεῖν with this kind of edge.[77] Moreover, this case complies with the observation that Galatians exemplifies the rhetoric of an ancient letter of ironic rebuke, so that the interpreter should be always alert to the double meaning of the language employed.[78]

The seams which protrude in the syntax of vv. 3–7,[79] and the problem of Paul's sarcastic irreverence toward those of repute when assumed to

---

Josephus, *Ant.* 20.197–203, attaches both senses of this language to those who opposed the actions of the Sadducean high priest Ananus and his cohorts in convening the Sanhedrin of judges which accused James of breaking the law and thus had him stoned. It appears that Josephus is referring to Pharisees when describing the opponents of Ananus's action against James who were "precise" or "rigorous concerning the Law": "those who seemed most equitable of the citizens, and such as were the most uneasy at the breach of laws [ὅσοι δὲ ἐδόκουν ἐπιεικέστατοι τῶν κατὰ τὴν πόλιν εἶναι καὶ τὰ περὶ τοὺς νόμους ἀκριβεῖς]" (201; emphasis added).

[76] Hay, "Indifference," 39–42, notes on 41: "Paul's indifference to the Jerusalem chiefs is grounded on God's." Hay helpfully develops several precedents in Jewish tradition for the indifference language of v. 6c in its appeal to God's impartiality toward human reputation: 1 Esd 4:39; Sir 4:22–28; 1QH 14, 19–20; cf. 2 Cor 5:12, 16! (42). See also David Wenham and A. D. A. Moses, "'There are Some Standing Here . . .': Did They Become the 'Reputed Pillars' of the Jerusalem Church? Some Reflections on Mark 9:1, Galatians 2:9 and the Transfiguration," *NovT* 36:2 (1994): 160 n 27, on the semantically similar Hebrew and Aramaic verb *caj* which means to "think, intend, plan, reckon," but in passive participial forms can mean "respectable," "of high esteem," e.g. b. *Gitt.* 59b.

[77] Barrett, "'Pillars,'" 2–3.

[78] See Nanos, *Irony of Galatians*.

[79] Cf. the discussions of B. Orchard, "The Ellipsis between Galatians 2,3 and 2,4," *Bib* 54:4 (1973): 469–81; *idem*, "Once Again the Ellipsis between Gal. 2,3 and 2,4," *Bib* 57:2 (1976): 254–55; A. C. M. Blommerde, "Is There an Ellipsis between Galatians 2,3 and 2,4?," *Bib* 56:1 (1975): 100–102; Burton, *Galatians*, 79–82; Betz, *Galatians*, 89–92; William O. Walker, Jr., "Why Paul Went to Jerusalem: The Interpretation of Galatians 2:1–5," *CBQ* 54 (1992): 503–10. See also J. Van W. Cronjé's discussion of how Paul's syntactical distortion here contributes to defamiliarization for the reader, thereby shifting their expectations of the author's meaning ("Defamiliarization in the Letter to the

be the other apostles, are surely perplexing, and have been the subject of much debate.[80] They paradoxically occur in the midst of his effort to otherwise explain his demonstration of respect for, and the subordination of his gospel to the Jerusalem apostles (after all, he has voluntarily laid his gospel before them to ensure that he was not and had not been running in vain; v. 2). If this suggestion is right, then Paul interrupted his larger discussion about the unanimous agreement of the apostles on the issue of Gentile equality apart from circumcision (vv. 1–2, 7–10), with Titus serving as an example (v. 3), by a digression in vv. 4–6.

This digression was intended to highlight the controversial nature of the unanimous decision of in-Christ Jewish leaders regarding the inclusion of and *koinōnia* with Gentiles in-Christ as Gentiles, not proselyte candidates. As is now the case in Galatia, others of repute within the larger Jewish communities may apply pressure to conform with other views of how to include Gentiles within the people of God (other inclusive "gospels" that conform to the prevailing "human" traditions insist on circumcision for entrance), such as these so-called "legitimate" inspectors/informants did in Jerusalem; however, "of what sort formerly[81] [cf. 1:13–14] they were does not make any difference to me, God does not discriminate [lit. 'take people at face value']," that is, in terms of "humanly constructed" categories of "appearance," with importance or status according to the terms of human agencies.[82] They may be "of

---

Galatians," in *A South African Perspective on the New Testament* [ed. J. H. Petzer and P. J. Hartin; Leiden: E. J. Brill, 1986] 220–21).

[80] Hay, "Indifference," 36–44, for a summary and bibliography. The usual interpretations of Paul's disrespect or perhaps dismissal of the significance and reputation of the other apostles, particularly any claims based on having been with Jesus, or of authority where gospel traditions are concerned, accent Paul's break with the Jerusalem leaders at this point in which he is seeking to demonstrate agreement and mutual respect. After all, Paul has brought his gospel to them. Furthermore, they create conflict with the plain meaning of 1 Cor 15:1–11.

[81] Barrett, "'Pillars,'" 19 n. 1: "It is impossible to decide with certainty whether ποτέ is to be taken with ὁποῖοι ('What*ever* they were . . .'), or with ἦσαν as a temporal particle ("What they *once* were . . .')."

[82] See Bruce W. Winter, *Seek the Welfare of the City: Christians as Benefactors and Citizens* (Grand Rapids: Eerdmans and Carlisle: The Paternoster Press, 1994) 137–40, for a discussion of the usage of "having a face" to designate legal status. Betz, *Galatians*, 93–95, discusses the perplexing problem of Paul's change in tenses here, with the imperfect verb ἦσαν ("they were") instead of the expected present tense as in the following phrases: οὐδὲν διαφέρει ("it makes no difference") and πρόσωπον [ὁ] θεὸς ἀνθρώπου οὐ λαμβάνει ("God shows no partiality to man"). "The discrepancy between the tenses is grammatically awkward and makes one suspect that Paul created it intentionally, because he wanted to distinguish between the past and the present" (93). Betz discusses

repute" by the appointment of men from other Jewish coalitions, and even by the consent of the other apostles who had allowed them to be present and their opinions considered, but God revealed the good news of Christ, and this revelation takes precedence over any other approaches or authorities, regardless of their position or long-held traditions, that is, regardless of their repute.[83]

In this light the digression of vv. 4–6, with its biting sarcasm, does not express Paul's view of the other apostles, but of the pseudo-brethren. The apostles of Paul's coalition are distinguished from these other human agents who base their authority in tradition when Paul introduces his purpose in going to Jerusalem to yield his proclamation of the good news of Christ for Gentiles, which is based in revelation, only to the apostles' coalition for confirmation: κατ' ἰδίαν δὲ τοῖς δοκοῦσιν, μή πως εἰς κενὸν τρέχω ἢ ἔδραμον: "but according to our *own* [*coalition's* norms]

---

the many proposals that have been put forward to try to explain what it was that the apostles once had that Paul appears to deny them now (they have died; they have lost positive qualities such as their physical knowledge of Jesus or advantageous situation at the time of the conference; or negative qualities such as their lack of education or failure at the passion of Jesus; the shifts of power from Peter to James, etc.), all assuming that the ones of reputation and the pillar apostles were one and the same. Betz suggests that the statement should be seen as a "proverbial present" which emphasizes this is a "matter of indifference" (*adiaphoron*), thus relativizing the "'authority' of the 'men of eminence' at Jerusalem," whom Betz assumes to be the Jerusalem apostles (94).

My point is made without pushing the limitations of the phrase as far as Betz does by simply removing the assumption that it is the Jerusalem apostles to whom Paul is referring. Instead, this reference may be to the change in status of the informers between the time or location of their authority in Jerusalem (which was already then suspect for Paul but tolerated because of the apostles), versus the case now as it applies to the Galatians (as would perhaps be the case anywhere, including Jerusalem, after the agreement was finalized), so that now no authorities who seek to circumcise Gentiles in-Christ (that is, "add something") are legitimate authorities in the eyes of God according to Paul. Just as the tension between pleasing God or man in Paul's former manner of life in Judaism is contrasted with his post-revelation-of-Christ life in this new Judaism, so too the situation has changed with respect to the authority of such influencers since the Jerusalem agreement confirmed that Gentiles in-Christ are not to be circumcised. Just as they added nothing to Paul in Jerusalem then, no one must be allowed to add something to the Galatian Gentiles in-Christ now.

[83] Betz, *Galatians*, 86–87, 92. Peter L. Berger, *The Sacred Canopy: Elements of a Sociological Theory of Religion* (New York: Doubleday, 1967) 98–100, discusses how "religious perspectives may *withdraw* the status of sanctity from institutions that were previously assigned this status by means of religious legitimation," which in the biblical tradition is witnessed in the way that, "before the face of God, the institutions are revealed as nothing but *human* works, devoid of inherent sanctity or immortality" (98–99, emphasis his). A sociological perspective on the fundamental "bad faith" evident in legal fictive role justification such as Paul seeks to demonstrate at work here is discussed in Berger (*Invitation*, esp. 160).

for ones of seeming repute (i.e., seeking a *private* meeting of the ostensible leaders of our coalition), [to ensure] that I am not running or had not somehow run in vain." The other apostles came separately by revelation to the same conclusion, and established at these meetings that Paul had nothing to fear in this regard (vv. 7–10).

Paul's dismissing of the legitimate right to authority on the matter of "revelation" at hand applies then specifically to those who sought the circumcision of Titus—though not as a formal but only a descriptive label—whether:

1) vigilante informants who were taking action (e.g., threatening and gathering incriminating data) they deemed necessary in view of the failure of the authorities to properly control this coalition;
2) inspectors who acted on behalf of the interests of the authorities in charge of all Jewish groups within Judaea, yet perhaps undermining their (mis)representation of the interests of this coalition in a subversive twist on their role, calling them informants;
3) legitimate representatives of the Jewish people in Roman terms (as puppets of the Roman regime), but undermining the legitimacy of their claim to inspect/investigate as though actually representing the interests of the Jewish people as the people of God;
4) or inspectors/informants perhaps in a way combining one or more features of these hypotheses.

As Paul tells the story, the "reputed" representatives of other Jewish interest groups failed to win the day because God had revealed otherwise. All of those in Christ, as represented by "the reputed to be *pillar* ones,"[84] formalized this understanding of the "truth of the gospel" by giving to Barnabas and Paul the "right hand of fellowship [*koinônia*]" (Gal 2:9). Thus, while Paul nuances his opinion of the apostles as "*reputed* pillars" in v. 9, this may not indicate that he did not regard them as of central importance (after all, he admits to having initiated this meeting to seek their confirmation), but that he also recognized them as "humans" subject to social anxiety (as he was formerly himself) within the larger framework of the many interest groups whom Paul regards now as merely "human agents" representing "human agencies." The apostles, like the inspectors in this sense, "seem" to be something in "the present

---

[84] For discussions of στῦλοι, see Barrett ("'Pillars,'" 1–19; Roger D. Aus, "Three Pillars and Three Patriarchs: A Proposal Concerning Gal 2:9," *ZNW* 70 [1979]: 252–61; Wenham and Moses, "There are Some," 146–63; U. Wilckens, *TDNT* 7.732–36).

evil age" even according to prevailing (traditional) "human" standards of measure.

The ironic edge perhaps explores the fact that the inspectors recognized the authority of these apostles as the leaders of this movement, although on grounds not of God's revelation, by which the claim to authority of this coalition actually appeals, but in terms of their ostensible standing at the head of the coalition, and thus subject to these social control agents' pressure to conform with the prevailing norms of Judean political constraints. These "seeming pillars" are thus open to criticism if they fail to "hold up" the principles upon which this coalition's claims are founded in the face of pressure to compromise in compliance with "other" communal norms.[85] They must "seek the approval of God, not such human agents or their agencies, or they will no longer be servants of Christ" (cf. 1:1, 10–11). The revelation of God in Christ must take precedence in the face of any claims by "human" authority or authorities.

In the context of the point being articulated for the benefit of the Galatians, namely, that "the truth of the gospel" might be preserved for them, Paul thus emphasizes that even these pillars were a bit shaky for a while (allowing these informants to intimidate them), when by the very nature of their esteemed roles and titles they should have been solid as a "rock."[86] In the end, with Paul's help, they did hold up the foundations of the faith; so too, now—regardless of their similar anxiety—must the Galatians.

This approach provides a snapshot of the thoroughly intra-Jewish nature of the social setting and polemic of Paul and the other early believers in Christ of the period. In many respects, it is not different from the stories of Jesus' interaction with such "spies" from rival Judaisms,

---

[85] While some irony does appear in the term "*reputing* to be pillars," it is not clear that Paul rejected the concept of their role or saw the label pillars as inappropriate, nor that the issue had anything to do with rejecting the merit of the fathers (the pillars are shown to be in agreement on the truth of the gospel!); *contra* Aus, "Three Pillars." He seems to be punning on the fact that pillars are foundational, they should be expected to make the structure "stand," which is, of course, that to which he calls the Galatians in this letter in the face of human agents who "trouble" them by maintaining the need for proselyte conversion (cf. 5:1–5).

[86] Paul's switch with reference to Peter from the normal use of the transliterated Hebrew name Cephas throughout the rest of the autobiographical material (1:18; 2:11, 14) frames the sudden change to the Greek name Petros in 2:7–9 (although manuscript discrepancies exist for v. 9). Both of course mean "rock." Perhaps Paul has made this switch here to ensure that the ironic level is not missed among his presumably Greek but not Hebrew speaking Gentile addressees in Galatia.

who were "carefully observing" his teaching in order to bring him into compliance, or else (Luke 20:20),[87] or from those investigators of the earliest movement of Jewish believers in Jesus such as Stephen.

The Matters of "Freedom" and "Gospel" at Stake in Jerusalem

Paul states that the purpose of his refusal to yield to the supervisory authority of the pseudo-brethren was not general, but very specific. The point by which they sought to "bring us into bondage [ἡμᾶς καταδουλώσουσιν],"[88] that is, under their social control,[89] was with regard to "our *freedom* which we have in Christ Jesus."[90] This is a most revealing point. With respect to exactly what are Paul and the other Jewish believers in Jesus free that these pseudo-brethren are seeking to now prohibit? Is it a matter on which the pseudo-brethren are themselves free? Would the pseudo-brethren consider their own present state, which they expect Paul and the apostles to share, "bondage"? Even if we strip this term of Paul's value judgment, so that we speak of the issue as a boundary obligation, the question arises: Would the pseudo-brethren consider the discarding of the obligation to circumcision or Torah-observance for themselves "freedom"? Would the Jerusalem apostles? Would Paul?

Paul and the others at this meeting, with the notable exception of Titus (the only Gentile we are made aware of), are not "free" with respect to circumcision. They are circumcised and have a mission to the same. Moreover, we have no evidence that any (male) Jewish believers in

---

[87] Hay, "Indifference," 41.
[88] καταδουλώσουσιν has the literal meaning of "absolute subjection or the loss of autonomy" (K. H. Rengstorf, *TDNT* 2.279).
[89] Betz, *Galatians*, 91 n. 310, notes that the term was originally political.
[90] Sederberg, *Terrorist Myths*, 15, helpfully defines the kind of political language which we find in this context: "Generally, liberty seems to imply some idea of space; most basically, a literal space within which to move; more *figuratively, a 'space' to express a range of opinions or engage in a variety of lifestyles.* Positively, liberty may suggest the possession of resources necessary to make use of the available 'space.' In any case, space is always restricted to some extent. In no community are either liberties or the resources needed to realize them unlimited. Harm to a person's liberty, therefore, involves the imposition of restrictions *beyond* those that have been *conventionally* established. *Of course, the definition of the 'appropriate' limits on liberty, and thus where harm begins, often is disputed*" (emphasis added). Paul, of course, is arguing that the boundaries of convention have been altered by revelation by God and not the consensus of the people in authority (i.e., tradition), thus challenging the definition of "the 'appropriate' limits on liberty" and thus of the point where "harm begins." Paul thus sees their action as coercion by Sederberg's definition: "*coercion includes all acts intended to harm others or their valued possessions*," with the stress on the intention of harm (11, emphasis his; cf. 13–19).

Christ, including Paul, regarded themselves as free with respect to circumcision, their own or that of their sons. Or that they cared to be. Jews simply do not look upon non-circumcision as "freedom," but as the loss of freedom, as a bondage to a pagan agenda rejected in the Maccabean revolt. Circumcision is a sign of privileged covenant status. It was God's idea for his people; who would want to be "free" of it? To the contrary, all the evidence indicates their continued zeal for Jewish identity and Torah observance. At the very least, they would be expected to live by Paul's "rule" of remaining in the state of circumcision in which they were called, leading their life appropriately, that is, as circumcised ones "keeping the commandments of God" (1 Cor 7:17–24), which would certainly apply to the circumcision of their sons.

Moreover, this would clearly mean, for one who was circumcised, the complete observance of Torah, even on Paul's teaching (Gal 5:3). The implicit logic of this warning is too often overlooked. Paul makes the rhetorical point in 5:3, to Gentiles seeking circumcision, that they thereby become bound to observe the whole Torah. But what prevents these Gentiles from simply answering Paul thus?

> We just want what you have Paul. We want the status of Jewish identity and the access to goods that identity provides (whether religious, political, economic, psychological, etc.). Since that does not seem to oblige you to observe the whole Torah, why should it do so for us?

In other words, for Paul's rhetorical point to carry any weight, particularly with the Galatians—among whom Paul has lived and taught in the past as a circumcised Jew, and about whom they are expected to know a great deal (cf. 1:9, 13; 4:12–20)—they are expected to recognize him to be Torah observant. Otherwise they would dismiss his point as irrelevant to their present concern for circumcision—that is, for the honored status of proselyte Jews with concomitant access to resources—regardless of any interest in full Torah observance they may have had (or not had) in the past.

Now Titus is "free," you might say, with respect to circumcision: he is a Gentile. The commonly noted Greco-Roman cultural offense at such "mutilation," or the very real apprehension of any grown man, especially at this time with regard to the primitive practice of medicine, makes it easy to understand the concern for "freedom from the knife." But that is unlikely to be Paul's meaning here in language inclusive of Jewish believers in Jesus: "*our* freedom," or more literally rendered: "the freedom of *us* which *we* have in Christ Jesus." Rather, is his point not probably that "we," that is, Jewish believers in Jesus, are free because of "the truth of the gospel" to regard Gentiles in-Christ who are not circumcised (such as Titus) as their *equals in status* among the people of God, fellow children of Abraham, and thus *to indulge in indiscriminate fellowship* ("our freedom") with them? Naturally, this freedom belongs to the Gentiles as well; they are free to regard themselves as children of God in-Christ, of *equal status with Jews without proselytizing*, that is, without circumcision identity to achieve such equal status.

This freedom was at the cutting edge of the revelation of Christ ("the truth of the gospel") that Paul presses in the message of this letter: both circumcised and uncircumcised are now equal before God in Christ. This position was a departure from the prevailing interpretations of the traditions of the fathers which guided the opinions of most other Jewish groups of which we are aware, for those of Pharisaical nature,[91] or those collaborating with the Roman regime in the administration of prevailing norms, but not in conformity with Paul's understanding of God's promises as set forth to Abraham in Scripture. Or so he argues![92] For Paul understands the revelation of this freedom contained in the truth of the gospel not as a new idea, but as the realization of the promise made to the fathers—a very old and thoroughly Jewish idea, you might say. He has not discarded the traditions of the fathers, in fact, he still speaks of them in the present as an aspect of his own continuing actions (1:14: "the traditions of *my* fathers"). Paul maintained, as did presumably the Jerusalem apostles, that the good news of this present reality was promised to Abraham (3:8–9, 14; cf. Acts 11:17–18; 15:14–21), that is, to the fathers. The revelation of Christ, Paul argues, must now alter, in this age, the interpretation of these traditions where Gentile inclusion is concerned, for the awaited age has dawned.

In other words, the issues are not of circumcision and Torah observance *per se*, that is, for Jews in-Christ as well as Gentiles, as many

---

[91] See Goodman, *Ruling Class*, 97–108.

[92] Here one may sense tensions set forth by Paul that are similar to those found in the often cited rabbinic incident of Eliezer ben Hyrcanus (a leading scholar in the period just after the destruction of the Temple) in the Babylonian Talmud's *Bava Metzia* 59b. In this halakhic dispute even revelation "proof" by God on the side of Eliezer (including the heavenly voice crying out on his behalf!) is insufficient evidence to overrule the consensus of the majority: "we do not pay attention to a [heavenly] voice, for You already wrote in the Torah at Mount Sinai: 'After the majority to incline,'" to which God replied: "'My sons have defeated Me, My sons have defeated Me,'" furthermore, after this ruling Eliezer was excommunicated (Steinsaltz transl.).

interpreters state or imply. Such universalizing of perspective is absent from this discussion and the whole of Galatians. To the observance of these Jewish norms Jewish believers in Jesus, including Paul, are by implication committed without reflection. They are not "the truth of the gospel" in question. These are simply not issues for them: They are not the topics of concern that have brought Paul to Jerusalem, nor to which he attends in his application of this story to the Galatians. The argument implies that the representatives of this coalition are all practicing Jews for whom Torah observance is not "bondage," though the particular interpretation of proper behavior by these rival pseudo-brethren inspectors or vigilantes is so regarded, in this case, concerning the issue of circumcising the Gentile Titus. For Paul, the representation of their authority if not also intention is suspect, it is harmful coercion ("bondage") toward the members of this coalition in view of the revelation received from God in Christ.

Conclusion

The issue in Jerusalem, and now in Galatia, was with regard to the ritual processes and observances incumbent upon Gentile believers in Jesus, a process which would be interpreted and administered by these Jews (the "yoke" or "bondage" of circumcising male Gentiles).[93] This naturally folds into the concomitant halakhic issue of appropriate social behavior governing the interaction of Jewish believers in Jesus who mix with these Gentiles. It is on this point that Paul, an apostle, and the other apostles in Jerusalem, are in full agreement on the decision regarding Titus.

Paul legitimates his power to instruct the Galatian Gentiles in the face of rivals by appealing to the symbolic importance of the earlier public institutionalizing of authority (dependence) demonstrated by the ritualized agreement[94]—not disagreement—in Jerusalem. This Judaism embraces the theology and practice of not circumcising Gentiles in Christ, and at the same time regards them not as merely "guests" or "liminal personae," but as indiscriminate equals, which Paul bundles together con-

---

[93] This understanding of the yoke mentioned in Acts 15:10 as proselyte conversion was suggested by Rebecca Denova ("James and the Fulfillment of Prophecy in Acts" [paper presented at the 1996 SBL Annual Meeting]).

[94] Cf. David I. Kertzer, *Ritual, Politics, and Power* (New Haven and London: Yale University Press, 1988) 51.

cisely in his phrase, "the truth of the gospel." This is the case regardless of the fact that other Jewish groups, including those which may otherwise have some legitimate supervisory capacity where this Jewish coalition is concerned, may find their position (of regarding and interacting with these Gentiles as though "already" equals) disputable, or the situation threatening. As far as we can be certain, except for the reference in Acts 15:1–5[95] to "some" Jewish believers in Jesus who were "from the sect of the Pharisees"—who believed at that point in time that Gentiles in-Christ should proselytize, a position with which the rest apparently had not agreed in the past and which they ruled against then—so too do all Jewish believers in Jesus of this period, whether Pharisees or not.[96]

Titus thus functions as an example of the parallel situations of the apostles in Jerusalem, when Paul was among them, and the Galatians now.[97] Both situations involve interaction with influential authorities from other Judaisms who do not share the view of Paul or the other apostles about "the truth of the gospel," which they claim to have received by the revelation of Christ. If they do not agree that the awaited time of Israel's restoration—and thus that of the whole creation—has begun, they would naturally disagree about the "freedom" that is claimed on the basis of the equal inclusion of the nations/Gentiles who turn to Israel's God as the One God of all humankind, that is, apart from completion of the ritual process of proselyte conversion, which provides for such inclusion in the present age, as agreed by all other Jewish groups (of whom we are aware).

This claim to the realization of the arrival of the age to come in this present age, with such attendant consequences as the indiscriminate incorporation of Gentiles who turned to Israel's God as their God too, was not derived from the prevailing majority interpretation of the traditions of the fathers, though, to Paul's mind, it was presupposed by them, for "the gospel was proclaimed beforehand to Abraham" (3:8). Yet this position naturally implies the (un)realized situation of the other Judaisms, and

---

[95] Is this also to whom the letter of the apostolic decree addressed to Gentiles of Antioch and Syria and Cilicia refers in 15:24 as "some persons from among us who have troubled you with words, unsettling your minds, although we gave them no instruction"?

[96] Bauckham, "James," 471–75, also notes that such evidence is lacking for the post-70's. See too Hill, *Hebrews*, 115, 149–92.

[97] Koptak, "Rhetorical Identification," 165: "Like Titus, the Galatians have been affirmed as believers without the requirement of circumcision, and have avoided the enslavement of those who would require it." He further notes: "The Galatians are also encouraged to identify with Titus, who, with Paul's help, responded to the circumcision-free gospel of Christ instead of the human desires of the false brothers."

judges their current views and methods on the issue at dispute, regardless of their prevailing authority, as "out of date." Such a position constitutes therefore an implicit if not always explicitly articulated insult or threat to the leaders of the dominant Jewish groups, to those in particular who are charged with the maintenance of order within the larger community(s) in which all these Jewish groups mix.[98]

The mechanisms of social control would thus be engaged to bring the proponents of this "deviant" view into conformity with the concerns of Israel's leaders as expressed under current religious and political constraints. In this case, they would seek to convince the leaders of this coalition to make proselytes of Gentiles seeking "full" admission, as is the prevailing position on the matter at hand in "this" age. This position provides many benefits, not the least of which, for those in positions of authority, are the protection of the covenant people from compromise (from a level of "freedom" which threatens the interests of those they protect)[99] and from infiltration by representatives of the intruding dominant society (from "sleeping with the enemy"),[100] not to mention the natural concerns of self-beneficence inherent in demonstrating their continued control of revelation, ritual, and interpretation over against the claims of the leaders of this new Jewish group to the contrary. Paul insists that the Galatians must now resist the pressure of the influencers to adopt circumcision, just as Paul and the other apostles had resisted the influence of the "pseudo-brethren," who did not successfully carry the (ultimate) decision in Jerusalem on this point (they did not turn them away to a different gospel; cf. 1:6),[101] even if they had or assumed some authority to exercise such influence, and possibly had succeeded at some level in applying such pressure, perhaps even on this point, until Paul set them straight.[102]

---

[98] Cf. Berger, *Sacred Canopy*, 44.

[99] This is indicated similarly in Paul's own concern elsewhere, when functioning as an agent of social control, to limit behavior he deems inappropriate and thus harmful, even if it may be argued as an expression of freedom (e.g., Gal 5; Rom 14; 1 Cor 8–10).

[100] See Fredriksen, *From Jesus*, 154–56.

[101] Richardson, *Israel*, 96, notes similarly: "Since, in Jerusalem, Titus (a Gentile) was not *compelled* to be circumcised, you must not allow anyone to compel you to be circumcised (2:3ff.; cf. 5:2ff.; 6:12ff.). False brethren in Jerusalem were responsible for this attempt, working from inside the Christian community; so also you must beware of those who are encouraging this from inside your own community (2:4; cf. 4:17; 5:8: 6:12f.)" (emphasis his).

[102] Burton, *Galatians*, 77, 81–82.

The collection mentioned at the close of this account is, I suggest, linked with the socio-economic fallout which results from just such dangerous and "shameless" behavior by this coalition. The message to the Galatians is a call for just this kind of suffering by choosing to resist the pursuit of honor on the terms of the dominant and majority Jewish culture (though itself constituting a minority group in Galatia in terms of the dominant and majority pagan culture) as determined by the prevailing interpretations of the fathers which clash with the revelation of Christ, not because the traditions were wrong, but because their interpretation needs to be "now" reconsidered. This marginalization may be shameful and involve very real socio-economic and religious deprivation in what Paul regards as this "present evil age" (1:4); nevertheless, as Christ is "portrayed as crucified" (3:1) and Paul "bear[s] on [his] body the marks of Jesus" (6:17), what else can the Galatians expect if they are to "become as [Paul is]" (4:12) in their lifestyle as full children of God, thereby called to walk "straightforward towards the truth of the gospel" (2:14)? These are, after all, the ultimate Jewish values, as set out in the Torah, and confirmed by the expression of the Holy Spirit for those who walk in Christ (5:14–25).

APOSTOLIC IDENTITY AND THE CONFLICTS IN CORINTH AND GALATIA

N. H. TAYLOR
University of Zululand, South Africa

That apostleship of Christ was a defining aspect of Paul's self-identity is widely recognised in scholarship.[1] That this apostolic consciousness, and the authority claimed on the basis thereof, were crucial to the conflicts which overshadowed much of Paul's recorded ministry, is perhaps less widely acknowledged, particularly among scholars who emphasise the theological nature of the controversies in which Paul was engaged. While early Christian history can no longer be reduced to Pauline and anti-Pauline camps, there is a lingering tendency to view the conflicts in which Paul was involved in such terms.[2] Despite attempts to demonstrate alternative backgrounds to opposition to Paul's authority and theology,[3] the notion of a single, concerted, anti-Pauline movement of so-called Jewish-Christian origin continues to be maintained in some scholarly circles.

I wish to argue that the parties Paul opposes in his letters must be examined individually, and not defined exclusively in terms of their opposition to Paul, but rather in terms of their own broader theological, missiological, and ecclesiastical agenda. I wish to argue also that the conflicts reflected in the Pauline literature cannot be understood simply in terms of doctrinal differences. Rather, the central issue is one of legitimate teaching and disciplinary authority in and over the early Christian communities. Paul's letters are assertions of authority, and claims to legitimacy where his authority is contested. Apostleship was a fundamental concept in Paul's rhetoric of authority, particularly, but in very different ways, in the conflicts reflected in Galatians and 2 Corinthians. I shall argue that these letters reflect hostility between Paul on the one hand and on the other groups of Christian Jewish missionaries who cannot be

---

[1] Cf. Dunn 1998; Taylor 1993.
[2] Barrett 1985; Lüdemann 1989.
[3] Georgi 1986; Jewett 1970; Munck 1959.

identified with each other. Whatever theological and missiological principles these may have held in common, their agenda are quite disparate, but the contested notion of apostleship is central both to Paul's authority claims and to attempts to supersede his authority in the churches. A study of the construction of apostolic identity can therefore shed useful light on the struggle for power in early Christianity, and, by extension, on the theological disputes which accompanied the contest for authority.

It is not necessary for the present purpose to discuss the origins and derivation of the term ἀπόστολος and the usage it acquired in early Christianity.[4] It is sufficient to note that the term would have been readily understood, even if not in widespread use, in the ancient world. The principle and practice of sending agents and messengers were well known, even if technical details regarding the scope and limitations of such representation were disputed.[5] ἀπόστολος gained currency in early Christian usage, referring very generally to messengers and representatives of Christian communities (cf. 2 Cor 8:23; Phil 2:25). It acquired at an early date also a very much more specific sense, referring to those sent to proclaim the gospel (cf. Acts 14:4, 14). Paul's self-conception, as reflected in Galatians in particular and also in 2 Corinthians and other isolated texts, is derived from this usage, but gives apostleship very much greater theological weight, and claims greater authority on the basis thereof.[6] The fact that Paul's self-designation was controversial and contested indicates that he was not alone in loading ἀπόστολος (Χριστοῦ) with theological, ideological, and rhetorical weight. Later usage of the term in Matthew, Mark, and Luke-Acts,[7] and its ultimate restriction to the circle previously known as the δώδεκα and a very few privileged others, similarly suggests that that term early became one of authority, and was used in articulating claims to authority in the Church. The concept was recognised, even if its definition and criteria, and the exercise of the authority attached to the title, varied considerably during the earliest decades of Christianity.

---

[4] For discussion see Ehrhardt 1958; Hanson 1961; Klein 1961; Mosbech 1948; Munck 1949; Rengstorf 1933; Schmithals 1971b; Schnackenburg 1970.

[5] For discussion see Buckland & McNair 1952; Jones 1956.

[6] I have argued this position more fully in my 1992 and 1993, and depend on these studies for much of the treatment which follows.

[7] Matt 10:2; Mark 6:30; Luke 6:13; 9:10; 11:49; 17:5; 22:14; 24:10; Acts 1:2, 26; 2:37, 42, 43; 4:33, 35, 36, 37; 5:2, 12, 18, 29, 34, 40; 6:6; 8:14, 18; 9:27; 11:1; 14:4, 14; 15:2, 4, 6, 22, 23, 33; 16:4. Cf. 1 Pet 1:1; 2 Pet 1:1; 3:2; Jude 17; Rev 2:2; 18:20; 21:14.

Paul's definition of his apostolic authority derives from a specific historical context. The extant letters all date from the period after his confrontation with Peter and Barnabas at Antioch (Gal 2:11–14) which ended his association with the church there.[8] Paul had hitherto been a functionary of the church of Antioch, engaged in its mission to Cyprus and parts of Asia Minor (cf. Acts 13:1–3).[9] Galatians in particular reflects Paul's reconstruction of his apostolic identity after ceasing to be a representative and missionary of the church of Antioch. It would therefore be helpful at this stage to consider such evidence as we may have of the nature of the apostleship to which the church of Antioch commissioned Barnabas, Paul, and presumably many others.

APOSTLESHIP OF THE CHURCH OF ANTIOCH

Acts 13:1–3 relates the church of Antioch commissioning Barnabas and Paul, described as προφῆται and διδάσκαλοι, for undefined work to which they had been called by the Holy Spirit. There follows the narrative of the so-called first missionary journey, and Barnabas and Paul are described as being ἀφορίσατε by the community and ἐκπεμφθέντες by the Holy Spirit. While ἀπόστολος and its derivatives are not used in this pericope, Barnabas and Paul are twice described as ἀπόστολοι in the ensuing narrative (Acts 14:4, 14), the only such designation of either of them in Acts. The absence of such terminology in 13:1–3 does not in any way mean that it is illegitimate to speak of Barnabas and Paul as apostles of the church of Antioch.[10] If there is any significance to the word usage, it indicates no more than Luke's reticence with the title and the relative unimportance of personal designations in the work of Christian mission at this early date.

In 1 Cor 9:1–6 Paul indicates that he and Barnabas did not receive economic support for their work of Christian ministry. This text is significant for several reasons. While it is clear that Barnabas and Paul did not claim any support from the churches, it is equally clear that there was a generally recognised right of Christians fully committed to the work of

---

[8] Brown & Meier 1983; Dunn 1983; Holmberg 1980; Taylor 1992.
[9] Dunn 1993: 25; Holmberg 1980; Murphy-O'Connor 1996; Taylor 1992; cf. Riesner 1998.
[10] Barrett 1994/1998: 598–601; Taylor 1992: 88–95.

the Gospel to do so.[11] Paul cites as ἀπόστολοι who exercised this right Peter and the brothers of Jesus, all of whom were associated, at least initially, with the church of Jerusalem.[12] The place in and from where Barnabas and Paul exercised a common apostleship was Antioch. This would seem to suggest that the custom of apostles' not receiving financial support from the churches in which they worked may have originated in Antioch. This was a practice which Paul continued during his years of independent mission. As the custom of the church of Antioch, this practice would not have been at issue in Galatians, even though it was to become controversial in Corinth, as will be discussed below.

A further indication of Antiochene apostleship may be found in Paul's account of the Jerusalem conference (Gal 2:1–10; cf. Acts 15:6–21/29).[13] In Gal 2:8 Paul uses the term ἀποστολή to describe the work of proclaiming the gospel, rather than the personal designation ἀπόστολος.[14] The former expression, while applied explicitly to Peter and the Jerusalem church and only implicitly to Barnabas, Paul, and the Antiochene mission, suggests a more fluid and less personalised conception of apostleship than is reflected in Paul's conception of his own apostleship. The work of Christian mission, rather than the status of individuals, is at issue.[15] In a context in which the status and authority of individuals are not of primary concern, the term ἀπόστολος could be applied to any person involved in ἀποστολή. It may therefore not be insignificant that the only occasion in which Barnabas and Paul are referred to as ἀπόστολοι in Luke-Acts is in the account of their mission from Antioch (Acts 14:4, 14). A similar usage is found in 1 Thess 2:7, where Silvanus and Timothy are included in the description Χριστοῦ

---

[11] The wariness of claimants to financial support evident in later Christian writings in itself indicates that the claim was or had been regarded as legitimate, Matt 10:8–10; Mark 6:8–9; Luke 9:3–4; 10:4–5; *Did.* 11.6, 12; 13.1–2. There is no indication elsewhere in the tradition that the right was exclusively associated with those who claimed the title ἀπόστολος. See further Taylor 2003.

[12] As we are concerned here with the criteria and nature of apostleship, we do not need to concern ourselves at this point with whether or not Paul acknowledged Peter and the brothers of Jesus as apostles in this text, or similarly James in Gal 1:19.

[13] For discussion of the correlation between the Acts and Galatians accounts of Paul's visits to Jerusalem and the Jerusalem conference see Taylor 1992: 51–54, 95–122, 140–42, and refs.

[14] Betz argues that Paul cites the actual words of a formal agreement at this point, 1979: 98. Cf. Dunn 1982: 473; R. Longenecker 1990: 56; McLean 1991: 67.

[15] Cf. Holmberg 1980: 18; McLean 1991.

ἀπόστολοι. This text may be particularly relevant if Silvanus represented an Antiochene notion of apostleship.[16]

In summary, the apostles of the church of Antioch, so far as we have been able to reconstruct, were deployed by that church to proclaim the Christian gospel in other centres. They were supported either from their own resources or by the sending church, but not by the communities they established. They were defined not by status but by the nature of their commission, and were sent by and were presumably accountable to the church of Antioch. If Paul's acquaintance with Andronicus and Junia (Rom 16:7) dated to his Antiochene period, this would suggest that the apostolate of the church of Antioch was not exclusively male.[17] As will be clear from our study of the relevant sections of Galatians, Paul departs from this notion of apostleship very fundamentally in his conception of the origin of his commission as an apostle.

In place of, and over against, the commission and authority he himself had previously derived from the church of Antioch, Paul expounds a conception of apostleship derived directly from God, superior in origin and authority to that of those whom he opposes. That this has shaped subsequent Christian notions of apostleship, and of Paul himself, requires caution in the reading of texts and reconstruction of the Christian mission and life which lies behind them. "Paul's discourse, which is situational, rhetorical, embattled to lesser and greater degrees, and in competition with other discourses, is imbued by later interpreters with the hegemonic status it seeks to claim."[18] Galatians and 2 Corinthians must be examined bearing this in mind.

Apostleship and the Conflict in Galatia

The churches in Galatia, to whom the letter is addressed, were established by Barnabas and Paul under the auspices of the church of Antioch.[19] In

---

[16] For discussion of the role of Silvanus in Paul's mission, and his previous connections with the churches of Jerusalem and Antioch, see Taylor 1992: 148–52, and refs.

[17] It might be argued on the basis of 1 Cor 9:5 that a husband-wife apostolic team would have been more characteristic of the circles associated with Peter and the brothers of Jesus. However, Barnabas and Paul are the only Antiochene apostles known by name, and 1 Cor 9:6 could indicate that Barnabas and Paul were exceptional even among this group in not being accompanied by wives. Cf. Conzelmann 1975: 153.

[18] Castelli 1991: 33.

[19] For the purposes of this study I am presupposing the so-called south Galatia

understanding Paul's ideology of apostolic authority asserted in the letter, we need to be aware of the situation both of the communities addressed and of Paul himself at the time of writing. The church of Antioch was the parent community of the Galatian churches, and Paul's relationship with the latter had hitherto been governed by his position as an apostle of the former. Antioch did not cease to be the parent congregation of the Galatian churches when Paul lost his position in that community. On the other hand, Paul's ceasing to be an apostle of the Antiochene church meant that he no longer had a recognised authority relationship with the churches of Galatia. His purpose in the letter is to create such a relationship. Paul does this in two ways. First, he claims an apostolic authority that is independent of the church of Antioch, deriving directly from God. Secondly, he claims in this capacity to have been the founder of the Galatian churches, and by implication not to have been acting on any commission from the church of Antioch. Paul's objective is therefore in effect to replace the oversight of the church of Antioch with his own apostolic authority in the Galatian churches. It is in the context of this conflict that Paul's claims to apostolic authority in Galatians are to be understood.

Paul's authority claims are most explicit in the epistolary greeting (Gal 1:1-2) and in the (auto)biographical narrative (Gal 1:11-2:14). Before these texts can be considered in detail, some attention to the rhetorical structure of Galatians is required.[20] While this section of the letter is clearly the narratio, its parameters and purpose are both disputed.[21] Several scholars have argued that Paul is concerned not so much with his own apostolic authority as with the content of the gospel he preaches.[22] Others have argued that Paul portrays himself as an example to the Galatian Christians,[23] or that he is seeking to persuade the Galatians to conform to his interpretation of the gospel.[24] The last point might be

---

hypothesis and an early date for Galatians, argued in my 1992: 45–46, and subsequently supported by Dunn 1993; Longenecker 1998. *Contra* Murphy-O'Connor 1996.

[20] The use of rhetorical criticism in the study of Galatians has been criticised by Kern 1996. While he is undoubtedly correct that a too rigid application of the categories of the rhetorical handbooks of Cicero and Quintilian could be misleading, we nonetheless need to be aware in general terms of the conventions which influenced the composition of speeches and letters.

[21] For review of literature and discussion see Taylor 1993: 66–69.

[22] Brinsmead 1982: 50; Kennedy 1984; Lategan 1988; Smit 1989.

[23] Aune 1987: 189–90; Gaventa 1986; Lyons 1985: 75–176.

[24] Hall 1991; Hester 1991: 282; Kennedy 1984: 146; Smit 1989: 23.

regarded as self-evident from even a cursory reading of Galatians. However, it is crucial that we recognise that Paul was not participating in a free exchange of ideas regarding Christian living in the abstract, but asserting his position unequivocally in a specific and concrete ecclesiastical situation. His example would not be followed, nor would his injunctions regarding Christian life be observed, unless Paul's authority to regulate the life of the Galatian churches was acknowledged. As we have already noted, Paul was addressing a situation in which his authority would not be accepted without question. His rhetoric is accordingly directed to establishing his authority, in order that he might govern the lives of the Galatian Christians in accordance with his interpretation of the gospel.[25]

It is clear from the way in which Paul qualifies his self-designation as ἀπόστολος in Gal 1:1 that the term was capable of alternative interpretation, and that the theological weight and authority claims Paul attaches to the term are at least potentially controversial.[26] Paul cites nowhere any paradigm of apostleship, other than claiming for ἀπόστολοι pre-eminence in the church (1 Cor 12:28). Where criteria of apostleship are reflected in the letters, it is not clear to what extent these criteria were generally current in the early Church, and to what extent they reflect Paul's self-conception and ideological and rhetorical agenda in a particular letter (1 Cor 9:1–5; 15:7; 2 Cor 12:12; Gal 1:16; 2:7–9). Paul could recognise another as an apostle only as that person met the criteria on which Paul based his own apostolic self-identity. At the same time, if Paul was to assert authority within established churches, as he does in Galatians, as well as in establishing new churches, he needed to define himself in terms of those who were able to exercise authority effectively in the various Christian communities.

The leaders of the Jerusalem church were the most effective wielders of authority in the Church of this period, and were acknowledged as pre-eminent by the church of Antioch (cf. Gal 2:1–14).[27] Paul therefore needed to model himself on them so far as he could, irrespective of whether they used the title ἀπόστολος or accorded it to anyone else. Paul could not claim to have been a disciple of Jesus,[28] and his reference to σαρκὶ καὶ αἵματι in Gal 1:16 may be wilful disparagement of this

---

[25] Betz 1979; Taylor 1993.
[26] Dunn 1993: 25–26; R. Longenecker 1990: 4; cf. Betz 1979: 39.
[27] Cf. Brown & Meier 1983; Dunn 1982; 1983; Holmberg 1980; Taylor 1992.
[28] For discussion see Hengel 1991; Riesner 1998: 33–58.

criterion of authority as well of James's blood relationship with Jesus (cf. 2:2, 6; 2 Cor 5:16).[29] Perhaps more significantly, Paul did not have the support or commission of any community, such as the churches of Jerusalem or Antioch, on which to base his claim to authority. He was alienated from the eschatological centre of Christianity and could derive no authority from that centre without affirming the higher authority of the Jerusalem church in communities over which he asserted authority. Paul was obliged therefore to claim for his conversion experience the significance attributed to other prominent Christians' experiences of the risen Christ (Gal 1:16; cf. 1 Cor 9:1; 15:1–8), and, moreover, to derive from it that authority which he defined as apostleship.[30] There is little evidence that anybody else was concerned at this time with personalising, or even with defining, the Christian apostolate.[31] Paul therefore does not need to counter one explicit definition of apostleship with another, but rather to match the authority exercised by others with his own, which he linked to his self-designation ἀπόστολος. Galatians was written early in Paul's period of independent mission and therefore early in the process in which he sought to articulate his conception of his personal apostolic vocation.

The Galatian Christians had previously encountered apostles, including Paul himself and Barnabas, who had been commissioned by the church of Antioch (cf. Acts 13:1–3; 14:4, 14). Insofar as they acknowledged any specifically Christian usage of the term, therefore, the Galatian Christians would have understood it in the Antiochene sense. Paul accordingly articulates against Antiochene conceptions of apostleship familiar in Galatia his ideology of apostolic authority derived from and accountable only to God.

Apostleship and the Rhetoric of Authority

Paul articulates his claim to authority over the Galatian churches in terms of an apostleship derived directly from God (Gal 1:1). The fact of

---

[29] Cf. Boyarin 1994: 109–13; Betz 1979: 72–73; Dunn 1993: 67–68; R. Longenecker 1990: 32–35.

[30] Cf. Dunn 1982: 463; Kim 1981: 55–56; Stendahl 1976: 7–11. The identification of Paul's revelatory vision of the risen Christ as a criterion for apostolic authority does not, however, imply that his vocation to apostleship was received in that vision. Cf. Taylor 1992: 63–67.

[31] A significant exception may be Paul's opponents in Corinth, who will be considered below.

preaching the gospel is no longer an adequate qualification for apostleship in the ecclesiastical and rhetorical context Paul is addressing. Paul's apostleship διὰ 'Ιησοῦ Χριστοῦ καὶ θεοῦ πατρός is contrasted with apostleship οὐκ ἀπ' ἀνθρώπων οὐδὲ δι' ἀνθρώπου. Paul's notion of his own apostleship is highly personalised and theologised. The exclusion of any human principal, including by implication a Christian community such as that of Antioch, and claim to direct and unmediated divine revelation and vocation, serve both to entrench Paul's claim to authority and to exclude rival claimants.[32] Paul's apostolic self-conception is radically different from that of the missionaries of the church of Antioch among whom he had previously worked, and with at least some of whom the Galatian Christians would have been acquainted. The possibility needs to be considered that it is precisely this pattern of apostleship to which Paul is contrasting his own apostolic identity.[33]

In seeking to identify the party Paul opposes in Galatians, a number of further factors need to be considered in addition to those identified above. One is that it is not clear that Paul himself knew precisely who they were (cf. Gal 1:6–9; 4:20; 5:10).[34] It would seem clear from Gal 5:2–3 that Paul is attacking a party influencing the (Gentile) Galatian Christians to undergo circumcision. His argument that the obligation to observe Torah in full is a corollary of circumcision would militate strongly against any figurative interpretation of περιτομή.[35] In place of token incorporation into Israel signified by circumcision, Paul articulates the inheritance by Gentile Christians into the promises made to Abraham (Gal 3:14–18; 4:21–31). The position Paul opposes seems similar to that which was repudiated at the Jerusalem conference (Acts 15:6–21; Gal 2:1–10), and which is excluded by the Apostolic Decree (Acts 15:23–29).[36] There is no indication that the crisis reflected in Gal 2:11–14 concerned circumcision of Gentile Christians, but rather the appropriate degree of commensality between Christians of Jewish and Gentile origin.[37] Apart from a passing mention of calendrical observations (4:10), Paul makes no reference in

---

[32] Cf. Boyarin 1994: 107–109; Burton 1921: 37–39; Dunn 1993: 25.
[33] Cf. Dunn 1993: 14–17; Murphy-O'Connor 1996: 193–94.
[34] Kümmel 1975: 300; Martyn 1985: 313–14.
[35] Betz 1979: 259–61; Dunn 1993: 265–67; R. Longenecker 1990: 226–27.
[36] The Apostolic Decree is treated here as a document or position reached after the Jerusalem conference and the subsequent incident in Antioch. See fuller discussion in Borgen 1988; Taylor 1992: 110–22, 140–42.
[37] Brown & Meier 1983: 36–44; Dunn 1983; Holmberg 1998; Howard 1990: 14; Taylor 1992: 124–38.

Galatians to any specific judaising practice other than circumcision (5:2, 3, 6; 6:12, 13, 15). There are very general allusions to Torah observance in 2:14–3:14 and elsewhere. While Paul may not respond to every aspect of the teaching he opposes,[38] or may caricature it,[39] it is nonetheless surprising that he makes in the probatio and peroratio no reference to table fellowship and dietary laws which had been at issue in Antioch. On the contrary, Paul intimates that those he opposes demand circumcision to the exclusion of other observances (5:2–3), and he attacks an antinomian tendency in the Galatian churches (5:13–26). These factors suggest that the leadership of the churches of Jerusalem and Antioch cannot be identified with the party Paul opposes in Galatia. While tension between Paul and the Jerusalem church is clearly reflected in Galatians (1:16–2:14; cf. 4:21–31), there is no evidence that either the Jerusalem or the Antioch church came to regard circumcision as obligatory for Gentile Christians.[40] There may well have been pressure on the Jerusalem church (cf. Gal 6:12; 1 Thess 2:14–16) not to allow the conversion of Gentiles to abrogate the distinction between Israel and the Gentile world.[41] Such pressure may well have contributed to the confrontation between Paul and Peter in Antioch (Gal 2:11–14).[42] There is nevertheless no indication of a fundamental departure from the consensus established at the Jerusalem conference, and the agenda of Paul's antagonists are quite contrary to implementation of the Apostolic Decree.[43]

In view of the difficulties in identifying Paul's antagonists with the Jerusalem and Antioch churches and their leadership, the majority of recent scholars argue that they represent a faction in the Jerusalem or Antioch church, but not the leadership of either community.[44] That there was a faction in the Jerusalem church which sought the imposition of the Mosaic law on Gentile Christians, and that they were active in the Antiochene church as well as Jerusalem, is clear from Acts 15:1–5 and Gal 2:3–5.[45] This group were overruled at the Jerusalem conference, but

---

[38] Barclay 1988: 38.
[39] Cf. Hall 1991: 311.
[40] This position continues to be maintained in recent scholarship, e.g. Barrett 1985: 6, 22; Watson 1986: 59–61. See also Slee 2003; Zetterholm 2003.
[41] Reicke 1984; Taylor 1996.
[42] Dunn 1983; Taylor 1992: 124–38.
[43] Borgen 1988; Taylor 1992: 110–22; 140–42. Cf. Murphy-O'Connor 1996: 193–94.
[44] Betz 1979: 7; Burton 1921: lvi; Dunn 1993: 14–17; Gunther 1973: 298; Koester 1971: 144–45; R. Longenecker 1990: xcv; Murphy-O'Connor 1996: 193–94.
[45] Cf. Watson 1986: 50–51.

pressure from them may have influenced James's subsequent despatch of emissaries to Antioch (Gal 2:12). However, there is no indication that James's delegation made demands comparable to those of the judaistic faction.[46] They may, however, have had the same motivation, to ameliorate pressure on the Jerusalem church by reinforcing the distinction between Jew and Gentile in ethnically mixed churches (cf. Gal 5:11; 6:12; 1 Thess 2:14–16). The resolution of this second crisis in the Apostolic Decree would have been a second defeat for this party. They may have taken matters into their own hands, either in response to the Apostolic Decree or by taking advantage of the crisis in the Antiochene church resulting from the confrontation between Peter and Paul, before the Apostolic Decree had been formulated and adopted. Churches established under Antiochene auspices, but remote from the oversight of that church, may have seemed susceptible to their influence, and have posed an opportunity to shape Christian communities in accordance with their vision.[47] It is entirely possible that this movement was represented in Galatia by apostles of the church of Antioch, who had been known previously to the Christian communities there.

Some scholars argue that the party Paul opposes was unconnected with the churches of Jerusalem and Antioch.[48] Their apparently selective imposition of the Mosaic law, involving no more than token incorporation into Israel, noted above, may count against an association with these churches. Even allowing for the diversity of Judaism,[49] and of Gentile conformity with Christian[50] and other forms of Judaism,[51] a movement which stressed circumcision cannot easily be identified with communities which waived circumcision for Gentile Christians while imposing other observances on them (cf. Acts 15:22–29).[52] Therefore, if attached to the Jerusalem or Antioch churches, this movement would have been

---

[46] Cf. Taylor 1992: 128–31, and refs.
[47] Cf. Barclay 1988: 58–59; Taylor 1992: 138–42.
[48] Barclay 1988: 42–44; Brinsmead 1982: 104; Gaston 1984: 64; Howard 1990: xiv–xix; Martyn 1985; Munck 1959: 129–32; Schmithals 1965: 9–10.
[49] Sanders 1977; 1992. Cf. Martyn 1985: 308–11.
[50] Taylor 1995.
[51] Cohen 1986.
[52] Another consideration is whether they regarded Paul as being unduly dependent upon the Jerusalem church, rather than as defying the authority of that community, as representatives of the Jerusalem and Antioch churches would maintain. Persons unconnected with the Jerusalem church, on the other hand, could have accused Paul of being unduly subservient to that community. Cf. Brinsmead 1982: 104; Munck 1959: 129–32; Schmithals 1965: 9–10.

something of a dissident faction, but nevertheless possibly one which enjoyed more support than Paul.

The convoluted manner in which Paul defines his relationship with the Jerusalem church and its leaders[53] indicates that this relationship is very much at issue. While there is no clear link between the party Paul opposes and the Jerusalem church, or that of Antioch, Paul's relationship with the former and its leadership is integral to defining his apostolic identity in Galatians. This is particularly clear in the autobiographical narrative (1:11–2:14).[54] The narratio interprets selected events in Paul's life from his conversion to the time of writing in order to substantiate his authority, before proceeding in the remainder of the letter to articulate the position of Gentile Christians in relation to the Mosaic law. Galatians may well be the earliest attempt to limit apostleship as an office or vocation belonging to particular people.[55] In order to define his own apostleship as independent of any human or ecclesiastical authority, Paul closely identifies his reception of the gospel (conversion) with his vocation to preach it (Gal 1:16).[56] He models his account of his conversion on the Hebrew tradition of prophetic vocational oracles, as reflected in Jer 1:5, claiming to have been chosen for his apostolic work before his birth (Gal 1:15).[57] It is arguable that Paul, in claiming to have been called directly by God, claims a higher vocation than that of apostles sent by Jesus.[58] It is doubtful, however, whether this distinction would have been recognised either by those thereby relegated to an inferior status, or by Christians who acknowledged the authority of the latter.[59] Paul's close association of Jesus and God as the authors of his own vocation (Gal 1:1) and frequent self-designation as ἀπόστολος Χριστοῦ (1 Cor 1:1; 2 Cor 1:1; cf. Rom 1:1; 1 Thess 2:7) would also militate against such a reading, as would his explicit claim to have been sent by Christ (1 Cor 1:17).

---

[53] Dunn 1982; Taylor 1992.

[54] Scholars debate the parameters of this section of the letter. For discussion see Taylor 1993.

[55] Schmithals 1971b: 86; cf. Munck 1949: 100–101; Taylor 1992: 155–70.

[56] Cf. Schütz 1975: 134; Segal 1990. Some scholars continue to equate Paul's conversion with his vocation as apostle to the Gentiles, Kim 1981: 55–66; McLean 1991: 67; Stendahl 1976: 7. For discussion see Taylor 1992: 62–67.

[57] For discussion see Malina & Neyrey 1996: 40–41; Munck 1959; Sandnes 1991; Segal 1990.

[58] Boyarin 1994: 107–109; Malina & Neyrey 1996: 40–41.

[59] It would not require a high christology to regard those sent by Jesus as being at the same time called by God.

Paul assimilates his conception of ἀπόστολος into his self-identity. While anxious not to imply any hostility to the Jerusalem church, but rather to stress the unity between them, Paul articulates his self-understanding as ἀπόστολος of God and of Christ, independent of any human principal. He superimposes this on his account of his career as an ἀπόστολος of the church of Antioch. This serves both to legitimate his claim to continuing authority over the Galatian churches, and to counter any authority claims made by the party he opposes.[60] There is no suggestion in the letter that these identified themselves as ἀπόστολοι, in any sense of the word and especially in none that conveyed a claim to special status and authority. Paul does not compete with any authority claims made by the group he opposes, as he does in 2 Corinthians 10–13. Rather, he claims acknowledgement by the leaders of the Jerusalem church of his status, authority, and mission to the Gentiles. The distinction therefore needs to be maintained between Paul's attack on his rivals in Galatia and assertions, however ambiguous and uncomplimentary, about the Jerusalem church.[61]

Apostleship in the Autobiographical Narrative

Paul begins the autobiographical narrative (Gal 1:11–12) with a refutation of real or hypothetical contentions about the gospel he preaches similar to those about his apostleship which he refutes in Gal 1:1.[62] While the verbal parallels are not precise, the correlation is nonetheless clear and significant. Gospel and apostleship alike do not derive from any human source. Just as his acquisition of Christian convictions had been without human intervention, so was Paul's apostolic vocation received without human mediation. By associating his reception of the Christian gospel with his vocation to preach it, and claiming direct divine revelation as the source of both, Paul is able to assert an authority in Galatia which transcends that of the church of Antioch which had sent him to proclaim the gospel there.

Paul denies having sought an interpretation of his conversion experience from any human authority (Gal 1:16),[63] and explicitly having travelled to Jerusalem to consult those who were already ἀπόστολοι

---

[60] For more detailed discussion see Taylor 1992; 1993.
[61] Betz 1979: 92; Smith 1985: 191.
[62] Cf. Betz 1979: 62.
[63] Dunn 1982: 463; cf. Kim 1981: 55–59.

(Gal 1:17). The mention of τοὺς πρὸ ἐμοῦ ἀποστόλους indicates Paul's apostleship as the key issue in the autobiographical narrative, even if it had not been so at the time of the events related. While making no explicit statement that he was already an apostle, Paul nonetheless, intentionally if implicitly, conveys this impression.[64] This reinforces Paul's claim, implicit in his use of the title ἀπόστολος, to authority independent of the Jerusalem church, and by implication also that of Antioch. At the time of writing he is operating independently of any Christian community, and the implication that he had begun his Christian missionary work without reference to the Jerusalem church serves to justify this.[65] His subsequent participation in the apostolate of the church of Antioch does not mean that that church was the source of his apostolic authority.

After arguing the basis of his independent and absolute apostolic authority, Paul reports his first visit to Jerusalem after his conversion. He identifies his purpose as ἱστορῆσαι Κηφᾶν (Gal 1:18). Any casual overtones to this phrase[66] are rhetorical rather than historical. Paul seeks to demonstrate unity of purpose with Peter, and also with James, and leads the recipients to infer that they acknowledged the claim to apostolic authority he makes in the letter.[67] It would seem to follow that Peter at least is one of those τοὺς πρὸ ἐμοῦ ἀποστόλους (Gal 1:17), and any ambiguity in the reference to James in Gal 1:19, while significant for Paul's rhetorical purpose in the letter, is of less importance for reconstructing early Christian nomenclature.[68] Any others who could claim to be apostles senior to Paul are, by implication, of no consequence. While claiming acknowledgement by Peter and James, Paul is nonetheless concerned not to accord them, or anyone else who could claim apostolic title, any jurisdiction over his ministry which others, particularly those he opposes in Galatia, would recognise or claim for themselves.

Paul next travelled to Jerusalem, as the junior partner to Barnabas, as a representative of the church of Antioch (Acts 15:2; Gal 2:1).[69] Perhaps

---

[64] Taylor 1993: 71–72.
[65] Cf. Schütz 1975: 155.
[66] Betz 1979: 76; Campenhausen 1969: 69; Hofius 1984: 77–78; cf. Dunn 1982: 463–65.
[67] Cf. Malina & Neyrey 1996: 42–43.
[68] Cf. Betz 1979: 77–78; Dunn 1993: 76–77; Howard 1977; R. Longenecker 1990: 38; Schmithals 1971b: 64–65; Trudinger 1975.
[69] Taylor 1992: 102. The details of the issues discussed and resolved, or left unresolved, are not of significance for the present purpose. For discussion see Dunn 1982; Murphy-O'Connor 1996; Taylor 1992: 96–122.

more than any other section of the autobiographical narratio, Paul reinterprets the Jerusalem conference in the light of his situation at the time of writing Galatians. The church of Antioch is conspicuously not mentioned, and Paul's purpose in travelling to Jerusalem is stated in the singular. Paul distances himself from Barnabas, whose presence he acknowledges only in Gal 2:1 and 2:9, while his use of the singular in 2:2, 6–8 implicitly ignores him. Paul shifts the focus from issues between Jews and Gentiles in the Antiochene church to his own apostolic authority and the gospel he associates therewith (Gal 2:2).[70]

Paul relates that he had submitted his gospel to the scrutiny of the leadership of the Jerusalem church (Gal 2:2), and that these had affirmed his preaching (Gal 2:6). The redefining of the issue at stake in Gal 2:2 in terms of Paul's apostolic preaching and authority is followed here by the vindication of Paul's gospel. Affirmation by the Jerusalem church of the gospel preached at Antioch becomes Paul's claim that his own teaching and practice, and by implication his apostolic authority, were recognised by the Jerusalem leadership. Paul had been entrusted with τὸ εὐαγγέλιον τῆς ἀκροβυστίας, just as Peter had been entrusted with the (gospel) τῆς περιτομῆς (Gal 2:7). The parallelism between the gospels preached in and from Jerusalem and Antioch[71] is co-opted by Paul in defence of his own gospel and preaching. He claims further that the Jerusalem leaders recognised that God operates through Peter εἰς ἀποστολὴν τῆς περιτομῆς and through Paul εἰς τὰ ἔθνη (Gal 2:8). Two aspects of these statements are remarkable. εἰς τὰ ἔθνη designates the scope of Paul's work, whereas in the previous clause he had used ἀκροβυστίας (Gal 2:7), indicating the distinctive character of the gospel he preached. This alteration[72] reflects and emphasises Paul's later apostolic claims (cf. Rom 1:5; 11:13; Gal 1:16), signifying his notion of his own unique and all but exclusive apostleship to the Gentiles. Paul, in defence of his personalised notion of his own apostleship, uses the term ἀποστολή of Peter's mission but not explicitly of his own (Gal 2:8).[73] Reference is made to the ministry

---

[70] Cf. Betz 1979: 81; Schütz 1975: 140; Taylor 1993.
[71] See discussion in Taylor 1992: 110–22.
[72] Argued more fully in Taylor 1992: 166. Cf. also Betz 1979: 95–99; Dunn 1993: 105–107; R. Longenecker 1990: 55–56.
[73] Betz 1979: 98 suggests that Paul is citing the actual words of the agreement, with the implication that Peter was recognised as an apostle, but not Paul. The implication, however, is doubtful, in that the noun governing the first of two parallel phrases would be implied in the second; repetition of ἀποστολή would therefore be redundant. Cf. R. Longenecker 1990: 56; McLean 1991, who argue that Paul's citation of the agreement is not verbatim.

exercised, not the title of the one exercising it. The work of ἀποστολή, in which several members of the two churches were presumably engaged, was the issue of the original agreement, and not the personal status of the various missionaries. The personalised concept of apostolic office has become important for Paul on account of his having ceased to be engaged in the apostolate of the Antiochene church, and forfeited the authority which derived from that commission. For apostles of churches whose authority is reinforced by the commissioning community, personal status is not so important. But for Paul, without any commissioning church after the Antioch incident, his authority needed to be sufficient in itself to be effective.

Paul briefly paraphrases the practical implication of the agreement: ἡμεῖς εἰς τὰ ἔθνη αὐτοὶ δὲ εἰς τὴν περιτομήν (Gal 2:9). I have argued previously that the agreement originally consisted in the mutual recognition of diverse interpretations of the Christian gospel by the two churches of Jerusalem and Antioch, and not in the division of the missionary fields along racial or geographical lines.[74] This does not mean that Paul does not imply precisely such an interpretation in order to substantiate his claim to jurisdiction in Galatia and to exclude rival authorities from involvement there. In this respect Paul's inclusion of Barnabas once again may be significant. He can plausibly argue that the agreement meant that the church of Jerusalem exercised no oversight of the Galatian churches, but he could not on that basis exclude the jurisdiction of the church of Antioch. Therefore, in order to maintain his claim to exclusive apostolic authority in Galatia, Paul needs to discredit the church of Antioch, and Barnabas in particular, which he does in relating the subsequent incident in Antioch.

Paul portrays as the sequel to the Jerusalem conference his confrontation with Peter and Barnabas in Antioch (Gal 2:11–14). While Paul does not criticise Peter's presence in Antioch as violating a division of influence, he condemns the violation of commensality by Peter when under pressure from James. The Jewish Christians of Antioch, including Barnabas, had at the very least acquiesced in Peter's withdrawal from table fellowship with Gentile Christians, if indeed it was not their prevailing custom with which Peter was conforming. The implication is that the church of Antioch had abandoned τὸ εὐαγγέλιον τῆς ἀκροβυστίας

---

[74] Taylor 1992: 112–15. Cf. Bornkamm 1971: 39–40; Dunn 1993: 111–12; Gaston 1984: 65; Georgi 1965: 22; Holmberg 1980: 30–31; Schütz 1975: 156.

(Gal 2:7), at least as Paul understood it, and had thereby forfeited its oversight of the Galatian churches.[75] This episode is significant for Paul's assertion of authority in Galatia also in demonstrating that he did not regard Peter and Barnabas as beyond his reproach. Paul's repudiation of any authority which conflicts with his interpretation of the gospel is unequivocal. The implication is that, if Paul had authority to take issue not only with Peter and Barnabas, but also by extension with James and the Jerusalem church, his authority in the Galatian churches is unqualified.[76]

In conclusion, Paul uses his notion of apostleship to articulate his claim to jurisdiction over the Galatian churches. His self-identity serves also to define his relationship with other effective bearers of authority in early Christianity, and in particular his unity with but independence of the leaders of the Jerusalem church. Paul's self-conception as apostle is, yet more significantly, the basis of his claim to continuing oversight of the Christian communities of Galatia after forfeiting his position in the church of Antioch and its mission. While Paul provides evidence that his notion of apostleship, and the authority he derives from it, would be contested, there is no indication that the party he opposes claimed any similar status. This was not the case in Corinth, which we now turn to consider.

The Crisis in Corinth

The situation in Corinth which overshadowed the closing years of Paul's ministry belongs to a very different context to that of Galatians. Paul had established the church in Corinth during his period of independent mission (cf. Acts 18:1–18). The community therefore had no connection with the church of Antioch or any other parent congregation. Whatever continuing connection Priscilla and Aqilla may have had with the Corinthian church, there is no evidence that Paul's position as founder of that community was questioned (cf. 1 Cor 3:6). Rather, opposition to Paul either originated within the Corinthian church itself, or with rivals who entered the community after Paul's mission. In this study we are not concerned with a detailed discussion of opposition to Paul in Corinth, but

---

[75] Cf. Dunn 1993: 124–26.
[76] Cf. Sampley 1980: 39.

specifically with conflict in which apostleship, and claims to authority derived from use of such title, played a role.

The Situation Prior to 2 Corinthians

There is considerable disagreement in scholarship as to the nature of the troubles which afflicted the Corinthian church and Paul's relationship with it.[77] In particular, it is unclear how the controversies reflected in 1 Corinthians relate to the conflict evident in 2 Corinthians.[78] 1 Corinthians clearly reflects a fractious atmosphere in the church (1:10–13). Despite the mention of Peter (1:12; cf. 9:5; 15:5), there is no evidence that he or his followers had been in Corinth, and it is the continuing influence of Apollos (1 Cor 1:12–13; 3:4–9, 22; 4:6) which occasioned Paul's anxiety.[79] The competing inclinations and ambitions of the leaders of the various house churches in Corinth were at least as important a factor in the strife as any external influences, at the time 1 Corinthians was written.[80]

Paul makes a number of potentially significant, if tangential, statements concerning apostles in 1 Corinthians. His identification of himself as ἀπόστολος Χριστοῦ διὰ θελήματος θεοῦ in the epistolary greeting (1:1) gives no hint that Paul expected his self-designation to be contentious in the eyes of the recipients. The rhetorical question at 1 Cor 9:1 would seem to confirm this. While some scholars see this section as a response to a challenge to Paul's apostolic authority,[81] this interpretation does not take adequate account of the place of the passage in the structure of 1 Corinthians. In the context of admonishing the Corinthians regarding the consumption of meat which had been offered in pagan rituals (1 Cor 8:1–11:1), Paul cites the example of his renunciation of the

---

[77] For discussion see Chow 1992; Georgi 1986; Gunther 1973; Horrell 1996; Marshall 1987; Sumney 1990; Theissen 1982.

[78] I am presupposing for the purposes of this discussion the reconstruction of the composition of 2 Corinthians and the history behind it argued in Taylor 1991. I argued the following sequence of letters: A. that including 2 Cor 6:14–7:1, alluded to in 1 Cor 5:9; B. 1 Corinthians; C. 2 Cor 10:1–13:10; D. 2 Cor 2:14–6:13; 7:2–4; E. 2 Cor 1:1–2:13; 7:5–8:24; F. 2 Cor 9:1–15.

[79] Cf. Holmberg 1980: 67–69; Robertson & Plummer 1914: 16; Sellin 1987: 3015; Watson 1986: 81. For contrary views, see Barrett 1982: 1–39; Conzelmann 1975: 34; Hurd 1965: 214; Munck 1959: 167; Schmithals 1965: 105.

[80] See discussion by Chow 1992; Horrell 1996: 88–125; Marshall 1987; Meeks 1983: 56–63; Theissen 1982: 69–143; Winter 2001.

[81] *Contra* Conzelmann 1975: 151–53; Fee 1987: 390–94; Hurd 1965: 126–31; Lüdemann 1989: 65–67; cf. Horrell 1996: 205–16.

rights and freedom to which he is entitled as an apostle.[82] This would be possible only if Paul's apostleship and the rights attached thereto were not being contested in Corinth at the time.

An indication of Paul's understanding of his commission is provided in 1 Cor 1:17 where he states that ἀπέστειλέν με Χριστὸς ... εὐαγγελίζεσθαι. That proclamation of the gospel is the essence of Paul's interpretation of the apostolic vocation is corroborated or implied at several points in his letters (Rom 1:2; 11:13; Gal 1:16), not least in Paul's identification of himself as founder of the church of Corinth (1 Cor 3:6, 10; 9:2). This correlates with identification of apostleship as the highest calling in the Church in 1 Cor 12:28, notwithstanding the sarcastic deprecation of that office at 4:9. The rights of apostles to material compensation for their efforts, which Paul waives (1 Cor 9:1–6), have already been discussed.

1 Corinthians 15:7 (cf. 9:1) implies that a vision of the resurrected Christ, presumably accompanied by some form of vocational oracle, was the defining credential of apostleship.[83] Irrespective of the origins and parameters of the tradition Paul is citing,[84] his appending his own resurrection vision and defining it as the last (15:8–9) are both significant. Paul claims for his conversion christophany the same vocational connotations as the resurrection experience of the original followers of Jesus (cf. Matt 28:19; Luke 24:47; Acts 1:8). This claim may have been contentious elsewhere in the early Church, but there is no indication that it was so in Corinth at the time 1 Corinthians was written (cf. 9:1).[85] That Paul is constrained to justify including himself among the ἀπόστολοι on the basis of his vision of the risen Christ, confirms very clearly that such visions were an important criterion of authority in the early Church. However, there is no evidence that there was at this time a more general association of apostleship with resurrection christophanies. Paul implicitly denies that any such vision subsequent to his own could have the same vocational significance as his (1 Cor 15:8). Paul therefore by implication defines out of legitimacy any later challenger to his authority. It is at least potentially significant that this argument is nowhere repeated in 2 Corinthians,

---

[82] Barrett 1968: 197; Mitchell 1991: 243–50; Sumney 1999: 58; Willis 1985: 35.
[83] Cf. Conzelmann 1975: 305; Moray-Jones 1993; Mosbech 1948; Munck 1949; Rengstorf 1933: 431; Schmithals 1961; Schnackenburg 1970; Taylor 1992: 176–94.
[84] Allo 1956: 341; Barrett 1968: 341–42; Conzelmann 1975: 299–303; Fuller 1971: 14–29; Gaston 1984: 66; Héring 1962: 158; Robertson & Plummer 1914: 335; Schmithals 1971b: 74; Schütz 1975: 96–97.
[85] Cf. Rowland 1982: 376; Taylor 1992: 190–94.

where Paul's authority and the credentials thereof have clearly been challenged.

The Opponents in 2 Corinthians

2 Corinthians 10–13 reflects the most intense conflict between Paul and the Corinthian church, and also the zenith of influence in Corinth of Paul's opponents. The identity of these latter remains a matter of contention in scholarship, but they are generally understood to be interlopers rather than Corinthian Christians.[86] Some scholars identify them as delegates, subordinate or otherwise, of the Jerusalem church.[87] A minority identify Paul's opponents as Gnostics.[88] Perhaps a majority identify them as Palestinian or Diaspora Jewish Christians, independent of the Jerusalem church.[89] For the present purpose this issue is of importance only insofar as it concerns the basis of the challenge to Paul's authority.

The expression ὑπερλίαν ἀποστόλων in 2 Cor 11:5 and 12:11 is a potentially significant indicator as to the identity of Paul's opponents. However, it needs first to be established whether the term refers to persons present in Corinth, or to other figures, such as the leadership of the Jerusalem church. If the latter, the question arises as to whether it is a self-designation or positive attribution, or whether ὑπερλίαν has sarcastic overtones. Much therefore depends on whether the ὑπερλίαν ἀποστόλων are to be identified with the ψευδαπόστολοι of 2 Cor 11:13. It has been argued that ὑπερλίαν ἀποστόλων refers to the Jerusalem apostles, and ψευδαπόστολοι to Paul's opponents in Corinth.[90] The former expression is used precisely in contexts in which Paul refers to implied comparisons between himself and others whose activities the Corinthian Christians must clearly have witnessed.[91] ὑπερλίαν ἀποστόλων can therefore refer to leaders of the Jerusalem church only if these were present in Corinth in person.[92] If this were the case, it would be surprising that Paul makes no claim to previous acknowledgement by the Jerusalem

---

[86] *Contra* McClelland 1982.
[87] Barrett 1971; 1982: 1–39; Gunther 1973; Holmberg 1980: 45–46; Käsemann 1942; Lüdemann 1989: 83–95; Thrall 1980.
[88] Bultmann 1985; Kümmel 1975: 209; Schmithals 1971a; Wilson 1982.
[89] Black 1984; Bornkamm 1971: 169–72; Crafton 1991: 54; Furnish 1984: 52–55; Georgi 1986; Sellin 1987: 3023; Sumney 1990; Theissen 1982: 27–77; Watson 1986: 81–82.
[90] Barrett 1971; Käsemann 1942: 20–24. *Contra* Bultmann 1985; Georgi 1986: 32.
[91] Cf. Furnish 1984: 503–505.
[92] Cf. Barrett 1971; Käsemann 1942. For a different view, Furnish 1984: 480–81.

apostles (cf. Gal 2:1–10). Given that, on whatever reconstruction, Paul had already encountered his opponents with humiliating consequences (2 Cor 2:1) by the time 2 Corinthians 10–13 was written, he could have been in no doubt as who they were and on what basis they legitimated their intervention in the Corinthian church.[93] It has been argued that ὑπερλίαν ἀποστόλων was a self-designation of pneumatic Christians in Corinth rather than intruders.[94] This view requires the unlikely reading that a Corinthian Christian should have used his Jewish pedigree as a basis on which to challenge Paul's authority (cf. 2 Cor 11:22). Furthermore, such a reading would require that Paul, elsewhere so defensive of his own apostleship (Galatians 1–2; cf. 1 Cor 9:1–6; 15:7–11) and exclusive in his claims (cf. Rom 11:13), and patriarchal in his dealings with his churches (cf. 1 Thess 2:11), should give even the most tacit assent to such self-attribution among the Corinthian Christians. It is therefore more likely that Paul's opponents were interlopers, and that, despite his labelling them ψευδαπόστολοι (11:13), they must have had a reasonable claim to the designation ἀπόστολοι, even in terms of Paul's particular conception thereof. Otherwise, he would have refuted their claim altogether in 2 Cor 11:5 and 12:11, rather than merely asserting his equality with them, and indicating an intent to undermine their claims (11:12). While Paul's opponents cannot be identified with the leadership of the Jerusalem church, their claim to status in the Church, and to the designation ἀπόστολοι, is clearly incontrovertible. ἀπόστολος is not necessarily their only self-designation, and ἐργάται in 11:13 and διάκονοι in 11:15 could indicate that these titles were also in use.[95] Nevertheless, it is apostleship that is crucial for Paul's self-understanding and assertion of authority, and it is the claim to apostleship which constitutes the opponents' threat to Paul's position in the Corinthian church.[96]

Paul's polemic against his opponents, while clearly directed to regaining his authority in Corinth, extends beyond his claims to apostolic authority and jurisdiction to the content of their teaching. Their legitimacy cannot be undermined on the basis of apostolic credentials or lack thereof, and Paul therefore delegitimates them on the basis of their doctrine. His reference to ἄλλον Ἰησοῦν ... ἢ πνεῦμα ἕτερον ... ἢ εὐαγγέλιον ἕτερον (2 Cor 11:4; cf. Gal 1:6–8) is not substantiated by

---

[93] *Contra* Thrall 1980: 48. See discussion in Taylor 1991.
[94] McClelland 1982: 82–84.
[95] Cf. Crafton 1991: 54; Georgi 1986: 27–40.
[96] Cf. Crafton 1991: 57.

any detail of his rivals' teaching, or refutation thereof on the basis of interpretation of Scripture. Labelling the teaching as deviant serves to categorise the teachers as illegitimate and unworthy bearers of the apostolic authority they claim. The vilification of his opponents as ψευδαπόστολοι, ἐργάται δόλιοι, μετασχηματιζόμενοι εἰς ἀποστόλους Χριστοῦ (2 Cor 11:13), and ἄγγελον [φωτός] (11:14–15) is further deviancy labelling, or as it was known in the rhetorical schools, vituperatio.[97] This reinforces the impression that Paul is unable to repudiate the credentials of his opponents on any objective basis. The fact that apostleship is explicitly cited in the contest for authority and legitimacy, and the designation subject to caricature, suggests strongly that authentic representation of Christ lies at the heart of the conflict. The issue is not so much of the content of the Christian gospel as the relationship of the preacher of that gospel to the community created through his preaching and the manifestation of the Spirit in his activities (cf. 2 Cor 6:1–10; 12:12).[98]

The absence of substantial theological differences suggests that Paul's rivals represented an essentially similar interpretation of Christianity to his own. They may nevertheless have been as forthright in their condemnation of Paul as he was of them.[99] They may have held a less narrow and individualistic conception of apostleship than Paul, and not have recognised the exclusive and territorial aspect Paul as church founder attached to his notion of apostleship (cf. Rom 1:5; 11:13; 1 Cor 3:6, 12; 9:2; Gal 1:6; 2:8–9). While they clearly challenged Paul's authority in Corinth (cf. 2 Cor 10:10), and did not see themselves merely as working in continuity with him, they presumably regarded their activities as consistent with their own apostolic self-conception. We are dealing therefore with conflicting notions of apostleship. There is no indication that Paul's rivals differed from him in locating proclamation of the gospel at the heart of their apostolic consciousness. However, Paul's self-conception as a church founder (Rom 15:20; 1 Cor 3:6, 12) was presumably not shared by his opponents, who, like Apollos, were entirely willing to water what another had planted, and to build on the foundation laid by another without conforming to his plan (cf. 1 Cor 3:5–15).[100]

---

[97] Cf. Barclay 1995: 122–25; Wanamaker 1995.
[98] Cf. Crafton 1991: 54; Sumney 1990; Theissen 1982: 40–54.
[99] Cf. Green 1985: 58; Wanamaker 1995.
[100] Cf. Watson 1986: 81–84.

A practice which distinguished Paul from his opponents was that of receiving financial support from the Corinthian church (2 Cor 11:9; 12:13–18; cf. 11:20). The right of apostles to financial support is one which Paul had affirmed in 1 Cor 9:1–6, even though he himself did not avail himself of that right, at least not in Corinth (cf. Phil 4:15–18).[101] If we have been correct in associating Barnabas and Paul's custom with the church of Antioch, this would exclude that church as the origin of Paul's opponents, but would not in itself associate them with the church of Jerusalem. Given that Paul recognises the right, but makes a virtue of not exercising it (1 Cor 9:1–6; 2 Cor 11:7–11; cf. 1 Thess 2:9), the difference with his opponents is not one of substance or of apostolic self-conception. Paul's decision had become contentious not so much because his opponents chose differently, but because they interpreted Paul's waiving of his rights as evidence that his apostleship was deficient. Moreover, Paul's refusal of financial support kept him independent of the patronage networks of Christian householders, which would have cost him goodwill and social support during the crisis.[102] The issue of financial support therefore does not constitute a significant difference in apostolic self-conception between Paul and his opponents in Corinth.

The use of letters of recommendation by Paul's opponents (2 Cor 3:1), presumably to gain influence and credibility in the community,[103] is a practice Paul clearly abhors. This, however, does little to identify their origins and agenda.[104] The source of the letter/s is unclear, even if Paul knew the identity of the authors.[105] 2 Corinthians 3:1–3 implies that the Corinthian Christians themselves could have issued letters, so any Christian community could presumably have commended Paul's opponents to the church in Corinth. The letters carried by the opponents do not imply that they were ἀπόστολοι in the sense of being emissaries of another church. If this were the case, Paul would surely have capitalised on it, and relegated them to an inferior status, comparable to those of

---

[101] Cf. Crafton 1991; Hock 1980; Taylor 2003.
[102] Chow 1992: 172; Hock 1980: 50–65; Horrell 1996: 210–16; Marshall 1987.
[103] Cf. Marshall 1987: 268–72.
[104] Furnish 1984: 193; Georgi 1986: 244–45; Watson 1986: 83–84. *Contra* Barrett 1973: 40–41, who argues that the letter came from Jerusalem; cf. Holmberg 1980: 45–46.
[105] In Acts 18:27 it is reported that Apollos received a letter of introduction from the church in Ephesus when he travelled to Corinth. If the involvement of Aquila and Priscilla is at all historical, this would count against identifying Apollos with the opposition to Paul reflected in 2 Corinthians, as Paul evidently remained well disposed towards them (Rom 16:3). Cf. Watson 1986: 83–84.

2 Cor 8:23. The letters rather indicate a willingness and intent to move from one Christian community to another established congregation. Unlike Paul (Rom 15:20), his opponents do not limit their activities to planting new churches, or their assertion of authority to communities they themselves had founded. Rather, they are itinerants who assert apostolic authority wherever opportunity presents itself (cf. *Did.* 11.6).

To conclude, the conflict between rival claimants to apostolic authority in 2 Corinthians concerns not so much the essence of Christian apostleship, but the context in which it is legitimately exercised. Paul's apostolic self-conception, moulded at least partly in response to his alienation from the church of Antioch, embraces continuing and exclusive jurisdiction over churches he had established. His opponents differ from him not so much in doctrine as in knowing no boundaries to their apostolic activities. They would appear not to be church founders so much as itinerant missionaries exercising influence in established Christian congregations. They sought this influence through dramatic manifestation of pneumatic power, portraying theirs as greater than that which Paul had been able to exercise in the Corinthian church.

Conclusions

We have considered two situations in which Paul uses letters to assert authority over churches, and employs the self-designation ἀπόστολος to define his authority over against that which is being exercised effectively in the churches. In Galatians, Paul is seeking to regain oversight of communities he had established while an apostle of the church of Antioch. He defines himself as an ἀπόστολος called by God, and claims that this status has been acknowledged by the leaders of the Jerusalem church. He therefore enjoys greater authority than those currently influencing the Galatian Christians towards circumcision. In 2 Corinthians, on the other hand, Paul is seeking to regain authority over the Corinthian church, which has been undermined by persons claiming an apostolic authority similar to but greater than his own. Paul claims, as the founding ἀπόστολος of the Corinthian church, an exclusive jurisdiction there, whereas his opponents represent a model of itinerant apostleship which knows no boundaries and does not acknowledge any limitation of their jurisdiction.

It is clear that the title ἀπόστολος became an effective vehicle for the assertion of authority at an early date in Christian history. While Paul may have been instrumental in developing a notion of apostolic authority independent of sponsoring Christian communities, the evidence of 2 Corinthians suggests that he was not alone in doing so. Paul was distinctive, it would seem, in defining an apostolic authority with geographical and ethnic boundaries, conceptual if not practical, which excluded others from jurisdiction where he had begun to work.

ἀπόστολος, as the designation of an authority bearer with a mission to proclaim the gospel, may have been in wider use in the early Church than the New Tetsament would seem to indicate. The use of the title where authority was contested suggests that the term was not rigidly defined, and that the authority asserted by any claimant to the designation would not necessarily be recognised by rival claimants or by Christian communities over whom that authority was asserted. As an aspect of institutionalisation of authority in early Christianity, the notion of apostleship of Christ merits further examination, not least in situations of conflict, of which those involving Paul are only an example.

WORKS CITED

Allo, E.-B. (1956) *Saint Paul seconde Épître aux Corinthiens*. Paris: Lecoffre.
Aune, D. E. (1987) *The New Testament in its Literary Environment*. Cambridge: Clarke.
Barclay, J. M. G. (1988) *Obeying the Truth*. Edinburgh: T. & T. Clark.
——. (1995) "Deviance and Apostasy", in *Modelling Early Christianity*, ed P. F. Esler. London: Routledge, 114–27.
Barrett, C. K. (1968) *A Commentary on the First Epistle to the Corinthians*. London: A. & C. Black.
——. (1971) "Paul's Opponents in II Corinthians", *NTS* 17: 233–54.
——. (1973) *A Commentary on the Second Epistle to the Corinthians*. London: A. & C. Black.
——. (1982) *Essays on Paul*. London: SPCK.
——. (1985) *Freedom and Obligation*. London: SPCK.
——. (1994/1998) *A Critical and Exegetical Commentary on the Acts of the Apostles*. 2 vols. Edinburgh: T. & T. Clark.
Betz, H. D. (1979) *Galatians*. Philadelphia: Fortress.
Black, D. A. (1984) *Paul, Apostle of Weakness*. New York: Lang.
Borgen, P. (1988) "Catalogues of Vices, the Apostolic Decree, and the Jerusalem Meeting", in *The Social World of Formative Christianity and Judaism*, ed. J. Neusner et al. Philadelphia: Fortress, 126–41.
Bornkamm, G. (1971) *Paul*. London: Hodder & Stoughton.
Boyarin, D. (1994) *A Radical Jew*. Berkeley: University of California Press.
Brinsmead, B. H. (1982) *Galatians—Dialogical Response to Opponents*. Chico, CA: Scholars.
Brown, R. E. & Meier, J. P. (1983) *Antioch and Rome*. New York: Paulist.
Buckland, W. W. & McNair, A. D. (1952) *Roman Law and Common Law*. Cambridge: Cambridge University Press.
Bultmann, R. (1985) *The Second Letter to the Corinthians*. Minneapolis: Augsburg.
Burton, E. deW. (1921) *A Critical and Exegetical Commentary on the Epistle to the Galatians*. Edinburgh: T. & T. Clark.
Campenhausen, H. F. von (1969) *Ecclesiastical Authority and Spiritual Power in the Church of the first three Centuries*. London: A. & C. Black.
Castelli, E. A. (1991) *Imitating Paul*. Louisville: Westminster.
Chow, J. K.-M. (1992) *Patronage and Power*. Sheffield: Sheffield Academic Press.
Cohen, S. J. D. (1989) "Crossing the Boundary and Becoming a Jew", *HTR* 82: 13–34.
Conzelmann, H. (1975) *1 Corinthians*. Philadelphia: Fortress.
Crafton, J. A. (1991) *The Agency of the Apostle*. Sheffield: Sheffield Academic Press.
Dunn, J. D. G. (1982) "The Relationship between Paul and Jerusalem according to Galatians 1 and 2", *NTS* 28: 461–78.
——. (1983) "The Incident at Antioch", *JSNT* 18: 3–57.
——. (1993) *Galatians*. Peabody, MA: Hendrickson.
——. (1998) *The Theology of Paul the Apostle*. Edinburgh: T. & T. Clark.
Ehrhardt, A. A. T. (1958) *The Apostolic Ministry*. Edinburgh: Oliver & Boyd.
Fee, G. D. (1987) *The First Epistle to the Corinthians*. Grand Rapids: Eerdmans.
Fuller, R. H. (1971) *The Formation of the Resurrection Narratives*. London: SPCK.
Furnish, V. P. (1984) *II Corinthians*. New York: Doubleday.
Gaston, L. (1984) "Paul and Jerusalem", in *From Jesus to Paul*, ed. G. P. Richardson & J. C. Hurd. Waterloo: Wilfrid Laurier, 61–72.

Gaventa, B. R. (1986) "Galatians 1 and 2: Autobiography as Paradigm", *NovT* 28: 307–26.
Georgi, D. (1965) *Die Geschichte der Kollekte des Paulus für Jerusalem*. Hamburg: Reich.
——. (1986) *The Opponents of Paul in Second Corinthians*. Edinburgh: T. & T. Clark.
Green, W. S. (1985) "Otherness within: Towards a Theory of Difference in Rabbinic Judaism", in *'To See Us as Others See Us'*, ed. J. Neusner & E. S. Frerichs. Chico: Scholars, 49–69.
Gunther, J. J. (1973) *St. Paul's Opponents and their Background*. Leiden: E. J. Brill.
Hall, R. G. (1991) "Historical Inference and Rhetorical Effect: Another Look at Galatians 1 and 2", in *Persuasive Artistry*, ed. D. F. Watson. Sheffield: Sheffield Academic Press, 308–20.
Hanson, A. T. (1961) *The Pioneer Ministry*. London: SCM.
Hengel, M. (1991) *The Pre-Christian Paul*. London: SCM.
Héring, J. (1962) *The First Epistle of St. Paul to the Corinthians*. London: Epworth.
Hester, J. D. (1991) "Placing the Blame: The Placing of Epideictic in Galatians 1 and 2", in *Persuasive Artistry*, ed. D. F. Watson. Sheffield: Sheffield Academic Press, 281–307.
Hock, R. F. (1980) *The Social Context of Paul's Ministry*. Philadelphia: Fortress.
Hofius, O. (1984) "Gal 1 18: ἱστορῆσαι Κηφᾶν", *ZNW* 75: 73–85.
Holmberg, B. (1980) *Paul and Power*. Minneapolis: Fortress.
——. (1998) "Jewish versus Christian Identity in the Early Church?", *RB* 105: 397–425.
Horrell, D. G. (1996) *The Social Ethos of the Corinthian Correspondence*. Edinburgh: T. & T. Clark.
Howard, G. (1977) "Was James an Apostle? A Reflection on a New Proposal for Gal.i.19", *NovT* 19: 63–64.
——. (1990) *Paul: Crisis in Galatia*. Cambridge: Cambrige University Press.
Hurd, J. C. (1965) *The Origin of I Corinthians*. London: SPCK.
Jewett, R. (1970) "The Agitators and the Galatian Congregation", *NTS* 17: 198–212.
Jones, J. W. (1956) *Law and Legal Theory of the Greeks*. Cambridge: Cambridge University Press.
Kennedy, G. A. (1984) *New Testament Interpretation through Rhetorical Criticism*. Chapel Hill: University of North Carolina Press.
Käsemann, E. (1942) *Die Legitimität des Apostels*. Darmstadt: Wissenschaftliche Buchgesellschaft.
Kern, P. J. (1996) *Rhetoric and Galatians*. Cambridge: Cambridge University Press.
Klein, G. (1961) *Die zwölf Apostel*. Göttingen: Vandenhoeck & Ruprecht.
Koester, H. (1971) "*Gnomai Diaphoroi*: The Origin and Nature of Diversification in the History of Early Christianity", in *Trajectories through Early Christianity*, ed. J. M. Robinson & H. Koester. Philadelphia: Fortress, 144–57.
Kümmel, W. G. (1975) *Introduction to the New Testament*. London: SCM.
Lategan, B. C. (1988) "Is Paul Defending his Apostleship in Galatians?" *NTS* 34: 411–30.
Longenecker, B. W. (1998) *The Triumph of Abraham's God*. Edinburgh: T. & T. Clark.
Longenecker, R. N. (1990) *Galatians*. Waco: Word.
Lüdemann, G. (1989) *Opposition to Paul in Jewish Christianity*. Minneapolis: Fortress.
Lyons, G. (1985) *Pauline Autobiography*. Atlanta: Scholars.
McClelland, S. E. (1982) "'Super-Apostles, Servants of Christ, Servants of Satan': A Response", *JSNT* 14: 82–87.
McLean, B. C. (1991) "Galatians 2.7–9 and the Recognition of Paul's Apostolic Status at the Jerusalem Conference: A Critique of G. Luedemann's Solution", *NTS* 37: 67–76.
Malina, B. J. & Neyrey, J. H. (1996) *Portraits of Paul*. Louisville: Westminster.
Marshall, P. (1987) *Enmity in Corinth*. Tübingen: Mohr Siebeck.
Mitchell, M. M. (1991) *Paul and the Rhetoric of Reconciliation*. Tübingen: Mohr Siebeck.

Moray-Jones, C. R. A. (1993) "Paradise Revisited (2 Cor 12:1–12): The Jewish Mystical Background of Paul's Apostolate", *HTR* 86: 177–217, 265–92.
Mosbech, H. (1948) "Apostolos in the New Testament", *ST* 2: 166–200.
Martyn, J. L. (1985) "A Law-observant Mission to the Gentiles: The Background of Galatians", *SJT* 38: 307–24.
Meeks, W. A. (1983) *The First Urban Christians*. New Haven: Yale University Press.
Munck, J. (1949) "Paul, the Apostles, and the Twelve", *ST* 3: 96–110.
———. (1959) *Paul and the Salvation of Mankind*. London: SCM.
Murphy-O'Connor, J. (1996) *Paul: A Critical Life*. Oxford: Oxford University Press.
Reicke, B. I. (1984) "Judaeo-Christianity and the Jewish Establishment, AD 33–66", in *Jesus and the Politics of his Day*, ed. E. Bammel & C. F. D. Moule. London: SCM, 145–52.
Rengstorf, K. H. (1933) "ἀπόστολος", *TDNT* 1: 398–406.
Riesner, R. (1998) *Paul's Early Period*. Grand Rapids: Eerdmans.
Robertson, A. & Plummer, A. (1914) *A Critical and Exegetical Commentary on the First Epistle of St. Paul to the Corinthians*. Edinburgh: T. & T. Clark.
Rowland, C. C. (1982) *The Open Heaven*. London: SPCK.
Sampley, J. P. (1980) *Pauline Partnership in Christ*. Philadelphia: Fortress.
Sanders, E. P. (1977) *Paul and Palestinian Judaism*. London: SCM.
———. (1992) *Judaism, Practice and Belief*. London: SCM.
Sandnes, K. O. (1991) *Paul—One of the Prophets?* Tübingen: Mohr Siebeck.
Schmithals, W. (1965) *Paul and James*. London: SCM.
———. (1971a) *Gnosticism in Corinth*. Nashville: Abingdon.
———. (1971b) *The Office of Apostle in the Early Church*. London: SPCK.
Schnackenburg, R. (1970) "Apostles Before and During Paul's Time", in *Apostolic History and the Gospel*, ed. W. W. Gasque & R. P. Martin. Exeter: Paternoster, 287–303.
Schütz, J. H. (1975) *Paul and the Anatomy of Apostolic Authority*. Cambridge: Cambridge University Press.
Segal, A. F. (1990) *Paul the Convert*. New Haven: Yale University Press.
Sellin, G. (1987) "Hauptprobleme des ersten Korintherbriefes", *ANRW*. Berlin: De Gruyter, 2940–3044.
Slee, M. (2003) *The Church of Antioch in the First Century CE*. London: Sheffield Academic Press.
Smit, J. (1989) "The Letter of Paul to the Galatians: A Deliberative Speech", *NTS* 35: 1–26.
Smith, T. V. (1985) *Petrine Controversies in Early Christianity*. Tübingen: Mohr Siebeck.
Stendahl, K. (1976) *Paul among Jews and Gentiles*. London: SCM.
Sumney, J. L. (1990) *Identifying Paul's Opponents*. Sheffield: Sheffield Academic Press.
———. (1999) *'Servants of Satan', 'False Brothers', and Other Opponents of Paul*. Sheffield: Sheffield Academic Press.
Taylor, N. H. (1991) "The Composition and Chronology of Second Corinthians", *JSNT* 44: 67–87.
———. (1992) *Paul, Antioch and Jerusalem*. Sheffield: Sheffield Academic Press.
———. (1993) "Paul's Apostolic Legitimacy: Autobiographical Reconstruction in Galatians 1:11–2:14", *Journal of Theology for Southern Africa* 83: 65–77.
———. (1995) "The Social Nature of Conversion in Early Christianity", in *Modelling Early Christianity*, ed. P. F. Esler. London: Routledge, 128–36.
———. (1996) "Palestinian Christianity and the Caligula Crisis: I. Social and Historical Reconstruction", *JSNT* 61: 101–24.
———. (2003) "Paul and the Historical Jesus Quest." *Neot* 37: 105–26.
Theissen, G. (1982) *The Social Setting of Pauline Christianity*. Edinburgh: T. & T. Clark.
Thrall, M. E. (1980) "Super-Apostles, Servants of Christ, and Servants of Satan", *JSNT* 6: 42–57.

Trudinger, L. P. (1975) "ἕτερον δὲ τῶν ἀποστόλων οὐκ εἶδον εἰ μὴ Ἰάκωβον: A Note on Galatians 1 19", *NovT* 17: 200–202.
Wanamaker, C. A. (1995) "The Rhetoric of Uncivil Society: Deviance Labelling as Uncivil Discourse", in *Religion and the Construction of Civil Society*, ed. J. W. de Gruchy & S. Martin. Pretoria: Unisa, 304–15.
Watson, F. B. (1986) *Paul, Judaism and the Gentiles*. Cambridge: Cambridge University Press.
Willis, W. L. (1985) "An Apostolic Apologia? The Form and Function of 1 Corinthians 9", *JSNT* 24: 33–48.
Wilson, R. McL. (1982) "Gnosis at Corinth", in *Paul and Paulinism*, ed. M. D. Hooker & S. G. Wilson. London: SPCK, 102–14.
Winter, B. W. (2001) *After Paul left Corinth*. Grand Rapids: Eerdmans.
Zetterholm, M. (2003) *The Formation of Christianity in Antioch*. London: Routledge.

REFLECTIONS CONCERNING PAUL'S "OPPONENTS" IN GALATIA[1]

JOHN C. HURD
Trinity College
Toronto, ON, Canada

What follows is by way of a reflection on an aspect of Paul's life about which I have often taught but never published. It is not a research paper in the usual sense, since at this point I have been retired almost twelve years and have given away most of my professional library. I do, however, welcome the chance to talk, as it were, about this fascinating topic. Further, I discover that this talking involves a welcome occasion to revisit a conversation with my friend and one-time colleague John Knox.

1. PAUL'S BIOGRAPHY

A new era in the study of Paul's life began with the publication of John Knox's modest volume, *Chapters in a Life of Paul*, in 1950.[2] There, after discussing the relative historical value of the Book of Acts and Paul's letters, he concluded,

> Thus of our two sources the letters of Paul are obviously and incomparably the more trustworthy. The truth in principle of this last statement no serious student of Paul's life is likely to deny, but its meaning in practice is not so widely or so clearly seen.[3]

---

[1] Almost twenty years ago now I was honored by an invitation to contribute to the Festschrift for Paul Meyer, now published as *Faith and History: Essays in Honor of Paul W. Meyer* (ed. John T. Carroll, Charles H. Cosgrove, and E. Elizabeth Johnson; Atlanta: Scholars Press, 1990). Paul while at Yale had directed my dissertation in 1958–61. I regret to say that I failed in that commitment, but the topic of this essay was originally intended for Paul, and it is to him that I now dedicate this more modest effort with respect and gratitude.

[2] New York: Abingdon-Cokesbury, 1950; London: A. & C. Black, 1954; 2nd ed. rev. by author with a preface by Douglas R. A. Hare (Macon, GA: Mercer University Press, 1987). It is important to notice that Knox had already published the essentials of his approach in two earlier journal articles: "'Fourteen Years Later': A Note on the Pauline Chronology," *JR* 16 (1936): 341–49; and "The Pauline Chronology," *JBL* 58 (1939): 15–29.

[3] *Chapters*, 31 (2nd ed. 18).

He was pointing to the distinction between primary and secondary historical sources. Paul's letters are first-hand, coming to us (more or less) directly from Paul. Acts, however, is secondary as a source for our knowledge of Paul, not only for his thought *but also* for the events in his life. He summed up this point with the pithy statement:

> We can justly say that a fact only suggested in the letters has a status which even the most unequivocal statement of Acts, if not otherwise supported, cannot confer.[4]

Knox then proceeded to construct an outline of the events in Paul's life on the basis of this principle. He discovered, somewhat to his surprise, that, like Acts, the biographical information which the letters give us is organized around visits by Paul to Jerusalem. We cannot do better than to cite Knox's words exactly:

    I. Conversion in Damascus—Gal 1:15–17
    II. Three years or more, spent largely or entirely in Syria and Arabia—Gal 1:17–18
    III. First visit to Jerusalem after the conversion ("acquaintance"), and departure for Syria and Cilicia—Gal 1:18–21
    IV. Eleven years or more, presumably passed in activity as an apostle—Gal 2:1
    V. Second visit to Jerusalem ("conference")—Gal 2:1–10
    VI. Activity in churches of Galatia, Asia, Macedonia, and Greece, especially in connection with raising the offering for the poor at Jerusalem—Gal 2:10; 1 Cor 16:1–4 (also 2 Cor 8–9); Rom 15:25–32
    VII. Final visit to Jerusalem ("offering")—1 Cor 16:4; Rom 15:25–32[5]

Knox then went on to argue that, unlike Acts, the letters clearly indicate that these three visits are the only visits to Jerusalem that Paul made or intended to make. His argument has three steps. (i) In the outline above (III) was his first visit, and no previous visits can have occurred. (ii) Paul in Gal 1:18–2:10 was demonstrating to the Galatians the limited nature of his contact with the Jerusalem apostles. There cannot therefore have been an additional visit or visits to Jerusalem between (III) and (V) above. Therefore (V) was indeed Paul's second visit. (iii) Knox then made the case that Gal 2:10 ("only they would have us remember the poor, which very thing I was eager to do") indicates the inception of the "Collection for the poor among the saints at Jerusalem" (Rom 15:26; 1 Cor 16:1; 2 Cor 8:4; 9:1). The Collection began at (V) and ended at

---

[4] *Chapters*, 33 (19).
[5] *Chapters*, 51 (34).

(VII), a two- or three-year project in Knox's estimation. There is no hint or real probability that a Jerusalem visit intervened between the inception of the Collection and its delivery (VII).

Knox concluded this analysis by pointing out that the above outline means that the bulk of Paul's missionary work preceded his second visit to Jerusalem, that is, it occurred in period (IV) above. Gone are the fourteen (Gal 2:1) so-called "silent years" of the Acts chronology.[6] Paul went to the "conference" visit (V) with Gentile churches already established in Galatia, Asia, Macedonia, and Achaia.

At this point Knox turned his attention to Acts and the fascinating question of how its author re-worked the traditions available to him into the narrative which we now have. Then with the data from both Acts and the letters in hand he addressed the problem of assigning absolute dates to the events in Paul's life. In the course of this discussion he did touch on the sequence of the letters, although not in any systematic way. In fact, he said specifically, "On the question of the chronological order of the letters of Paul our scheme has little bearing."[7] Galatians, he said, must have followed the "Conference" visit (V). He put 1 Thessalonians before the "Conference" visit and quite soon after the founding of the church in that city, although noting that 1 Thess 1:8–9 could be taken to indicate a lapse of some time. He placed 1 Corinthians; 2 Corinthians 1–9, 10–13; and Romans between (V) and (VII). For Philippians, Colossians, and Philemon, the "imprisonment" letters, he suggested no particular occasion in light of Paul's reference to his many imprisonments (2 Cor 11:23). For Knox therefore these letters have no firm anchor point in the sequence of the letters, although he was inclined to put them in Ephesus before the "Conference" because they do not mention the Collection. (Knox showed his Chicago origins by taking Ephesians to be a pseudepigraphic, general letter.)[8] The rest of his book is devoted to an interesting presentation of Paul's beliefs and character on the sole basis of the information contained in his letters.

Knox's observation that the "meaning in practice" of the logical distinction between the letters and Acts was "not so widely or so clearly

---

[6] A large number of scholars, having equated the first visit in Galatians (1:18) with the first visit in Acts (9:26–29), match the Gal 2:1–10 visit "after fourteen years" with the next visit in Acts, viz. 11:27–30. Since in Acts Paul's first missionary journey began with this visit, the preceding fourteen years are therefore "silent."

[7] *Chapters*, 85 (71).

[8] On the work of Edgar J. Goodspeed on Ephesians see James I. Cook, *Edgar Johnson Goodspeed: Articulate Scholar* (Chico, CA: Scholars Press, 1981), Chapter 2.

seen" can be applied to subsequent Pauline studies as well as those that Knox had in mind. The temptation to harmonize Acts and the letters is so overwhelming that I can think of no treatment of Paul's life that confines itself solely to the letters. There are, however, a few Pauline biographers who accept Knox's axiom absolutely. Donald Riddle's *Paul: Man of Conflict*, was an early attempt (1940).[9] Charles Buck and Greer Taylor's *Saint Paul: A Study in the Development of his Thought* appeared in 1969.[10] Knox considered this book to be the most serious attempt to put his basic principle into practice, until, that is, the appearance of Gerd Lüdemann's *Paulus, der Heidenapostel* in 1980. Knox himself wrote an enthusiastic preface to the English translation, which appeared in 1984.[11] Then in 1996 Jerome Murphy-O'Connor published *Paul: A Critical Life*.[12] In its Preface (p. vi) he wrote concerning Knox's axiom, "Recent lives of Paul (e.g. Fitzmyer, Baslez, Légasse) all pay lip-service to this principle, but in practice they not only permit Luke to exercise decisive control over the presentation of Paul's career, but fail to recognize the problems of extracting historical data from the Acts of the Apostles." A number of Pauline scholars who write in areas other than Pauline biography have also gone on record as affirming Knox's approach.[13] We

---

[9] Donald W. Riddle's *Paul, Man of Conflict: A Modern Biographical Sketch* (Nashville: Cokesbury, 1940). Riddle was one of Knox's professors at Chicago, and this fact plus the date of his book ten years before Knox's *Chapters* has led some scholars to think that Knox had derived his approach to Paul from Riddle, which implies that Knox had copied without proper acknowledgment. In 1976 in an informal communication sent to me and a few other friends Knox expressed his disappointment that such writers had missed his two articles dated 1936 and 1939 (cited above), which contain the essentials of his approach. In fact, as Knox related it, Riddle had actually telephoned him in the summer of 1936 to say that he had just read Knox's article in *JR*, that he was convinced of its truth, was very much excited by it, and was going to write a book about Paul based on this approach.

[10] New York: Scribner, 1969. Buck was my first New Testament professor and Greer Taylor was my classmate at the Episcopal Theological School, Cambridge, MA, in 1949–1952. I attempted to express my major indebtedness to Buck in the preface to the second edition of my book, *The Origin of 1 Corinthians* (London: SPCK, 1965; 2nd ed. Macon, GA: Mercer University Press, 1983). Buck's courses on Paul made significant use of Knox's *Chapters*, which had only just appeared.

[11] *Paul, Apostle to the Gentiles: Studies in Chronology* (Philadelphia: Fortress, 1984). In the preface to the 2nd ed. of *Origin* I expressed my admiration for Lüdemann's grasp of the American discussion.

[12] Oxford: Clarendon, 1996. The book is an incredible mine of information. However, the argument begins by assigning absolute dates to the events in Paul's career, a highly risky business, rather than with a treatment of the sequential data of the letters, which constitute evidence known to us with a high level of probability. Further, the material from Acts is ubiquitous.

[13] For example, E. P. Sanders, *Paul and Palestinian Judaism* (Philadelphia: Fortress,

await, however, an attempt to write the story of Paul's life solely on the basis of the letters.[14]

Let me be clear. The difference between the letters and Acts is not a difference in degree. It is not acceptable merely to give more weight to one source as compared to the other. It is a difference in kind. The letters must be treated first and treated as though Acts did not exist. Then Acts can be approached to see what it can add to the story. However, to say this is not to say enough. When we deal with the letters, we are accustomed to think of ourselves as dealing with Paul's mind. In the same way, when we deal with Acts, we must consider its author's mind. When material from Acts is considered, it must be considered in the light of its author's intentions before attempting to relate it to what Paul is telling us.

The usual procedure, however, is to put all the pieces of information on the table at once like a great jig-saw puzzle.[15] Only when two pieces vie for the same location in the solution does the analyst consider the question of method. At this point the scholar may give somewhat more weight to the piece from Paul as compared to the piece from Acts. The concern with method is limited to the question of just how much more weight to give the Pauline pieces. The result, however, is that the uncontested pieces are put in place without real discussion, and, since the pieces from Acts far outweigh those from the letters both in number and vividness, it is the Acts picture of Paul that emerges.

If much of the study of Pauline biography since Knox has been less than ideal, at least part of the blame can be assigned to Knox himself. Let me be clear about my admiration for and gratitude to John Knox, who autographed my copy of *Chapters in a Life of Paul*, "To John Hurd, friend and colleague, with great admiration and affection." His achievement with this book was enormous, and I have returned to it again and again with profit. However, in my opinion he aborted his analysis in two ways: (i) when dealing with the information from the letters, he was constantly looking over his shoulder at Acts. In fact, after his short chapter on the

---

1977), who said, "My own position on the use of Acts for the general study of the career of Paul is that of John Knox" (432).

[14] There are considerable differences among the works just listed. I refrain from attempting here to assess their relative merits. Rainer Riesner in his comprehensive work, *Paul's Early Period: Chronology, Mission Strategy, Theology* (Grand Rapids: Eerdmans, 1998) 27–28, concludes that these differences mean that the Knox program is a failure and that we must either use Acts or go without dates for Paul's career, an odd justification for his reliance on Acts.

[15] An example is Robert Jewett, *A Chronology of Paul's Life* (Philadelphia: Fortress, 1979).

basic outline of Paul's life as found in the letters (see above), he jumped directly to "The Evidence of Acts." Knox could have extracted so much more from the letters; Acts could have been held at bay much longer. Then (ii) he went from there directly to the problem of assigning absolute dates to the resulting outline. What he failed to do was to deal with the letters sequentially, that is, in relation to one another.[16] An archaeologist organizes his data stratigraphically, that is, sequentially, and then at a second stage attempts to assign absolute dates.[17] If we consider each letter as a stratum, then Knox moved directly to stage two without establishing a relative stratigraphy, that is, a sequence of the letters. He was quite willing to lump Philippians with Colossians on the basis of their common reference to external events (Paul's imprisonment).[18] To my mind and that of many scholars there is a world of difference in thought and style between these two letters. At several points subsequent to *Chapters* he toyed with the notion of Galatians as Paul's last letter.[19] He considered 1 Thessalonians to have been written shortly after Paul founded that congregation, not because of its early eschatology, but presumably because of 1 Thess 2:17, "since we were bereft of you, brethren, *for a short time.*" Bauer-Arndt-Gingrich-Danker, however, suggest that πρὸς καιρὸν ὥρας, *pros kairon horas* might also be understood as "for the present time,"[20] which makes more sense in light of the Thessalonians' own missionary activity (1:7–9) and Paul's repeated attempts to revisit them (2:18). My point, however, is not the date of 1 Thessalonians, but the fact that Knox

---

[16] Knox attempted to deal with this criticism in his article, "On the Pauline Chronology: Buck-Taylor-Hurd Revisited," in *The Conversation Continues: Studies in Paul & John in Honor of J. Louis Martyn* (ed. Robert T. Fortna and Beverly R. Gaventa; Nashville: Abingdon, 1990) 258–74. There is an air of unreality about this paper since, as explained above, neither my "Chronology" article nor that in the *Interpreter's Dictionary of the Bible: Supplementary Volume*, was intended to present my own views. To do so would require at least a book. Moreover, as explained in the preface to the 2nd ed. of *Origin*, Buck-Taylor-Hurd are virtually one person, since both Taylor and I were Buck's pupils.

[17] I am far from ready to assign dates. Such assignment should come only after all the sequential evidence has been thoroughly analyzed. The only dates that I am presently willing to consider are the famine in Judea in 46 CE as a possible background for the Collection project and Caligula's attempt to erect his statue in the Jerusalem Temple in 40 CE as perhaps the cause for the Thessalonians' fear that the Parousia had passed them by (2 Thess 2:1–12).

[18] Later Knox in "Buck-Taylor-Hurd" (262) pronounced Buck's theological argument for dating Philippians between 1 Corinthians and 2 Corinthians 1–9 "quite impressive" but set it aside on the grounds that the letter makes no mention of the Collection.

[19] See "Buck-Taylor-Hurd," 265.

[20] *BAGD*, see καιρός, *kairos*.

focused on relating the letters to external events rather than also considering their mutual relationship.

2. Pauline Chronology and Pauline Theology

It was with the above thoughts in mind that I wrote "Pauline Chronology and Pauline Theology," my over-long contribution to Knox's Festschrift, published on the occasion of his retirement in 1966 from Union Seminary in New York.[21] There I rehearsed the work of Knox and Riddle in greater detail than the above brief account. I noted that Riddle had picked up from Knox the distinction between the letters and Acts as historical sources.[22] I further noted that Knox had added a second distinction, the distinction between Paul's outer or external life—where he was and what he was doing—and his inner or internal life—Paul's beliefs and character. What I faulted Knox for (and Riddle) was his failure to use the letters in relation to one another. It may have been because the letters do not belong simply either to Paul's inner life or to events around him. They are a bridge between the two. Instead Knox used the letters as a sort of quarry from which to mine specific events in Paul's life. As originally envisioned, this article was to end with a demonstration of the high level of agreement among those relatively few scholars who had made

---

[21] *Christian History and Interpretation: Studies Presented to John Knox* (ed. W. R. Farmer, C. F. D. Moule, and R. R. Niebuhr; Cambridge: Cambridge University Press, 1967) 225–48. I was invited to contribute, I imagine, because Knox went from Union to the Episcopal Theological Seminary of the Southwest upon his retirement. We were therefore colleagues there until I moved to Trinity College, Toronto, in the spring of 1967.

[22] In 1967 at the time that I wrote my contribution to Knox's Festschrift, I was unaware of how sensitive this matter was for Knox, and I unwittingly failed to emphasize sufficiently the priority of Knox to Riddle, although as the article makes clear I was myself in no doubt about it. Some time later in conversation with Knox in his office one day I asked him about what he had learned from Riddle (since I had learned so very much from my teacher, Charles H. Buck [see the preface to the 2nd ed. of *Origin*]), and the chill in the conversation made me break off. It was not until an exchange of letters in 1976 that Knox in accepting my apology pronounced everything to be "so very right between us." However, in his final publication, "Reflections," in *Cadbury, Knox, and Talbert: American Contributions to the Study of Acts* (ed. Mikeal C. Parsons and Joseph B. Tyson; Atlanta: Scholars Press, 1992) 107–13, Knox in publishing his 1976 informal communication (see n. 9 above), enlarged on it to express his hurt over an unnamed contribution to his Festschrift which demonstrated the lack of clarity in the scholarly world over this matter. Clearly the article was mine, and I apologize posthumously to Knox for offending him.

comments about the relative order of two or more letters on the basis of evidence from the letters alone. I had realized that a hidden consensus already existed, although the evidence was widely scattered. In the end, the editors and I agreed to omit the last third of the article and to leave the first two parts to stand alone. Shortly later, however, Eugene Fairweather, my colleague at Trinity College, Toronto, and editor of the *Canadian Journal of Theology*, solicited me for a contribution to the journal, and I submitted that final section under the title, "The Sequence of Paul's Letters."[23] At that point, however, as a young scholar I was concerned merely to catalogue the work of others, and I did not venture my own opinion. I thought (and still think) that it is interesting that, while most Pauline scholars derived their ideas about Pauline chronology by using Acts to control the letters, the occasional suggestions that had appeared in the literature about sequencing pairs of letters based on internal evidence, when added up, pointed to a single sequence, namely:

Thess → "Prev. Let." → 1 Cor → Phil → 2 Cor 1–9 → Gal → Rom → Col → Eph.[24]

---

[23] *CJT* 14 (1968) 189–200, republished in the collection of my essays, *The Earlier Letters of Paul—and Other Studies* (Studies in the Religion and History of Early Christianity 8; Frankfurt am Main: Lang, 1998) 31–45.

[24] In his hasty survey of the problem Robert Jewett (*Chronology*, 76) missed the facts that my early article did not claim either to represent my own view or to be "deciding historical questions by majority rule." Riesner (*Paul's Early Period*, 15–16) seems to base his knowledge of my article on Jewett for he picks up Jewett's "majority principle" comment, and he, like Jewett, seems unaware of my discussion in the article of the work of J. R. Richards ("Romans and I Corinthians: Their Chronological Relationship and Comparative Dates," *NTS* 13 [1966/67]: 14–30) and my reasons for setting it aside. Riesner also thinks that my survey was "within the Knox school," which it emphatically was not.

As far as my own conclusions about the sequence of events in Paul's life are concerned, I have never published a full account. As said, the 1967 "Sequence" article catalogues the work of others. When I wrote the article "Pauline Chronology" for *The Interpreter's Dictionary of the Bible: Supplementary Volume* (Nashville: Abingdon, 1976) 166–67, I considered it my duty to reflect the views of responsible scholars and not to argue for my own views. Finally, in the 1980 seminar on Pauline chronology, the transcript of which was published in *Colloquy on New Testament Studies: A Time for Reappraisal and Fresh Approaches* (Macon, GA: Mercer University Press, 1983) 263–364, I served as moderator, summarizing the views of others in order to keep the discussion focused.

For the record, however, I present the following as my opinion as to the sequence of Paul's letters: 2 Thess → 1 Thess → "Prev. Let." → 1 Cor → "Severe Let." → Phil → 2 Cor 1–9 → Gal → Rom → 2 Cor 10–13 → Col/Phlm → Eph.

3. The Pauline Collection and the Previous Letter to Corinth

One of the strengths of Knox's presentation of Paul's career is the prominence he gave to the Pauline Collection. He took the references in 1 Corinthians 16, 2 Corinthians 8 and 9, and Romans 15 to point to a single undertaking of considerable importance. He proposed that this Collection occupied the entire interval between the "Conference" visit of Paul to Jerusalem (V, in his outline above) and his anticipated and presumably final visit to Jerusalem described in Rom 15 (VII, the "Offering" visit; cf. 1 Cor 16:3–4). To make this proposal he argued in some detail that Gal 2:10, "only they would have us remember the poor, which very thing I was eager to do," points to the inception of the Collection project.[25]

In my book *The Origin of 1 Corinthians* I was primarily concerned to reconstruct the contents of the "Previous Letter" (1 Cor 5:9–11).[26] I concluded that this earlier lost letter contained:

1. Injunctions to avoid immorality, specifically immoral persons and the danger of immorality for unmarried persons.
2. Injunctions to avoid idolatry, specifically meat sacrificed to an idol.
3. Some words of caution about charismatic enthusiasm, perhaps on the grounds that it smacked of pagan cults.
4. Reassuring words about the safe resurrection of those believers who die before the Parousia (cf. 1 Thess 4:13–18).
5. The announcement of the Collection project.

The Corinthians in their Reply Letter (also lost) then queried each of these items to some extent. It is this letter which Paul took up in 1 Cor 7:1, "Now concerning the matters about which you wrote...." As background to the Previous Letter I set what we can know of Paul's original

---

[25] This connection is not widely made within Pauline scholarship, since it depends on the conclusion that Paul had pushed his Gentile mission as far west as Corinth (or Illyricum, Rom 15:19?) prior to the Conference visit. Both James D. G. Dunn, *The Epistle to the Galatians* (BNTC; London: A. & C. Black, 1993) 114, and J. Louis Martyn, *Galatians* (AB 33A; New York: Doubleday, 1997) 207, 222–28, reject this connection on the grounds that Paul's Gentile mission had hardly begun at the time of the Conference visit. The connection is one of the new possibilities opened up by Knox's axiom.

[26] See especially, *Origin*, Chapter 7, "The Apostolic Decree and Paul's Previous Letter" 240–70.

preaching and practice when founding the congregation at Corinth. He had preached an imminent apocalypticism such as we find in 2 and 1 Thessalonians. He had led them to believe that all his converts would live to welcome the Lord Jesus Christ from heaven. In view of the nearness of the end he had recommended asceticism for married couples, and discouraged the marriage of unmarried converts. He had neither observed nor required dietary restrictions. He spoke in tongues, and allowed the practice to spread within the congregation.

The Corinthians in their Reply Letter called to Paul's attention the contrast between what Paul had originally taught and what he was now saying in his Previous Letter. Paul then devoted 1 Corinthians 7–16 to their comments. In each case he was careful to affirm his original message and practice but at the same time to explain the reasons why some modifications were necessary. Thus his arguments seem to favor first one opinion and then another in a somewhat confusing way.

I then raised the question: Why should Paul at the time at which he composed the Previous Letter have become so cautious on the subject of immorality and idolatry. These cautions struck me as somewhat un-Pauline. Noting that the Collection project had been announced in the same letter, I reached the following reconstruction of the negotiations which took place at the Conference Visit (Gal 2:1–10).

1. As Knox had argued, Paul agreed to raise money for the benefit of the Jerusalem Church among the churches that he had founded in Galatia, Asia, Macedonia, and Achaia during the "fourteen year" period preceding the Conference.
2. In return, the Jerusalem apostles gave Paul authority as apostle to the Gentiles, that is, they and Paul reached a comity agreement "that we should go to the Gentiles and they to the circumcised" (2:9). Thus the Collection project was to be Paul's side of a bargain.
3. At this point I added a third element to the bargain. In view of items #1–3 in the preceding list I ventured to adopt from Acts the pre-Lukan tradition of the so-called "Apostolic Decree": "to abstain from the pollutions of idols and from unchastity and from what is strangled and from blood" (Acts 15:20; cf. 15:29 and 21:25). Within Judaism these were the traditional conditions laid by Jews on Gentiles who wished to live in a Jewish context. It seemed to me that the evidence of 1 Corinthians that "idol meat" was indeed an issue at Corinth supported the connection that the author of Acts had made between these provisions and the admission of Gentiles into the believing

community. Thus I concluded that, when Paul and the Jerusalem apostles reached their comity agreement concerning the Gentile mission, the Jerusalem church also imposed the Apostolic Decree. I could see no reason why the author of Acts should have created this connection, since very probably it did not reflect the practice of his own readership.

This last suggestion is not important to the present discussion. However, the connection between Paul's apostleship and the Collection is important and formed for this period the basis of the relationship between Paul and the Jerusalem church. On Paul's side, the completion of the Collection at an acceptable level was vital to what he understood his God-given role to be: Apostle to the Gentiles. He explained to the Romans that, in spite of his desire to visit them directly and pass on to the west carrying the gospel as far as Spain, he was presently obligated to travel to Jerusalem to deliver the Collection (15:25–29). He was planning to make this visit in spite of the fact that he viewed it with some apprehension. He asked the Romans to pray, not only for his safety in Jerusalem, but also "that my service may be acceptable to the saints" (15:31). On Jerusalem's side, the church undoubtedly had great hopes for the Collection and followed Paul's fund-raising efforts closely.

Paul's collection strategy seems to have been to revisit all his churches by traveling from Jerusalem through Galatia, Asia (Ephesus), and Macedonia (Philippi and Thessalonica), ending finally in Corinth. Writing from Ephesus he told the Corinthians, "I will visit you after passing through Macedonia" (1 Cor 16:5). From Corinth the collection would go to Jerusalem (1 Cor 16:3). It is highly probable that announcement of the Collection was contained in the Previous Letter to Corinth, and if he had written to the Corinthians, he probably wrote to others of his churches as well. After the initial announcement, however, Paul's anxiety about the size of the Collection's goal caused him to raise the level of the collection procedure. In 1 Cor 16:2 Paul explained to the Corinthians that the Collection was not to be considered a one-time "passing the hat." It was to be a weekly offering during the period preceding Paul's arrival. He said that he had already given these directions to the churches of Galatia (16:1), presumably when he passed through Galatia prior to his arrival in Ephesus.

4. Second Corinthians and the Crisis in Asia

The first thing that Paul wanted to tell the Corinthians in the letter that we have as 2 Corinthians 1–9[27] was about his release after his near-death experience "in Asia." He opened with an emphatic disclosure formula, "For we do not want you to be ignorant, brethren, . . ." Paul's announcement, therefore, was news to the Corinthians. His reference to "the sentence of death" implies that he had been put in prison[28] and, if in prison, then on a capital charge.

Since for reasons of the development of Paul's thought[29] I place Philippians between 1 and 2 Corinthians, I identify the imprisonment from which Paul wrote to the Philippians with the "affliction in Asia" about which Paul wrote to the Corinthians.[30] Presumably this imprisonment was in Ephesus, where Paul had planned to stay "until Pentecost" (1 Cor

---

[27] Victor Paul Furnish, *II Corinthians* (AB 32A; Garden City, NY: Doubleday, 1984) 35–48, presents a clear exposition of the case for considering canonical 2 Corinthians to have been produced by an early editor who combined two of Paul's letters to Corinth: 2 Cor 1–9 and a later letter, 2 Cor 10–13.

[28] So Furnish, *II Corinthians*, 122–23.

[29] I might say a word about what I mean by "development." I specifically do not mean a kind of organic growth or the result of a process of abstract reflection. As I understand Paul, he reacted theologically to the problems that arose in the course of his turbulent ministry. When the first few converts died before the expected Parousia, Paul created the scheme of a preliminary resurrection of just those persons at the time of the Parousia so that God's promise that all believers should be included in the Kingdom would not fail. That message is contained in 1 Thess 4:13–18 and was not a part of his original preaching. Once such a scheme had been created, however, it became part of his theological tool box, reappearing in subsequent letters, in this instance, in 1 Cor 15 and Phil 3:20–21, until his total view of eschatology changed. When Judaizers became a threat, Paul developed the doctrine of justification by faith not works. There is the merest hint in Phil 3:9 where Judaizers are on the horizon, but the full development occurs in his response to the Galatian situation. Once articulated, the doctrine reappeared in Romans where the problem of Judaizers was not on the table but where Paul wished to make it clear that he was not an antinomian. When faced with death during the imprisonment from which he wrote to the Philippians, Paul developed his idea of redemptive suffering (Phil 3:10–11), whereas previously he had considered the suffering of believers to be evil and the grounds for the destruction of those who caused it (2 Thess 1:6–10; 1 Thess 2:14–16). Redemptive suffering then appears in later letters written when he was no longer experiencing unusual suffering (e.g., 2 Cor 6:4–10 where he boasts of his suffering; Rom 5:3–5; and Col 1:24–26). The diet of believers was a present problem at the time of 1 Corinthians; an echo of Paul's argument to the Corinthians then appears as Romans 14, written to those for whom it was not a problem. As I understand him, Paul's theological initiatives were born in conflict over real pastoral issues. Once born, they became part of his theological repertoire.

[30] So also Furnish, *II Corinthians*, 122–23: "This hypothesis seems at least as likely as any other."

16:8). Clearly the imprisonment was of some duration. There was time for the news to reach Philippi, time for the Philippians to send him money by the hand of Epaphroditus, time for Epaphroditus to fall seriously ill, time for news of this misfortune to reach Philippi, time for news of the Philippians' concern to reach Epaphroditus, and time for Epaphroditus to recover (Phil 2:25–30).

Since we know that the news of Paul's plight spread to Philippi, presumably as the result of the casual comings and goings of church members engaged in commerce, it seems likely that this news had gone elsewhere as well. Paul's "disclosure" in 2 Cor 1:8–11 is therefore probably not the news that he had been imprisoned but the news that he had been released in vindication of God's plan for his mission.

At this point Paul had traveled north from Ephesus looking for Titus, who had carried the "Severe Letter" to Corinth (see 2 Cor 2:3–4; 7:8–12), written by Paul just before his imprisonment. This letter concerned a disciplinary problem in Corinth, perhaps the matter of the immoral man of 1 Cor 5:1–5 (cf. 2 Cor 2:5–11). The letter also contained the threat of a follow-up inspection visit from Ephesus to Corinth and back, after which Paul planned to resume his Collection circuit traveling counter-clockwise around the Aegean Sea. His imprisonment interrupted his plans, and on reflection Paul decided that it would be prudent to hear what Titus had to say about the reception of the "Severe Letter" by the Corinthians before visiting Corinth again. Paul had traveled north upon his release. Titus must therefore have been directed to return overland via Macedonia and Asia. Paul had reached Troas without meeting Titus, and so he had crossed to Macedonia (2 Cor 2:12–13). There he did indeed meet Titus and rejoiced at the news Titus brought of the obedience of the Corinthians. Paul was now back on the route he had originally planned for the Collection project. Second Corinthians 1–9 was his joyful response to these events.

However, Paul's joy was not without a cloud. A new element had entered the picture in the form of two traveling "brothers." They were on their way to Corinth, and thus, since Titus was also traveling to Corinth carrying 2 Corinthians 1–9, they were to accompany him on the journey. In 2 Corinthians 8–9 Paul introduced and commended the "brothers" to the Corinthians.

What do we know of these two unnamed persons?

1. They were believers in the Way, since Paul called them "brothers" (8:18, 22, 23; 9:3, 5).
2. They were "apostles" (ἀπόστολοι, *apostoloi*, 8:23).

3. One of them was "famous among all the churches for his services on behalf of the gospel" (8:18). The other was someone with whom Paul had had previous satisfactory dealings.
4. They were traveling on behalf of the Collection (8:18–9:5).
5. They had been appointed by "the churches" (8:19, 24). Commentators differ over the meaning of this designation.[31] Most take it to mean the Macedonian churches, although Paul's reference to "some of the Macedonians [who] might come with me" as a separate group (9:4) seems to make this conclusion unlikely. If not the Macedonian churches, then which churches? I cannot escape the conclusion that only Jerusalem could be said to embody the collective authority of "the churches."[32] Two travelers implies one appointment, since traveling alone was precarious, especially when sums of money were involved. It is therefore easier to imagine that this pair had been appointed in one place rather than two or more. Certainly Jerusalem was the locus of temporal authority in Paul's mind, at least with respect to the Collection (Rom 15:31b). Further, "apostles" is a rather formal term to use of local appointees, and to refer to them as "the glory of Christ" also seems to give them a larger role.
6. They had independent fiscal authority concerning the Collection. Paul specifically said that they would be in charge of Collection arrangements in Corinth, although he added that this authority was to be only until his arrival (9:5). Presumably therefore they had been in charge of Collection arrangements on the preceding legs of the journey. Paul viewed them in the role of independent auditors before whom he wished to avoid "blame" (8:20–21).

Paul seems to have put the best face on the situation that he could. He cast himself in the role of the one who was sending these brothers to Corinth (8:18; 9:3). He expressed his pleasure that outside auditors had been sent in, so that "no one should blame us about this liberal gift which we are administering" (8:20). He enthusiastically commended them to the Corinthians as "the glory of Christ" (8:23). However, it does not take much imagination to read between the lines and see Paul's annoyance, anxiety, and frustration at their intrusion.[33]

---

[31] See the careful survey by Furnish, *II Corinthians*, 433–38.

[32] Keith F. Nickle, *The Collection: A Study in Paul's Strategy* (SBT 48; London: SCM, 1966) 18–22, whose focus is the Collection as a whole, also considers that it was the churches of Judea that Paul was referring to.

[33] Hans Dieter Betz, *2 Corinthians 8 and 9* (Hermeneia; Philadelphia: Fortress, 1985)

What can account for the appearance at this juncture of these two individuals? It seems reasonable to suppose that the Jerusalem church had heard of Paul's imprisonment in the manner described above and, fearing for the Collection project, had sent two of their number to take his place. Paul, on the other hand, had believed that he had an agreement with Jerusalem that he alone would be in charge of the Gentile mission—including the Collection—and that the Jerusalem apostles were to confine themselves to the mission to the Jews (Gal 2:9). However, Paul's imprisonment was an unforseen situation. Jerusalem considered that the comity agreement had been at least suspended if not nullified. Paul considered it still in force. We hope that the Jerusalem church had some concern for Paul's plight and were not acting purely out of self-interest. In any case, we can understand their decision to supplant Paul. The situation, however, had the makings of conflict, to say the least.

5. Paul's Opponents in Galatia

Now at last we turn to the question of the "opponents" in Galatia who have caused Paul so much anxiety and anger. Instead of the customary Thanksgiving section with which Paul opened all but one of those letters whose opening address has survived, Paul substituted an expression of astonishment. In this letter more than in any other we can sense Paul's emotional state, at least the state which he wished to project to his Galatian readers. The result is that it is universally assumed, as far as I am aware, that if Paul considered these visitors to the Galatian congregations to be interlopers and adversaries—in a word, his enemies—then they must have considered Paul to be their enemy.[34] Yet a moments reflection

---

73, notes that Paul seems to have the habit of naming his friends and associates (1 Cor 16:10–15; Rom 16; Col 4:7–10), but of omitting the names of his adversaries (1 Cor 3:10–15; 5:1, 5; 2 Cor 2:5–11; 7:12). We might add Gal 3:1.

[34] Hans Dieter Betz, *Galatians: A Commentary on Paul's Letter to the Churches in Galatia* (Hermeneia; Philadelphia: Fortress, 1979) 5–9, surveyed the history of proposals about various types of opponent. He himself concluded, "In the view of the opponents, Paul and his mission are illegitimate and an embodiment of everything they abhor and warn against." Martyn, *Galatians* 117–26, prefers to call them "the Teachers," and, citing his earlier article, "A Law-observant Mission to the Gentiles," *SJT* 38 (1985): 307–24, thinks of them as having a parallel mission of their own with a Jewish-Christian basis. The trouble occurred when they intruded into Paul's territory. He does, however, allow the possibility that they had a specifically anti-Pauline bias. Dunn (*Galatians*, 11) accepts Martyn's thesis and uses the term "the other missionaries," but considers their antipathy to Paul as "clearly implied."

should show the fallacy of the assumption. It is clear that Paul considered that their version of the Christian message differed from his own, and undoubtedly there was some difference, although we have only Paul's word for it. Paul, however, was quite capable of exaggeration when engaged in polemic. Thus the actual position of the visitors could have ranged all the way from a somewhat innocent and unreflective gospel message, a portion of which had unwittingly offended Paul, to studied hostility to Paul with a vigorous attempt to subvert his work in Galatia and elsewhere.

What do we know of Paul's opponents? We cannot do better than to summarize the list of characteristics of these persons given by James Dunn in his commentary on Galatians (9–11).

1. They recommended circumcision for Gentile followers of Jesus the Christ (5:2–12; 6:12–13).
2. They were themselves circumcised, that is, they were Jews ("fairly obvious").
3. They were also followers of Jesus. Paul was contesting their version of the "gospel of Christ."
4. They were apostles. Thus Paul insisted on the superiority of his apostleship vis à vis theirs.
5. Their authority came from the Jerusalem apostles. Hence Paul's emphatic account of his commissioning by the same Jerusalem apostles.

Clearly their view of the need for circumcision differed from Paul's. "It is those who want to make a good showing in the flesh that would compel you to be circumcised" (6:12). There is a measure of authority in the verb "compel," used twice earlier in Galatians of the imposition of circumcision on Gentile Christians by the authority of (some at least of) the Jerusalem apostles (2:3, 14). In 6:12, however, Paul continued, "and only in order that they may not be persecuted for the cross of Christ." Part of his scorn seems to be that they did not see the theological implications of their recommendation but made it on purely practical grounds: the avoidance of persecution. Earlier in the letter he had also linked circumcision with avoidance of persecution: "If I, brethren, still preach circumcision, why am I still persecuted?" (5:11). Whatever the precise situation under Roman administration in that place and time concerning treatment of Jews, we may take Galatians as evidence that Paul, his "opponents," and the Galatians all knew that Jews enjoyed a toleration that Christians did not.

It is revealing further that Paul continued by saying that his opponents are not only non-theological but also non-observant, that is, they do not keep the Jewish Law: "For even those who receive (or, have received) circumcision do not themselves keep the law" (6:13). That these Judaizers should be non-observant is so unexpected that some commentators suggest that Paul was referring not to them but to a small, otherwise unmentioned group of Gentile converts in Galatia who had already accepted circumcision and whom Paul criticized for not undertaking the whole burden of the Law. However, the second half of the verse, "they desire to have you circumcised," points more probably to the visiting missionaries. Paul was calling into question the full Jewishness of these preachers, at the same time emphasizing his own credentials as an apostle by solemn agreement of the Jerusalem hierarchy (Gal 2:1–10), and further his divine appointment as *the* Apostle to the Gentiles (Gal 1:1).

6. Mystery Unraveled?

The reader will have guessed by this point where this exposition is leading. It seems to me probable that the two "brothers" who, I have argued, were appointed and sent from Jerusalem to look after the Collection in Paul's presumed absence were the same as the ones who caused Paul so much heartache and anger because of their preaching in Galatia. Galatia was certainly involved in the Collection project (1 Cor 16:1). Thus the two brothers from Jerusalem would have needed to stop there. When among the Galatians, they would certainly have been called upon to preach. It is equally certain that their message would not have sounded like Paul's. We know that circumcision was a continuing interest of the Jerusalem church, and we would expect that its representatives would include it in their message, if only as a practical device for avoiding persecution.

The two brothers traveled faster than the news of the effect that their preaching had had in Galatia. Thus Paul, although he had mixed feelings about their intrusion into his Collection project, could nevertheless swallow his pride and recommend them to the Corinthians. Shortly thereafter, however, news of the Galatians' sympathetic reception of these Jerusalem apostles reached Paul, and Paul in response composed and sent his angry letter to Galatia.

Let us compare what has been proposed above about these two groups.

Galatian "opponents"	"Brothers" of 2 Corinthians
1. They were Christians.	1. They were Christians.
2. They were also Jews.	2. Coming from Jerusalem they were quite likely Jews.
3. They were apostles.	3. They were apostles.
4. They were authorized representatives of the Jerusalem church.	4. They were authorized representatives of the Jerusalem church.
5. They visited the Galatian churches.	5. They visited the Galatian churches.
6. They preached circumcision.	6. (No occasion to preach.)
7. (No direct evidence in Galatians, but it may be significant that Paul does *not* mention the Collection.)	7. They were traveling on behalf of the Collection.

On this last point, Knox took Paul's silence in Galatians about the Collection as evidence that the Collection had already been delivered to Jerusalem and thus favored a very late dating for Galatians. However, if the Galatian "opponents" had been sent to administer the Collection, then their visit to Galatia would have ended the project as far as the Galatians were concerned. There would be no more putting something aside every week. Paul could perhaps have commended them for whatever they may have contributed (if he knew), but in this angry letter it is easy to understand why explicit commendation found no place. Note, however, that Paul did allude to alms-giving as he brought the letter to a close. It is interesting that the Book of Common Prayer has picked up Gal 6:10 as an Offertory Sentence: "As we have opportunity, let us do good unto all men; and especially unto them that are of the household of faith."

There is an inherent plausibility in characterizing the Galatian "opponents" as Paul's co-workers. The Galatian churches were composed of Paul's converts (Gal 4:12–16). It would therefore have been far easier for persons who could present themselves to the Galatians as Paul's associates to gain a sympathetic audience among them, than if they began by attacking Paul's message. In fact we have positive evidence of their claimed association with Paul. Paul felt it necessary to protest that he did *not* preach circumcision as they presumably alleged (Gal 5:11); he was *not* one of them. I have always thought that the problem of gaining acceptance in Galatia by persons hostile to Paul's mission is not sufficiently considered in the usual depiction of Paul's opponents.

Further, when we boil down the message of these visitors to Galatia, the single element that remains is the recommendation of circumcision, and even this recommendation is based on a practical rather than a theological consideration. We do not get the picture of a full, anti-Pauline gospel. Thus these two groups of apostles are like two pieces of a picture puzzle which fit together, and, since both pieces are from the letters, in my opinion they should be joined.

7. Conclusion: Probability Estimate

I think that Knox's insight (Section 1 above) is axiomatic and frees us from the distorting influence of Acts on the Pauline chronology. Sections 2–3 of this paper present a "cover story" as I call such constructions. The narrative has many points of contact with the letters, but it is not itself evidence. I view my reconstruction of Paul's career as plausible, even probable. It is, at least, as probable as I can make it. However, alternate stories are possible to fit the same or different conclusions. The essential argument is in Sections 4–6, where the basic characteristics of these two groups of "apostles" are identified and compared. A number of the paired characteristics are highly probable; others perhaps less so. However, the probability is cumulative. Each additional pair that is accepted adds to the overall probability. The argument is not of the "If A, then B, and if B, then C" type, where each additional step reduces its overall credibility.

I have frequently warned graduate students against the fallacy of merging the identity, for example, of persons with the same names—the various John's in the New Testament or the Mary's—attractive as such identifications may seem. Within the population of early Christian women whose name was Mary, the probability that two New Testament references to the unmodified name "Mary" refer to a single person is very low. In our case, however, the population of "apostles" sent from Jerusalem into Paul's Gentile mission is very small, and the probability that these two groups are actually the same group is correspondingly high. That the two "brothers" that we meet in 2 Corinthians 8–9 were the "opponents" of the letter to the Galatians seems to me probable at about the 66% level, which means that the above reconstruction would be the most likely solution currently offered to this small problem within Pauline studies.

I conclude, therefore, that it is Paul's "opponents" from Galatia that we meet in 2 Corinthians 8 and 9. It seems to me probable that they had come from Jerusalem, were traveling on behalf of the Collection, and had visited the Galatian churches on their way to Macedonia. They presented themselves to Paul's converts in Galatia as Paul's colleagues and associates in the Collection project. The reader will have guessed what is coming. Paul, if the expression had been current in his day, could well have said, "With friends like these, who needs enemies?"

DID PAUL HAVE OPPONENTS IN ROME AND WHAT WERE THEY OPPOSING?

STANLEY E. PORTER
McMaster Divinity College
Hamilton, ON, Canada

1. INTRODUCTION

In the most thorough, comprehensive and detailed treatment of Paul's opponents, Jerry Sumney excludes treatment of the book of Romans for the following reasons. He says that "We exclude Romans, even though its purpose is still a matter of much debate, because the church at Rome was not a Pauline church in the sense that those in Corinth, Thessalonica and elsewhere were. Furthermore, since Paul had not been to Rome, anti-Pauline activity is not as probable. In addition, Romans was clearly not written as a response to anti-Pauline activity. We may take it, then, that the primary purposes of Romans do not involve opponents."[1] Virtually every one of the reasons that Sumney gives for dismissing treatment of Romans can be and has been questioned—and sometimes can be done in terms of the strictures of Sumney's book itself. Sumney is correct that the purpose of Romans is still much debated. The important volume, *The Romans Debate*,[2] makes clear that the continued discussion has done

---

[1] J. L. Sumney, *'Servants of Satan', 'False Brothers' and Other Opponents of Paul* (JSNTSup 188; Sheffield: Sheffield Academic Press, 1999) 31. My comments here are not designed in any way to minimize the work of my friend, Jerry Sumney. I was very pleased to accept his second volume for publication in the series that I then edited, and his volume has pushed discussion decidedly forward. See also his *Identifying Paul's Opponents: The Question of Method in 2 Corinthians* (JSNTSup 40; Sheffield: JSOT Press, 1990), where he first worked out his methodology. Other important books on the question of Paul's opponents include: J. J. Gunther, *St. Paul's Opponents and their Background: A Study of Apocalyptic and Jewish Sectarian Teachings* (NovTSup 35; Leiden: E. J. Brill, 1973); G. Lüdemann, *Opposition to Paul in Jewish Christianity* (trans. M. E. Boring; Minneapolis: Fortress, 1989). There are, of course, many volumes on the individual letters.

[2] K. P. Donfried (ed.), *The Romans Debate: Revised and Expanded Edition* (Peabody, MA: Hendrickson, 1991), significantly enlarged in size from the first edition (Minneapolis: Augsburg, 1977). See also J. W. Drane, "Why Did Paul Write Romans?" in D. A. Hagner and M. J. Harris (eds.), *Pauline Studies: Essays Presented to Professor F. F. Bruce*

nothing to diminish theorizing regarding the purpose and occasion of Romans, but has only promoted more discussion. In this respect, however, Romans is no different from many others of Paul's letters, where there remains major debate over the purpose and occasion of the particular writing—and the nature of Paul's opponents. Sumney himself has focused upon the Corinthian correspondence,[3] but he has also undertaken such difficult letters as Colossians and the Pastoral epistles.[4] However, Sumney, as his statement above makes clear, does not require that such issues of occasion and purpose be solved before undertaking to examine the Pauline opponents. Sumney further states that the church at Rome was not a Pauline church as were the churches in Corinth, Thessalonica and elsewhere. No doubt Paul was instrumental in the bringing of Christianity to the people in such cities as Corinth and Thessalonica, as well as Galatia and Philippi. Sumney includes the letter to the Colossians as well, however, but most do not believe that Paul had actually been to Colossae when he wrote the letter—if he did indeed write the letter to the Colossians.[5] His sending of Epaphras to Colossae (Col 1:7; 4:12, 13) was no doubt different than the founding of the Roman church,[6] but Paul's second-hand knowledge of the situation in Rome and Colossae would have been somewhat similar.[7] Further, I am not convinced that Paul actually had to have physically been to a given city to generate anti-

---

on his 70th Birthday (Exeter: Paternoster; Grand Rapids: Eerdmans, 1980) 208–27; A. J. M. Wedderburn, *The Reasons for Romans* (Edinburgh: T. & T. Clark, 1988); and L. A. Jervis, *The Purpose of Romans: A Comparative Letter Structure Investigation* (JSNTSup 55; Sheffield: JSOT Press, 1991).

[3] Sumney, *Servants of Satan*, 33–133; cf. his *Identifying Paul's Opponents*.

[4] Sumney, *Servants of Satan*, 188–213 and 253–302, respectively. Colossians has been even more problematic ever since M. D. Hooker's "Were there False Teachers in Colossae?" in B. Lindars and S. S. Smalley (eds.), *Christ and Spirit in the New Testament: Studies in Honour of Charles Francis Digby Moule* (Cambridge: Cambridge University Press, 1973) 315–32, a question not adequately answered by most who examine Colossians. The Pastoral epistles are problematized by the issue of pseudonymous authorship, which (if true, and I remain unconvinced) creates a "double pseudonymy." See D. Meade, *Pseudonymity and Canon* (WUNT 39; Tübingen: Mohr Siebeck, 1986) 127.

[5] I believe that he did. See L. M. McDonald and S. E. Porter, *Early Christianity and its Sacred Literature* (Peabody, MA: Hendrickson, 2000) 471–76.

[6] The founding of the Roman church rests in mystery, and probably always will.

[7] The standard view is by J. B. Lightfoot, *St. Paul's Epistles to the Colossians and to Philemon* (London: Macmillan, 1879) 1–72. On whether Paul actually did visit Colossae, see B. W. R. Pearson, *Corresponding Sense: Paul, Dialectic, and Gadamer* (BIS 58; Leiden: E. J. Brill, 2001).

Pauline activity.[8] If the letter of James is early, as I believe that it is, it suggests that Paul caused theological *Angst* in a variety of quarters where he had not been, and generated a poignant response.[9] The question is not whether the word of someone could go ahead of him, since we know that it could, and that seems to be one of the premises of Paul's letter to the Romans, but the question is whether there is any evidence that such word had already prompted a response among the Romans. I argue below that there is some indication that it had. Lastly, whereas Romans as a letter is much, much more than simply a response to anti-Pauline sentiment, at a minimum it contains such a response within it. It is this sentiment that is worth examining to see whether we can discover something of Paul's opponents at Rome. One of the constant bedevilments of such discussion in Pauline studies, however, is the definition of what constitutes an opponent. This issue will need to be addressed as well.

Once such a definition of opposition is in place, I believe that it is possible to detect at least an anti-Pauline hesitancy, if not outright opposition, addressed by Paul in his comments to the Romans that merit further consideration.

2. The Evidence for Pauline Opposition in Romans

Discussion of Paul's letter to the Galatians has been the focal point for much discussion of Paul's opponents, perhaps rivaled only by the Corinthian letters.[10] Many of the issues that are discussed in Galatians overlap significantly with Romans, especially in terms of such topics as works, the law, and the like.[11] Discussion of Galatians usually focuses

---

[8] I do not, however, believe that there was necessarily a consistent and universal anti-Paulinism, even if there was widespread opposition, especially among some Jewish Christians (see below). See, e.g., Lüdemann, *Opposition to Paul*, 35–115; M. Goulder, *A Tale of Two Missions* (London: SCM Press, 1994); cf. *idem*, *Paul and the Competing Mission in Corinth* (Library of Pauline Studies; Peabody, MA: Hendrickson, 2001).

[9] Even if the positions are reconcilable. See McDonald and Porter, *Early Christianity*, 532–33; L. T. Johnson, *The Letter of James* (AB 37A; New York: Doubleday, 1995) 118–21. Cf. M. Hengel, "Der Jakobusbrief als antipaulinische Polemik," in G. F. Hawthorne with O. Betz (eds.), *Tradition and Interpretation in the New Testament: Essays in Honor of E. Earle Ellis* (Grand Rapids: Eerdmans; Tübingen: Mohr Siebeck, 1987) 248–78; *contra* J. B. Mayor, *The Epistle of St. James* (London: Macmillan, 3rd edn, 1913) xci–cii, clxxxiii–clxxxviii.

[10] See, e.g., M. D. Nanos (ed.), *The Galatians Debate* (Peabody, MA: Hendrickson, 2002) 321–433.

[11] E.g., R. K. Rapa, *The Meaning of "Works of the Law" in Galatians and Romans*

upon treatment of these issues, since it is in terms of these topics that Paul seems to be most vexed in his direct engagement with the Galatians.[12] However, even though there is such conceptual and theological similarity between Galatians and Romans, I do not believe that the sections of Romans concerned with such issues (esp. chs. 3–5, but also 9–11 and 14–15; see below) necessarily offer direct insight into the Roman situation and Paul's opponents, but are perhaps more characteristic of the elements of Romans as a letter essay.[13] Such indicators of potential if not outright antagonism are to be found in other portions of the letter. There are a number of comments by Paul at both the beginning and ending of the letter that indicate that there had been some sort of anticipation and possible reaction on the part of those in Rome to Paul's attempts to come to Rome. It is these passages that I wish to concentrate upon.[14]

Before one can examine these passages, however, one must examine what is meant by the notion of opponent and opposition. Sumney works from a fairly broadly defined notion of what constitutes opposition, although he wishes to restrict his investigations to evidence from the individual letters, especially those that were to churches known first-hand to Paul. Like many New Testament scholars who discuss such an issue,

---

(Studies in Biblical Literature 31; New York: Lang, 2001). In fact, much of the recent discussion of Paul and the law focuses upon these two Pauline letters. For a summary of some of the recent discussion, as it focuses upon the so-called New Perspective, see S. Westerholm, *Perspectives Old and New on Paul: The "Lutheran" Paul and his Critics* (Grand Rapids: Eerdmans, 2004) 101–258; idem, "The 'New Perspective' at Twenty-Five," in D. A. Carson, P. O'Brien and M. A. Seifrid (eds.), *Justification and Variegated Nomism*. II. *The Paradoxes of Paul* (Tübingen: Mohr Siebeck; Grand Rapids: Baker, 2004) 1–38.

[12] This is seen in numerous ways, including his deleting of the thanksgiving in the letter, his abbreviated ending, and his strong language of rebuke: e.g. Gal 1:6–8; 2:11, 17; 3:1, 3; 5:12; etc.

[13] See M. L. Stirewalt, Jr., *Paul the Letter Writer* (Grand Rapids: Eerdmans, 2003) 107–12; cf. idem, "The Form and Function of the Greek Letter-Essay," in Donfried (ed.), *Romans Debate*, 147–71; K. P. Donfried, "False Presuppositions in the Study of Romans," in Donfried (ed.), *Romans Debate*, 102–25, esp. 122–25.

[14] Wedderburn (*Reasons for Romans*, 102–42), utilizing a method somewhat similar to mine, has identified 1:16a and Paul's statement regarding not being ashamed of the gospel as reflecting the fact that "*some in Rome had in fact claimed that* [Paul] *indeed ought to be ashamed of his gospel and his proclamation*," and that "*the argument of the rest of Romans from this point to the end of chapter 11 is a defence of Paul's message and ministry against charges which claimed that it was indeed shameful*" (p. 104; italics his). Wedderburn, however, fails to consider the literary formulation of 1:16a and the timeless nature of 1:16b–17, and in essence reduces the body of Romans to an answer to a single question, confusing the purpose of Romans with its occasion, to say nothing of the opponents.

howevever, Sumney does not offer an explicit definition of what is meant by an opponent, but assumes an understanding of the notion. Others work from more specific definitions, such as Barnett's in terms of "outsiders who have penetrated the Pauline assemblies."[15] Whereas there is much to commend a clear and explicit definition such as Barnett's, such a definition can overly restrict discussion. In fact, it is difficult to see how Barnett's definition is even applicable to all of the letters that he discusses in his treatment of the issue, since in many instances it is difficult to show that what Paul speaks against is constituted mainly by outsiders and that this has penetrated the Pauline churches.[16] As a result, I will work from a tacit definition that attempts to describe the nature and content of any opposition or antagonism to Paul or his mission, as found in explicit or implied statements in his letter to the Romans, especially statements that pertain to direct interaction between the parties.

a. *Romans 1:9–10—Frustrated Expectation of Paul's Arrival*

In the thanksgiving to the letter to the Romans (1:8–15 [17]), Paul lays out the grounds for his thanksgiving to God for the believers in Rome.[17] The thanksgivings of Paul's letters have a consistency to them that is worth noting.[18] The two major features of the Pauline thanksgiving are that it "provides a general orientation to the relationship between Paul and the particular church," a relationship that is then "developed in the rest of the leter," and it is full of "giving thanks to God for the faithfulness of

---

[15] P. W. Barnett, "Opponents of Paul," in G. F. Hawthorne, R. P. Martin and D. G. Reid (eds.), *Dictionary of Paul and his Letters* (Downers Grove, IL: InterVarsity Press, 1993) 644–53, here 644.

[16] E.g. if Arnold is correct about the situation at Colossae, the problem is religious syncretism that was part of the local folk religion. See C. E. Arnold, *The Colossian Syncretism* (WUNT 2.77; Tübingen: Mohr Siebeck, 1995) esp. 5.

[17] For my working outline of the letter, see McDonald and Porter, *Early Christianity*, 461.

[18] Important studies of the Pauline thanksgiving include: P. Schubert, *Form and Function of the Pauline Thanksgivings* (BZNW 20; Berlin: Töpelmann, 1939); W. G. Doty, *Letters in Primitive Christainity* (Philadelphia: Fortress, 1973) esp. 31–33; P. T. O'Brien, *Introductory Thanksgivings in the Letters of Paul* (NovTSup 49; Leiden: E. J. Brill, 1977); F. Schnider and W. Stenger, *Studien zum neutestamentlichen Briefformular* (NTTS 11; Leiden: E. J. Brill, 1987) esp. 42–49; J. L. White, "Ancient Greek Letters," in D. E. Aune (ed.), *Greco-Roman Literature and the New Testament* (SBLSBS 21; Atlanta: Scholars Press, 1988) 85–105, esp. 96–100; J. Murphy-O'Connor, *Paul the Letter-Writer: His World, His Options, His Skills* (Collegeville, MN: Liturgical, 1995) esp. 55–64; J. T. Reed, "Are Paul's Thanksgivings 'Epistolary'?" *JSNT* 61 (1996) 87–99.

the congregation" and offering intercession on their behalf.[19] In none of the letters addressed to churches, including those that have intercessory prayer sections, does Paul mention an anticipated visit to the church concerned. It is only in 2 Timothy that Paul mentions a longing to be with Timothy (1:4), but he does not mention this in terms of his visiting Timothy or explaining why such a meeting has not occurred. This is one of the major differences regarding the thanksgiving in Paul's letter to the Romans. He uses the thanksgiving as a way of addressing the issues for which he appears to have been criticized.

The first of these items of criticism appears to revolve around the sincerity of his actual desire to see the Christians in Rome and what has prevented this meeting from taking place. We do not know how much knowledge Paul had of the Christian church in Rome,[20] but we do know several apparent facts: (1) that he knew a number of people in Rome (e.g. 16:1, 3, 7, 8, 9, 10, 11, 12, 13), presumably people whom he had met or had some form of contact with in the course of his travels or communication;[21] (2) that at least some people from Rome had communicated with him, since he sends greetings to many of these people within the context of the church (see ch. 16 and references above) and appears at several places to be addressing issues that are of potential practical importance to the church in Rome (e.g. chs. 9–11 regarding the future of ethnic Israel and 14:1–15:13 on relations between the weak and strong, in which he identifies himself as one of the strong [15:1], even if he commends con-

---

[19] McDonald and Porter, *Early Christianity*, 383. On intercessory prayers, see G. P. Wiles, *Paul's Intercessory Prayers: The Significance of the Intercessory Prayer Passages in the Letters of Paul* (SNTSMS 24; Cambridge: Cambridge University Press, 1974) esp. 76–77.

[20] There have been a number of recent discussions of the church in Rome. See W. Wiefel, "The Jewish Community in Ancient Rome and the Origins of Roman Christianity," in Donfried (ed.), *Romans Debate*, 85–101; P. Lampe, *From Paul to Valentinus: Christians at Rome in the First Two Centuries* (trans. M. Steinhauser; ed. M. D. Johnson; Minneapolis: Fortress Press, 2003); J. S. Jeffers, *Conflict in Rome: Social Order and Hierarchy in Early Christianity* (Minneapolis: Fortress, 1991); J. C. Walters, *Ethnic Issues in Paul's Letter to the Romans: Changing Self-Definitions in Earliest Roman Chistianity* (Valley Forge, PA: Trinity Press International, 1993).

[21] This presumes that Romans 16 was addressed originally to the church at Rome, rather than being a separate letter or some form of cover letter sent to Ephesus. See H. Gamble, Jr., *The Textual History of the Letter to the Romans: A Study in Textual and Literary Criticism* (SD 42; Grand Rapids: Eerdmans, 1977), mostly in response to the so-called Ephesian hypothesis (pp. 36–55); and Lampe, *From Paul to Valentinus*, 153–83.

sideration of the weak);[22] (3) that Paul had already made clear, whether through previous personal communication or another means, his concern for the Christians in Rome by noting his unceasing mentioning of them in prayer (1:9–10); (4) that Paul had made known his intention to come to visit the church in Rome, but that that intention had been thwarted a number of times so that he had so far been unable to visit them (1:9–10); and (5) that Paul saw his intention to visit as in some way guided by the will of God and, previously at least, out of his control (1:10).

The fact that Paul had so far been unable to make the trip to Rome appears to have generated some form of opposition to him within the church there, so much so that he is aware of those questioning his intentions. Perhaps this had been communicated to him, whether directly or indirectly, by some of those he appears to have known in Rome. This opposition may have simply taken the form of those who expressed their doubt concerning Paul's regard for the church in Rome, but it may have taken a stronger form in which Paul was seen as intentionally avoiding coming to visit them (see e.g. below for discussion of this possibility). This lack of regard would, in their minds at least, account for his making excuses regarding his failure to visit, even to the point perhaps of using the notion of the will of God as the reason that he had so far been unable to make the trip to Rome. The composition of the Roman church probably exacerbated these tensions,[23] as the church was predominantly Gentile but with an increasing number of Jewish believers as they returned from the lapsed edict of Claudius under the reign of Nero.[24] Both

---

[22] I do not believe, however, that either chs. 9–11 or 14:1–15:13 is of central significance to the purpose of the letter, or to defining the opponents, although they will enter into the discussion (see below). Baur constructed his entire understanding around chs. 9–11. See F. C. Baur, *Paul the Apostle of Jesus Christ: His Life and Works, his Epistles and Teachings* (two volumes in one; Peabody, MA: Hendrickson, 2003; repr. of 1873–75 English trans. of 1845 German edn) 318–19; J. Munck, *Paul and the Salvation of Mankind* (trans. F. Clarke; London: SCM Press, 1959) 42–44. Those who put Rom 14:1–15:13 at the center include: P. S. Minear, *The Obedience of Faith: The Purposes of Paul in the Epistle to the Romans* (SBT Second Series 19; London: SCM Press, 1971) 6–22; R. J. Karris, "Romans 14:1–15:13 and the Occasion of Romans," in Donfried (ed.), *Romans Debate*, 65–84, with bibliography on p. 65 n. 6. See n. 44 below.

[23] For discussion of the composition of the Roman church, see McDonald and Porter, *Early Christianity*, 452–54, with reference to C. E. B. Cranfield, *A Critical and Exegetical Commentary on the Epistle to the Romans* (2 vols.; ICC; Edinburgh: T. & T. Clark, 1975, 1979) 1:17–22.

[24] The date of the edict has been disputed, but probably occurred in AD 49 (see the sources below for discussion). Opinion on those evicted has ranged from the few involved

sides of this debate may have been suspicious of Paul and his intention to visit Rome.[25] The Gentile believers, now separated from the synagogue, might have thought that Paul's arrival could have marked another re-organization of the structure of the Christian community and perhaps a restoration and even an enhancement of the roles and responsibilities of the Jews, possibly even a return to the synagogue. The Jews' having been exiled for a number of years, during which time the Christian church grew in significant ways under the direction of Gentile Christians, would have been perceived by some (Gentiles at least) as a sign that the church should be, if not a predominantly Gentile one, one at least led by the Gentiles who had remained. The Jews, on the other hand, would have perhaps been suspicious of Paul on the basis of his previous reputation in the West—if his correspondence with the Galatian churches were known, and if such stereotypes of his teaching as led to the need for James's response had become well known to them[26]—as one who did not insist upon following the requirements of the law. After all, Paul had represented himself to the Corinthians not too many years previously as being adaptable to the demands and needs of those to whom he ministered (1 Cor 9:19–22). This had resulted in his apparent abandoning of the Jewish distinctives such as food laws, circumcision and other celebrations, certainly for Gentiles, if not for Jews as well (Rom 14:1–15:13; see below on Paul's antagonism in Jerusalem).

---

in insurrection (E. M. Smallwood, *The Jews under Roman Rule: From Pompey to Diocletian* [Leiden: E. J. Brill, 2nd edn, 1981] 210–16) to all Jews, including Christians (Wiefel, "Jewish Community," 93). Probably most Jews were involved, apart from those with Roman citizenship (see Lampe, *From Paul to Valentinus*, 11–16, esp. 14). Though there was no formal repeal of Claudius's edict, it probably lapsed with his death (see F. F. Bruce, *New Testament History* [New York: Doubleday, 1969] 290–99; *contra* Wiefel, "Jewish Community," 94, 96 who contends that the edict was repealed, but provides no evidence, apart from a reference to H. Leon, *The Jews of Ancient Rome* [Peabody, MA: Hendrickson, 1960] 27–28, who provides no such evidence).

[25] Some have thought that the edict of Claudius was the motivating factor for writing the letter to the Romans. See W. Marxsen, *Introduction to the New Testament* (trans. G. Buswell; Oxford: Blackwell, 1968) 100–101; Walters, *Ethnic Issues*, 56–66. It no doubt plays a role, but is not the only factor.

[26] We cannot know how much was known, but there is nothing that prevents communication. See B. Rapske, "Acts, Travel and Shipwreck," in D. Gill and C. Gempf (eds.), *The Book of Acts in its Greco-Roman Setting* (BAFCS 2; Grand Rapids: Eerdmans, 1994) 1–48; S. R. Llewelyn, *New Documents Illustrating Early Christianity* (New South Wales: Macquarie University, 1994) 1–92; E. R. Richards, *Paul and First-Century Letter Writing: Secretaries, Composition and Collection* (Downers Grove, IL: InterVarsity Press, 2004) 188–209.

Paul addresses this opposition head on. His response includes three elements. First is in terms of how Paul characterizes and then addresses those who have raised questions regarding his sincerity or effort in coming to visit the church in Rome. In any such reconstruction or mirror reading (as it is wont to be called these days),[27] we do not know the other side of the conversation by definition. As Bruce says, "we often find ourselves in the position of people listening to one end of a telephone conversation and trying, not very successfully, to reconstruct what is being said at the other end."[28] That does not mean that we should not try to overhear what they are saying, however. In this case, Paul does not address his opponents as if they were overly vociferous, but tacitly acknowledges in v. 10 that there have been questions that have been raised, by virtue of the fact that he is able to mention what appears to be some question regarding his plans and intentions for such a visit. In the second and third elements of his response, Paul focuses upon himself, rather than those who might be questioning his motives and intentions. The second response is for Paul to invoke God as his witness to the actions that he has taken on behalf of the Christians in Rome. Paul has acknowledged in v. 8 that the faith of the Christians in Rome is being discussed throughout the world, and he gives thanks to God for this. In essence, Paul is invoking God as his witness in both regards—for the Roman believers and on his own behalf as one who is unceasingly making mention of them. Paul thanks God for the Roman Christians and calls upon God as support for the fact that he continues to intercede on their behalf for their continued faithfulness. The third element follows from the second. Paul has invoked God as his witness for his prayer on their behalf, and now he extends that prayer to include requesting of God that he might at last be able to visit the Romans. The apparent presumption is that Paul has on previous occasions tried to come to Rome, but that something has hindered him, perhaps to the point that some are questioning Paul's intentions. Perhaps the edict of Claudius figured into Paul's delay, but as a citizen he may well have been exempt from such a restriction.[29] In any case, the language Paul uses indicates that there may have been no one single reason, but many. Paul links here his continuing prayer for the Roman Christians with his

---

[27] See J. M. G. Barclay, "Mirror-Reading a Polemical Letter: Galatians as a Test Case," *JSNT* 31 (1987): 73–93.
[28] F. F. Bruce, *1 and 2 Corinthians* (NCB; London: Oliphants, 1971) 23.
[29] See Walters, *Ethnic Issues*, 127 n. 16, who notes that steps could, nevertheless, be taken, and so caution may still have been warranted.

own request to be able to visit them. The same God to whom he addresses his prayers on their behalf is the one in whose hands his intention of coming to them rests, i.e. it rests with God's will. Paul's counter to the incipient and perhaps growing criticism of his failure to come to them is that the God who is the object of their faith is the same one who holds it in his will to allow Paul to come to them. Criticism of his intention is tantamount to a criticism of God's will for Paul.

b. *Romans 1:11–12—Questions Regarding Charismatic Experience*

One of the persistent questions in discussion of the purpose and occasion of Romans is the relationship between the Christian foundation of the church and Paul's desire to visit the church.[30] It has been posited that one of the reasons that Paul might have been interested in visiting the church at Rome was to provide for it the kind of apostolic foundation that he had given to other churches and that the church at Rome presumably lacked. Most scholars do not accept this analysis, for a number of good reasons. One of these is that there does not seem to have been a need within the early Church for specific churches to have an apostolic foundation in order to be authentic churches. Another is that it has not been clearly established what the advantage would be to having an apostolic foundation. In other words, there is no discernible difference between a Pauline and a non-Pauline church in so far as an apostolic foundation is concerned.[31]

In the light of this discussion, the question might legitimately be raised by the Romans themselves regarding exactly what it was that Paul would have brought to them in Rome. Romans 1:11–12 seems to raise this question. In the light of the questions raised regarding Paul's sincerity of intention in visiting the church at Rome, it appears that there were some who may have raised the question of what sort of benefit Paul would have brought. The comments in vv. 11–12 raise questions in two regards concerning Paul's visit. On the one hand, the thought might have been that Paul's failure to visit Rome—regardless of the reason—had not apparently in any way created a deficiency in the Roman community. On the other hand, the Christians in Rome, perhaps because of communication between the Roman and Corinthian churches (e.g. Rom 16:3–4, regard-

---

[30] The classic essay in this regard is G. Klein, "Paul's Purpose in Writing the Epistle to the Romans," in Donfried (ed.), *Romans Debate*, 29–43.

[31] See McDonald and Porter, *Early Christianity*, 458.

ing Prisca and Aquila), may have become suspicious of Paul on the matter of so-called grace gifts (χαρίσματα), usually linked with being gifts of the Spirit. Apart from two references in the Pastoral epistles (1 Tim 4:14; 2 Tim 2:16), and a singular references in 2 Corinthians (1:11), all of the Pauline references to χάρισμα are in Romans (1:11; 5:15, 16; 6:23; 11:29; 12:6) and 1 Corinthians (1:7; 7:7; 12:4, 9, 28, 30, 31). The controversy in Corinth over manifestations of the grace gifts, especially as seen in 1 Corinthians 12, might have raised questions in the minds of the Roman believers regarding what it was exactly that Paul was intending to bring to them. There is little other evidence from the letter to the Romans that spiritual gifts or their manifestations were a problem for them, or at least that Paul thought of them as a problem for them, but his raising of the issue at the outset of the letter and his linking it throughout Romans to the gracious work of God seems to have been a strategy to alleviate any possible opposition that might have been raised in the light of how he handled the issue of spiritual gifts in Corinth.

Paul's first strategy is to make the matter of grace gifts reciprocal. In v. 11 Paul says that he wishes to impart some spiritual grace gift to the Roman believers for the purpose of their being strengthened. The strengthening of believers is something that Paul advocates elsewhere (see, e.g., 1 Thess 3:2, 13; 2 Thess 2:17; 3:3), although it is noteworthy that he does not use this language when speaking of gifts and their manifestations in 1 Corinthians 12. There the gifts are given for the common good (see 1 Cor 12:7, and vv. 12–27 with the body metaphor). Perhaps sensitive that this might appear as advocacy of his particular position on gifts, something that he had to combat at Corinth, Paul rephrases his advocacy in terms of a mutual encouragement of each other's faith (v. 12). This mutuality is directly in line with Paul's advocacy of the use of grace gifts for the common good. Paul's second strategy is in terms of placing grace gifts within the larger economy of God's salvific work. In Romans 5, Paul uses the language regarding grace gifts again (vv. 15–16). In this instance, the grace gifts are seen in opposition to transgressions and condemnation and leading to righteousness. Rather than being concerned with manifestations, grace gifts are interwoven with the fabric of forgiveness for sins and the gracious gift of God through Jesus Christ (see also Rom 6:23, where the same framework is in place). In Rom 11:29, at the end of his discussion of the role of national Israel in his plan of salvation of Gentiles, Paul notes that the gifts and the calling of God are not revocable, including both Israelites and those who are otherwise disobedient. By the time that he arrives at the parenetic section of Romans

(12:1–15:33)³² and the discussion of specific manifestations of gifts within his treatment of the body of Christ (12:3–8), there is nothing of the disputatious treatment found in 1 Corinthians 12. Instead, Paul makes the sharing of grace gifts to be a mutually beneficial practice.

c. *Romans 1:13; 15:22–23—Dispelling Rumors of Avoidance*

I have already discussed above the issue of Paul's delay in traveling to Rome, introduced in 1:10–11. In those verses Paul creates unity around the witness of God. Here Paul confronts more directly the possible rumour that he had tried specifically to avoid the Roman church. This is a theme that he returns to in ch. 15, giving further evidence that this is a sensitive issue for the Roman Christians.

In Rom 1:13, Paul begins with a disclosure formula.³³ Paul uses several different types of disclosure formulas in his letters. These include οὐ θέλω ὑμᾶς ἀγνοεῖν (Rom 1:13; 11:25; 1 Cor 10:1; 12:1; 2 Cor 1:8; 1 Thess 4:13), θέλω ὑμᾶς εἰδέναι (1 Cor 11:3; Col 2:1), γνωρίζω ὑμῖν (1 Cor 12:3; 15:1; 2 Cor 8:1; Gal 1:11), and γινώσκειν ὑμᾶς βούλομαι (Phil 1:12). What these formulaic phrases seem to have in common is that they are used at points where Paul wishes for his audience to recognize something that he considers to be important but that is quite possibly not yet or thoroughly known by them, though they should know it. There is not a necessary correlation between the use of disclosure formulas and addressing opponents in Paul's letters, although in most instances the usage is linked to a controversial issue within one of the letters where opposition is usually recognized, such as Corinth, Thessalonica and Colossae.

What Paul wants the Roman believers to know consists of four things, which together suggest that there is opposition that he wishes to clear up. The first is that he had intended (προεθέμην) to visit them many times (πολλάκις). Paul uses here a verb of purpose and an adverb whose sense

---

³² See McDonald and Porter, *Early Christianity*, 461 regarding the outline of Romans, and p. 385 on parenesis. There is some discussion regarding Pauline parenesis in terms of letter structure. See Doty, *Letters*, 37–39; Schnider and Stenger, *Studien*, 75–107.

³³ On the disclosure formula, see J. L. White, "Introductory Formulae in the Body of the Pauline Letter," *JBL* 90 (1971): 91–97, esp. 93, 94; idem, *The Body of the Greek Letter* (SBLDS 2; Missoula, MT: Society of Biblical Literature, 1972) 11–15; T. Y. Mullins, "Formulas in New Testament Epistles," *JBL* 91 (1972): 380–90, esp. 382–83.

is that of multiple occasions. The language indicates that Paul's intention has not been haphazard or casual, but that it has been purposeful but rebuffed on numerous and persistent occasions. The second is that he was hindered up to the present time. Paul uses a passive verb, ἐκωλύθην, without specifying the agent of the hindering (see also 15:22, where he uses a different verb for hinder, ἐνεκοπτόμην, and the adverbial τὰ πολλά, and 15:23, where he reiterates his having a longing or desire to come to them for many years).[34] It could be that he has a specific agent in mind that he chooses not to specify or, more likely, he simply does not know what the various factors are that have limited his coming. Nevertheless, this hindering has persisted right up to the time of writing this letter to the Romans. The third item of information is that the purpose of his visit is to "produce fruit" in the Roman church that is equivalent to what has been produced among the rest of the nations or Gentiles to whom he has been ministering. Paul's desire for the Roman believers is no less than it is for any of his churches, and that is to see the same work come to fruition among them as he has already seen in other of his churches. The fourth item is that, as 15:23 states, Paul has run out of places to evangelize in the regions in which he has been working, that is, in Asia and Greece. This last statement might seem to provide fuel for his opponents, who see Paul as neglecting the Christians in Rome. Instead, I think that it indicates that Paul has put the Romans on the same level as his other evangelistic efforts. He was occupied with work in the areas of Asia and Greece, but now that these areas have been satisfactorily "exhausted," he is now turning to new places, with the sense not that they are lesser but that they are equally deserving of the spread of the gospel.

---

[34] Some scholars have made much of the difference between the use of the aorist verb ἐκωλύθην and the imperfect ἐνεκοπτόμην. In response to Schmithals (W. Schmithals, *Der Römerbrief als historisches Problem* [SNT 9; Gütersloh: Mohn, 1975] 167), who contends that Rom 1:13 indicates that "the hindrance still remains," whereas 15:23-25 indicates specific travel plans, Wedderburn asserts (*Reasons for Romans*, 197–98) that Schmithals's understanding of 1:13 would be stronger with a present or perfect verb tense-form, while agreeing that the imperfect in 15:22 does indicate that "the hindrance has clearly ceased." The verbal tense-forms indicate nothing of the sort either way, but only the context indicates the endurance of the hindrance. The hindrance is clearly still in place, since Paul believes he must go to Jerusalem before travelling west. Misunderstanding of the Greek verbal tense-forms persists, despite a plethora of recent work. For a convenient summary, see S. E. Porter, *Idioms of the Greek New Testament* (Biblical Languages: Greek 2; Sheffield: Sheffield Academic Press, 2nd edn, 1994) 20–49.

d. *Romans 15:25–27—Abandoning Judaism?*

In Romans 9–11, Paul raises and answers the question regarding the place of Israel within God's economy now that the message of salvation has been extended to Gentiles. He insists that it is not as though God has abandoned his chosen people. To the contrary, Paul asserts, God has a continuing plan so that all Israel might be saved (11:26). Besides the problem of fitting these three chapters with particular theological systems, Romans 9–11 has posed difficulties in most outlines of Paul's letter to the Romans.[35] They clearly are not part of the parenetic section, since their emphasis and orientation is contrary to the kind of moral exhortation found in such a section. Neither do these three chapters at first glance fit well with the argument of the body of Paul's letter, which is so well structured around the progress of salvation from sinfulness to life in the Spirit. In any case, Romans 9–11 can be seen as a non-specific (I hesitate to use the word "abstract") treatment of the subject of God's faithfulness despite Israel's rejection, supported by use of the very Scriptures of Israel.[36]

Even though Paul concludes Romans 9–11 with the clear statement that all Israel will be saved, which leads to praise for God, the potential practical problem of the place of Judaism in the new dispensation of Gentile inclusion in the Church remains.[37] It appears from Rom 15:25–27

---

[35] See S. E. Porter, "A Newer Perspective on Paul: Romans 1–8 through the Eyes of Literary Analysis," in M. D. Carroll, D. J. A. Clines, and P. R. Davies (eds.), *The Bible in Human Society: Essays in Honour of John Rogerson* (JSOTSup 200; Sheffield: Sheffield Academic Press, 1995) 366–92.

[36] As noted above, for a number of scholars, Romans 9–11 has constituted the focal point of the entire letter. Discussion of these chapters continues. See G. Lüdemann, *Paulus und das Judentum* (Munich: Kaiser, 1983) 30–35; J.-N. Aletti, *Israël et la loi dans la lettre aux Romains* (Lectio Divina 173; Paris: Cerf, 1998) 167–265; C. Grenholm and D. Patte (eds.), *Reading Israel in Romans: Legitimacy and Plausibility of Divergent Interpretations* (Harrisburg, PA: Trinity Press International, 2000) esp. 127–245, for essays by J. Sievers, G. Wasserberg, W. S. Campbell, M. D. Nanos, and D. Patte. I agree with R. N. Longenecker that Romans 9–11 is not analogous with Galatians and should not be read as a "polemical [thrust] against a Judaizing threat (whether lurking or actual; whether arising from within or outside of the various Roman congregations)," but is consistent with Paul's method throughout the book ("Prolegomena to Paul's Use of Scripture in Romans," in R. N. Longenecker, *Studies in Paul, Exegetical and Theological* [New Testament Monographs 2; Sheffield: Sheffield Phoenix Press, 2004] 67–95, here 91–92).

[37] There are numerous interpreters who attempt to get around Paul's statement regarding the inclusion of ethnic Israel by spiritualizing it in terms of the Church. This strikes me as an example where theology dictates exegesis (and often results in contortionist

that Paul had felt pressure regarding his relationship to Judaism, and more particularly the "founding" church in Jerusalem. Having just noted that he had had every intention of visiting the church in Rome, that he was coming to them so that they might have mutual benefit, but that he had been delayed and the way had now been cleared, Paul must now once more delay his coming. He explains why this is so in terms of his visit to Jerusalem.

One might be tempted to claim that Paul's inclusion of these details regarding his anticipated visit to Jerusalem in the light of the collection that he had been making in Macedonia and Achaia[38] is simply an attempt to be complete in his narrative and to stave off further criticism of a delay in his coming. This might well be true. However, there is no compelling reason why Paul had to give specific details regarding this delay, when he had not provided such details for his previous delays. Nor does he need to go into the details of the collection, especially since he had not provided an opportunity for the Roman church to be a part of this project that had occupied so much of his time in his previous travels. This might appear to be working contrary to the very idea of mutuality that Paul had promoted at the outset of his letter (1:12). It has been suggested that one of the purposes for the writing of Romans is that Paul was concerned about how he was going to be treated by the Christians in Jerusalem.[39] His fears were warranted, as we see from Acts 21, where Paul appears to have been put in an untenable situation (whether intentionally or inadvertently) by the leaders in Jerusalem, such as James.[40] The purpose of Romans in this analysis is to provide a letter of apology for his behavior with regard

---

eisegetical gymnastics). See the recent, helpful discussion of K. Haacker, *The Theology of Paul's Letter to the Romans* (New Testament Theology; Cambridge: Cambridge University Press, 2003) 77–96.

[38] On the collection, see K. F. Nickle, *Collection: A Study in Paul's Strategy* (London: SCM Press, 1966); D. Georgi, *Remembering the Poor: The History of Paul's Collection for Jerusalem* (Nashville: Abingdon, 1992).

[39] See, e.g., J. Jervell, "The Letter to Jerusalem," in Donfried (ed.), *Romans Debate*, 53–64.

[40] See S. E. Porter, *The Paul of Acts: Essays in Literature, History and Theology* (WUNT 115; Tübingen: Mohr Siebeck, 2000) 179–84. Cf. also W. Schmithals, *Paul and James* (SBT 46; London: SCM Press, 1965) 87–93; A. J. Mattill, Jr., "The Purpose of Acts: Schneckenburger Reconsidered," in W. W. Gasque and R. P. Martin (eds.), *Apostolic History and the Gospel: Biblical and Historical Essays Presented to F. F. Bruce on his 60th Birthday* (Exeter: Paternoster, 1970) 108–22, esp. 115–16; M. Hengel, *Acts and the History of Earliest Christianity* (trans. J. Bowden; London: SCM Press, 1979) 123–24.

to the churches of Asia and Greece. There are numerous problems, however, with the idea that Paul writes an apology to Jerusalem in the east by sending a letter to Rome in the west, including its indirectness and the relative insignificance of the collection to the entire letter.[41]

Another explanation is that there was opposition to Paul and his behavior toward Jerusalem in a number of locations. These places would certainly include Jerusalem, where Paul was seen to be suspicious by the leaders of the church there, to the point of insisting upon his being involved in a temple ritual that played into the hands of Jewish Pauline opponents from Asia. However, we know that Paul had Jewish opponents elsewhere as well. These included opponents in Galatia to be sure, but possibly in other places (that is one of the major discussions regarding Paul's opponents—the nature of the opponents and whether they were Jewish).[42] One of those places may also have been Rome. Paul clearly was not facing the kind of opposition from outside or within the church that he faced in Galatia, but there are several indications that the internal problems of the Roman church regarding Jewish and Gentile factions resulted in tensions that ended up focusing upon Paul. As noted above, the church at Rome was probably primarily Gentile in composition, due to the fact that Jewish Christians were forced to leave Rome under the edict of Claudius. However, with Claudius's death and the probable suspension of that edict, Jewish Christians had returned to the church, now controlled and led by Gentile Christians. There were bound to be problems of two sorts. On the one hand, there would be the inevitable socio-cultural clashes between those who were occupying positions of power and those who were not, those who believed they had the rights to authority and had power and those who believed they had such rights but did not have power, those who had feelings of entitlement and those who believed that they had earned such privilege, and the like.[43] On the other hand, there would be the religious and theological clashes between those who believed that they were from the trunk of the organism and those who were perceived to be the expendable branches, those who believed that their being grafted into the trunk gave them equality and those who

---

[41] See McDonald and Porter, *Early Christianity*, 457.

[42] For a summary of suggestions, see Sumney, *Servants of Satan*, passim; Gunther, *St. Paul's Opponents*, passim.

[43] For a recent discussion of the social context, see P. F. Esler, *Conflict and Identity in Romans: The Social Setting of Paul's Letter* (Minneapolis: Fortress, 2003) esp. 19–39.

believed that the later grafts were always and only grafts, and the like. There were quite probably also problems caused by those who had been in exile picking up comments about Paul from those in other cities. We know that some of those who returned to Rome, such as Prisca and Aquila, were Jews who had been located in other cities of the Mediterranean world. Some of these cities were Pauline church cities, and they may well have picked up some of the controversy that surrounded Paul (since we have seen that there is discussion of Paul's opponents in most, if not virtually all, of the other cities with which he is associated).

We can surmise that the controversy over Jewish right and privilege may have revolved to some extent over at least whether certain Jewish boundary markers were to be maintained or not. These would have included food laws, circumcision and festivals and other special days. We can find reference to and treatment of these in Rom 14:1–15:13.[44] Paul characterizes the one who is weak in faith as one who attends to restrictions in food laws (e.g. 14:3), who celebrates certain holidays (e.g. 14:6), and who uses such distinctive behavior as a means of judging others (e.g. 14:10). It would be easy, in the light of Paul's beliefs as seen here in Romans (e.g. 14:14, 17) and elsewhere, for Paul to have sided with the strong who did not feel compulsion in such areas. Paul recognizes that the arguments are on the side of those who are the strong in faith (15:1), but that there are compelling reasons in the light of what God has done in Christ not to insist upon one's rights but to move one's behavior to a higher plain that does not compel such distinctions (e.g. 14:15–17, 19–20), especially if they might cause a fellow believer in some way to stumble in their walk with God (e.g. 14:21; 15:2). Paul does not concede to the mandates of Judaism, nor does he endorse libertine practices, but he promotes accommodation for the greater mutual good. In terms of the collection, he puts it into the context of those who are financially more fortunate being able to help those who are less fortunate, since the former

---

[44] Those who continue to emphasize this section as central to understanding Romans include: F. Watson, *Paul, Judaism and the Gentiles: A Sociological Approach* (SNTSMS 56; Cambridge: Cambridge University Press, 1986); R. Morgan, *Romans* (New Testament Guides; Sheffield: Sheffield Academic Press, 1996) 63–65; M. D. Nanos, *The Mystery of Romans: The Jewish Context of Paul's Letter* (Minneapolis: Fortress, 1996) esp. 85–165; M. Reasoner, *The Strong and the Weak* (SNTSMS 103; Cambridge: Cambridge University Press, 1999); A. A. Das, *Paul and the Jews* (Library of Pauline Studies; Peabody, MA: Hendrickson, 2003) 49–77; M. J. Gorman, *Apostle of the Crucified Lord* (Grand Rapids: Eerdmans, 2004) 342. The major issue currently revolves around whether the weak were Christian or non-Christian Jews. Despite some arguments to the contrary, I believe that the evidence still points to the weak being Christian Jews.

Gentiles are indebted to the Jews for Jesus who has brought spiritual life (15:26–27). Paul concludes by arguing that there is a mutuality in terms of ministering to both material and spiritual needs.

e. *Romans 15:28–29—Apostolic Appointment Questioned*

One of the constant and recurring criticisms that Paul apparently faced was his status as an apostle. There were those who wished to deny him the position of apostle, and with it apostolic standing and authority, since he had not actually been one of the original twelve disciples or functioned in the personal circle of Jesus' associates. In various places, this controversy erupted to the point of becoming a significant point in Paul's dealings with various churches, such as the Corinthian church as seen in 2 Corinthians 3–4. At numerous places in his letters, Paul reminds his readers that, although he was not an apostle in the same way as the original twelve, he did have apostolic credentials. His message was not humanly derived (e.g. Gal 1:11–12) but he was in the line of those who had received the entrusted traditions regarding Jesus Christ (e.g. 1 Cor 15:1).

Paul saw himself as the apostle to the Gentiles (Rom 11:13; 1:1).[45] He begins his letter to the Romans with this direct claim, labeling himself as a "called apostle" (1:1).[46] In the course of his argument regarding a future for Israel, he addresses the Gentiles as one who is their apostle (11:13). Thus, when he took the collection to Jerusalem and presented it to the church there, he saw that as his apostolic task on behalf of the Gentile believers, as part of their reciprocal spiritual and material obligations. He states that when he has finished making this presentation in Jerusalem and has put his seal on this fruit, then, in the course of going to Spain, he will come to the Roman church "in the fulness of the blessing of Christ" (15:29). We noted above that there is some scholarly discussion regarding the apostolic foundation of the church at Rome and that it is unclear what such an apostolic foundation would have added to what the church already had. Rather than the question of apostolic status rest-

---

[45] See D. J.-S. Chae, *Paul as Apostle to the Gentiles: His Apostolic Self-Awareness and its Influence on the Soteriological Argument in Romans* (Paternoster Biblical and Theological Monographs; Carlisle: Paternoster, 1997) esp. 21–37. Cf. L. J. Lietaert Peerbolte, *Paul the Missionary* (Leuven: Peeters, 2003) 177–201.

[46] This is found elsewhere in Paul's letters, including: 1 Cor 1:1; 2 Cor 1:1; Gal 1:1; Eph 1:1; Col 1:1; 1 Tim 1:1; 2 Tim 1:1; Titus 1:1.

ing with the church itself, it appears that there may have been a question in the Roman church regarding the status of Paul as apostle. This would have been consonant with such questioning elsewhere, but Paul's diffusing of the issue takes place in his claim to be continuing the task begun with the collection in his coming to Rome. The taking of the collection to Jerusalem is an event at which, as apostle of the Gentiles, Paul can put his seal on the transaction. This event, he says, is a necessary step that precedes his further travels from the east, in which his ministry is complete, to new destinations in the west. As he heads west, he continues to carry the fullness of the blessing of Christ on his work as he comes to Rome as a necessary stopping off point on his way to Spain.

3. Conclusion

There have been good reasons for scholars discerning Paul's opponents to resist undertaking the kind of detailed examination of Romans as they have of others of Paul's letters. As far as clear and manifestly hostile comments in Romans are concerned, Paul does not cite them nor does he seem to reflect them back. This may have been because of the nature of his circumstances with regard to the Roman church. It was a church with which he had had less contact than with many other churches—if for no other reason than it may have been difficult for him to gauge the level of antagonism that was present in the church at Rome. This brings us back to the question of what constitutes opposition and opponents. Even though the level of antagonism is not as great or explicit as it is in other letters, this does not mean that there were not those within the church at Rome who had questions regarding Paul. As discussed above, many of these issues may have been directly or indirectly related to the ethnic situation in Rome at the time, and how Paul would have been perceived as relating to each side in this dispute. There is the further matter, however, that Paul had traveled extensively in the Mediterreanean world, including Asia and Greece. He had admittedly had conflict with a number of his churches, or at least with significant factions within these groups, as well as with outside groups that had attempted with varying degrees of success to infiltrate the Christian communities in these cities. There had also been communication between some of these cities and Rome, and between some of these people and Paul. Paul appears to have had a number of items brought to his attention that he addresses in the letter. One of the major factors to note, however, is that Paul has not placed such disputes at the heart of the letter. In that sense, it is justifiable to recognize that the level of conflict that Paul has with antagonists in Rome is much less than it is in other cities. However, the alterations that we noted above in the thanksgiving portion of the letter, and the fact that Paul returns to a number of these issues at the end of the letter, do indicate that Paul was at least aware that there were some tensions in the Roman church that were specifically related to him. They do not appear to have been new issues that he had not confronted already (or would not confront again in some instances), but they appear to have been present strongly enough for him to respond to them. He addresses them in a measured yet direct way to help to ensure that his plans to visit the church in Rome would be at least as conducive to the promotion of his evangelistic purposes as they might be.

THE OPPONENTS AT COLOSSAE[1]

CHRISTIAN STETTLER
University of Zürich
Zürich, Switzerland

1. INTRODUCTORY REMARKS

Colossians is included in this collection of essays about Paul's opponents because in recent years there has been a growing tendency to regard it as possible or even probable that Colossians was written by Paul himself, or at least in Paul's lifetime and on behalf of Paul by a secretary (cf. 1:1 and 4:18) whose theology was very close to Paul's.[2] Therefore in this article Pauline authorship in the wider sense (by Paul or a secretary) is assumed, although I am conscious that a careful balancing of the arguments for and against Pauline authorship leads some to a different conclusion.[3] The arguments in this article remain valid if one assumes that

---

[1] The following article is based on a chapter in my book *Der Kolosserhymnus: Untersuchungen zu Form, traditionsgeschichtlichem Hintergrund und Aussage von Kol 1,15–20* (WUNT 2.131; Tübingen: Mohr Siebeck, 2000). For this English version the article has been considerably revised and updated.

[2] So for example E. Schweizer, *Der Brief an die Kolosser* (EKKNT; Zürich: Benziger and Neukirchen-Vluyn: Neukirchener, 1976) 27; W.-H. Ollrog, *Paulus und seine Mitarbeiter: Untersuchungen zu Theorie und Praxis der paulinischen Mission* (WMANT 50; Neukirchen-Vluyn: Neukirchener, 1979) 219–32; G. E. Cannon, *The Use of Traditional Materials in Colossians* (Macon, GA: Mercer University Press, 1983); J. D. G. Dunn, *The Epistles to the Colossians and to Philemon* (NIGTC; Grand Rapids: Eerdmans, 1996) 19, 38–39; J. N. Aletti, *Saint Paul, Épître aux Colossiens* (EB NS 20; Paris: Gabalda, 1993). Most German-speaking scholars still follow W. Bujard, *Stilanalytische Untersuchungen zum Kolosserbrief als Beitrag zur Methodik von Sprachvergleichen* (SUNT 11; Göttingen: Vandenhoeck & Ruprecht, 1973), despite its methodological problems (on the latter see especially K. J. Neumann, *The Authenticity of the Pauline Epistles in the Light of Stylostatistical Analysis* [SBLDS 120; Atlanta: Scholars Press, 1990] 10–13 and on statistics and style H. W. Hoehner, *Ephesians: An Exegetical Commentary* [Grand Rapids: Baker, 2004] 24–29).

[3] So with different results Marshall in I. H. Marshall, S. Travis and I. Paul, *Exploring the New Testament. Vol. 2: The Letters and Revelation* (London: SPCK, 2002) 159–60 (slight tendency in favour of Pauline authorship in the wider sense), and R. E. Brown, *An Introduction to the New Testament* (ABRL; New York: Doubleday, 1999) 610–17 (slight tendency against Pauline authorship).

Colossians was written after Paul's death, but still reflects a real situation.[4]

Scholarship is still far from a consensus about the character of the Colossian "heresy".[5] Most scholars assume that Colossians aims at a distinct group of heretics.[6] Their identity is defined in very different ways. Already in 1973, J. J. Gunther listed 44 different suggestions.[7] In the meantime, their number has increased considerably. Examples are: a syncretistic, gnostic group which combines an ascetic veneration of the elements, Jewish ritualism and Jewish speculation about angels;[8] Pytha-

---

[4] For Standhartinger, who assumes pseudo-pauline authorship, the situation addressed in the letter does not reflect the situation at Colossae at the time of writing, but a fictitious and typical situation, namely the "frustration and pessimism" which result from criticism from within the church and from non-Christians who "do not understand the worship practice of the church and therefore condemn it". Colossians aims at countering this by its "optimistic view of reality"; it seeks in the form of a "testament" to warn against possible future opponents, leaving by its imprecise language many options for identifying these opponents (A. Standhartinger, *Studien zur Entstehungsgeschichte und Intention des Kolosserbriefs* [NovTSup 94; Leiden: E. J. Brill, 1999] 193, 190, 194, 284). However, Daniel Harrington is certainly right in saying that "the situation presupposed by the letter seems real, not fictive", although he thinks Colossians to be written by "an admirer or student of Paul" ("Christians and Jews in Colossians," in J. A. Overman and R. S. MacLennan [eds.], *Diaspora Jews and Judaism: Essays in Honor of, and in Dialogue with, A. T. Kraabel* [South Florida Studies in the History of Judaism 41; Atlanta: Scholars Press, 1992] 153–61 here 154). And, as we shall see, much more can be said about the opponents in Colossians than is suggested by Standhartinger.

[5] See the the summaries in C. A. Evans, "The Colossian Mystics," *Bib* 63 (1982): 188–205 here 189–94 (until 1982); T. J. Sappington, *Revelation and Redemption at Colossae* (JSNTSup 53; Sheffield: JSOT Press, 1991) 15–19 (until 1991); C. E. Arnold, *The Colossian Syncretism* (WUNT 2.77; Tübingen: Mohr Siebeck, 1995) 1–3 (until 1995); Dunn, *Colossians*, 27–33 (until 1996); Standhartinger, *Studien*, 16–27 (until 1998); R. M. Royalty, "Dwelling on Visions: On the Nature of the So-Called 'Colossian Heresy,'" *Bib* 83 (2002): 329–57 here 329–30 (until 2002).

[6] So already J. B. Lightfoot, *Saint Paul's Epistles to the Colossians and to Philemon: A Revised Text with Introductions, Notes, and Dissertations* (9th ed.; London: Macmillan, 1890) 71–73.

[7] J. J. Gunther, *St. Paul's Opponents and Their Background* (NovTSup 35; Leiden: E. J. Brill, 1973) 3–4.

[8] Thus W. G. Kümmel, *Einleitung in das Neue Testament* (21st ed.; Heidelberg: Quelle & Meyer, 1983) 297. Christian Maurer ("Die Begründung der Herrschaft Christi über die Mächte nach Col 1,15–20," *WD* NS 4 [1955]: 79–93) even assumes a cult with pagan, Jewish, Christian and Gnostic influences and elements of the mystery cults! Cf. more recently H. W. Attridge, "On Becoming an Angel: Rival Baptismal Theologies at Colossae," in L. Bormann, K. del Tredici and A. Standhartinger (eds.), *Religious Propaganda and Missionary Competition in the New Testament World: Essays Honoring Dieter Georgi* (Leiden: E. J. Brill, 1994) 481–98 (a proto-gnosticism close to the Nag Hammadi tractate *Zostrianos*); R. Gebauer, "Der Kolosserbrief als Antwort auf die Herausforderung des Synkretismus," in R. Gebauer and M. Meiser (eds.), *Die bleibende Gegenwart des Evangeliums: Festschrift für Otto Merk* (MTS 76; Marburg: Elwert,

gorean philosophy;[9] the propagation of double membership in church and mystery associations;[10] a group close to the Essenes;[11] Jewish mystics;[12] or even John, the author of Revelation, and his apocalyptic circle.[13] For A. Thomas Kraabel,[14] Johannes Lähnemann,[15] and more recently Clinton E. Arnold, the background of the "heresy" is the syncretism of Lydia and Phrygia. According to Arnold, Jewish and Gentile Christians retained parts of their old beliefs alongside their new faith: fears and practices which included belief in many mediators between God and humans (called ἄγγελοι by the Jews); the invocation of these mediators for protection and help; ecstatic practices, partly including asceticism; and a strong belief in evil powers.[16] Lately Richard E. DeMaris identified the Colossian "philosophy" as Middle Platonism (with Jewish elements),[17]

2003). M. Goulder opts for a kind of proto-gnosticism which is no syncretism, but "a straightforward development of Jewish Christianity" and similar to the later Barbelo gnosticism ("Colossians and Barbelo," *NTS* 41 [1995]: 601–19).

[9] Schweizer, *Kolosser*, 100–104.

[10] Thus P. Vielhauer, *Geschichte der urchristlichen Literatur. Einleitung in das Neue Testament, die Apokryphen und die Apostolischen Väter* (Berlin and New York: De Gruyter, 1975) 194–95.

[11] For example Lightfoot, *Colossians* 88ff.; D. Guthrie, *New Testament Introduction* (4th ed.; Downers Grove, IL, and Leicester: InterVarsity Press, 1990) 550. Cf. more cautiously Harrington, "Christians," (159–)160: "in the Qumran scrolls and Colossians we have the Hebrew and Greek versions of a theological language that had developed among first-century Jews".

[12] So F. O. Francis, "Humility and Angel Worship in Col 2:18," and "The Background of Embateuein (Col 2:18) in Legal Papyri and Oracle Inscriptions," both in F. O. Francis and W. A. Meeks (eds.), *Conflict at Colossae: A Problem in the Interpretation of Early Christianity Illustrated by Selected Modern Studies* (SBLSBS 4; 2nd ed.; Missoula, MT: Scholars Press, 1975) 176–81 and 197–207; more recently Sappington, *Revelation* and J. H. Roberts, "Jewish Mystical Experience in the Early Christian Era as Background to Understanding Colossians," *Neot* 32 (1998): 161–89.

[13] Royalty, "Dwelling."

[14] A. T. Kraabel, "Judaism in Western Asia Minor Under the Roman Empire" (unpublished Ph.D. dissertation, Harvard University, 1968) 139–54.

[15] J. Lähnemann, *Der Kolosserbrief: Komposition, Situation und Argumentation* (SNT 3; Gütersloh: Mohn, 1971) 82–100.

[16] So Arnold, *Syncretism* (summary at 310–12). Cf. 269: "The purveyors of 'the philosophy' are offering a new means of appeasing the powers—through a unique mixture of their Christianity, Jewish and local Phrygian ascetic practices, mystery inititation concepts, visionary experience, and through invoking helpful angels." For Arnold, "the root question filling the minds of some of the Colossians" is: "do we need extra protection from the hostile 'powers' in addition to our faith in and union with Christ?" (p. 270).

[17] R. E. DeMaris, *The Colossian Controversy: Wisdom and Dispute at Colossae* (JSNTSup 96; Sheffield: JSOT Press, 1994) esp. 131–33: the opponents are neither Jews nor Proselytes, but they have a "Jewish orientation" and are "at some level" connected to the synagoge in Colossae; in addition, their language of "humility" shows "a Christian component" (p. 132).

while Troy W. Martin identified it as the Cynic philosophy.[18] For H. Van Broekhoven, the debate is not at all about a (conceptual) threat from inside or outside, but about different *social* profiles.[19] In recent years there has also been an increasing number of scholars who identify the opponents simply as the Jewish synagogue(s) at Colossae.[20]

What characterizes many of these attempts is either very imprecise language concerning the concrete religious phenomena (which is due to the kind of syncretism proposed, often without historical analogies being presented for it)[21] and/or a lack of methodology concerning the way in which allusions to the opponents in the letter to the Colossians are identified.[22]

This article seeks to avoid both pitfalls by a clearly defined methodology and by using only known historical phenomena as analogies. The outcome of the study largely depends on which passages of Colossians one takes to refer to the opponents. It is only from *explicit statements* about the opponents that we can gain certainty about their identity. Only on this basis we can identify indirect *allusions* to the opponents.[23] Sappington rightly points out that

---

[18] T. W. Martin, *By Philosophy and Empty Deceit: Colossians as Response to a Cynic Critique* (JSNTSup 118; Sheffield: Sheffield Academic Press, 1996).

[19] H. van Broekhoven, "The Social Profiles in the Colossian Debate," *JSNT* 66 (1997): 73–90.

[20] N. T. Wright, "Poetry and Theology in Colossians 1.15–20," *NTS* 36 (1990): 444–68 here 463–64; idem, *The Epistles of Paul to the Colossians and to Philemon* (TNTC 12; Grand Rapids: Eerdmans, 1986) 23–30; Dunn, *Colossians*, 33–35; W. Schenk, "Der Kolosserbrief in der neueren Forschung (1945–1985)," *ANRW* II 25,4 (Berlin: De Gruyter, 1987) 3327–64 here 3349–54; Harrington, "Christians."

[21] An exception is Arnold who identifies concrete Phrygian and Lydian beliefs and practices of the time.

[22] A recent example for jumping on seeming parallels without analysing the statements of Colossians first is Royalty, "Dwelling."

[23] J. L. Sumney, "Those Who 'Pass Judgment': The Identity of the Opponents in Colossians," *Bib* 74 (1993): 366–88 here 367 (emphasis mine); cf. 366–67. Sumney distinguishes between allusions and affirmations. I will not maintain this distinction since in terms of methodology there is no distinction between the two; both can only be determined as referring to the opponents by comparing them to the explicit statements. Cf. further J. L. Sumney, *Identifying Paul's Opponents: The Question of Method in 2 Corinthians* (JSNTSup 40; Sheffield: JSOT Press, 1990) 75–120; K. Berger, "Die impliziten Gegner: Zur Methode des Erschliessens von 'Gegnern' in neutestamentlichen Texten," in D. Lührmann and G. Strecker (eds.), *Kirche: Festschrift für Günther Bornkamm zum 75. Geburtstag* (Tübingen: Mohr Siebeck, 1980) 373–400 esp. 373–78; further M. Wolter, *Der Brief an die Kolosser. Der Brief an Philemon* (ÖTK 12; Gütersloh: Mohn, 1993) 156; DeMaris, *Controversy*, 41–45; Arnold, *Syncretism*, 4.

It is, of course, possible that teachings affirmed within the more expositional passages are also largely antithetical to the system of belief advocated by the errorists, and this is frequently assumed by many scholars. Yet one must also allow that relationships could be more subtle—that, for example, an exposition could simply contain teachings that are, at least in the mind of Paul, incompatible with the beliefs and practices of the errorists.[24]

To what extent this is the case can only be determined with any certainty from the explicit statements.

Second, we need to address an issue which considerably narrows down the possibilities of identification, namely the question if the letter addresses a group ("heresy") within the church or a threat from without.

Finally, we have to avoid a further mistake which many have made in that they press all explicit statements so that they fit one single religious phenomenon. Rather, we have to consider each statement individually, leaving open the possibility that the church at Colossae was under threat from more than one side. For this it is essential to pay attention to the structure of Colossians. Regarding this, I will largely follow the grammatical analysis of Col 1:3–3:4 by Léonard Ramaroson[25] and the rhetorical analysis of the argument of Colossians by Jerry L. Sumney,[26] which, although conducted independently, largely agree. 1:20–23 is the "basic thesis" of the letter, foreshadowed in 1:12–14 and restated in 2:6–7 and 3:1, "showing that the primary concern is to assure the readers of their salvation/reconciliation/forgiveness by holding to the teaching they had already received".[27] The first explicit warning (2:4) is found in the section 1:24–2:5, which recommends Paul as the one who in contrast to the deceivers teaches godly wisdom.[28] The next section is 2:6–19. It is opened by 2:6–7, a positive confirmation of the "basic thesis" of the letter. This is followed by three explicit warnings, each concluded by a positive statement about Christ and his work (8 with 9–15; 16–17a with 17b; 18 with 19).[29] 2:20–3:4 forms the next section. 2:20–23 is parallel to 2:16–19 in several respects: both passages "give a list of the opponents'

---

[24] Sappington, *Revelation*, 144.
[25] L. Ramaroson, "Structure de Col 1,3–3,4," *ScE* 29 (1977): 313–19 here 317–19.
[26] J. L. Sumney, "The Argument of Colossians," in A. Eriksson, T. H. Olbricht and W. Übelacker (eds.), *Rhetorical Argumentation in Biblical Texts: Essays from the Lund 2000 Conference* (Harrisburg, PA: Trinity Press International, 2002) 339–52 here 342–52.
[27] Sumney, "Argument," 344.
[28] Sumney, "Argument," 346.
[29] Verses 16–17 and 18–19 are two different arguments against the opponents; both appear to be conclusions from vv. 9–15 (see Sumney, "Argument," 349).

regulations (vv. 16, 21) and of what they attain (vv. 18, 23), in both the regulations and the attainments are rejected, and both distinguish between appearance and reality (vv. 17, 23)."[30] The opponents' teaching is contrasted to the new reality of the addressees: they have died with Christ and are dead to the world (2:20); they have risen with Christ and live according to that which is above (3:1–2); therefore they are both dead and alive (3:3), and their life will be revealed at Christ's coming (3:4). 3:1–4 connects the preceding and following parts: it is "the counterpart of 2:20–23" and at the same time introduces the exhortations of 3:5ff. which exemplify what it means to "seek the things that are above".[31] Whereas 2:4 introduces Paul's warnings in a general way, 2:20–3:4 summarizes his warnings and exhortations (at least 2:16 and 18, maybe also 2:8) by referring to the theme of dying and rising with Christ.

2. Heresy in the Church or Threat from Outside?

In 1973 Morna D. Hooker argued convincingly that contrary to most reconstructions of a Colossian "heresy", Colossians does not oppose a group within the Colossian church (with a specific heresy).[32] Paul praises the faith and love of the Colossian Christians without reservations (1:3–8; 2:5). He would not do so if some of the Christians had fallen away from the gospel as it had been preached to them.[33] Nowhere in his letter does Paul speak of such an apostasy, nor of any dissent between himself and the Colossian Christians. The only passage that could be interpreted in such a way is τί . . . δογματίζεσθε in 2:20. It can be translated "Why *do* you subject yourselves to regulations?", meaning that the Christians had

---

[30] Sumney, "Argument," 349 n. 62.

[31] See Sumney, "Argument," 350. Sumney rightly stresses that "the argument of Colossians does not stop at 2:23 . . . Rather, the instructions of 3:1 and following are an important part of the argument for his [i.e. the author's] understanding of what it means to be 'in Christ'" (352).

[32] On the following, see M. D. Hooker, "Were there False Teachers in Colossae?" in B. Lindars and S. Smalley (eds.), *Christ and Spirit in the New Testament: In Honour of C. F. D. Moule* (Cambridge: Cambridge University Press, 1973) 315–31 (reprinted in *idem, From Adam to Christ: Essays on Paul* [Cambridge: Cambridge University Press, 1990] 121–36). Hooker was followed e.g. by Wright, *Colossians*, 27; Dunn, *Colossians*, 26; Roberts, "Experience," 169.

[33] Thus already T. Zahn, *Grundriss der Einleitung in das Neue Testament* (Leipzig: Deichert, 1928) 40; E. Percy, *Die Probleme der Kolosser- und Epheserbriefe* (SHVL 39; Lund: Gleerup, 1946) 44.

already begun to submit to them. But it is also possible to translate "Why subject yourselves to regulations?" (cf. 1 Cor 10:30).[34] This is much more probable from the context.

The fact that there were no apostates or heretics within the church is the reason for the very different kind of argumentation compared to the harshness and personal directness and the extensive arguments in, for example, the letters to the Corinthians and Galatians.[35] Of course this does not mean that the church in Colossae was not really in danger so that Paul did not need to warn it[36]—on the contrary, he *did* warn it with his usual sharpness (see 2:4, 8, 17–19, 20, 21–22). But his attack falls on people from *outside* (2:4 etc.). The attack on these deceivers is hard: they not only tried to convince the church by plausible arguments (2:4, 8), they also "judged", i.e. condemned, the Christians (2:16) and denied their heavenly "prize", i.e. the reality of their salvation (2:18). In spite of these attacks the Christians had not yet left the foundation of the gospel, but were in danger of doing so. Therefore Paul sought to confirm this foundation by means of his letter, reminding the Christians of all the privileges they had received in Christ (cf. 1:12–23; 2:2–3, 6–7, 9–15, 17, 19; 3:1–4, etc.). This is why positive, didactic statements by far outweigh negative polemic in Colossians.

3. Explicit Statements about the Opponents

The warnings of 2:8, 16–17a, 18 differ from the introductory and concluding statements in 2:4 and 2:20–3:4 in that they address specific dangers which the Colossian Christians encounter. Whether they speak of three different dangers or of one and the same, we can only decide after a careful analysis of each of these three passages.

---

[34] Hooker, "False Teachers," 317–18. E. Haupt, *Die Gefangenschaftsbriefe* (KEK 8/9; 7th and 8th eds.; Göttingen: Vandenhoeck & Ruprecht, 1902) 111, translates as passive voice: "Why are regulations being imposed on you?", instead of middle voice: "Why do you let them impose regulations on you?" (In this article I will often refer to Haupt's commentary because its grammatical analysis is unsurpassed in many respects.)
[35] Hooker, "False Teachers," 316.
[36] Hooker, "False Teachers," 326.

a. *Colossians 2:4*

2:4, the first warning, is short and general: "so that no one may deceive you with plausible arguments".[37] In order to prevent that deception, Paul has referred to the "treasures" which are hidden in Christ (v. 3). τοῦτο (v. 4) refers back to this.[38] That which Paul aims to attain by the positive statement of v. 3 is expressed in the form of exhortation in vv. 6–7: he strengthens the Colossian Christians so that they continue to walk in Jesus as they got to know him through the teaching they had received.

b. *Colossians 2:8*

2:8 warns against the impressive wisdom of "the philosophy and empty deceit". The norm and source (κατά c. acc.[39]) of these teachings are "the human tradition"[40] and "the elements of the world". They stand in contrast to the norm and source of Christian teaching, namely the "Messiah". Therefore, the "elements of the world" are something which is parallel to the "human tradition", but contrasts the Messiah Jesus. It follows that "elements of the world" is a phrase that qualifies the teaching of the opponents in a negative way.[41] The expression cannot be a catchword of the opponents which Paul cites here, as is often assumed,[42] and it is very unlikely that it has something to do with the "angels" of v. 18.[43]

In the New Testament, φιλοσοφία ("philosophy") is found only here.[44] In the Septuagint, "the philosophers" denotes the magical priests (*asha-*

---

[37] This verse reflects the language of hellenistic polemic against philosophers, particularly sophists (see Standhartinger, *Studien*, 182).

[38] Haupt, *Kolosser*, 69.

[39] See Haupt, *Kolosser*, 76; P. Ewald, *Die Briefe des Paulus an die Epheser, Kolosser und Philemon* (KNT 10; 2nd ed.; Leipzig: Deichert, 1910) 363; W. Bauer, *A Greek-English Lexicon of the New Testament and Other Early Christian Literature* (trans. W. F. Arndt, F. W. Gingrich and F. W. Danker; Chicago: University of Chicago Press, 1979) 407.

[40] Literally: "the tradition of humans". The article is generic, thus denotes the "tradition of *humankind*" (or "*human* tradition") in contrast to true wisdom which is hidden in Christ (cf. v. 3). See E. G. Hoffmann and H. von Siebenthal, *Griechische Grammatik zum Neuen Testament* (2nd ed.; Riehen: Immanuel, 1990) 177–78 (§ 131b); Ewald, *Kolosser*, 364.

[41] So already Ewald, *Kolosser*, 364; Percy, *Probleme*, 167; G. Delling, "στοιχέω κ.τ.λ.," *TDNT* 7 (1971): 666–87 here 685–86; more recently, Sumney, "Identity," 374; Sappington, *Revelation*, 169. There will be more to say about the "elements of the world" in connection with v. 20 below.

[42] *Contra*, e.g., DeMaris, *Controversy*, 52–56; Arnold, *Syncretism*, 193–94.

[43] So also Sumney, "Identity," 377. See also below on v. 20.

[44] φιλόσοφοι is found in Acts 17:18.

phim) in the Babylonian court (Dan 1:20).[45] In Rabbinic Judaism, "philosopher" is used for members of Gentile philosophical schools or for Gentile orators and advisers of kings. In Rabbinic writings, many disputes between rabbis and "philosophers" are presented. They are typical, but might reflect the fact that similar disputes did actually take place.[46] The aim of these disputes is to show the superiority of the Jewish teaching over against hellenistic philosophy.[47] It follows that in rabbinic Judaism "philosophy" is something inferior to Judaism, even opposed to it. The term is never used by Rabbinic writings to denote Judaism itself.[48] More hellenized Jews, however, could call Judaism a "philosophy" and "philosophic" for apologetic reasons (see 4 Macc 5:22; Arist. 30–31).[49] Josephus calls the different Jewish parties "philosophical schools" (φιλοσοφίαι), Jewish education "philosophizing", and even the teachings of Scripture "philosophies".[50] For Philo, Judaism is the highest form of "philosophy".[51] However, as far as we can see, neither apocalyptic Jewish groups nor first-century Christians ever used "philosophy" as a self-designation, although they claimed to have special access to divine *sophia* (cf. 1 Cor 2:6).[52] Christians accepted the hellenistic-Jewish self-designation "philosophy" comparatively late, not before the time of Trajan and Hadrian, when Christianity entered wider and more educated circles.[53] It is therefore not probable that "philosophy" in Col 2:8 designates a (Jewish-) *Christian* group.

In principle, both Jewish usages of "philosophy" are possible for Col 2:8, i.e. "philosophy" as a designation of Gentile hellenistic philosophy, or as a propagandist self-designation of a Jewish group. Now in Col 2:8 "empty deceit" and "philosophy" are seen as a unity as is shown by the

---

[45] O. Michel, "φιλοσοφία, φιλόσοφος," *TDNT* 9 (1974): 172–88 here 179–80. In hellenistic usage, σοφισταί and φιλόσοφοι can denote enchanters and magicians. It is also possible that in Dan 1:20 we find a hellenization in content: then the two terms are to be understood as "teacher" and "researcher" according to hellenistic educational tradition (see ibid. n. 75).

[46] Michel, "φιλοσοφία, φιλόσοφος," 184.

[47] Michel, "φιλοσοφία, φιλόσοφος," 184.

[48] Michel, "φιλοσοφία, φιλόσοφος," 184.

[49] Michel, "φιλοσοφία, φιλόσοφος," 180–81.

[50] See the references in Michel, "φιλοσοφία, φιλόσοφος," 182–84.

[51] See Michel, "φιλοσοφία, φιλόσοφος," 181–82.

[52] Michel, "φιλοσοφία, φιλόσοφος," 187.

[53] M. Hengel and A.-M. Schwemer, *Paulus zwischen Damaskus und Antiochien: Die unbekannten Jahre des Apostels* (WUNT 108; Tübingen: Mohr Siebeck, 1998) 128 n. 531.

absence of the second article.⁵⁴ This leaves two possible interpretations. Syntactically the more straightforward one would be to understand the two terms as *identified*, i.e. shown to be synonyms, by the non-repetition of the article. In this case "philosophy" in itself would have a negative connotation as in Rabbinic writings and could even be translated by something like "would-be wisdom",⁵⁵ with "empty deceit" merely restating this negative connotation. Then of course "philosophy" would not refer to a self-designation of the opponents but only express Paul's negative assessment. The second possibility is that here "philosophy" in itself has a positive or at least neutral meaning, but is qualified negatively in a second step by the apposition of "empty deceit".⁵⁶ In this case "philosophy" could be a self-description of the opponents, either Gentiles⁵⁷ or Jews, and we could translate: "the seemingly positive philosophy which is in truth only empty deceit" (cf. similarly *Diogn.* 8.2). As we shall see below, Col 2:23 (the opponents' practices and teachings have an "appearance of wisdom") and the mention of circumcision in the passage directly following 2:8 point to the self-designation of a Jewish group.

Following this first specific warning, Paul praises Christ and his work in the church, using non-philosophical, biblical language (vv. 9–15).⁵⁸ The aim of these verses is to pause for a moment in the midst of polemic and to make clear once more the foundation on which Paul's argument is built.⁵⁹

---

⁵⁴ See Hoffmann and von Siebenthal, *Grammatik*, 178 (§ 131c). Similar to v. 4, this verse employs the language of hellenistic polemic against philosophers (see Standhartinger, *Studien*, 182–83).

⁵⁵ See H. G. Liddell and R. Scott, *A Greek-English Lexicon* (rev. ed.; Oxford: Clarendon Press, 1996) 1939 (φιλοσοφέω I.1.b); H. Menge, *Langenscheidts Grosswörterbuch der griechischen und deutschen Sprache. 1. Teil: Griechisch—Deutsch. Unter besonderer Berücksichtigung der Etymologie* (2nd ed.; Berlin: Langenscheidt, 1913) (= 20th ed. 1967) 730 (φιλόσοφος 2).

⁵⁶ In this case, καί is used as καί *epexegeticum* or *explicativum*, meaning "that is" (Hoffmann and von Siebenthal, *Grammatik*, 444, § 252:29).

⁵⁷ This is the view of R. E. DeMaris and T. W. Martin who start from "philosophy" as a self-designation of Gentile philosophers and try to fit in all the other statements about the opponents, clearly doing violence to the texts in many respects.

⁵⁸ "Through the expression 'in him,' which appears seven times in 2:6–15, the author ties his assertions about Christ to those about Christians. The assertion that Christians are 'in Christ,' and the exposition of the meaning of that assertion, are central argumentative goals of verses 6–15. At 2:11–15 the focus turns to the effects of the Colossians' conversion and the acts of God and Christ that made those things possible" (Sumney, "Argument," 347).

⁵⁹ C. Burger, *Schöpfung und Versöhnung: Studien zum liturgischen Gut im Kolosser- und Epheserbrief* (WMANT 46; Neukirchen-Vluyn: Neukirchener, 1975) 80.

c. *Colossians 2:16–17a*

Verses 16–17a turn to criticism levelled against the Colossian church "in matters of eating or[60] drinking or in matters of festival or new moon or sabbath". The Colossian Christians are under pressure to comply with regulations concerning food and festivals. The triad "festivals, new moons and sabbaths" often occurs in the Septuagint and denotes the festivals prescribed by the Torah (Hos 2:13; Ezek 45:17; 1 Chr 23:31; 2 Chr 2:3; 31:3; cf. Isa 1:13–14; Amos 8:5).[61] The same triad, together with other terms, is found in *Jub.* 1:14: "They will forget all of my laws and all of my commandments and all of my judgments, and they will err concerning *new moons, sabbaths, festivals*, jubilees, and ordinances."[62] Here the festivals are clearly *pars pro toto* of the whole law. It follows that the regulations mentioned in Col 2:16 are those of the Torah of Moses.[63] It has been said that the mention of the new moons rules out Essene influence on the opponents.[64] This is not the case; as we shall see, such an influence is improbable for different reasons. Of course the Essenes, also those in Qumran, kept all the festivals prescribed by the Torah.[65] In Ezek 46:4, 6 and the priestly text Num 28:9–15, the festival of the new moon is even more important than the sabbath.[66]

It goes without saying that in the Torah prescriptions about "eating" occupy a prominent place, especially in the purity laws. However,

---

[60] The most reliable "Alexandrian" manuscripts (ℵ, A) have ἤ, not καί as the Nestle-Aland edition.

[61] Cf. DeMaris, *Controversy*, 56; Arnold, *Syncretism*, 215; Sappington, *Revelation*, 163.

[62] Translation: *OTP*.

[63] So e.g. Wright, "Poetry," 463–64. Therefore it is difficult to understand how DeMaris can say that "there is no obvious polemic concerning the Law in Colossians" (*Controversy*, 51).

[64] Thus W. Wink, *Naming the Powers: The Language of Power in the New Testament* (Philadelphia: Fortress, 1984) 80 n. 91; F. F. Bruce, *The Epistles to the Colossians, to Philemon and to the Ephesians* (NICNT; Grand Rapids: Eerdmans, 1984) 115 n. 103.

[65] See E. Schürer, *The History of the Jewish People in the Age of Jesus Christ (175 B.C.–A.D. 135)* (3 vols.; revised new ed. by G. Vermes, F. Millar und M. Black; Edinburgh: T. & T. Clark, 1973–1987) 2:582 and the calender fragments 4QMishmarot in which the new moons are mentioned.

[66] On the history of the new moon festival until New Testament times see D. Fiebig (ed.), *Rosch ha-Schana* (= G. Beer and O. Holtzmann [eds.], *Die Mischna Vol. 2:8*) (Gießen: Töpelmann, 1914) 15–25. Also in Josephus, Philo, Samaritan and tannaitic writings the new moon is mentioned as a festival (see ibid. 20–25). For Fiebig, Col 2:16 is proof of the fact that the new moon festival was still kept in New Testament times (ibid. 72).

"drinking" in Col 2:16 does not seem to fit this explanation since in the Pentateuch there are no general prescriptions about drinking. But in the late Old Testament period such regulations were formulated because of intensified contact with the Gentile world. Daniel 1:8–16 is an example of this.[67] In Rabbinic Judaism it was strictly forbidden to drink wine produced by Gentiles.[68] A close parallel to Col 2:16 is Rom 14:1–23, where Paul speaks similarly about keeping regulations concerning food (vv. 2–3, 6, 14–17, 20–21, 23), drink (vv. 17, 21) and festivals (vv. 5–6). According to Rom 14:21 the dispute is about eating meat and drinking wine which had been consecrated to idols (the wine by means of libation).[69] So it is mainly the issue of defilement by idolatry rather than other issues of purity which is at stake.[70] It is most natural to assume that the same questions are referred to in Col 2:16, too. It is not necessary to recur to other religious phenomena, e.g. Nasirean customs (according to Num 6:3–4 Nasireans had to abstain from wine, cf. Matt 11:18[71]), or the special priestly regulation in Lev 10:9–10, or the "pure" drink at Qumran (cf. 1QS 6:20; 7:20; 4Q284a frg. 1; 11Q19 47:7; 49:7ff.),[72] or encratism (cf. 1 Tim 4:3; Philo, *Contempl.* 37; and the apocryphal Acts of the Apostles)[73] or other ascetic practices (after the destruction of the Temple some Jews abstained from meat and wine because the *tamid* and drink offerings could no longer be presented[74]).[75] The Jewish groups which did

---

[67] See further J. D. G. Dunn, "The Colossian Philosophy: A Confident Jewish Apologia," *Bib* 76 (1995): 153–81 here 163.

[68] See P. Billerbeck and H. Strack, *Kommentar zum Neuen Testament aus Talmud und Midrasch* (6 vols.; Munich: Beck, 1922–28 and 1956–61) 4/1:366ff.

[69] See P. Stuhlmacher, *Paul's Letter to the Romans: A Commentary* (trans. S. J. Hafemann; Louisville, KY: Westminster John Knox, 1994) 228.

[70] On defilement through idolatry in New Testament times see the discussion in my "Purity of Heart in Jesus' Teaching: Mark 7:14–23 as an Expression of Jesus' Basileia Ethics," *JTS* NS 55 (2004): 467–502 here 473–74. Harrington, "Christianity," 157 thinks of the "Jewish ritual purity regulations pertaining to foods and vessels"; he refers to "Do not handle, Do not taste, Do not touch" in Col 2:21. It is most likely that these issues are included in Col 2:16 and 21, but that the main thrust, as in Rom. 14:21, is on defilement by idolatry.

[71] Cf. W. S. LaSor, *The Dead Sea Scrolls and the New Testament* (2nd ed.; Grand Rapids: Eerdmans, 1983) 148.

[72] So W. D. Davies, *Paul and Rabbinic Judaism: Some Rabbinic Elements in Pauline Theology* (London: SPCK, 1948) 167. On the holy meal at Qumran, see LaSor, *Scrolls*, 71.

[73] Encratism is an element which unites the different apocryphal Acts of the Apostles, see G. Kretschmar, "Apokryphen (NT)," in H. Burkhardt et al. (eds.), *Das grosse Bibellexikon Vol. 1* (Wuppertal: Brockhaus and Giessen: Brunnen, 1987) 74–82, 77–78.

[74] *t. Sota* 15:11–15. See Billerbeck, *Kommentar*, 3:307–308 and J. Fossum, *The Name of God and the Angel of the Lord* (WUNT 36; Tübingen: Mohr Siebeck, 1985) 66 n. 128.

[75] It is grammatically possible, but nevertheless highly improbable to read ἐν (μέρει)

not belong to one of these ascetic groups only abstained from libation wine, not from wine in general (if *kosher* wine could be obtained), since wine played an important part in the Jewish festivals.[76]

This result is in accordance with v. 17: Paul can only call these regulations concerning food, drink and festivals "a shadow of what is to come" if for him they are commandments of God and not human traditions. As in Heb 8:5; 10:1, the "shadow" contrasts the reality which casts the shadow. This reality, the "body" which casts the shadow, belongs to "the Messiah" Jesus (v. 17b).[77] This corresponds to the use of "shadow" and "body" (or similar expressions) in Plato and—influenced by him—in Philo and Josephus,[78] but whereas in the latter the contrast is of a cosmic or metaphysical kind, in Hebrews and Colossians it is primarily temporal and eschatological.[79] According to Col 2:17, that which is present and real in the Messiah[80] had precast its shadow into the Old

---

in a temporal way "during (the time of)" (so Standhartinger, *Studien*, 185–89). Why should the opponents only refrain from judging Christians during meals and festivals?

[76] See U. Wilckens, *Der Brief an die Römer* (3 vols.; EKKNT 6; Zürich: Benziger and Neukirchen-Vluyn: Neukirchener, 1982–87) 3:96.

[77] Verse 17b is a nominal sentence (omitting ἐστιν), see Haupt, *Kolosser*, 102. It is not the church as the "body of Christ" which is in view here, see Haupt, *Kolosser*, 102–103; P. Benoit, "Leib, Haupt und Pleroma in den Gefangenschaftsbriefen," in P. Benoit, *Exegese und Theologie: Gesammelte Aufsätze* (Düsseldorf: Patmos, 1965) 246–79 here 252 n. 1; C. Rowland, "The Influence of the First Chapter of Ezekiel on Jewish and Early Christian Literature" (unpublished Ph.D. dissertation, Cambridge University, 1974) 296–97. T. W. Martin, "Let Everyone Discern the Body of Christ (Colossians 2:17)," *JBL* 114 (1995): 249–55, proposed that, since δέ is always a coordinating conjunction, τὸ δὲ σῶμα τοῦ Χριστοῦ must continue the beginning of v. 16, which results in the translation: "but (let everyone discern) the body of Christ". For a good refutation of this view, see H. R. Cole, "The Christian and Time-Keeping in Colossians 2:16 and Galatians 4:10," *AUSS* 39 (2001): 273–82 here 275. Cole's main point is that although δέ is always coordinating, "the equivalence required between coordinating clauses is that of their position within the hierarchy of the sentence, not that of their clause types . . . There is, therefore, no reason why, in Col 2:17, the expression τὸ δὲ σῶμα τοῦ Χριστοῦ should not be translated as an independent clause ('but the body [is] Christ's'), which is coordinated with the [immediately preceding] relative clause" (275). According to Cole, this interpretation is further supported by the parallel in Heb 10:1 (277).

[78] See the references in H.-F. Weiss, *Der Brief an die Hebräer* (KEK 13; Göttingen: Vandenhoeck & Ruprecht, 1991) 437 and S. Schulz, "σκιά κ.τ.λ.," *TDNT* 7 (1971): 394–400 here 396–97. For synonymous terminology, see W. C. Vergeer, "ΣΚΙΑ and ΣΩΜΑ: The Strategy of Contextualisation in Colossians 2:17," *Neot* 28 (1994): 370–93 here 383.

[79] See O. Michel, *Der Brief an die Hebräer* (KEK 13; 6th ed.; Göttingen: Vandenhoeck & Ruprecht, 1966) 291 n. 2; Weiss, *Hebräer*, 500; Schulz, "σκιά," 398. In Qumran and Rabbinic Judaism the concept of "shadow" and "reality" (or the like) cannot be found (see Schulz, "σκιά," 397).

[80] "What is to come" does not refer to the ultimate, eschatological consummation, but to its present realisation in Christ incarnate (see Michel, *Hebräer*, 331).

Testament. To speak of the Law as "shadow of what is to come" implies on the one hand that the Law is of lesser quality and reality than its *Urbild* so that it is only a representation of what is to come and not the real thing itself.[81] Thereby the validity of the regulations of the Law is limited to a certain *time* in salvation history. It follows that "shadow of what is to come" cannot be a catchword of the opponents at Colossae.[82] On the other hand, the concept also expresses the eminently positive character and greatness of the Law of the old covenant: its regulations are shadows of the *Messiah*, therefore ordinances of the God who revealed himself in Jesus. They point to him, they are closely related to him.[83] Of course—this is Paul's argument—nobody asks for the shadow, however great it is, once the reality has come.[84]

We can conclude: It is the most natural and straightforward solution to read Col 2:16–17a as referring to the Torah of Moses.[85] Those who "condemn" the Colossian Christians must then be the local Torah-observant Jews. Their point is that Christians do not observe the most prominent commandments of the Torah which mark out the elect people of God from the Gentiles.[86] "[T]he food laws were fundamental and defining features of Jewish identity";[87] the same is true of the sabbath and Jewish festivals.[88]

---

[81] See Weiss, *Hebräer*, 436–37; A. Strobel, *Der Brief an die Hebräer* (NTD 9:2; 4th ed.; Göttingen: Vandenhoeck & Ruprecht, 1991) 94; E. Riggenbach, *Der Brief an die Hebräer* (KNT 14; 3rd and 4th ed.; Leipzig and Erlangen: Deichert, 1922) 294.

[82] *Contra* Francis, "Humility," 182.

[83] See Haupt, *Kolosser*, 102–103; Weiss, *Hebräer*, 500.

[84] Cf. Philo, *Migr.* 12: "Monstrous it is that shadows should be preferred to substance or copy to originals" (see Vergeer, "ΣΚΙΑ," 382).

[85] Most of the scholars who see Col 2:18 as referring to Jewish ascetics and mystics (see below on v. 18), assume that 2:16 must speak about ascetic regulations as well (so Francis, "Humility," 182; Sumney, "Identity," 378). This is a further example of a methodologically problematic inference from one statement about the opponents to another.

[86] According to Martin, there is some evidence that the Pauline communities generally followed the Jewish calendar; see T. W. Martin, "Pagan and Judeo-Christian Time-Keeping Schemes in Gal 4.10 and Col 2.16," *NTS* 42 (1996): 105–19 here 108–11. But, as Martin admits, this "does not necessarily mean that they also practice Jewish religious rituals" (110).

[87] Dunn, "Philosophy," 162.

[88] See Dunn, "Philosophy," 163–64.

d. Colossians 2:18

Colossians 2:18 speaks of people who take pleasure[89] in "humility" and "worship of the angels".[90] Because ἐν refers to both "humility" and "worship of the angels", some take "humility" to be that of the angels, meaning that in humility one angel lets the other sing first in their adoration of God (as in *'Abot R. Nat.* 23a; *3 En.* 18; 35:6; 39).[91] But the repetition of "humility" in v. 23 shows that Paul has in view a virtue of his opponents, not of angels. In early Christianity, humility is a positive virtue (so also in Col 3:12), but here the word is used for something Paul rejects. In the Septuagint, ταπεινοφροσύνη is partly used in a technical way for fasting as a special expression of humility. In Lev 16:29, 31; 23:27, 32; Num 29:7; Ps 35:13; Isa 58:3, 5, ענה נפש (pi., literally "humiliating one's soul") means "fasting", and in Ezra 8:21 ענה (hitp., literally "humiliating oneself") also denotes fasting as a way of self-humilation before God (similarly Dan 10:2–3, 12).[92] This use of ענה (and equivalents) is widespread also in early Jewish (e.g. *1 En.* 108:7, 9; 11Q19 25:11–12; 27:7; cf. *1 En.* 108:7; *4 Ezra* 7:125) and early Christian writings (Herm., *Sim.* 5.3.7; *Vis.* 3.10.6).[93] In apocalyptic circles, fasting is a means of preparing oneself for visions (cf. Dan 9:3, 20–21; 10:2–3, 12; *4 Ezra* 5:20; 6:35; *2 Bar.* 9:2; 12:5; 21:1; 47:2).[94] In Col 2:18, "humility" is also connected with heavenly visions.[95] It is therefore very probable that here and in v. 23 "humility" is used in this technical sense, whereas in 3:12 the non-technical meaning is intended.[96]

---

[89] θέλειν ἐν is a Hebraism and stands for חפץ ב ("taking pleasure in, having a desire for"), so in 1 Kgdms 18:22; 15:26; 3 Kgdms 10:9; Ps 146:10 LXX etc., see Evans, "Mystics," 195; Bauer, *Lexicon*, 355; Haupt, *Kolosser*, 104.

[90] On the different options of lexical and syntactical interpretation, see Sappington, *Revelation*, 153–58.

[91] Francis, "Humility," 130; cf. Rowland, "Influence," 259–60; Sumney, "Identity," 376–77; Sappington, *Revelation*, 158–61.

[92] See W. Gesenius, *A Hebrew and English Lexicon of the Old Testament* (ed. F. Brown; Oxford: Clarendon Press, 1959) 776, ענה III. pi (4) and hitp. (3).

[93] See Evans, "Mystics," 195–96; Percy, *Probleme*, 148; C. F. D. Moule, *The Epistles of Paul the Apostle to the Colossians and to Philemon* (Cambridge: Cambridge University Press, 1968) 104; Francis, "Humility," 168; cf. W. Grundmann, "ταπεινός κ.τ.λ.," *TDNT* 8 (1972): 1–26 here 12–13.

[94] See Sappington, *Revelation*, 65–66. Fasting can be combined with mourning and confession of sins, see ibid. 66–67.

[95] On the visions, see below.

[96] *Contra* DeMaris, *Controversy*, 75, who fails to notice the difference between the technical and the non-technical use of "humility" and therefore wrongly assumes the same meaning in both passages. For the distinction between technical and non-technical use in general see J. Ysebaert, *Die Amtsterminologie im Neuen Testament und in der Alten Kirche: Eine lexikographische Untersuchung* (Breda: Eureia, 1994) 216.

More difficult is the phrase "worship of the angels". θρησκεία means religious veneration, cult or worship in a comprehensive sense: "The term is commonly used ... for the cultic activity of worshipping God. It can also be used with regard to the cultic veneration of the pagan gods."[97] θρησκεία τῶν ἀγγέλων therefore cannot bear the more specific sense of "invocation of angels" for help and protection[98] as it was practiced by some Jews in Asia Minor.[99] Around A.D. 100 there was an increase of interest in angels at the fringes of Judaism. It resulted in images and the invocation of angels.[100] In more orthodox Judaism, some texts speak of secret seals which mystics had to present to the watcher angels in the course of their *merkhabah* visions,[101] but this could not be called cultic worship either. Nor is a cultic veneration of angels attested in Qumran. In 4Q403 1 i 10–29, the angels[102] are "praised" or "blessed" (ברך). However, the subject of this praise is not humans, but the seven angel princes who do it in the name of God. In 4Q403 1 i 30–33 (תשבחות כול אלוהים), the angels are not the object of veneration, but they are in charge of praising *God*, as is clear from the context.[103] Only of the seven angel princes it is said in 4Q400 2:2 (= 14 i 8) that they receive honour:[104] "They are honoured in all camps of the gods (i.e. angels) and awe-inspiring for the

---

[97] Arnold, *Syncretism*, 93. Although the term can have different nuances of meaning (see Francis, "Humility", 180), it never loses its comprehensive sense of "religious veneration".

[98] *Contra* Arnold, *Syncretism*, 101. None of the passages that Arnold mentions in support of his view (ibid. 93–95) actually uses θρησκεία in this limited sense.

[99] See Schürer, *History*, 3/1:35 and especially Arnold, *Syncretism*, 8–102 (summaries at pp. 59 and 89).

[100] See the passages cited by P. Schäfer, *Rivalität zwischen Engeln und Menschen: Untersuchungen zur rabbinischen Engelvorstellung* (SJ 8; Berlin and New York: De Gruyter, 1975) 67–72; for an invocation of mediating angels see already Job 5:1; 33:23 and the warning in *y. Ber.* 13a: "If hardship comes over a man, he shall invoke neither Michael nor Gabriel, but he shall invoke me, and I will answer him." See also M. Bar-Ilan, "Prayers of Jews to Angels and Other Mediators in the First Centuries CE," in M. Poorthuis and J. Schwartz (eds.), *Saints and Role Models in Judaism and Christianity* (JCPS 7; Leiden: E. J. Brill, 2004) 79–95.

[101] See G. Scholem, *Major Trends in Jewish Mysticism* (New York: Schocken, 1955) 50.

[102] The parallel expression "all who walk in justice" also means the angels, see C. Newsom, *Songs of the Sabbath Sacrifice: A Critical Edition* (HSS 27; Atlanta: Scholars Press, 1985) 196.

[103] *Pace* A.-M. Schwemer, "Gott als König und seine Königsherrschaft in den Sabbatliedern aus Qumran," in M. Hengel and A.-M. Schwemer (eds.), *Königsherrschaft Gottes und himmlischer Kult im Judentum, Urchristentum und in der hellenistischen Welt* (WUNT 55; Tübingen: Mohr Siebeck, 1991) 45–118 here 100.

[104] Which is not necessarily identical with cultic worship; on the contrary, the monotheistic setting at Qumran makes this interpretation rather improbable.

foundations of men, too wonderful for gods and men."[105] But again the subject is angels, not humans. Consequently there is no evidence for a veneration of angels by humans at Qumran.

Centuries later there was a church at Colossae which was dedicated to Michael the ἀρχιστράτηγός.[106] But this in itself is no sufficient proof of a religious veneration of angels in Asia Minor in the sixties of the first century A.D. Generally, there is "no evidence of cultic activity in which Michael (or the other angels) was adored, sung to, sacrificed to, praised, and worshipped" by Jews in Asia Minor.[107] There is only proof for a *pagan* cult of an "angel", namely the cult of the goddess Hekate who could be called "angel".[108] But this cult is too far removed from our text— one would expect much sharper polemic if actual idolatry was in view (cf. 1 Cor 10:14–22).[109]

Later Christian polemic against Jewish angel veneration is clearly dependent on Colossians 2. The Kerygma Petri (first half of 2nd c. A.D.[110]) and the writings which are based on it[111] are not independent evidence of Jewish angel worship.[112] The Kerygma Petri intreprets θρησκεία τῶν

---

[105] Newsom, *Songs*, 111 and Schwemer, "Gott als König," 100 n. 153 translate נוראים as "reverenced". But according to M. Jastrow, *A Dictionary of the Targumim, the Talmud Babli and Yerushalmi and the Midrashic Literature* (2 vols.; New York: Pardes, 1950) 1:593, the participle nif'al of ירא always means "fearful, awe-inspiring" and never "reverenced". In the text under discussion this is further supported by a change of preposition (for angels: ב, for humans: ל).

[106] See the references in Arnold, *Syncretism*, 87.

[107] Arnold, *Syncretism*, 60, cf. 88–89.

[108] See Arnold, *Syncretism*, 88.

[109] Bar-Ilan cites *t. Hul.* 2:18 as evidence for an invocation of angels by Jews ("Prayers," 85–86), but the text could even be read as evidence for cultic veneration of angels by Jews: "He who slaughters for the sake of the sun, for the sake of the moon, for the sake of the stars, for the sake of the planets, for the sake of Michael, prince of the great host, and for the sake of the small earth worm—lo, this is deemed to be flesh deriving from the sacrifices of corpses." However, "sun, moon, stars, planets and the heavenly host" are clearly standard expressions of Jewish polemic against *idolatry*, see Deut 4:19; 17:3; Wis 13:2. According to Deut 4:19; 32:8, JHWH appointed the heavenly host to the Gentiles. Michael and the earth worm mark the extreme positions of animate creation (highest and lowest animate creature).

[110] See E. Hennecke and W. Schneemelcher (eds.), *Neutestamentliche Apokryphen* (2 vols.; 5th ed.; Tübingen: Mohr Siebeck, 1987–89) 2:35.

[111] See T. Zahn, *Einleitung in das Neue Testament* (2 vols.; 3rd ed.; Leipzig: Deichert, 1906–1907) 1:339 n. 6; N. Kehl, *Der Christushymnus im Kolosserbrief: Eine motivgeschichtliche Untersuchung zu Kol 1,12–20* (SBM 1; Stuttgart: Katholisches Bibelwerk, 1967) 145–48.

[112] Cf. Kehl, *Christushymnus*, 146 n. 26; *contra* Arnold, *Syncretism*, 58–59.

ἀγγέλων as "worship of angels". Furthermore it understands the observance of Jewish festivals (Col 2:16) as "worship of elements" (cf. Col 2:20), i.e. the sun, moon, etc. This has not much in common with the realities of first-century Judaism, but the text nevertheless shows that in the early second century Col 2:16–23 was understood by Gentile Christians as referring to Judaism.[113]

Furthermore, to read τῶν ἀγγέλων in Col 2:18 as an objective genitive makes no sense of the following relative clause which is a *constructio ad sensum* in which the relative pronoun in the neuter plural refers to the things which the person in question "has seen as he entered".[114] It follows that syntactically θρησκεία τῶν ἀγγέλων only makes sense if we read ἀγγέλων as a subjective genitive as in Ἰουδαίων θρησκεία (4 Macc 5:7; Josephus, *Ant.* 12.253).[115] In this case Paul speaks about the heavenly worship (of God) which is conducted by the angels and which is one of the main interests of early Jewish mystics.[116] This heavenly worship is described already in Isaiah 6 and then in the Songs of the Sabbath Sacrifice at Qumran (cf. also *Jub.* 2:18, 21, 30).[117] According to 4Q511 10:11, the members of the Qumran community worship in fellowship with the angels in the heavenly council (סוד, cf. 1Q28a 2:8–9; 1QS 11:8; 1QH 11[3]:19–23).[118] These writings are pre-New Testament evidence for the belief that the community of the just is united with the angels in wor-

---

[113] Cf. similarly already Zahn, *Einleitung*, 1:339.

[114] See F. Blass and A. Debrunner, *A Greek Grammar of the New Testament and Other Early Christian Literature* (trans. R. W. Funk; Chicago: University of Chicago Press, 1961) 155 (§ 296). That this construction is not at all difficult is shown by the parallel construction in vv. 16–17.

[115] Evans, "Mystics," 196–97; so already Luther and Melanchthon, see Haupt, *Kolosser*, 164 n. 2; cf. Bauer, *Lexicon*, 363. Arnold decides against this solution because he only looks for parallels in which "a divine being, or a typical object of worship" is subject of θρησκεία (*Syncretism*, 91). Such a limitation is unwarranted.

[116] On the definition of "mysticism," see Roberts, "Experience," 164–69; P. T. O'Brien, "Mysticism," in G. F. Hawthorne, R. P. Martin and D.G. Reid (eds.), *Dictionary of Paul and His Letters* (Downers Grove, IL, and Leicester: InterVarsity Press, 1993) 623–25 here 623; I. Gruenwald, "Major Issues in the Study and Understanding of Jewish Mysticism," in J. Neusner (ed.), *Judaism in Late Antiquity Vol. 2: Historical Syntheses* (Leiden: E. J. Brill, 1995) 1–49 here 7. For commonalities and differences between apocalyptic *merkhabah* experiences and the experiences of the later *merkhabah* mystics see Roberts, "Experience," 167, on the discussion about the nature of the historical links between the two phenomena ibid. n. 5. The "mystics" in Colossae seem to have been closer to the mystics of the time of Akibah than to the earlier apocalyptics, cf. Roberts, "Experience," 167, 171.

[117] For many additional references, see Francis, "Humility," 177–78.

[118] See Newsom, *Songs*, 114.

ship.[119] What we find at Qumran is strictly speaking not mystic experience as such but priestly knowledge drawing on mystic experience.[120] Therefore these texts are not on one level with the kind of experience which is described in Col 2:18. According to the latter, the opponents claim to have *seen* angels in their heavenly worship, and this happened as these mystics "entered" (ἐμβατεύειν) the heavenly council.[121] ἐμβατεύειν means "to enter" in a general sense.[122] The term is also found in some of the very few surviving inscriptions referring to mystery cults; there it is used for the entry of the mystagogue into the innermost part of the temple where he experiences the initiatory vision.[123] Although the verb is used in this context it never becomes a technical term for initiation: "There is absolutely no evidence that ἐμβατεύειν can stand alone for initiation."[124] It always keeps its non-technical meaning "to enter". As a consequence there is no need to assume that the Colossian opponents borrowed the term from mystery religions (via hellenistic Judaism where language of the hellenistic mystery cults found its way into Jewish religious language).[125] Rather, in Col 2:18, too, ἐμβατεύειν is to be understood in its ordinary, non-technical meaning "to enter": "The requirements of historical parallelism are satisfied when the simple sense of the verb together with its context answers to a profuse literary tradition."[126] In this case the verb stands for entry into heaven in order to behold the *merkhabah*, the throne vehicle of God, as it is the main interest of early Jewish *merkhabah* mysticism.[127] For this "entrance" the

---

[119] See the discussion in U. Mell, *Neue Schöpfung. Eine traditionsgeschichtliche und exegetische Studie zu einem soteriologischen Grundsatz paulinischer Theologie* (BZNW 56; Berlin and New York: De Gruyter, 1989) 96 n. 11.

[120] Cf. the discussion and references in Roberts, "Experience," 175 n. 13.

[121] See Evans, "Mystics," 197–98. The translation "because he entered the things he had seen" is grammatically less likely (*contra* Arnold, *Syncretism*, 123, cf. 155).

[122] Francis, "Humility," 171, 189–90 n. 31.

[123] See the references and discussion in Arnold, *Syncretism*, 109–27; Francis, "Humility," 172–73; idem, "Background," *passim*.

[124] Francis, "Humility," 172 (against M. Dibelius, *An die Kolosser, Epheser, an Philemon* [HNT 12; 2nd ed.; Tübingen: Mohr Siebeck, 1927]).

[125] On the use of language of the mystery cults in hellenistic Judaism, see M. Hengel, "Die Ursprünge der Gnosis und das Urchristentum," in J. Ådna, S. J. Hafemann and O. Hofius (eds.), *Evangelium—Schriftauslegung—Kirche: Festschrift für Peter Stuhlmacher zum 65. Geburtstag* (Göttingen: Vandenhoeck & Ruprecht, 1997) 190–223 here 208 (here further references); on Philo see Arnold, *Syncretism*, 151.

[126] Francis, "Humility," 176.

[127] See the many references at Francis, "Humility," 173–76; Rowland, "Influence," 264.

extant Greek fragments mostly use εἰσέρχεσθαι (so *1 En.* 14)[128] which is a synonym for ἐμβατεύειν. From the many texts using "entrance" language it is clear "that visionary transcendence was often characterized as entrance into heaven. More than this, . . . 'entrance' is not a phenomenon distinct from 'ascent' even when the entrance theme is predominant."[129]

We can conclude that in Col 2:18 some kind of Jewish mystic is in view. Because of his ascetic preparation and heavenly vision he thinks himself to be superior to those who do not share his experience.[130] Moreover, "a mystical interest did go hand in hand with a strict adherence to the law", and "a righteous life according to the torah seems to have been a prerequisite" for mystical visions.[131] Often, in turn, the content of apocalyptic revelations is an adhortation to be faithful to the Torah, including issues of calendar.[132] Paul denies the superiority and righteousness of these mystics and exposes that the true motivation behind the allegedly spiritual experience is carnal, not spiritual. The main reason for this evaluation is mentioned in v. 19: these mystics are not holding fast to Jesus, the "head".[133] This means that they are not Christians.[134] Nevertheless they make an impression on the Colossian Christians because the latter, too, know about the heavenly worship before God's throne. Paul's point is that the only thing that matters is holding fast to Jesus who is the "head" even of the heavenly powers (2:10). From him the church receives everything she needs for a growth which pleases God and is not motivated by the flesh.

---

[128] See further Francis, "Humility," 191 n. 44; Roberts, "Experience," 168.

[129] Francis, "Humility," 174.

[130] Standhartinger, *Studien*, 187–89 presents a very different reading which is grammatically possible, but, like her reading of v. 16, very improbable: "humility" is a virtue of the church (as in 3:12), "worship of the angels" is the worship service of the church, and θέλων ἐν stands for the willingness of the church. Therefore those who disqualify the church are, according to Standhartinger, those who "enter" church gatherings by accident and condemn "what they see" because they do not understand it.

[131] Roberts, "Experience," 174–75 n. 13; Sappington, *Revelation*, 63–65. In Daniel this includes abstinence from food and drink that was contaminated by consecration to idols (1:8, cf. Col 2:16).

[132] See Sappington, *Revelation*, 115–24.

[133] On the "head" language see my *Kolosserhymnus*, 222–28.

[134] "Clinging to the Lord of the Spirits" is found in *1 En.* 40:6; 46:7–8 and is the opposite of denying his name and not serving him (45:1; 46:6; see Roberts, "Experience," 183). Consequently Paul is not saying that the opponents "have separated themselves from Christ" (*contra* Sumney, "Identity," 369). Rather, they have never believed in him.

e. *Colossians 2:20–23*

Verses 20–23, the first part of 2:20–3:4, summarise the dangers the Colossians are facing. Here the commandments of the Torah (vv. 16–17a) and the mystics' pride of their asceticism and visionary experience (v. 18) are taken together. This is made obvious by the fact that v. 20 speaks of "being subjected to ordinances",[135] thereby referring to the "ordinances" of the Torah about food and drink (i.e. about purity and idolatry) and about festivals that are mentioned in v. 16. Verse 21 mentions three prohibitions which "are examples of the types of regulations the opponents impose".[136] They are typical of the regulations of the Jewish Scriptures concerning purity issues (including issues of impurity by idolatry), especially regarding food and drink.[137] They could also be typical of the ascetic abstinence of the mystics mentioned in v. 18, although it does not seem that these mystics explicitly *imposed* their asceticism on the Colossians. Rather, the visions they desired were their *own* goal. "The attitude is simply that 'my way is superior to yours; it achieves goals which you fall short of '."[138] However, they "disqualified" the Christians because of their lack of ascetic and mystic experience; in its effect, this hardly falls short of the "judging" mentioned in connection with the Torah (v. 16). It was no big step to understand their pride of their own ascetic practice as an implicit obligation. And it is hardly possible to understand the relative clause v. 23 in a different way: it refers back to the "human commandments and teachings" of v. 22 which in turn are interpretations of the purity regulations of the Torah (vv. 20–21). The Law has to do with "ordinances" which are related to "things that are destined to perish with use": "do not handle, do not taste, do not touch" (vv. 21–22; cf. 1 Cor 6:13), and the mystics' abstinence has to do with the same perishable things. Apart from this, there are more hints to the mystics of v. 18 in vv. 20–23. In v. 23 some catchwords of v. 18 are repeated: ἐθελοθρησκία refers to θέλων ἐν ... θρησκείᾳ τῶν ἀγγέλων, and ταπεινοφροσύνη as well as ἀφειδίᾳ σώματος to the ascetic preparation for visions called ταπεινοφροσύνη in v. 18. It follows that in vv. 20–23 the references to two explicit passages about opponents, vv. 16 and 18, are intertwined. This suggests that vv. 16 and 18 speak of the same

---

[135] On this translation see above.
[136] Sumney, "Identity," 370.
[137] See Dunn, "Philosophy," 164–65.
[138] Dunn, "Philosophy," 171.

group. This does not necessarily mean that the two kinds of criticism which they levelled at the Colossian Christians were closely linked in their own understanding, too; it is Paul who, in his negative evaluation, sees them as closely linked. So most probably vv. 16 and 18 speak of one and the same group, namely the Jews of the local synagogue who condemned the Colossian Christians because of their lack of Torah observance and because of their lack of ascetic commitment and visionary experience. Usually Jewish mystics were strictly Law-observant *and* adherent to ascetic practices.[139] In this respect, 2:16 applies to them, too; but because of the literal parallels in the Septuagint and because of v. 17, v. 16 cannot possibly refer to the ascetic practices of the mystics.

According to Paul's evaluation, these "ordinances" as well as the mystical traditions are meant for persons who still live "in the world", that is in the old aeon (v. 20); they are no longer valid for Christians who have died to the "elements of the world". So any teaching which demands that Christians keep these ordinances is on the side of merely "human commands and teachings" (v. 22). In regard to the mystical traditions, "human commands and teachings" disqualifies them as merely human invention. In regard to the Torah, "human commands and teachings" is more difficult to understand. The phrase cannot refer to the Torah itself because elsewhere Paul calls it "the Law of *God*" (Rom 7:22) which is "holy, just and good" (Rom 7:12). Nor can Col 2:22 refer to the *oral* Torah although it is called "human tradition" elsewhere (Matt 15:1–11 and parallels, citing Isa 29:13), for in Col 2:22 Paul not only summarises vv. 18–19, but vv. 16–17, too, where he calls these ordinances a "shadow of what is to come" (v. 17a). He would not have talked about the "oral Torah" in such a positive way. So the only way left to interpret vv. 20–23 is that the "human commands and teachings" refer to the *validity* of the Torah of Moses. Paul rejects any teaching that demands Christians to observe the Old Testament Torah. This is fully in accord with Paul's teaching in Romans, 2 Corinthians, Galatians and Philippians, and it is parallel to Jesus' criticism of the Pharisees "for their way of defining the will of God by means of Scripture".[140] What is in question is the *use* of Scripture, not human additions to Scripture.

In v. 23 these "human commands and teachings" are further characterised. The syntax of this verse is extremely difficult to untangle. Following

---

[139] See Rowland, "Influence," 239–98.
[140] A. Schlatter, *The History of Christ: The Foundation for New Testament Theology* (trans. A. Köstenberger; Grand Rapids: Baker, 1997) 219.

Erich Haupt,[141] I suggest to translate it as follows: "... which—although they have the reputation of wisdom for reasons of wished-for worship and fasting and severe treatment of the body, (but) not for the reason of something that is truly valuable (or honourable)—lead only to satisfaction of the flesh". Hidden "wisdom" was revealed by the visions of the early Jewish apocalyptics,[142] and the "wisdom" of the apocalyptics was a prerequisite for their visionary experience (cf. Dan 2:21; 12:10; *m. Hag.* 2:1).[143] The appearance of wisdom results from "aimed-at worship", "humility" and "severe treatment of the body". This means that these three terms stand for something apparently positive and praiseworthy which was seen positively also by the Colossian Christians.[144] "Humility" repeats v. 18 and therefore denotes ascetic practice, especially fasting. The "severe treatment of the body" merely restates this. ἐθελοθρησκία is more difficult to understand. According to the usual connotations of ἐθελο- it can have three meanings: (1) voluntary worship, (2) wished-for (or aimed-at) worship, (3) would-be worship.[145] "In all cases the differing nuances overlay the action of the will in relation to certain circumstances", i.e. here in relation to worship.[146] It follows that ἐθελοθρησκία is not "self-chosen worship" in the sense of merely human worship. This is also excluded because, as we have seen, from its context ἐθελοθρησκία must mean something positive. Therefore the word means "that certain Colossians chose/aspired to/gave pretence of some worship"[147]— more precisely, they aspired to seeing the heavenly worship of the angels. The meaning "wished-for worship" or "delighted-in worship" exactly matches to θέλων ἐν ... θρησκείᾳ τῶν ἀγγέλων in v. 18.[148]

To these only seemingly positive appearances, Paul contrasts sharply, by repeating ἐν and thereby indicating the contrast to μέν, that all this is nothing (truly) "valuable" or "honourable".[149] All these seemingly wise habits only lead to the "fullest satisfaction" of the (sinful) "flesh" (cf. 2:18b; 3:9).[150] After the coming of the Messiah (cf. v. 17), these ordinances only

---

[141] *Kolosser*, 113–17.
[142] See Sappington, *Revelation*, 59–62.
[143] See Sappington, *Revelation*, 63–65; Rowland, "Influence," 252.
[144] Haupt, *Kolosser*, 115–16; Sumney, "Identity," 371.
[145] See Francis, "Humility," 181–82.
[146] Francis, "Humility," 181–82.
[147] Francis, "Humility," 182.
[148] See Dunn, "Philosophy," 176.
[149] τιμή is a metonymy, cf. Phil 4:8 (Haupt, *Kolosser*, 166–67).
[150] Haupt, *Kolosser*, 118. Similarly, Paul says in Gal 6:12–13 that his opponents only

lead to carnal honour, to an outward appearance of wisdom, but they are without value in view of "that which is above, where Christ is" (3:1). Therefore, Christians are to raise their eyes from the earth to the Messiah who is inthroned at God's right hand and with whom their own "life" is hidden (3:1–3).

In this context Paul repeats the phrase "the elements of the world" (τὰ στοιχεῖα τοῦ κόσμου v. 20, cf. v. 8).[151] With Christ the Christians have died to these "elements", therefore they no longer live "in the world" (ἐν κόσμῳ) and are no longer to fix their thoughts on "that which is on earth" (τὰ ἐπὶ τῆς γῆς 3:2). Consequently the "elements of the world" are something which characterises the "world", i.e. the first creation, which is marred by sin, subject to destruction and therefore passing away (cf. Rom 8:18–25; 1 Cor 7:29–31; 2 Cor 4:16–18). Furthermore, those who died to these "elements" are no longer under the "ordinances" of the Law.[152] This is parallel to Gal 2:19: "I died to the law." As in Galatians, life under the "elements" is characterized as the way of the flesh (Col 2:23)—the teaching that those who have risen to new life through faith in Christ still have to observe the Law belongs to the "human commands and teachings", is motivated by the flesh and can only lead to honour in the flesh. This means that the "elements of the world" are related to this merely human teaching (which opposes Christ), and to the flesh and the old creation which is passing away. Eduard Schweizer and Dietrich Rusam have shown that up to New Testament times, "elements of the world" exclusively means the four or five physical elements the world consists of.[153] It is very unlikely that we find a different meaning in Colossians. Therefore in 2:8, 20, Paul warns the church not to become

---

wish "to make a good showing in the flesh". One could also translate the last part of Col 2:23: "are without value against the indulgence of the flesh" (see Sumney, "Identity," 371 with further references in n. 27).

[151] Here I can only make a few remarks about the complex and much discussed interpretation of this phrase. I am preparing a detailed study about it which I hope to publish soon.

[152] In 3 Macc 1:3 and Josephus, *Ap.* 1.42, δόγματα stands for the Law (see G. Kittel, "δόγμα, δογματίζω," *TDNT* 2 [1935]: 233–35 here 234).

[153] E. Schweizer, "Slaves of the Elements and Worshippers of Angels: Gal 4: 3, 9 and Col 2:8, 18, 20," *JBL* 107 (1988): 455–68; *idem*, "Altes und Neues zu den 'Elementen der Welt' in Kol 2,20; Gal 4,3.9," in K. Aland and S. Meurer (eds.), *Wissenschaft und Kirche: Festschrift für Eduard Lohse* (Bielefeld: Luther, 1989) 111–18; D. Rusam, "Neue Belege zu den στοιχεῖα τοῦ κόσμου (Gal 4,3.9; Kol 2,8.20)," *ZNW* 83 (1992): 119–25; cf. J. Blinzler, "Lexikalisches zu dem Terminus τὰ στοιχεῖα τοῦ κόσμου bei Paulus," in *Studiorum Paulinorum Congressus Internationalis Catholicus Vol. 2* (AnBib 18; Rome: Pontifical Biblical Institute, 1963) 429–43 here 439.

enslaved to earthly, physical things, which are destined to pass away (cf. v. 22a); the Christians would become enslaved if they listened to a teaching which is not centered on Christ (v. 19), but on "that which is on earth", namely upon issues of calendar, food, etc.[154] This is also the interpretation given by most Christian references to the "elements of the world" in the second century A.D., including the Kerygma Petri.[155] As in 1 Cor 7:29–31, Paul does not teach that Christians are already removed from the ordinances of the first creation, nor does he teach that Christians, as the Stoics, should live in an "inner distance to the goods and events of this world", but he "encourages (them) to live their present lives in the light of the future Kingdom of God . . .; in this he follows the teaching of Jesus".[156]

4. Synthesis: The Identity of the Opponents According to the Explicit Statements

We can now draw a conclusion from our analysis of the explicit statements. According to 2:16–17a the Christians at Colossae are condemned by the local synagogue because they do not keep those regulations of the Torah which are most crucial for Jewish identity, namely the laws about idolatry and purity (food and drink, especially meat and wine consecrated to idols), the Jewish festivals and the sabbath. Further, according to 2:18–19a, the Christians are despised by Jewish mystics who boast of their ascetic rigour and their consequent visions of angels and heavenly worship, but do not submit to Jesus as Messiah and "head". Verses 20–23 present the two threats referred to by vv. 16–17a and 18–19a as coming from one and the same group, namely the Jewish synagogue at Colossae. What is the relationship of these Jews to the "philosophy" mentioned in v. 8? Verse 8 can be read as an additional reference to the local synagogue which then would have used the self-designation "philosophy", or as a reference to a different danger from outside, namely "deception" by

---

[154] It is created things, namely the course of the stars, that influence the calendar, cf. 1QS 9:26–10:8; *Jub.* 2:9 (see Arnold, *Syncretism*, 179, 217).

[155] On the latter see above. In the 20th century T. Zahn, *Der Brief des Paulus an die Galater* (KNT 9; 3rd ed.; Leipzig: Deichert, 1922) 197–99 and H. Cremer, *Biblisch-theologisches Wörterbuch des neutestamentlichen Griechisch* (10th ed.; Gotha: Klotz, 1915) (= 11th ed. 1923) 1021–25, interpret the phrase in this way.

[156] F. Lang, *Die Briefe an die Korinther* (NTD 7; Göttingen: Vandenhoeck & Ruprecht, 1986) 100.

Gentile philosophy. Both views are historically possible, for on the one hand the Colossian church seems to have consisted wholly (or at least primarily) of former Gentiles (cf. 1:21, 27; 2:13; 3:5, 7)[157] who maintained bonds with at least some of their non-Christian family members and friends among whom there may have been members of philosophical schools. On the other hand it is very probable that there was a strong Jewish community in Colossae, which certainly took some notice of this new group of Gentiles who claimed to be true inheritants of Israel's blessings (cf. Col 1:12–14). According to Josephus, *Ant.* 12.147–153, Antiochus III (223–187 B.C.) deported 2000 Jewish families from Mesopotamia and Babylon to Phrygia and Lydia. From Cicero, *Pro Flacco* 28.68 we can deduce that in Laodicea and the surrounding area in the year A.D. 62 there were about 10,000 male Jews older than 20 years who paid the temple tax, not including women and children.[158] These Jews were in close contact with Jerusalem as is evidenced by their payment of the temple tax, by their participation in pilgrimage to the high festivals at the temple (Acts 2:9–11) and by the later move of Philipp and his daughters from Palestine to Hierapolis (Eusebius, *Hist. Eccl.* 3.31.2–5). Dunn assumes that about 2000–3000 of these Jews lived in Colossae.[159] If he is right, then there was more than one synagogue at Colossae,[160] and

---

[157] See Schweizer, *Kolosser*, 20; P. T. O'Brien, *Colossians, Philemon* (WBC 44; Waco, TX: Word, 1982) xxviii–xxix; Roberts, "Experience," 167–68; Harrington, "Christians," 154. According to Dunn, "Philosophy," 157, 159 it is possible that the church was a mixed group of mainly Gentile and some Jewish believers. On 2:13 see Schweizer, *Kolosser*, 114 ("uncircumcision of your flesh" can be understood literally as referring to their Gentile past, so also Dunn, "Philosophy," 160–61, or metaphorically, meaning that their uncircumcision consisted in their being dominated by the sinful "flesh").

[158] The calculations of different scholars differ slightly; see G. Kittel, "Das kleinasiatische Judentum in der hellenistisch-römischen Zeit: Ein Bericht zur Epigraphie Kleinasiens," *TLZ* 69 (1944): 9–20 here 11; Dunn, *Colossians*, 21 n. 4; J. M. G. Barclay, *Jews in the Mediterranean Diaspora from Alexander to Trajan (323 B.C.E.–117 C.E.)* (Edinburgh: T. & T. Clark, 1996) 266. On Judaism in Asia Minor, see further Kittel, "Judentum," *passim*; M. Hengel, *Juden, Griechen und Barbaren: Aspekte der Hellenisierung des Judentums in vorchristlicher Zeit* (SBS 76; Stuttgart: Katholisches Bibelwerk, 1976) 144–47; idem, *Judentum und Hellenismus: Studien zu ihrer Begegnung unter besonderer Berücksichtigung Palästinas bis zur Mitte des 2. Jahrhunderts vor Christus* (3rd ed.; WUNT 10; Tübingen: Mohr Siebeck, 1988) 478–79; P. R. Trebilco, *Jewish Communities in Asia Minor* (SNTSMS 69; Cambridge: Cambridge University Press, 1991) esp. 5–36, 167–90; Barclay, *Jews*, 259–81.

[159] *Colossians*, 22. DeMaris is more cautious: "Yet, if Colossae was anything like other Anatolian cities, it probably did have a Jewish community that by the first century C.E. could attract the attention, the interest, and perhaps even the favor of its pagan neighbours" (*Controversy*, 125).

[160] Dunn, "Philosophy," 155.

conflicts between these and the small group of Christians who believed that Jesus was the Jewish Messiah were unavoidable.[161] It is even possible that some Christians, e.g. former God-fearers, not only attended their house church, but also the local synagogue, as it is attested for later times by Origen and John Chrysostom.[162] Ephesians 2 is further evidence for the deep impression that Judaism made on Christians in the very same region. Therefore the "philosophy" mentioned in 2:8 could be Gentile philosophy or a Jewish self-designation. It would not be difficult to imagine that the Colossian church was under threat from two sides, from its Gentile and its Jewish environment.[163]

However, some of the catchwords of v. 8 are repeated in vv. 20 and 22, too: τὰ ἐντάλματα καὶ διδασκαλίαι ἀνθρώπων picks up ἡ παράδοσις τῶν ἀνθρώπων, and τὰ στοιχεῖα τοῦ κόσμου are mentioned again. σοφία in v. 23 could be understood as a reference to φιλοσοφία in v. 8, but it could also refer to the mystics since seeing visions of the *merkhabah* requires wisdom and is proof of the wisdom of the visionary. If σοφία refers to the "philosophy", then v. 8, too, speaks of the same group of opponents since v. 23 clearly speaks of the Jewish mystics. In that case the Jews of the synagogue in Colossae would have called their religion a "philosophy" for apologetic and propagandist reasons. Their rejection of Jesus, the Head (v. 19), would be referred to by "not according to Christ" in v. 8. In the other case, if "wisdom" in v. 23 is not an intended reference to "philosophy" in v. 8, it is possible that the church in Colossae was not only threatened by the synagogue, but also by Gentile philosophy. The fact that Paul speaks of the "human teaching" and the "elements of the world" in both contexts does not necessarily

---

[161] Roberts concludes from Paul's references "to the universalistic scope of the Gospel and the attending worldwide proclamation of its message" in 1:3–8 and 4:2–6 that the "point of contact" between Christians and Jews at Colossae is found "in the missionary outreach of the Christians into their environment" ("Experience," 173–75; similarly Harrington, "Christians," 158).

[162] See D. Stökel Ben Ezra, "Christians Observing Jewish Festivals of Autumn," in P. J. Tomson and D. Lambers-Petry (eds.), *The Image of Judeo-Christians in Ancient and Christian Literature* (WUNT 158; Tübingen: Mohr Siebeck, 2003) 53–73 here 66–70.

[163] This is what we find e.g. in the *Letter to Diognetes* where the author writes against Jewish practice and against Gentile religion and philosophy. Although in 4:1 he mentions the very issues of Col 2:16 and 18 (food, sabbath, fasting, new moons), the line of his argument against the Jews is very different from that in Colossians. He clearly is a Gentile Christian himself, not taking into account that the regulations of the Jewish Torah are in fact revelations of God (cf. Col 2:17), however temporarily limited in their validity. Interestingly, in characterizing Gentile philosophy in 8:2 he uses words very similar to Col 2:8, but neither in 4:1 nor in 8:2 does he seem to quote Colossians directly.

prove that he speaks about the same group of opponents. As we have seen, both phrases merely express a negative evaluation and are not part of the opponents' teaching itself, unlike "wisdom" and (possibly) "philosophy" or the "ordinances" and ascetic practices mentioned in vv. 8, 18, 20–23. So it is possible that as Paul characterises both Judaism "under the law" *and* Gentile religion as enslavement under the "elements of the world" in Gal 4:1–11, so here he stresses that both Gentile philosophy and the synagogue's criticisms have their ultimate source in a mind set on earthly things, not on "things which are above", namely the Messiah Jesus. As the teaching of these Gentile philosophers is not rooted in Christ ("not according to Christ" v. 8), so the Jews who criticise the Colossian Christians "are not holding fast to the Head", Jesus (v. 19).

In addition to the possible reference to the "philosophy" (2:8) by "wisdom" in 2:23, Paul mentions circumcision in the positive passage following 2:8 (see below section 5). This supports the view that the "philosophy" is either a pejorative reference to or a propagandist self-description of the local Jews. Furthermore, συλαγωγεῖν in 2:8 could be a derogatory pun on the word "synagogue" (συναγωγή).[164] For all these reasons it is more probable that in all explicit passages Paul speaks of one and the same group of opponents, namely the Jewish synagogues at Colossae.

It follows that there is no reason to assume that the opponents at Colossae were a *syncretistic* group of any kind.[165] Rather, they were Torah-observant Jews with an interest in asceticism, mystic experience and wisdom. It is possible that they called themselves "philosophy" for apologetic or propagandist reasons. This non-syncretistic character of the opponents fits excellently with what we know about the character of Judaism in Asia Minor in the first century A.D.[166] According to Josephus, most Jews in Asia Minor strictly observed the laws about food and festivals and consequently often faced conflicts with their Gentile environment.[167] In Sardes, Jewish influence was so considerable that the town

---

[164] So Wright, *Colossians*, 100.

[165] Cf. Harrington, "Christians," 160–61.

[166] This is also the conclusion of Harrington, "Christians," 161.

[167] See the references in Barclay, *Jews*, 270. Only from the second century A.D. onward more and more Jews held a public office and therefore became more adapted to Graeco-Roman culture, see Barclay, *Jews*, 280–81. There is no evidence that Jews from Asia Minor were involved in the two Jewish revolts in Palestine and in the revolt in Egypt in A.D. 116–117. From this Barclay concludes that "their mood was far removed from the antagonistic spirit which came to dominate in Judaea, Egypt and Cyrene" (*Jews*, 281). But this is an argument from silence and therefore problematic.

officials who were in charge of the market had to ensure that *kosher* food was publicly available.[168] There is evidence in Ignatius that Christians in Asia Minor in the early second century were in fact strongly attracted by the synagogue (*Phld.* 6:1–2; *Magn.* 8.1; 9.1–2; 10.3).[169]

5. Further Evidence by Indirect Allusions to the Opponents

Indirect allusions to the opponents in Colossae cannot be defined independently from the explicit statements. The wide variety of suggestions about the identity of the opponents offered by scholars in the past reflects the arbitrary nature of finding allusions to the opponents independently of the explicit statements. But starting from the explicit polemic against the opponents, we can identify further allusions to them with a certain probability.

Most important is the question whether circumcision played any part in the opponents' teaching. If the opponents were in fact the local Torah-observant Jews, one would expect that circumcision played a prominent part in their criticism of the mostly uncircumcised Colossian church. For first-century Judaism, exclusive worship of the one God, circumcision, purity and the sabbath were the most important God-given "badges of identity" which marked out the elect, Torah-obedient people of JHWH from the Gentiles. Now circumcision is mentioned in Col 2:11, 13 and 3:11. While 2:11, 13 contrasts bodily uncircumcision[170] and the true "spiritual" circumcision effected by Christ in baptism, 3:11 stresses that in the Church being Greek or Jewish, circumcised or uncircumcised is of no importance. The repetition of the issue ("neither Greek nor Jew" is repeated by "neither circumcision nor uncircumcision") is an additional hint that circumcision was important in the Colossian conflict although it is not mentioned in the explicit passages against opponents.[171] If this is true, then Paul "is here rejecting the reproach which the opponents directed against the congregation that they have no claim to salvation

---

[168] Josephus, *Ant.* 14.261, see Barclay, *Jews*, 276.
[169] Further evidence gives Melito of Sardes, Apollinaris of Hierapolis and Miltiades, see Barclay, *Jews*, 280.
[170] Thus with Dunn, "Philosophy," 160–61; on the different possibilities of interpretation see above n. 157.
[171] Dunn, "Philosophy," 161.

without becoming Jews through circumcision".[172] Anyway we can assume that the laws concerning food, drink and festivals (2:16) are only examples of those "ordinances" Jews thought to be indispensible for the truly elect people. Similarly, in Galatians Paul can speak of circumcision (5:2; 6:12–15) or of festivals (4:10) as examples for the commandments which his opponents tried to impose on the Galatian Christians. The fact that Paul mentions circumcision in the positive statement directly following 2:8 makes it very likely that the "philosophy" does not denote Gentile philosophy, but is either a pejorative word for the Jewish opponents who tried to persuade the Colossian Christians by means of convincing arguments (cf. 2:4) or a self-designation of these Jewish opponents.

In prominent places Paul stresses that the believers fully participate in the "heritage" of the "elect" people; they *are* the "holy and beloved elect ones of God" (1:12; 3:12). To this claim of a small group of Gentiles a "denunciation and pronouncement of disqualification (as in 2,16 and 18) would be a natural riposte . . . the reaction was to dismiss these Gentiles' claim to a share in Israel's heritage as fanciful and unfounded".[173]

Further Paul mentions forgiveness of sins and reconciliation several times (1:14, 20–22; 2:13–15; 3:13). The reason for this is certainly that the local Jews were passing judgment on the Christians (2:16) and denied their heavenly "prize" (2:18); Paul answers this by stressing the real "prize" which they already possess.[174]

Paul emphasises several times that the Christians have been filled with knowledge and wisdom because Jesus himself is God's wisdom in person (1:9–10, 15–17; 2:2–3). He thereby opposes deceit by a kind of philosophy which is not rooted in the Messiah Jesus, or, more likely, he opposes deceit by the alleged wisdom of Jewish mystics[175] and the claim

---

[172] Roberts, "Experience," (169–)170.

[173] Dunn, "Philosophy," (158–)159.

[174] Cf. Sumney, "Identity," 379. According to Sumney, the purpose of the didactic material in Colossians is "to assure the Colossians of their place before God in Christ, especially of the forgiveness of their sins . . ., not to establish the position of Christ" (387). This is a false alternative: the assurance of their forgiveness is rooted in the position and work of Christ, as is shown, for example, in 1:12–23, where the "hymn" focuses on Christ's person and work in order to present the foundation for the assurance of forgiveness in 12–14 and 21–23; see my *Kolosserhymnus*, 76–79 and Roberts, "Experience," 175–76 (with further references).

[175] Cf. Sumney, "Identity," 381.

by orthodox Jews that the Torah is the ultimate and unsurpassed embodiment of divine wisdom (cf. Sir 24:23; Bar 4:1).[176]

Furthermore, there are three enumerations of "principalities and powers" in Colossians (1:16; 2:10, 15). It has often been thought that these "powers" must have played an important role in the Colossian "heresy". Many scholars also counted the "elements of the world" (2:8, 20), understood to be "elemental spirits", among these "powers" and identified them with the "angels" the "heretics" worshipped (2:18).[177] As we have seen, the "elements of the world" and the "worship of angels" cannot be understood in this way. The enumerations of "powers" are found in a context where in dense and traditional christological language the Colossians are assured of the lordship of Christ and of their own position in him. Christ's victory and lordship over the "powers" is an essential part of early creedal texts.[178] So in Colossians the "powers" are mentioned several times in order to emphasise that if even they owe their existence to Christ, the mediator of creation, and are submitted to him, then his lordship encompasses everything. A secondary link to the opponents may be seen in that if Christ is Lord over the angelic powers, then the mystic vision of the angels in their heavenly adoration (2:18) loses its importance compared to the indwelling of Christ in his Church and the Church's close live relationship to him (cf. 1:27; 2:10, 19; 3:3).[179]

Finally, in 3:1–2 "Paul redefines seeking the 'things above' as living the ethical life set out in 3:5ff.".[180] "Seeking the things above" is not striving for heavenly visions, but an ethical life according to the pattern of him who is the "image of God" (3:10, 13; cf. 1:15).

---

[176] On the embodiment of divine Wisdom in the Torah and in Christ, respectively, see M. D. Hooker, "Where is Wisdom to be Found?" in D. F. Ford and G. N. Stanton (eds.), *Reading Texts, Seeking Wisdom* (London: SCM Press, 2003) 116–28, and my *Kolosserhymnus*, 133–65.

[177] In this they are following O. Everling, *Die paulinische Angelologie und Dämonologie: Ein biblisch-theologischer Versuch* (Göttingen: Vandenhoeck & Ruprecht, 1888) 93–101. Recent examples are Dunn, "Philosophy," 167–70; T. H. Olbricht, "The Stoicheia and the Rhetoric of Colossians: Then and Now," in S. E. Porter and T. H. Olbricht (eds.), *Rhetoric, Scripture and Theology: Essays from the 1994 Pretoria Conference* (JSNTSup 131; Sheffield: Sheffield Academic Press, 1996) 308–28 here 325; Gebauer, "Kolosserbrief," 156–57.

[178] This was first stressed by O. Cullmann, *Die ersten christlichen Glaubensbekenntnisse* (ThSt(B) 15; 2nd ed.; Zollikon-Zürich: Evangelischer Verlag, 1949) 53–56. See further my *Kolosserhymnus*, 194–98.

[179] Cf. Sumney, "Identity," 380: "there is no evidence in explicit statements that these powers play a part in the opponents' teachings" (cf. 384–85).

[180] Sumney, "Identity," 381.

6. Conclusion

In this study we could identify four characteristics of the opponents at Colossae:[181] (1) they tried to persuade the Colossian Christians by using seemingly convincing arguments; (2) they were Torah-observant Jews who denied the salvation of the Colossian Christians because the latter did not keep the Torah, i.e. were not proselytes; (3) they were mystics who sought to attain visions by means of rigorous asceticism and who claimed to have entered heaven and seen the angelic worship of God; they despised the Colossian Christians because the latter could not boast of similar experiences and therefore could not be wise and righteous; (4) they were not Christians. It is also possible, but less probable, that characteristic (1) refers to a different group, namely members of a Gentile philosophical school (2:8).

---

[181] Roberts' characterisation is close to this one, see "Experience," 169–75.

PAUL AND "WORKS OF LAW" LANGUAGE IN LATE ANTIQUITY

CRAIG A. EVANS
Acadia Divinity College
Wolfville, NS, Canada

INTRODUCTION

In his polemical letter to the churches of Galatia Paul affirms in 2:16 that οὐ δικαιοῦται ἄνθρωπος ἐξ ἔργων νόμου ἐὰν μὴ διὰ πίστεως Ἰησοῦ Χριστοῦ, καὶ ἡμεῖς εἰς Χριστὸν Ἰησοῦν ἐπιστεύσαμεν, ἵνα δικαιωθῶμεν ἐκ πίστεως Χριστοῦ καὶ οὐκ ἐξ ἔργων νόμου, ὅτι ἐξ ἔργων νόμου οὐ δικαιωθήσεται πᾶσα σάρξ ("a person is not justified from works of law but by faith in Jesus Christ; and we have believed in Christ Jesus, in order that we might be justified from faith in Christ and not from works of law; for no flesh will be justified from works of law"). Against whom was Paul addressing himself?

I am inclined to agree with Robert Jewett and others who have argued that in Galatians Paul is criticizing Jewish Christians, who, acting with Jerusalem's authority, were attempting to "complete" Paul's work, by bringing his converts to perfection in the new faith.[1] This perfection would be achieved through obedience of certain works of the law thought to be essential. Accordingly, it is important to try to understand what a phrase like "works of (the) law" would bring to mind in the thinking of Jews in late antiquity.

---

[1] R. Jewett, "The Agitators and the Galatian Congregation," *NTS* 17 (1970–71): 198–212; reprinted in M. D. Nanos (ed.), *The Galatians Debate: Contemporary Issues in Rhetorical and Historical Interpretation* (Peabody, MA: Hendrickson, 2002) 334–47; G. E. Howard, *Paul—Crisis in Galatia: A Study in Early Christiain Theology* (SNTSMS 35; Cambridge: Cambridge University Press, 1979) 1–19; R. N. Longenecker, *Galatians* (WBC 41; Dallas: Word Books, 1990) lxxxviii–xcvi.

WORKS OF LAW IN THE SCRIPTURES

The emphasis placed on "works of law" (ἔργα νόμου) should hardly occasion surprise, for words like "works" (ἔργα) and "working" (ἐργάζεσθαι) are closely associated with righteousness and divine approval in many passages in Israel's sacred writings. A review of these materials will help us appreciate more fully the context in which Paul's argument took place and would have been understood.

The Prophets

At least three prophets—Isaiah, Jeremiah, and Jonah—contain expressions that link works to righteousness, reward, and judgment. There is also a passage in Lamentations, which—in keeping with ancient views of authorship—will be cited and discussed in connection with Jeremiah.

Isaiah 32:17

וְהָיָה מַעֲשֵׂה הַצְּדָקָה שָׁלוֹם וַעֲבֹדַת הַצְּדָקָה הַשְׁקֵט וָבֶטַח עַד־עוֹלָם׃

And the work of righteousness shall be peace; and the labor of righteousness (shall be) quietness and confidence for ever.

καὶ ἔσται τὰ ἔργα τῆς δικαιοσύνης εἰρήνη καὶ κρατήσει ἡ δικαιοσύνη ἀνάπαυσιν καὶ πεποιθότες ἕως τοῦ αἰῶνος.

And the works of righteousness shall be peace; and righteousness shall obtain rest, and (the righteous) shall be confident for ever.

This passage is part of an oracle that warns the women of Jerusalem of coming judgment (Isa 32:9–20). The time is coming when they will grieve over the loss of vineyards and pleasant field. Agricultural land will be unplanted and will become infested with thorns. These woes will continue until God pours forth his Spirit (v. 15). Then the wilderness will again become fertile. Justice will dwell in the wilderness and righteousness will abide in the fertile field (v. 16). The work (מַעֲשֵׂה/ἔργα), or outcome, of righteousness (ἡ δικαιοσύνη/הַצְּדָקָה) will be peace, quietness, and confidence (v. 17).[2]

The Greek personalizes the text somewhat, with the masculine plural participle πεποιθότες. Whereas the Hebrew expands on the results of the

---

[2] On the nuance of מַעֲשֵׂה in this context, see H. Wildberger, *Isaiah 28–39: A Continental Commentary* (Minneapolis: Fortress, 2002) 256.

"labor of righteousness," as leading to quietness and confidence, the Greek says "they shall be confident." The context suggests that it is the righteous who will be confident. The Aramaic seems to be moving in the same direction, saying, וִיהוֹן עָבְדֵי צִדְקְתָא ("and those who do righteousness . . ."). The association of work(s) and righteousness and hints of eschatological salvation ("quietness" in the Hebrew and "rest" in the Greek) are interesting. Indeed, the Aramaic goes on to paraphrase v. 20: "Happy are you, the righteous; you have made good deeds for yourselves . . ."[3]

Jeremiah 31:16

כֹּה אָמַר יְהוָה מִנְעִי קוֹלֵךְ מִבֶּכִי וְעֵינַיִךְ מִדִּמְעָה כִּי יֵשׁ שָׂכָר לִפְעֻלָּתֵךְ
נְאֻם־יְהוָה וְשָׁבוּ מֵאֶרֶץ אוֹיֵב:

Thus says the LORD: "Keep your voice from weeping, and your eyes from tears; for your work shall be rewarded, says the LORD, and they shall come back from the land of the enemy."

οὕτως εἶπεν κύριος διαλιπέτω ἡ φωνή σου ἀπὸ κλαυθμοῦ καὶ οἱ ὀφθαλμοί σου ἀπὸ δακρύων σου ὅτι ἔστιν μισθὸς τοῖς σοῖς ἔργοις καὶ ἐπιστρέψουσιν ἐκ γῆς ἐχθρῶν (LXX = 38:16).

Thus says the Lord: "Let your voice cease from weeping, and your eyes from your tears; for there is reward for your works, and they shall return from the land of (their) enemies."

This text links work(s) (לִפְעֻלָּתֵךְ/τοῖς σοῖς ἔργοις) and reward. The promise of return from the land of captivity lends the passage an eschatological potential.[4] In the Aramaic the word "righteous" is added: אֲרֵי אִית אֲגַר לְעוּבָדֵי אֲבָהָתָךְ צַדִּיקַיָּא (". . . for there is a reward for the deeds of your righteous fathers . . ."; cf. *Tg. Jer* 12:5 ". . . what I am going to do for your righteous fathers [לַאֲבָהָתָךְ צַדִּיקַיָּא] who were of old, who ran like the horses to do good works [עוּבָדִין טָבִין] . . ."). The association of doing good works and being regarded as righteous is significant.

---

[3] B. Chilton, *The Isaiah Targum* (ArBib 11; Wilmington, DE: Michael Glazier, 1987) 65.
[4] R. P. Carroll, *Jeremiah* (OTL; London: SCM Press; Philadelphia: Westminster, 1968) 599; W. Holladay, *Jeremiah 2: A Commentary on the Book of the Prophet Jeremiah Chapters 26–52* (Hermeneia; Minneapolis: Fortress, 1989) 188–89; G. Keown, P. Scalise, and T. G. Smothers, *Jeremiah 26–52* (WBC 27; Dallas: Word, 1995) 120.

Lamentations 3:64

תָּשִׁיב לָהֶם גְּמוּל יְהוָה כְּמַעֲשֵׂה יְדֵיהֶם׃

You will requite them, O LORD, according to the work of their hands.

ἀποδώσεις αὐτοῖς ἀνταπόδομα κύριε κατὰ τὰ ἔργα τῶν χειρῶν αὐτῶν.

You will repay them a repayment, Lord, according to the works of their hands.

The context is clearly punitive and is directed against the wicked. What is relevant is the affirmation of the principle that judgment is "according to works" (מַעֲשֵׂה/ἔργα).

Jonah 3:10

וַיַּרְא הָאֱלֹהִים אֶת־מַעֲשֵׂיהֶם כִּי־שָׁבוּ מִדַּרְכָּם הָרָעָה
וַיִּנָּחֶם הָאֱלֹהִים עַל־הָרָעָה אֲשֶׁר־דִּבֶּר לַעֲשׂוֹת־לָהֶם וְלֹא עָשָׂה׃

When God saw their works, how they turned from their evil way, God repented of the evil that he had said he would do to them; and he did not do it.

καὶ εἶδεν ὁ θεὸς τὰ ἔργα αὐτῶν ὅτι ἀπέστρεψαν ἀπὸ τῶν ὁδῶν αὐτῶν τῶν πονηρῶν καὶ μετενόησεν ὁ θεὸς ἐπὶ τῇ κακίᾳ ᾗ ἐλάλησεν τοῦ ποιῆσαι αὐτοῖς καὶ οὐκ ἐποίησεν.

And God saw their works, that they turned from their evil ways, and God repented of the evil that he had said he would do to them, and he did not do it.

When God saw the "works" (מַעֲשֵׂיהֶם/τὰ ἔργα αὐτῶν) of the people of Nineveh, he decided not to destroy the city. Of course, the Ninevites are not said to be "righteous," but it is significant that it is their works (particularly seen in their repentance)[5] that saves them from divine wrath.

Writings

Several books that eventually find themselves gathered in the Bible as "writings" or as "apocrypha" (or deutero-canonical books) link the vocabulary of works with righteousness or other expressions of approval.

---

[5] In what ways the Ninevites repented becomes a point of interest in later Jewish and Islamic interpretation. On this point, see J. Limburg, *Jonah* (OTL; Louisville: Westminster/John Knox Press, 1993) 87–88.

Proverbs 10:16

פְּעֻלַּת צַדִּיק לְחַיִּים תְּבוּאַת רָשָׁע לְחַטָּאת׃

The wage of the righteous leads to life, the harvest of the wicked to sin.

ἔργα δικαίων ζωὴν ποιεῖ καρποὶ δὲ ἀσεβῶν ἁμαρτίας.

The works of the righteous makes life, but the fruits of the impious (makes) sins.

This wisdom saying supports the idea that works (ἔργα) performed by the righteous will result in life. The original meaning concerned life in this world.[6] The Targum renders the verse literally, but in the midrash on Proverbs, references to life (as in v. 17) are taken as references to life in the world to come.

Sirach 16:22

ἔργα δικαιοσύνης τίς ἀναγγελεῖ ἢ τίς ὑπομενεῖ μακρὰν γὰρ ἡ διαθήκη.

Who will announce the works of righteousness, or who will await them? For the covenant is far away.

With reference to ἔργα δικαιοσύνης, Moshe Segal reconstructs the underlying Hebrew מַעֲשֵׂה צֶדֶק.[7] This passage is part of the skepticism introduced in v. 17 ("I shall be hidden from the Lord, and who from on high will remember me?"). Ben Sira, speaking for the skeptic, wonders who will report his "works of righteousness" (or, RSV: "acts of justice"). He wonders this because the "covenant seems far away," that is, the hope of reward for righteous deeds is remote and uncertain. Skepticism notwithstanding, this passage evidently presupposes that "works of righteousness" should result in reward.[8]

---

[6] C. H. Toy, *A Critical and Exegetical Commentary on the Book of Proverbs* (ICC; Edinburgh: T. & T. Clark, 1899) 209.

[7] M. Segal, *The Book of Ben-Sira Completum* (Jerusalem: Bialik, 1953) 96. The passage is not preserved in the Masada fragments or in the materials recovered from the Cairo genizah.

[8] P. W. Skehan and A. A. Di Lella, *The Wisdom of Ben Sira* (AB 39; Garden City: Doubleday, 1987) 275.

Sirach 51:30

⁹מעשיכם עשו בצדקה והוא נותן לכם שכרכם בעתו

Do your works in righteousness, and he will give to you your reward in his time.

ἐργάζεσθε τὸ ἔργον ὑμῶν πρὸ καιροῦ καὶ δώσει τὸν μισθὸν ὑμῶν ἐν καιρῷ αὐτοῦ.

Do your work before the appointed time, and in God's time he will give you your reward.

None of the aforementioned skepticism is present in this passage. The reward (ὁ μισθός), of which Ben Sira speaks, is wisdom.[10] It is a short step from the hope of receiving wisdom, to the hope of gaining life in the world to come. One thinks of the promise of a later sage: "It is not your part to finish the task, yet you are not free to desist from it. If you have studied much in the Law much reward will be given to you, and faithful is the taskmaster who shall pay you the reward of your work. And know that the recompense of the reward of the righteous is for the time to come" (*m. 'Abot* 2:16).[11]

The Hebrew of the Cairo genizah text reads differently. In place of "before the appointed time" (πρὸ καιροῦ) we have "in righteousness" (בצדקה). The two-fold appearance of καιρός in the Greek version serves well the parallelism, so is probably original. It may be that the Hebrew version is a later qualification of "your works." If so, it is interesting to observe the tendency to link works with righteousness.

Wisdom 6:18

ἀγάπη δὲ τήρησις νόμων αὐτῆς προσοχὴ δὲ νόμων βεβαίωσις ἀφθαρσίας.

But love is keeping her laws, and observance of (her) laws is assurance of immortality.

The definition of love as keeping the laws alludes to Exod 20:6 (". . . They who love me keep my commandments"). There is no mention of works

---

[9] For Hebrew text, see I. Lévi, *The Hebrew Text of the Book of Ecclesiasticus* (Semitic Study Series 3; Leiden: E. J. Brill, 1904) 76.
[10] Skehan and Di Lella, *The Wisdom of Ben Sira*, 579.
[11] Translation is an adaptation of H. Danby, *The Mishnah* (Oxford: Clarendon Press, 1933) 449.

in this passage, but "keeping her laws" (τήρησις νόμων αὐτῆς) is the equivalent. In fact, from the sage's point of view, keeping the laws of God is the highest form of righteous work. What is significant about this passage is the explicit linkage of keeping the law with immortality (ἀφθαρσία). What is meant here by "immortality" is not obvious. The author may have in mind nothing more than a long-lasting, honored reputation. Eschatological conclusions are hazardous.[12] However, these sentiments could well take on eschatological connotations in other and later writers (e.g., 4 Macc 17:12 "the prize was immortality [ἀφθαρσία] in endless life").[13] In *Joseph and Aseneth*, the righteous Joseph describes himself as a man who has eaten the "blessed bread of life" and has drunk the "blessed cup of immortality [ἀφθαρσίας]" (8:5). After her repentance, an angel tells Aseneth: "Courage, chaste virgin. For behold, your name was written in the book of the living in heaven; in the beginning of the book, as the very first of all, your name was written by my finger, and it will not be erased forever. Behold, from today, you will be renewed and formed anew and made alive again, and you will eat blessed bread of life, and drink a blessed cup of immortality [ἀφθαρσίας], and anoint yourself with blessed ointment of incorruptibility" (15:3–4). There is no doubt here that the "immortality" of Aseneth refers to eschatological salvation. Readers of Wis 6:18, in late antiquity, may well have interpreted this passage the same way.

Wisdom 9:12

> καὶ ἔσται προσδεκτὰ τὰ ἔργα μου καὶ διακρινῶ τὸν λαόν σου δικαίως καὶ ἔσομαι ἄξιος θρόνων πατρός μου.
>
> And my works shall be acceptable and I shall judge your people justly and I shall be worthy of the throne of my father.

The fictive Solomon prays that his works (ἔργα) will be acceptable to God and that he will govern the people of Israel in a just manner and so, therefore, will be worthy to succeed his father David. In this passage works have no saving or eschatological implications.

---

[12] Perhaps even "hopeless," as remarked by A. T. S. Goodrick (ed.), *The Book of Wisdom* (London: Rivingtons, 1913) 176.

[13] See comments in W. J. Deane, *ΣΟΦΙΑ ΣΑΛΩΜΩΝ: The Book of Wisdom. The Greek Text, the Latin Vulgate and the Authorised English Version* (Oxford: Clarendon Press, 1881) 143.

Psalms of Solomon 9:3–5

οὐ γὰρ κρυβήσεται ἀπὸ τῆς γνώσεώς σου πᾶς ποιῶν ἄδικα καὶ αἱ δικαιοσύναι τῶν ὁσίων σου ἐνώπιόν σου κύριε καὶ ποῦ κρυβήσεται ἄνθρωπος ἀπὸ τῆς γνώσεώς σου ὁ θεός. τὰ ἔργα ἡμῶν ἐν ἐκλογῇ καὶ ἐξουσίᾳ τῆς ψυχῆς ἡμῶν τοῦ ποιῆσαι δικαιοσύνην καὶ ἀδικίαν ἐν ἔργοις χειρῶν ἡμῶν καὶ ἐν τῇ δικαιοσύνῃ σου ἐπισκέπτῃ υἱοὺς ἀνθρώπων. ὁ ποιῶν δικαιοσύνην θησαυρίζει ζωὴν αὐτῷ παρὰ κυρίῳ. . . .[14]

For everyone who does unrighteousness cannot hide from your knowledge, and the righteous deeds of your holy ones are before you, O Lord. And where will a man hide from your knowledge, O God? Our works are in (our) choice and in the power of our soul, to do righteousness and unrighteousness in the works of our hands; and in your righteousness you visit the sons of men. The one who does righteousness stores up life for himself from the Lord. . . .

This is a very important passage. In context we have commentary on the exile and an argument that God was just in allowing this judgment to befall Israel. Because of sin, the nation was expelled from its land. Those who do unrighteousness cannot hide from God's knowledge, and so forth. What is interesting is the assertion that what is done, whether righteous or unrighteous, is a human being's responsibility; and he will be judged (i.e., "visited") accordingly. He who does righteousness "stores up life for himself." What is in mind here is surely more than the prolonging of life in this world; eschatological hopes are probably present. The parallels with dominical tradition in Matthew 6 (v. 20: "store up treasures in heaven") encourage us to think this.[15]

Psalms of Solomon 14:1–2

πιστὸς κύριος τοῖς ἀγαπῶσιν αὐτὸν ἐν ἀληθείᾳ τοῖς ὑπομένουσιν παιδείαν αὐτοῦ τοῖς πορευομένοις ἐν δικαιοσύνῃ προσταγμάτων αὐτοῦ ἐν νόμῳ ᾧ ἐνετείλατο ἡμῖν εἰς ζωὴν ἡμῶν.

The Lord is faithful to those who truly love him, to those who walk in the righteousness of his commandments in the law, which he commanded to us for our life.[16]

---

[14] For Greek text (numbered slightly differently), see H. E. Ryle and M. R. James, *Psalms of the Pharisees, Commonly Called the Psalms of Solomon: The Text Newly Revised from all the MSS* (Cambridge: Cambridge University Press, 1891) 90–91. The Syriac reads essentially the same; cf. J. L. Trafton, *The Syriac Version of the Psalms of Solomon: A Critical Evaluation* (SBLSCS 11; Atlanta: Scholars Press, 1985) 99.

[15] See Ryle and James, *Psalms of the Pharisees*, 90–91.

[16] The Syriac reads: "He gave us the law for our life"; cf. Trafton, *The Syriac Version*

The principal reference is to life in this world (as in Lev 18:5), but the text leaves open the possibility of eschatological meaning, as references to "forever," "paradise," and "trees of life" in the next verse could suggest.

Psalms of Solomon 18:8

> κατευθῦναι ἄνδρα ἐν ἔργοις δικαιοσύνης φόβῳ θεοῦ καταστῆσαι πάντας αὐτοὺς ἐνώπιον κυρίου.
>
> To direct man in works of righteousness, in the fear of God; to make them all stand before the Lord.[17]

The language of this passage in itself is suggestive; all the more so, in light of the fuller context of chs. 17–18. In these chapters the hope of a coming messianic son of David is expressed. When the Messiah comes, he will gather a holy people and lead them in righteousness (17:26). He will purge Jerusalem, making it holy, as it was in the beginning (17:30). He will drive out sinners (17:36) and discipline Israel (17:43). The psalmist prays that God will cleanse Israel "for the appointed day when his Messiah will reign" (18:5). The Messiah will "direct man in works of righteousness," that "all may stand before the Lord" (18:8). The context is clearly restorative; and the eschatology of *Psalms of Solomon* should be understood in that sense. The author is not talking about celestial judgment and/or heaven. Nevertheless, the implication that "works of righteousness" (ἐν ἔργοις δικαιοσύνης) are required, in order to stand before the Lord, is very significant.

Tobit 4:6

> [18]כי בעשות ה[אמת . . . יה[וה עמך . . .
>
> For in doing the tr[uth . . . the Lo]rd shall be with you . . .
>
> διότι ποιοῦντός σου τὴν ἀλήθειαν εὐοδίαι ἔσονται ἐν τοῖς ἔργοις σου.
>
> For if you do the truth, your ways will prosper in your deeds.

Although the Greek and Hebrew versions differ, they agree that if one does the truth, one will benefit. The Greek promises prosperity, while the Hebrew, whose text is poorly preserved, states either that "the Lord shall

---

of the Psalms of Solomon, 131. The Syriac may be a more faithful rendering of the underlying Hebrew.

[17] This portion of the chapter is not preserved in the Syriac.
[18] The text is taken from 4Q200 frg. 2 line 5.

be with you," or perhaps that the "prosperity of the Lord shall be with you" (cf. Deut 15:10). In any case, the promise has in view benefits in this life. The next two passages from Tobit are more suggestive of eschatological implications.

Tobit 4:10–11

> διότι ἐλεημοσύνη ἐκ θανάτου ῥύεται καὶ οὐκ ἐᾷ εἰσελθεῖν εἰς τὸ σκότος. δῶρον γὰρ ἀγαθόν ἐστιν ἐλεημοσύνη πᾶσι τοῖς ποιοῦσιν αὐτὴν ἐνώπιον τοῦ ὑψίστου.

> For almsgiving delivers from death and keeps you from entering the darkness; for almsgiving is a good gift for all who do it in the presence of the Most High.

Tobit tells his son Tobias that "almsgiving delivers from death," yet it was Tobit's piety in securing burial for the dead that resulted in his blindness and his lending to a relative that has resulted in his financial distress. Although the primary reference is to a blessed life in this world (as in Prov 10:2), the promise of being delivered from death and from entering darkness may well have implications for life in the world to come.[19]

Tobit 12:9

> ἐλεημοσύνη γὰρ ἐκ θανάτου ῥύεται καὶ αὐτὴ ἀποκαθαριεῖ πᾶσαν ἁμαρτίαν οἱ ποιοῦντες ἐλεημοσύνας καὶ δικαιοσύνας πλησθήσονται ζωῆς.

> For almsgiving delivers from death, and it will purge away every sin. Those who perform deeds of charity and of righteousness will have fullness of life.

The point being made here is essentially the same as in 4:10–11. Carey Moore again states that afterlife is not in view.[20] But one cannot rule out a more expanded interpretation that early readers of Tobit may have entertained. The Latin tradition takes it this way:

> *quoniam elemosyna a morte liberat et ipsa est quae purgat peccata et faciet invenire vitam aeternam.*

> For alms(giving) delivers from death and likewise purges away sins and makes (it possible) to find eternal life.

---

[19] *Pace* C. A. Moore, *Tobit* (AB 40A; Garden City: Doubleday, 1996) 168: "There is, however, no hint here of belief in an afterlife."

[20] Moore, *Tobit*, 270. Moore says that early or premature death is in view.

One need not insist that eschatological implications were an original part of the author's thinking. The point is that affirmations of deliverance from judgment and death—through good works—could be interpreted by others, as in the case of the Latin translator, as pertaining to life in the world to come.

1 Esdras 1:21

καὶ ὠρθώθη τὰ ἔργα Ιωσιου ἐνώπιον τοῦ κυρίου αὐτοῦ ἐν καρδίᾳ πλήρει εὐσεβείας.

And the works of Josiah were upright in the sight of the Lord, for his heart was full of godliness (1:23).

The righteous works of Josiah are given in 2 Kgs 23:24–25.[21] The righteousness of Josiah did not spare him defeat and death at the hands of Pharaoh Necco at Megiddo. These works (ἔργα/מעשי) are said to be "upright" (ὀρθοῦν) before the Lord. The text does not hint at any eschatological implications.

1 Maccabees 2:51

καὶ μνήσθητε τὰ ἔργα τῶν πατέρων ἃ ἐποίησαν ἐν ταῖς γενεαῖς αὐτῶν καὶ δέξασθε δόξαν μεγάλην καὶ ὄνομα αἰώνιον.

And remember the works of your fathers, which they did in their generations and received great glory and an everlasting name.

The admonition of the dying Mattathias to his sons that they remember the works of their fathers no doubt is meant to recall the achievements extolled in Sirach 44–49 (esp. 44:1 "Let us now praise famous men, and our fathers in their generations"). The hope for an "everlasting name" (ὄνομα αἰώνιον) did not necessarily imply belief in an afterlife,[22] but the language invites this possibility.[23]

---

[21] On the Hebrew Vorlage, with commentary, see Z. Talshir, *1 Esdras: A Text Critical Commentary* (SBLSCS 50; Atlanta: Society of Biblical Literature, 2000) 38–39.

[22] H. A. Fischel, *The First Book of Maccabees: A Commentary* (New York: Schocken Books, 1948) 31.

[23] W. Fairweather and J. S. Black (eds.), *The First Book of Maccabees* (Cambridge: Cambridge University Press, 1936) 84: "Whether this craving for renown was the only immortality present to their minds is another question."

4 Maccabees 7:9

> σὺ πάτερ τὴν εὐνομίαν ἡμῶν διὰ τῶν ὑπομονῶν εἰς δόξαν ἐκύρωσας καὶ τὴν ἁγιαστίαν σεμνολογήσας οὐ κατέλυσας καὶ διὰ τῶν ἔργων ἐπιστοποίησας τοὺς τῆς θείας φιλοσοφίας σου λόγους.
>
> You, father, strengthened our loyalty to the law through your glorious endurance, and you did not abandon the holiness that you praised, but by your works you made your words of divine philosophy credible.

These words are part of a panegyric on Eleazar the righteous elder who suffered martyrdom at the hands of Antiochus IV Epiphanes (cf. 2 Macc 6:18–31; 4 Macc 5:1–6:30). The panegyric refers to Eleazar's "works" (ἔργα). Will these faithful works result in Eleazar's salvation? Evidently, they will, for the righteous man affirms: "The fathers will receive me as pure, as one who does not fear your violence even to death" (5:37). Eleazar's statement implies afterlife, whether in terms of resurrection (which in 4 Maccabees is doubtful, but is affirmed explicitly in 2 Maccabees 7) or in some other form.[24] Eleazar has remained loyal to God's law, lending credibility to it by his works.

Jubilees 30:17, 23

> Proclaim this testimony to Israel: "See how it was for the Shechemites and their sons, how they were given into the hand of the two children of Jacob and they killed them painfully. And it was a righteousness for them and it was written down to them for righteousness.... And on the day that the children of Jacob killed Shechem, he wrote (on high) for them a book in heaven that they did righteousness and uprightness and vengeance against the sinners and it was written down for a blessing."[25]

This passage is part of a rewritten account of the violent vengeance that Levi and Simeon took on behalf of their sister Dinah (Gen 33:17–34:31). According to *Jubilees*, this act of vengeance is regarded as a righteous work and was recorded in heaven as such.[26] The Latin version of this text

---

[24] On afterlife ideas in 4 Maccabees, see G. W. E. Nickelsburg, *Resurrection, Immortality and Eternal Life in Intertestamental Judaism* (HTS 26; Cambridge: Harvard University Press, 1972) 109–11; *idem, Jewish Literature Between the Bible and the Mishnah* (Philadelphia: Fortress, 1981) 223–27.

[25] The translation is based on the Ethiopic and is from O. S. Wintermute, "Jubilees," in J. H. Charlesworth (ed.), *The Old Testament Pseudepigrapha* (2 vols.; ABRL; New York: Doubleday, 1983–85) 2:113–14. See also R. H. Charles, "The Book of Jubilees," in *APOT* 2:59.

[26] On the author's reorientation of the story, so as to make it possible to regard the

may contain an important scriptural allusion, which will be taken into account below.

1 Enoch 10:16

ואכרת עולה מן] אנפי ארעא וכול עובד באישותא יעדא ותתחזא נ[צבת קושטא
ותהו[א ברכה ועובדי קושטא לעלם בחדוה יתנצבון].

And destroy iniquity from [the face of the earth, and every work of evil do away; and make the p]lant of truth [appear.] It will be a [blessing, and the deeds of truth will be planted in joy forever.][27]

καὶ ἀπόλεσον τὴν ἀδικίαν πᾶσαν ἀπὸ τῆς γῆς, καὶ πᾶν ἔργον πονηρίας ἐκλειπέτω, καὶ ἀναφανήτω τὸ φυτὸν τῆς δικαιοσύνης καὶ τῆς ἀληθείας εἰς τοὺς αἰῶνας· μετὰ χαρᾶς φυτευθήσεται.

And destroy all wrong from the earth and let every work of evil come to an end; and let the plant of righteousness and truth appear forever. With joy it shall be planted.

The more expansive Ethiopic version reads:

Destroy all perversity from the face of the earth; and let every wicked deed be gone; and let the plant of righteousness (and truth) appear, and it will become a blessing; (and) the deeds of righteousness (and truth) will be planted forever with joy.[28]

This passage is part of God's instructions to Michael the angel, to purge and renovate the earth (10:16–11:2).[29] Part of this renovation will be cultivation of "deeds of righteousness" or "truth." Although this part of *Enoch* is a retelling of old stories from Genesis (in this case, the recovery of the earth following the flood), the text goes on to foretell a time when the blessings of heaven will shower the earth, a time when humans will be righteous (cf. 10:20–11:2).

---

vengeance of Levi and Simeon as honorable, see the comments in Charles, "The Book of Jubilees," in *APOT* 2:58.

[27] For Hebrew, see 4Q204 5:3–4. The reconstructions come from M. G. Abegg, Jr. et al., as presented in the Qumran module for Accordance. The Hebrew reconstruction evidently has been influenced by the Ethiopic version.

[28] Translation based on G. W. E. Nickelsburg, *1 Enoch 1: A Commentary on the Book of 1 Enoch, Chapters 1–36; 81–108* (Hermeneia; Minneapolis: Fortress, 2001) 216.

[29] For commentary, see Nickelsburg, *1 Enoch 1*, 226–28.

1 Enoch 38:2, 1 Enoch 41:1

> When the Righteous One shall appear before the face of the righteous, those elect ones, their works are hung upon[30] the Lord of the Spirits . . .[31]

> And after that, I saw all the secrets in heaven, and how a kingdom breaks up,[32] and how the actions of the people are weighed in the balance.[33]

1 Enoch 38:2 and 41:1 are found in the *Similitudes of Enoch*, a large portion of *Enoch* not found at Qumran and not extant in Greek manuscripts. It is preserved in the Ethiopic tradition. The first passage describes the assessment of the works of the righteous, while the second passage describes the assessment of actions of humans in general. In *1 En.* 61:8, the Messiah (a.k.a. "Elect One") will judge the angels in the same manner.

1 Enoch 100:7

> οὐαὶ ὑμῖν οἱ ἄδικοι ὅταν ἐκθλίβητε τοὺς δικαίους ἐν ἡμέρᾳ ἀνάγκης στερεᾶς καὶ φυλάξητε αὐτοὺς ἐν πυρί, ὅτι κομιεῖσθε κατὰ τὰ ἔργα ὑμῶν.

> Woe to you, unrighteous, when you afflict the righteous on a day of severe need, and burn them in fire; for you will be recompensed according to your works.

Literally, the text reads "guard" or "imprison them in fire" and may allude to Daniel 3, where the Jewish youths are cast into a furnace of fire. The wicked will someday find themselves imprisoned and cast into the fires of hell (as in v. 9: "in blazing flames you will burn"). Because their works (ἔργα) were evil, the wicked will be paid back accordingly.[34]

1 Enoch 102:6

> ὅταν ἀποθάνητε, τότε ἐροῦσιν οἱ ἁμαρτωλοὶ ὅτι εὐσεβεῖς κατὰ τὴν εἱμαρμένην ἀπεθάνοσαν, καὶ τί αὐτοῖς περιεγένετο ἐπὶ τοῖς ἔργοις αὐτῶν;

> When you die, then the sinners will say: "The pious have died according to fate, and what did they gain from their works?"

---

[30] Or: "are weighed by the Lord of the Spirits."
[31] Translation based on E. Isaac, "1 (Ethiopic Apocalypse of) Enoch," in *OTP*, 1:30.
[32] Or: "is divided."
[33] Translation based on Isaac, "1 (Ethiopic Apocalypse of) Enoch," 1:32.
[34] See Nickelsburg, *1 Enoch 1*, 506.

Sinners think that there is no benefit to be had for being righteous—not in this life, nor in the life to come (as seen in v. 11, where sinners think the righteous simply perish and descend into Sheol). Of course, from the author's point of view, the sinners are quite wrong; the righteous will indeed derive benefit, even if they die painfully.

1 Enoch 103:2–4

> ἀν[έγνων] γὰρ τὰς πλάκας τοῦ οὐρανοῦ καὶ εἶδον τὴν γραφὴν ἀναγκαίαν· ἔγνων τὰ γ[εγραμμέ]να ἐν αὐταῖς καὶ ἐγκεκολαμμέν[α περὶ] ὑμῶν, ὅτι ἀγαθὰ καὶ ἡ χαρὰ καὶ ἡ [τιμὴ] ἡ ἡτοίμασται καὶ ἐγγέγραπται ταῖς [ψυχαῖς] τῶν ἀποθανόντων εὐσεβῶν· καὶ χαιρήσονται καὶ οὐ μὴ ἀπόλωνται τὰ πνεύματα αὐτῶν οὐδὲ τὸ μνημόσυνον ἀπὸ προσώπου τοῦ μεγάλου εἰς πάσας τὰς γενεὰς τῶν αἰώνων.

> For I have r[ead] the tablets of heaven and I have seen the writing of what must be; and I know the things written in them and inscrib[ed concerning] you, that good things and joy and [honor] have been prepared and written down for the [souls] of the pious who have died. And their spirits shall rejoice and in no wise perish, nor their memorial, from the face of the Great One for all the generations forever.

The passage reads somewhat differently in the Ethiopic:

> For I know this mystery; I have read the tablets of heaven and have seen the holy writings, and I have understood the writing in them; and they are inscribed concerning you. For all good things, and joy and honor are prepared for and written down for the souls of those who died in righteousness. Many and good things shall be given to you—the offshoot of your labors. Your lot exceeds even that of the living ones.[35]

The tablets and writings evidently have recorded the works of the righteous, as well as the sins committed against them. It will be on the basis of these records that God will render judgment. Presumably the "good things" written down (according to the Greek), which will be given to the pious (so the Ethiopic) presuppose the principle of judgment "according to works."[36]

Sibylline Oracles 3:233

> τοῦ πεπλανῆσθαι ὁδούς τ' ἀγαθὰς καὶ ἔργα δίκαια.

> ... so that (they) are misled as to good ways and righteous works.

---

[35] Translation based on Isaac, "1 (Ethiopic Apocalypse of) Enoch," 1:83.
[36] For commentary, see Nickelsburg, *1 Enoch 1*, 522–23.

This brief quotation is part of a long oracle tracing the history of the Jewish people, from Abraham, to Egypt, to the exodus, to the conquest of the land, to exile, and to restoration. The line cited above is in reference to foolish Gentiles who engage in astrology and teach errors. On account of this, many Gentiles "are misled as to good ways and righteous works." In contrast, the Jews teach righteousness and not out of hopes of money (line 235). Apart from peace and prosperity in the land of Israel, the benefits of the good ways and righteous works are not spelled out.

Testament of Reuben 4:1

> μὴ οὖν προσέχετε, τέκνα μου, κάλλος γυναικῶν, μηδὲ ἐννοεῖσθε τὰς πράξεις αὐτῶν· ἀλλὰ πορεύεσθε ἐν ἁπλότητι καρδίας, ἐν φόβῳ κυρίου, καὶ μοχθοῦντες ἐν ἔργοις καλοῖς, καὶ ἀποπλανώμενοι ἐν γράμμασι, καὶ ἐν τοῖς ποιμνίοις ὑμῶν, ἕως οὗ ὁ κύριος δώῃ ὑμῖν σύζυγον, ἣν αὐτὸς θέλει, ἵνα μὴ πάθητε, ὡς κἀγώ.

> Pay no heed, therefore, my children, to the beauty of women, nor set your mind on their activities. But walk in singleness of heart, in the fear of the Lord, laboring on good works, and being led away[37] on study, and on your flocks, until the Lord give you a mate, whom He will, lest you suffer as I did.

The patriarch urges his sons to fear the Lord, "laboring on good works" (μοχθοῦντες ἐν ἔργοις καλοῖς). If they pursue good works and avoid sin, they will also avoid hell (cf. v. 6).

Testament of Levi 13:5

> ποιήσατε δικαιοσύνην, τέκνα μου, ἐπὶ τῆς γῆς, ἵνα εὕρητε ἐν τοῖς οὐρανοῖς.

> Do righteousness, my children, upon the earth, in order that you find (it) in heaven.

Doing "righteousness" (δικαιοσύνη) may refer to almsgiving.[38] What is remarkable here is the exact correspondence between doing righteousness on earth, so that it will be found in heaven. This idea coheres with expressions of laying up treasure in heaven, some of which have been

---

[37] "Being led away" is an attempt to make sense of the participle ἀποπλανώμενοι. "Being led astray" hardly seems appropriate. R. H. Charles remarks that the text, as it is, is "untranslatable"; cf. R. H. Charles, *The Testaments of the Twelve Patriarchs* (London: A. & C. Black, 1908) 9. He suspects corruption in the underlying Hebrew text.

[38] So Charles, *The Testaments*, 52.

considered above (also see *4 Ezra* 7:77; 8:33). In Hebrew "do" is עשׂה, whose nominal form "deed" or "work" is מעשׂה. Doing righteousness (צדקה) is found in the Hebrew Bible (e.g., Gen 18:19; 1 Kgs 10:9), which will be discussed further below.

Testament of Naphtali 8:4

> ἐὰν ἐργάσησθε τὸ καλόν, τέκνα μου, εὐλογήσουσιν ὑμᾶς καὶ οἱ ἄνθρωποι καὶ οἱ ἄγγελοι· καὶ θεὸς δοξασθήσεται δι' ὑμῶν ἐν τοῖς ἔθνεσι, καὶ ὁ διάβολος φεύξεται ἀφ' ὑμῶν, καὶ τὰ θηρία φοβηθήσονται ὑμᾶς, καὶ ὁ κύριος ἀγαπήσει ὑμᾶς, καὶ οἱ ἄγγελοι ἀνθέξονται ὑμῶν.[39]

> If you work that which is good, my children, both men and angels will bless you; and God shall be glorified through you among the Gentiles, and the devil will flee from you, and the beasts will fear you, and the Lord will love you, and the angels will seek you.

Working the good (ἐργάζεσθαι τὸ καλόν) will result in human praise and divine blessing. Life in this world is what is in view, but assurance of divine praise for doing good deeds is important to note.

Testament of Benjamin 11:4

> καὶ ἐν βίβλοις ἁγίαις ἀναγραφόμενος, καὶ τὸ ἔργον καὶ ὁ λόγος αὐτοῦ· καὶ ἔσται ἐκλεκτὸς θεοῦ ἕως τοῦ αἰῶνος.

> And in the holy books he is written, both his work and word; and he shall be chosen of God forever.

Again we find the idea of one's deeds (and words, too, in this case) recorded in heaven. Although not explicitly stated, it seems that the designation "chosen of God forever" (ἐκλεκτὸς θεοῦ ἕως τοῦ αἰῶνος) implies some sort of afterlife.

Letter of Aristeas 18

> μεγάλην γὰρ εἶχον ἐλπίδα, περὶ σωτηρίας ἀνθρώπων προτιθέμενος λόγον, ὅτι τὴν ἐπιτέλειαν ὁ θεὸς ποιήσει τῶν ἀξιουμένων· ὃ γὰρ πρὸς δικαιοσύνην καὶ καλῶν ἔργων ἐπιμέλειαν ἐν ὁσιότητι νομίζουσιν ἄνθρωποι ποιεῖν, κατευθύνει τὰς πράξεις καὶ τὰς ἐπιβολὰς ὁ κυριεύων ἁπάντων θεός.

> For I had great hopes with regard to the salvation of people since I was assured that God would grant a fulfillment of my prayer. For when men

---

[39] Charles (*The Testaments*, 146) brackets off καὶ οἱ ἄγγελοι ἀνθέξονται ὑμῶν as based on a corrupt Hebrew dittography. Perhaps, but not all follow him.

from pure motives plan some action in the interest of righteousness and the performance of noble deeds, Almighty God brings their efforts and purposes to a successful issue.

The contribution that this passage makes to the concerns at hand is the notion that God gives assistance to those whose works are good (καλὰ ἔργα) and well intentioned, aimed toward some righteous goal (δικαιοσύνην). It is also interesting to observe that these good deeds are motivated out of a desire for the "salvation of people" (περὶ σωτηρίας ἀνθρώπων). This salvation (or deliverance) may be primarily political or economic, in the present context,[40] but some readers in late antiquity would probably have seen further implications.

Ps.-Philo, Biblical Antiquities 64:7

Et dixit ad eum Samuel: Ut quid me inquietasti, ut elevares me? Putavi quod approprinquasset tempus reddendi merces operum meorum.

And Samuel said to him, "Why have you disturbed me and raised me up? I thought the time to receive the reward for my works had arrived."

Ps.-Philo retells here the story of King Saul's raising the spirit of Samuel, for a consultation (1 Sam 28:14–15). Samuel's declarative "I thought the time to receive the reward for my works had arrived" firmly links eschatological reward (*merces*) with works (*opera*). The implication is that the day of judgment has arrived.[41] Rabbinic tradition interprets the story similarly.[42]

History of the Rechabites 12:8–9

καὶ οἱ ἄγγελοι τοῦ θεοῦ οἰκοῦσιν μεθ' ἡμῶν κατὰ πᾶσαν ἡμέραν καὶ λέγουσιν ἡμῖν πάντα τὰ περὶ ὑμῶν· καὶ χαίρομεν μετὰ τῶν ἀγγέλων ἕνεκεν τῶν ἔργων τῶν δικαίων, ἐπὶ δὲ τὰ ἔργα τῶν ἁμαρτωλῶν λυπούμεθα . . .

And the angels of God dwell with us every day and they tell us all things concerning you; and we rejoice with the angels, on account of the works of the righteous; but we grieve over the works of the sinners . . .

---

[40] See the comment in H. G. Meecham, *The Letter of Aristeas: A Linguistic Study with Special Reference to the Greek Bible* (Publications of the University of Manchester 241; Manchester: Manchester University Press, 1935) 189.

[41] So D. J. Harrington, "Pseudo-Philo," in *OTP*, 2:377.

[42] As noted by H. Jacobson, *A Commentary on Pseudo-Philo's Liber Antiquitatum Biblicarum, with Latin Text and English Translation* (2 vols.; AGJU 31; Leiden: E. J. Brill, 1996) 2:1210.

The grammar is somewhat ambiguous. It can read "on account of the works of the righteous," or "on account of the righteous works." However, the former rendering is preferred, because of the parallelism with "over the works of the sinners," where there is no ambiguity. The passage speaks of a contrast between the works of the righteous and the works of the sinful. What is interesting about this text is the idea that the angels of God rejoice on account of the works of the righteous, which encourages us to see linkage between good works and eschatological salvation. Indeed, a Christian scribe, writing in Syriac, seems to have understood the passage this way. He adds five or six verses, in which he speaks of the "salvation of mortals" (v. 9a), "salvation of your lives" (v. 9e), and the hope of inheriting "the kingdom of God" (v. 9g).[43]

WORKS OF LAW AT QUMRAN

In some of the Dead Sea Scrolls we find references to "doing the Law." Commenting on Hab 2:3b ("If it tarries, be patient . . ."), the pesher explains: "This refers to those loyal ones, who do the Law [עושי התורה], whose hands will not cease from loyal service even when the Last Days seems long to them" (1QpHab 7:10–12). We hear this again, in reference to "all those who do the Law [עושי התורה] among the Jews whom God will rescue from among those doomed to judgment, because of their suffering and their loyalty to the Teacher of Righteousness" (8:1–3). The pesher on Micah probably has a similar expression, though it has to be restored (cf. 1Q14 frgs. 8–10 lines 5–9). The pesher on Psalm 37 speaks of a "plot to destroy those who do the Law [עושה התורה] who are in the party of the Community" (4Q171 frgs. 1–2 ii 14). According to the Florilegium, most of Israel will be deceived and led astray by Belial. But then "shall be left behind a remnant of [chosen on]es, the pre[des]tined. They shall perform the whole of the Law [ועשו את כול התורה]" (4Q174 frgs. 1–3 ii 2; for additional examples, see 4Q176 frg. 17 line 7; 4Q470 frg. 1 line 4).

The Scrolls also speak of the "works of the Law" (מעשי תורה), particularly in reference to candidates for admission into the Community: "When anyone enters the covenant—to live according to all these ordinances, to make common cause with the Congregation of Holiness—they

---

[43] For discussion of this Syriac interpolation, see J. H. Charlesworth, "The History of the Rechabites," in *OTP*, 2:457–58.

shall investigate his spiritual qualities as a community, each member taking part. They shall investigate his understanding and his works in the Law [ומעשיו בתורה]" (1QS 5:21). And again, we hear later in the Community Rule: "When he has passed a full year in the Community, the general membership shall inquire into the details of his understanding and his works in the Law [ומעשיו בתורה]" (1QS 6:18). If a candidate's knowledge is found wanting, "the Overseer [shall instruct him] before the Community concerning [the works] of the law [ב]מעש[י התורה]" (4Q265 frg. 4 ii 6). Not only is one's understanding of the works of the Law essential for entry; it is also a criterion for determining rank within the Community: "They are to be enrol[led by rank, one man higher th]an [his] fellow[—as the case may be—by virtue of] his understanding and works in the law [ומעשו בתורה]" (4Q261 frg. 1a–b 2–3; for additional examples, see 4Q174 frgs. 1–2 i 7; 4Q258 2:1, 3).

It has also been suggested, persuasively in my opinion, that the sobriquet "Essene" is a transliteration from "those who do" (עשי), that is, those who "do the Law" (e.g., 1QpHab 7:11; 8:1; 12:4–5; 4Q171 frgs. 1–2 ii 14).[44] Indeed, we may have the translated equivalent in Paul, when he counters that only "doers of the Law will be justified [οἱ ποιηταὶ νόμου δικαιωθήσονται]" (Rom 2:13), implying that, of course, no one actually can do the Law. The epithet also appears in James, who asserts: "But if you judge the law, you are not a doer of the law [ποιητὴς νόμου] but a judge" (Jas 4:11). James's admonition to members of his community, to be "doers of the word [ποιηταὶ λόγου], and not hearers only" (Jas 1:22) is similar (see also Jas 1:23, 25).

This manner of speaking is not hard to explain, for "doing" (עשה) the "Law" (תורה) is found in Scripture. This language is found several times in Deuteronomy (e.g., Deut 27:26 "'Cursed be he who does not confirm the words of this law by doing them.' And all the people shall say, 'Amen'"; see also 29:28[E29] "that we may do all the words of this law"; 31:12; 32:46; Josh 1:7 "Only be strong and very courageous, being careful to do according to all the law which Moses my servant commanded you"). Indeed, this kind of language appears in Paul also, who speaks of "doing the Law" (Rom 2:14), "practicing the Law" (Rom 2:25), "keeping

---

[44] On this point, see S. Goranson, "Others and Intra-Jewish Polemic as Reflected in Qumran Texts," in P. W. Flint and J. C. VanderKam (eds.), *The Dead Sea Scrolls after Fifty Years: A Comprehensive Assessment* (2 vols.; Leiden: E. J. Brill, 1998–99) 2:534–51, here 537–40.

the righteous precepts of the Law" (Rom 2:26), and "fulfilling the Law" (Rom 13:8), to mention the most obvious.

The text at Qumran that has generated the most interest in this topic is the *Halakic Letter*, or *Miqsat Maʿase ha-Torah* ("Some of the Works of the Law"; a.k.a. 4QMMT).[45] After reviewing a series of "works of the Law," which in the opinion of the author are essential, the letter draws to a close:

> Remember David, he was a pious man, [and] indeed he [was] delivered from many troubles and forgiven. Now, we have written to you some of the works of the Law [מקצת מעשי התורה], those which we determined would be beneficial for you and your people, because we have seen that you possess insight and knowledge of the Law. Understand all these things and beseech Him to set your counsel straight and so keep you away from evil thoughts and the counsel of Belial. Then you shall rejoice at the end time when you find the essence of our words to be true. And it will be reckoned to you as righteousness [ונחשבה לך לצדקה], in that you have done [בעשותך] what is right and good before Him, to your own benefit and to that of Israel. (C25–32; cf. 4Q398 frgs. 14–17 ii 1–8 = 4Q399 frg. 1 i 9–11 + ii 1–5)

The references to "works of the Law," rejoicing at the "end time," and being "reckoned righteous," along with the assurance that the recipients "have done what is right and good," require comparison with Paul's theology, especially as expressed in his letters to the Christians of Rome and in various locations in Galatia. 4QMMT's "works of the Law" (מעשי התורה) is the linguistic equivalent of Paul's ἔργα νόμου (e.g., Rom 3:20, 28; Gal 2:16; 3:2, 5, 10). The scriptural allusion, "and it will be reckoned to you as righteousness" (ונחשבה לך לצדקה), parallels Paul's similar appeals (Rom 4:3, 5, 6, 22, 23; Gal 3:6). References to "rejoicing," "end time," and "doing what is right and good" all find linguistic and conceptual approximations in Paul. Scholars have rightly concluded that we have in 4QMMT an important parallel to Paul's discussion of "works of the Law" and how they relate to righteousness.[46]

---

[45] There are six fragmentary copies of this letter (4Q394–399), which overlap at places, making restoration of much of the original letter possible. See E. Qimron and J. Strugnell, *Qumran Cave 4. V: Miqṣat Maʿśe Ha-Torah* (DJD 10; Oxford: Clarendon Press, 1994) 3–13 + pls. I–III.

[46] M. G. Abegg, Jr., "Paul, 'Works of the Law,' and MMT," *BAR* 20/6 (1994) 52–55, 82; idem, "4QMMT C27, 31 and 'Works Righteousness'", *DSD* 6 (1999): 139–47; idem, "4QMMT, Paul, and 'Works of the Law'," in P. W. Flint (ed.), *The Bible at Qumran: Text, Shape, and Interpretation* (Studies in the Dead Sea Scrolls and Related Literature; Grand Rapids: Eerdmans, 2001) 203–16; M. Bachmann, "4QMMT und Galaterbrief, מעשי התורה und ΕΡΓΑ ΝΟΜΟΥ," *ZNW* 89 (1998): 91–113; J. D. G. Dunn, "4QMMT and Galatians,"

Since the publication of E. P. Sanders's influential *Paul and Palestinian Judaism*,[47] much of the discussion has focused on the concepts of "getting in" (i.e., into the covenant or into the community of God's people) and "staying in" (i.e., in the covenant and the community of God's people). Recently, several scholars have argued that for both the author of 4QMMT and Paul the "works of the Law" are requirements—not for getting in—but for staying in the covenant, however that is understood. For example, agreeing with James Dunn, Martin Abegg concludes that the author of 4QMMT wishes to protect those in his community, promising that if his interpretations are followed, "good standing" in the covenant will be the result, so that his adherents "will be reckoned righteous."[48] I have no particular quarrel with this aspect of the debate.

However, I am intrigued with the point that Simon Gathercole has raised recently.[49] He has shifted the focus away from "getting in" and "staying in" to final judgment. He finds a number of texts that suggest works of the Law will play an important role in eschatological judgment. From the survey of the texts above, I am inclined to agree. Isaiah affirms that the "work of righteousness shall be peace" (32:17); Jeremiah promises that one's "work will be rewarded" (31:16); and according to Jonah, the works of the Ninevites saved them (3:10). Later writers add to this idea, with the author of the *Testaments of the Twelve Patriarchs* promising that "work that is good" will result in God's love (*T. Naph.* 8:4), or the author of *Biblical Antiquities* imagining, as expressed through Samuel, that works will be the basis of reward (*LAB* 64:7).

The perspective of 4QMMT fits this general expectation. One may well gain entry into God's covenant and be numbered among God's people because God is gracious. But there were teachers who insisted that

---

NTS 43 (1997): 147–53; *idem, The Theology of Paul the Apostle* (Grand Rapids: Eerdmans, 1998) 357–58; J. A. Fitzmyer, "Paul and the Dead Sea Scrolls," in Flint and VanderKam (eds.), *The Dead Sea Scrolls after Fifty Years*, 2:599–621, esp. 614; P. J. Tomson, *Paul and the Jewish Law: Halakha in the Letters of the Apostle to the Gentiles* (CRINT 3/1; Assen: Van Gorcum; Minneapolis: Fortress, 1990) 66; N. T. Wright, "Paul and Qumran," *Bible Review* 14/5 (1998): 18, 54.

[47] E. P. Sanders, *Paul and Palestinian Judaism: A Comparison of Patterns of Religion* (London: SCM Press; Philadelphia: Fortress, 1977).

[48] Abegg, "4QMMT C27, 31 and 'Works Righteousness'," 146.

[49] S. J. Gathercole, *Where is Boasting? Early Jewish Soteriology and Paul's Response in Romans 1–5* (Grand Rapids: Eerdmans, 2002).

Law be obeyed—and sometimes obeyed in a very strict and peculiar fashion—or one faced judgment. The contrasting understandings of "reckoned righteous" in Paul and in 4QMMT seem to support this point.

To make his point that people are justified by faith—not by works of the Law—Paul appeals to the example of Abraham, who "believed God, and it was reckoned to him for righteousness [ἐπίστευσεν τῷ θεῷ, καὶ ἐλογίσθη αὐτῷ εἰς δικαιοσύνην]" (Gal 3:6). Paul has cited Gen 15:6, where Abraham responds in faith to God's promises. For Paul the example of Abraham becomes the pattern for all who are saved, whether Jew or Gentile. It was Abraham's faith—not his works (circumcision, willingness to offer up Isaac, etc.)—that resulted in his righteous standing before God. Faith is what made "getting in" possible for the Galatian Christians, which is what Paul recalls: "O foolish Galatians! . . . Let me ask you only this: Did you receive the Spirit by works of the law, or by hearing with faith? Are you so foolish? Having begun with the Spirit, are you now ending with the flesh?" (3:1–3). For Paul, the point is not "staying in," but moving forward to maturity and eventual eschatological judgment. "Getting in" was not achieved by works of the Law; neither will "finishing the course" be achieved by works of the Law.

The author of 4QMMT could not possibly agree with Paul's argument. For him, being "reckoned righteous" is on the basis of doing "works of the Law." If they "do what is right and good" they will "rejoice at the end time." In other words, in sharp contrast to what Paul enjoins on the Galatians, the author of 4QMMT urges compliance with "works of the Law" to guarantee a happy finish. Of course, he does not appeal to the example of Abraham's faith, he appeals to the example of priestly zeal on the part of Phineas:

> Then Phinehas stood up and interposed, and the plague was stayed. And that has been reckoned to him as righteousness [וַתֵּחָשֶׁב לוֹ לִצְדָקָה] from generation to generation for ever. (Ps 106:30–31)

We suspect that it is to Psalm 106 that the author of 4QMMT has appealed, for its verbal form agrees with the form found in 4QMMT (i.e., the niphal), whereas a different form is used in Genesis 15 (i.e., the qal). Moreover, the example of a zealous priest, willing to kill false priests, would likely have been inspirational to the priestly Essenes, who were bitterly critical of Jerusalem's priestly establishment.

At this point we should return to the passage from *Jubilees* cited above. According to the Latin version, the violent action taken by Levi and Simeon "was reckoned [*et conputatum est*] for righteousness."⁵⁰ Gathercole remarks that *et conputatum est* probably translates καὶ ἐλογίσθη, which itself translates וַתֵּחָשֶׁב.⁵¹ In all probability we have a second text from late antiquity that has appealed to the example of Phineas, as idealized in Psalm 106. Only in this case, the reckoning for righteousness has been retrojected into history and applied to Phineas's patriarchal ancestors, Levi and Simeon. Brothers Levi and Simeon acted in vengeful zeal, and were reckoned by God as righteous, just as Levi's descendant Phineas would act. It is on the basis of such zeal for God's Law—a zeal needed in the desperate struggle against Antiochus IV, out of which the Essenes would eventually emerge—that a paradigm was fashioned. The praise of Mattathias in 1 Macc 2:54 offers yet a third text, in which the zealous Phineas is said to have "received the covenant of everlasting priesthood." 4QMMT and *Jubilees* (esp. in the Latin version) reflect this way of thinking. The Christian Paul does not.⁵²

Before one suggests that the terminology shared by Paul and Qumran hints at direct contact, one should also take into account several other terminological overlaps. First, there are some interesting ecclesiastical words and phrases. In 2 Cor 2:5–6 Paul speaks of "punishment by the many [ὑπὸ τῶν πλειόνων]," which appears to be the semantic equivalent of Qumran's "the many" (הרבים), which is sometimes translated "general membership" or "the majority" (cf. CD 13:7; 14:7, 12; 15:8; 1QS 5:22; 6:1, 7–9, 11–21, 25; 7:3; *passim*). Paul's reference to ἐπισκόποις in Phil 1:1 ("with overseers and deacons") appears to approximate the meaning of המבקר in the Scrolls (cf. 1QS 6:12, 20; CD 9:18–19, 22; 13:6–7; *passim*). Paul's frequent epithet ἡ ἐκκλησία τοῦ θεοῦ (e.g., 1 Cor 1:2; 10:32; 11:16; 15:9; 2 Cor 1:1; Gal 1:13; 1 Thess 2:14; 2 Thess 1:4)

---

⁵⁰ Translation based on J. C. Endres, *Biblical Interpretation in the Book of Jubilees* (CBQMS 18; Washington: Catholic Biblical Association, 1987) 135; Gathercole, *Where is Boasting?* 60–61.

⁵¹ The Vulgate translates *et reputatum est*.

⁵² In my view some serious reservations have been raised against the idea that "works of Law" were not understood as meritorious or as having eschatological, saving significance in the minds of many Jews. On this, see C. E. B. Cranfield, "'The Works of the Law' in the Epistle to the Romans," *JSNT* 43 (1991): 89–101; Jacqueline C. R. De Roo, "The Concept of 'Works of the Law' in Jewish and Christian Literature," in S. E. Porter and B. W. R. Pearson (eds.), *Christian-Jewish Relations through the Centuries* (JSNTSup 192; Sheffield: Sheffield Academic Press, 2000) 116–47; R. H. Gundry, "Grace, Works, and Staying Saved in Paul," *Bib* 66 (1985): 1–38. See James Dunn's reply in "Noch einmal 'Works of the Law': The Dialogue Continues," in I. Dunderberg, C. M. Tuckett, and K. Syreeni (eds.), *Fair Play: Diversity and Conflicts in Early Christianity: Essays in Honour of Heikki Räisänen* (NovTSup 103; Leiden: E. J. Brill, 2001) 273–90.

seems to be the equivalent of Qumran's קהל אל (cf. 1QM 4:10; 4Q249g frg. 3 vii 1). Secondly, Paul and Qumran share some theological expressions, besides "works of law." One thinks of δικαιοσύνη θεοῦ (e.g., Rom 1:17; 3:21), whose equivalents צדקות אל and צדקת אל are found in the Scrolls (cf. 1QS 1:21; 10:23 and 1QS 10:25; 11:12, respectively). Paul's references to ἡ χάρις τοῦ θεοῦ (e.g., Rom 5:15; 1 Cor 1:4; 3:10; 15:10; 2 Cor 1:12) approximate Qumran's חסדי אל (cf. 1QS 11:12). And finally, Paul's καινὴ διαθήκη (e.g., 2 Cor 3:6) approximates Qumran's references to בברית החדשה (cf. 1QpHab 2:3; 1Q34bis frg. 3 ii 6; CD 6:19; 8:21; 20:11–12; 4Q509 frg. 97–98 i 8).[53] The common language, including the language concerned with works of the Law and doing the Law, reflects the Jewish world of late antiquity, of which Paul was a part.

Conclusion

The principal point this brief overview hopes to make clear is how natural it was in Paul's time for Jews to speak of "works of the Law" and "doing the Law." This language is well rooted in the Hebrew Scriptures themselves and was deeply entrenched in Jewish thought of late antiquity. Indeed, one should recall the conversation that Jesus had with a legal authority, who asked, "What shall I do to inherit eternal life?" (Luke 10:25). It is interesting that Jesus replies, making no mention of faith or grace. He asks, "What is written in the law? How do you read?" (v. 26). The man cites the two Great Commandments (v. 27) and Jesus commends him, "You have answered right; do this, and you will live" (v. 28). The words "do this, and you will live" (τοῦτο ποίει καὶ ζήσῃ) allude to Lev 18:5 "You shall therefore keep my statutes and my ordinances, by doing which a man shall live [אֲשֶׁר יַעֲשֶׂה אֹתָם הָאָדָם/ἃ ποιήσας ἄνθρωπος ζήσεται ἐν αὐτοῖς]: I am the LORD." Keeping in mind that the original

---

[53] For further discussion of the potential parallels between Paul and the Dead Sea Scrolls, see J. A. Fitzmyer, "The Qumran Scrolls and the New Testament after Forty Years," *RevQ* 13 (1988): 613–15; idem, "Paul and the Dead Sea Scrolls," 599–621; K. P. Donfried, "Paul and Qumran: The Possible Influence of סרך on 1 Thessalonians," in L. H. Schiffman, E. Tov, and J. C. VanderKam (eds.), *The Dead Sea Scrolls: Fifty Years after Their Discovery. Proceedings of the Jerusalem Congress, July 20–25, 1997* (Jerusalem: Israel Exploration Society and the Israel Antiquities Authority, 2000) 148–56; H. Räisänen, "Paul's and Qumran's Judaism," in A. J. Avery-Peck, J. Neusner, and B. D. Chilton (eds.), *Judaism in Late Antiquity. Part Five: The Judaism of Qumran: A Systemic Reading of the Dead Sea Scrolls. Volume Two: World View, Comparing Judaisms* (HO 57; Leiden: E. J. Brill, 2001) 173–200.

question concerned "eternal life," Jesus' pronouncement is quite significant. In essence he has said that if a person does the Law, he has eternal life. And in fact, this is how Lev 18:5 had come to be understood in late antiquity, as we see in the Aramaic paraphrase and in a quotation of it in the Damascus Covenant (cf. CD 3:12–21).

Seen in the context of the materials that have been surveyed in this essay, it seems that Paul's claim that "no human being will be justified from works of law" was a remarkable position to take in his time and was one sure to be controversial, in Christian Jewish circles and non-Christian Jewish circles alike.

PAUL AND THE IMPERIAL CULT

Ross Saunders
Macquarie University, N.S.W. Australia

Introduction

In this paper I do not propose to outline the history of the Imperial Cult during the first century of our era. This has been done by several scholars expert in this field.[1] The Imperial Cult was the only one expanding its influence at a time when the traditional cults were losing ground with the people. In spite of the growing influence of this cult, there is very little mention of it in the New Testament generally.

Some years ago while staying in the village of Ancient Corinth, I had a long conversation with the director of the American archaeologists there, Charles Williams III. He told me he believed that Paul's greatest enemy in Corinth was the Imperial Cult. Since then, I have come to see that the Imperial Cult played an important role in the growth of Christianity, especially from A.D. 64. That was when Christianity lost its imagined protection as a sect of Judaism under the persecution of Nero.

It is very important to understand that the cultic practices and attitudes of the Imperial Cult varied from place to place. We should perhaps refer to the "imperial cults". But their purpose and effects were the same: to unify the empire around the figure of the emperor. This was why Christians were regarded as atheists and accused of being disloyal to their fatherland.

I want to begin by noting echoes of the Imperial Cult in the Gospels.

---

[1] E.g. S. R. F. Price, *Rituals and Power: The Roman Imperial Cult in Asia Minor* (Cambridge: Cambridge University Press, 1984). Since Paul is involved mostly in the Greek East, Price is especially relevant. A. D. Nock, "Religious Developments from the Close of the Republic to the Death of Nero," in *The Cambridge Ancient History vol. X: The Augustin Empire 44 B.C.–A.D. 70* (Cambridge: Cambridge University Press, 1982) gives a good general overview.

The Gospels

The first direct echo of the Imperial Cult in Mark comes in 12:1–17, where the Pharisees and the Herodians try to trick Jesus into taking sides with Rome or Jerusalem in the matter of paying taxes to Caesar.[2] Jesus calls for a denarius and asks the question, "Whose likeness and inscription is this?" We all remember that the likeness is Caesar Augustus. But do we know what the inscription was? On one side was CAESAR AUGUSTUS, while on the other side was DIVUS IMPERATOR PATER PATRIAE.[3] Put together all that comes to a claim that Emperor Augustus Caesar is a divine being and father of the country. When Jesus said, "Render to God the things that are God's", Jesus was also saying that the Pharisees and Herodians should not render to Caesar the divinity that belongs to God alone, nor allow Caesar to be called the father of Jerusalem.

There's an earlier indirect echo in Mark. In 10:35–44 James and John ask Jesus to appoint them to the senior positions in the coming Kingdom. Part of Jesus' reply can be seen as a stinging attack on the Imperial Cult: "You know that those who are supposed to rule over the Gentiles lord it over them, and their great men exercise authority over them." The verb for "lord it over" is κατακυριεύω = "be another lord over." Bearing in mind that at that period κύριος = god or divine, then Jesus is plainly reminding the disciples that the leaders of the Gentiles, i.e. the Caesars, were acting like gods, and that this kind of behaviour should be no part of the attitude of followers of Jesus. Nor should those Judeans who made such a song and dance about their loyalty to God be so effusive in their acceptance of the lordship of Caesar. We should also remember that at this time Rome allowed all male adult Hebrews in Palestine and throughout the dispersion to pay a temple tax to Jerusalem for the upkeep of their temple. When Titus destroyed the temple in A.D. 70, Rome annexed this tax for the upkeep of the Capitoline temple in Rome. It is interesting that, while Matt 20:20–28 reports on this incident, Luke does not. One of Luke's concerns is to show that the Jesus movement was no threat to Roman imperialism.

I make no reference to the apocalyptic discourses in the Gospels, because it is very difficult to establish the exact frame of reference for

---

[2] See my article "What is Not Caesar's," *Interchange* 50 (1993): 19–24.

[3] G. L. Archer, "Coins," in *The Zondervan Pictorial Encyclopedia of the Bible* (ed. Merrill C. Tenney; Grand Rapids: Zondervan, 1975).

these. The same goes for the Apocalypse. There may be references to the Imperial Cult there. Certainly the next generation of Christians, reflecting on the persecutions they were suffering at the hands of Roman officialdom, saw those experiences reflected in the author's prophecies. But whether that was what the author had in mind is difficult to establish. It is also interesting to point out how careful Luke is with his language when he dates the beginning of the mission of John the Baptist: "In the fifteenth year of the reign of Tiberias Caesar . . ." The word Luke uses is ἡγεμονία = chief command, sovereignty. He avoids the titles that the Caesars themselves used because of the implications of divinity. The book of Acts contains no direct references to the Imperial Cult, no doubt because of the concern of Luke to show Rome as protector of the Jesus movement. The conflict is always with Judaism and Judean believers from Jerusalem.

AIM OF THE IMPERIAL CULT

It is well to remember that to both the Greek and Roman minds, one of the primary purposes of a state religion was to provide a focus for patriotism, like Orthodoxy in Greece, Serbia and Russia; or Catholicism in Italy, Croatia, Poland and many Latin-American countries, and Anglicanism in Great Britain today. The British and American National Anthems are hymns—a focus of loyalty and patriotism.

So it was with the state religions in the ancient world. There was no system of dogma and ethics that set off one religion against another. As a citizen of the Roman Empire, one paid tribute to the official religion as part of one's responsibility as a citizen, pretty much the way a homeowner today pays rates and taxes to the local council. The Roman citizen no more believed in his gods than we believe in our local council. The council, like the god, is there, and we pay it due respect and our taxes.

What Roman citizens worshipped first were the imperial virtues—Victoria (Victory) Augusti, Concordia (Harmony) Augusti, Clementia (Mercy) Augusti, Pax (Peace) Augusti etc.—supernatural beings that emanated from the emperor and were capable of bestowing benefits on humanity.

Personal religion, as we understand and practice, was not part of Roman religion. With the Imperial Cult being so strongly bound to the Caesar, it is no wonder that the Christians found it necessary to think carefully about how they should respond during official festivals, athletic games and oaths of loyalty. It is also well to remember that when Christians became emperors, they were not immediately able to abolish the ceremonial trappings of imperial office, including bowings, the extravagant language of royal compliments and homage to imperial insignia and images.

We must also remember that up to the end of the first century A.D., the priest of the state religion was not a separate class of person, specially trained in the dogma and ritual of the cult. The priest of a province was usually some high-status rich person who accepted the position for one, two or three years. He was also the president of the provincial assembly. The position did not bring him any income. On the contrary, it cost him a great deal because, as priest, he had to stage various festivals, games and processions and provide for the daily sacrifices at his own expense. He was prepared to do this because of the power and prestige that went along with being the priest. In the west the priest was called *flamen* or *sacerdos*, while in the east he was called *archierius*. The emperor himself was *pontifex maximus*—the supreme high priest for the empire.

It is only during the second century A.D. that the Imperial Cult became organized, like the Zeus cult, with a separate priesthood and a highly developed and powerful bureaucracy.

This is also the period when the Christians organized themselves into a more centralised Church, with regions and local heads and an ordained ministry. Up until the end of the first century A.D., the Church was a loosely organized group of congregations, not looking to any special place as its centre. What was left of the original group of Jesus' apostles plus Paul, Barnabas, Timothy, Titus and one or two others were looked to as their founders.

THE THREAT TO CHRISTIANITY

Two events caused the Christian congregations to unite and form a central point of reference: the fire of Rome in A.D. 64 with the first official persecution of Christians by the Roman state, and the destruction of Jerusalem by Titus in A.D. 70 with the resultant reduction in persecution by the Judeans. Whereas persecution by Judeans could be handled locally, persecution by the state was best handled centrally. This was when the congregations in Rome, capital of the state, started to become important and be looked to in the battle against the state and the state religion. This was when bishops of Rome began to emerge as powerful leaders of the Christian diaspora.

IMPERIAL CULT IN NON-PAULINE EPISTLES

Before looking at Paul's comments on the Imperial Cult, I want to refer briefly to a couple of references in other epistles.

James

James has an interesting phrase in 4:4, "Do you not know that friendship with the world is enmity with God?" Here κόσμος is being used in the same way that the author of the Fourth Gospel uses it: humankind organized against God. κόσμος is rarely, if ever, used in a good sense in the New Testament. In this case ἡ φιλία τοῦ κόσμου is clearly a reference to acting in a way that is claiming some kind of friendliness towards Caesar, who claimed to rule the world, and thus deserving to be called ἐχθρὸς τοῦ θεοῦ (inimical to God).

1 Peter 2:13–17

> For the Lord's sake accept the authority of every human institution, whether of the emperor as supreme, or of governors, as sent by him to punish those who do wrong and to praise those who do right. For it is God's will that by doing right you should silence the ignorance of the foolish. As servants of God, live as free people, yet do not use your freedom as a pretext for evil. Honour everyone. Love the family of believers. Fear God. Honour the emperor.

This needs to be read very carefully in the light of 2:9, where the author states that "you are a chosen race, a royal priesthood, a holy nation, God's own people . . ." When he says, "Be subject for the Lord's sake to all that mankind created", he is clearly talking about purely civil obedience. When a Christian is conscious of being a member of a royal priesthood that is God's own people, then there is no way that such a Christian can accept the divinity and high priesthood of the Roman emperor. So being subject "to the emperor as supreme or to governors as sent by him to punish those who do wrong and to praise those who do right" is conditional upon rendering a higher obedience to the true God and the Great High

Priest. The Christian, says 1 Peter, has the right, as a member of a holy nation that is God's own people, to live in freedom, having been freed from the power of sin. But this right to freedom must be exercised in the knowledge that we are first of all servants of God. One honours the emperor, but does not worship him, nor accept his claims to divinity and high priesthood.

PAUL AND THE IMPERIAL CULT

Romans 13:1–7

> Let every person be subject to the governing authorities; for there is no authority except from God, and those authorities that exist have been instituted by God. Therefore whoever resists authority resists what God has appointed, and those who resist will incur judgment. For rulers are not a terror to good conduct, but to bad. Do you wish to have no fear of the authority? Then do what is good, and you will receive its approval; for it is God's servant for your good. But if you do what is wrong, you should be afraid, for the authority does not bear the sword in vain! It is the servant of God to execute wrath on the wrongdoer. Therefore one must be subject, not only because of wrath but also because of conscience. For the same reason you also pay taxes, for the authorities are God's servants, busy with this very thing. Pay to all what is due them—taxes to whom taxes are due, revenue to whom revenue is due, respect to whom respect is due, honour to whom honour is due.

This is an exhortation to the Christians in Rome to obedience to lawful authority. Paul is very careful with his language here. Notice he does not insist on unthinking obedience to the emperor. That Paul does not refer to the Caesar, as you might have expected since he was writing to Christians who lived where Caesar's throne was, is crucial to a proper understanding of Paul here. Whereas Nero was honoured as a god and claimed absolute power over his subjects, to Paul only God had absolute authority, and could dispense it through whomever God chose.

"There is no authority except from God . . ." I believe we should pay careful attention to what Paul is writing here, and see how he carefully constructs the kind of authorities we should submit ourselves to. No ruler who claims to be divine could ever be God's servant!

Notice carefully his summary: "Pay to all what is due to them . . ." Paul does not say, "Pay to all what they claim they have a right to claim from you". How are Christians to work out what God says these human authorities have a right to claim? "... there is no authority except from God". When the Caesar as a god claims the right to tax and respect and honour, then no Christian needs to obey. But when governing authorities claim the civic right to be obeyed and respected, then Christians are free to obey what is in accord with Godly justice. "Pay to all what is due to them—taxes to whom taxes are due, revenue to whom revenue is due, respect to whom respect is due, honour to whom honour is due".

What Paul does not say is that all human institutions in their current form were created by God and must be absolutely obeyed. Only those human institutions that reflect the character of God as revealed in Christ merit such obedience. It is the link between the character of God and the institution and its leadership which is the key to understanding Paul's rhetoric about obeying civil authority.

One of the distinguishing features of Christianity was the direct link between faith and ethics, between cult worship and personal morality. This was inherited from Judaism but refined by Jesus in a more direct and personal way. It was the character of God and the human example of Jesus that were at the very core of all Christian institutions from the household to the house church. Human institutions reflected the character of their human leadership. For Christians, the notion of the emperor as a god was abhorrent. Those institutions led by such divinities could not be included in those institutions that have been instituted by God.

Paul was writing to congregations in the Empire's capital. He must not be seen as an anarchist inciting Christians to civil disobedience and thus threatening the *pax romana*. He had also to be careful that he was not seen as trying to replace the Caesar with Christ as the civil ruler of the Empire. The readers/listeners of this epistle would know exactly what Paul meant about how they were to obey human authorities, whereas any non-Christians who came across Paul's words would think that Paul was telling Christians to obey the emperor, no matter what.

1 Corinthians 6:1–8

> When any of you has a grievance against another, do you dare to take it to court before the unrighteous, instead of taking it before the saints? Do you not know that the saints will judge the world? And if the world is to be judged by you, are you incompetent to try trivial cases? Do you not know that we are to judge angels—to say nothing of ordinary matters? If you have ordinary cases, then, do you appoint as judges those who have no standing in the church? I say this to your shame. Can it be that there is no one among you wise enough to decide between one believer and another, but a believer

goes to court against a believer—and before unbelievers at that? In fact, to have lawsuits at all with one another is already a defeat for you. Why not rather be wronged? Why not rather be defrauded? But you yourselves wrong and defraud—and believers at that.

Paul criticises the Corinthian Christians for taking their disputes to the secular courts. Notice how he contrasts the "unrighteous" with the "saints"? He uses here ἄδικος—those with an absence of rightness—to describe the lawyers and judges at the courts of Corinth.

What we need to remember is that the Roman legal system was an extension of the imperial powers. Tiberius used to sit regularly in the courts at Rome, and often gave orders as to how a judgement should be made. What made civil courts unrighteous, then, was not their bad legal process, but their link with the Imperial Cult.

For Paul, then, the only justice that was right was that coming through Christ, and so when Christians went to civil courts they were denying the justice of God and favouring the injustice that emanated from the civil gods.

1 Corinthians 8:4–6

Paul draws attention to the differences between earthly "so-called" gods and the one true heavenly God; between the "many gods and many lords" and the "one God, the Father . . . and one Lord, Jesus Christ". In Corinth there was the temple to Augustus's sister, Octavia; and of course Aphrodite was the patron god of the whole city. This passage can be seen as a direct attack on the Imperial Cult.

The Epistle to the Ephesians, whether or not written by Paul, is remarkable for its absence of any reference to obedience of authorities. The passage in chs. 5 and 6 about husbands and wives, parents and children, masters and slaves, at one level is incomplete because it has no reference to obedience to those in authority over us. But there is an interesting passage earlier in chapter 1:21 where the writer is talking about Christ "triumphant over all rule and authority and power and dominion and above every name that is named . . ." One of the words there is κυριότης = dominion or lordship; an obvious reference to Caesar, as is the παντὸς ὀνόματος (all titles).

Colossians 1:15

Paul refers to Christ as "the image (εἰκών) of the invisible God" in contrast, surely, in Asia Minor, to the many images of Augustus and Tiberius that had been set up in all the pagan temples there. Again there is no inclusion of general obedience to Roman authority in ch. 3 when dealing with the household.

The Pastoral epistles, whether or not written by Paul, are again remarkable for having not one single word about obedience to civil authorities. Showing some evidence of the centralised organization round the episcopate that was slowly developing, one would expect some reference to teaching the faithful to be good and obedient citizens. I suspect that because the Roman Empire was now well and truly built around the divinity of the emperor, and with the growing power and authority of the Imperial Cult, Paul would place obedience to the only true God well above obedience to any civil authority. He therefore handles ethical matters in a doctrinal and religious way, not in a legal way.

Paul's Personal Experience of Roman Authority

The picture that Acts gives is one where Paul's main enemies are his own people, while the Roman authorities protect him, sometimes from his own people. His first major encounter with the Roman authorities was in Philippi (Acts 16:16–40). For some reason Paul does not declare his Roman and Tarsian citizenships and ends up in prison after a severe flogging for allegedly advocating anti-Roman customs and breaking the *pax romana*. The next morning the magistrates send police to the prison to order his release. They had obviously decided that Paul and Silas were innocent of the charges the owners of the fortune-telling slave-girl had brought against them. Paul then declares his Roman citizenship and demands a personal apology from the magistrates. They come to the prison in great embarrassment, apologise, and ask them to leave the city.

Shortly after this Paul goes on to Thessalonica and once again his own people are upset with him and cause a city-wide uproar (Acts 17:1–9). This time, Paul and Silas are hidden by some Christians there while the mob attacks a leading believer called Jason. The mob accuses Jason and some of his fellow-Christians of causing a rebellion by setting up another

Caesar called "Jesus". Jason and his friends pay a fine and are released. Paul is not directly affected by this, but has to go off under cover of night to Beroea.

In Corinth it is once again Paul's own people who bring him before the Roman proconsul Gallio, charging Paul with an offence against their religion (Acts 18:12–17). But Gallio refuses to hear them because they are not charging Paul with any offence against any Roman religion. This is probably a reference to the Imperial Cult since there was a small temple to Octavia—temple E—in the main part of the city. Once again the Roman authorities act as protectors to Paul.

Acts 19 reports the riot generated by the silversmiths in Ephesus who experience a great loss of business in Artemis artefacts because of the large drift away from the Artemis cult to Christianity. Once again the Roman authorities protect Paul, but this time from their own people and not from his own people.

On his return to Jerusalem it is once again the Roman authorities who protect Paul from the Judean temple authorities and finally provide him with a military escort to Rome (Acts 21–28:16). There is not one clear hint of any problems with the Imperial Cult.

Paul has used his Roman citizenship to appeal directly to the Caesar against the charges laid against him by the Judean authorities. That Caesar is Nero. But when Paul finally arrives in Rome he discovers that the Judean authorities have not sent any official accusations against him to Nero (Acts 28:21). He is allowed to stay outside of the prison under house arrest for two years. This is about A.D. 61–63.

Paul's own personal experience of being a Christian leader and evangelist in the Roman Empire, where adherence was permitted only to those religions officially recognised by Rome, is a positive one. This needs to be born in mind when assessing Paul's statements about how Christians should react towards state authorities.

But what finally happened to Paul's appeal to Nero? The only official papers presented to Nero would be those of Agrippa and Festus, both of whom had declared him innocent of any crime against the *pax romana* (Acts 26:30–32).

There is, sadly, no historical evidence that can reliably ascertain Paul's fate. My own view is that he did finally appear before Nero who was soon to blame Christians for setting the fire in Rome, and waging the first official persecution against Christians. Nero probably would have demanded that Paul sacrifice to him as divine and then order his execution for his refusal to do so. So it was his final rejection of the Imperial Cult that ended his life and his ministry.[4]

Conclusion

Wherever Paul travelled around the Roman Empire, he would have encountered countless images of the imperial cults in city after city. As a Roman citizen he had the protection of the authorities against unjust treatment. Yet he had an aversion, as a Christian, to any emperor who claimed divine power during his own lifetime. He was bound to steer a careful course so as not to hinder his work for the gospel, but that did not also involve him in supporting such a blasphemous regime.

Right until the very end, Acts shows Paul succeeding in helping many Greeks, Romans and his own Hebrew people, from a wide variety of social statuses, to adopt the new religion based around a man who claimed true divinity. It is clear that Paul did not wage any overt campaigns against the Imperial Cult. But in his epistles he uses very carefully crafted language to help converts distinguish between authorities who exercise a legitimate right to command obedience and taxes because of their authoritative position in the Roman administration, and any human authority who claimed divinity as a right to exercise power over them.

An Afterword

When we move from the Church as it displays itself in the first century to the Church as it emerges in the second century, we see almost a complete transmogrification. From being a loose collection of house groups

---

[4] I do not propose to enter the debate on Paul's possible release and later execution under Nero. So much depends on the interpretation and dating of the Pastoral epistles that it is virtually impossible to be certain. The more interesting question for me is why the author of Acts does not say what the final outcome of Paul's trial was. My own view, impossible to validate, is that the "Theophilus" to whom he addressed Acts already knew the outcome. He may have been there at Paul's trials at Caesarea and was interested to know more about the beginnings of Christianity and how Paul fitted into it. After reading J. A. T. Robinson's *Redating the New Testament* (London: SCM Press, 1976), I am convinced that the onus is on his critics to prove him wrong, rather than on other scholars to prove him correct.

with local leaders, not apparently looking to any one centre as its authority for either doctrine or practice, we discover a highly centralised series of linked congregations dominated and ruled by a small band of specially ordained men, themselves under the rule of a single leader now known as ἐπίσκοπος, "bishop".

Believers are graded according to their status of initiation and level of knowledge, with these being made visible by the places they occupied when at worship in the congregation. When meeting places were built for congregational worship, they were a copy of the basilica form adopted by the Imperial Cult when special buildings were erected for the god-emperor. This happened at the same time as the Imperial Cult priesthood became a separate class.

It seems to me, then, that a realistic explanation of the dramatic change in the organization of the Church can be seen in the increasing power of the Imperial Cult in the Roman Empire, and its growing persecution of all religions—especially Christianity—that encouraged what they saw as disloyalty to the emperor and empire. The Church needed to centralise in order to protect itself from the Imperial Cult. It decided to set up an organization that was capable of matching the power and authority of the Imperial Cult priesthood.

Thus, the Imperial Cult became both the enemy and the model for the Christian Church.

INDEX OF ANCIENT SOURCES

OLD TESTAMENT

Gen 15	223	Ezra 8:21	183
Gen 15:6	223		
Gen 18:19	217	Job 2:9	193
Gen 33:17–34:31	212	Job 2:18	186
		Job 2:21	186
Exod 20:6	206	Job 2:30	186
		Job 5:1	184
Lev 10:9–10	180	Job 33:23	184
Lev 16:29	183		
Lev 16:31	183	Ps 35:13	183
Lev 18:5	209, 225–26	Ps 37	219
Lev 23:27	183	Ps 106	223–24
Lev 23:32	183	Ps 106:30–31	223
		Ps 146:10 LXX	183
Num 6:3–4	180		
Num 28:9–15	179	Prov 10:2	210
Num 29:7	183	Prov 10:16	205
		Prov 10:17	205
Deut 4:19	185		
Deut 15:10	210	Isa 1:13–14	179
Deut 17:3	183	Isa 28–39	202
Deut 27:26	220	Isa 29:13	190
Deut 29:28	220	Isa 32:9–20	202
Deut 31:12	220	Isa 32:15	202
Deut 32:8	185	Isa 32:16	202
Deut 32:46	220	Isa 32:17	202, 222
		Isa 58:3	183
Josh 1:7	220	Isa 58:5	183
1 Sam 16:7	86	Jer 1:5	110
1 Sam 28:14–15	218	Jer 26–52	203
		Jer 31:16	203, 222
1 Kgdms 15:26	183	Jer 38:16 LXX	203
1 Kgdms 18:22	183		
		Lam 3:64	204
1 Kgs 10:9	217		
		Ezek 45:17	179
2 Kgs 23:24–25	211	Ezek 46:4	179
		Ezek 46:6	179
3 Kgdms 10:9	183		
		Dan 1:8–16	180
1 Chr 23:31	179	Dan 1:20	177
		Dan 2:21	191
2 Chr 2:3	179	Dan 9:3	183
2 Chr 31:3	179	Dan 9:20–21	183

Dan 10:2–3	183	3 Macc 1:3	192
Dan 10:12	183		
Dan 12:10	191	4 Macc 5:1–6:30	212
		4 Macc 5:7	186
Hos 2:13	179	4 Macc 5:22	177
		4 Macc 5:37	212
Amos 8:5	179	4 Macc 7:9	212
		4 Macc 17:12	207
Jonah 3:10	204, 222		
		Sir 4:22–28	86
Hab 2:3b	219	Sir 16:17	205
		Sir 16:22	205
Bar 4:1	199	Sir 24:23	199
		Sir 44–49	211
1 Esd 1:21	211	Sir 44:1	211
1 Esd 1:23	211	Sir 51:30	206
1 Esd 4:39	86		
		Tob 4:6	209
1 Macc 2:51	211	Tob 4:10–11	210
1 Macc 2:54	224	Tob 12:9	210
2 Macc 6:13–31	212	Wis 6:18	206–207
2 Macc 7	212	Wis 9:12	207
		Wis 13:2	183

New Testament

Matt 6	208	Luke 20:20	90
Matt 6:20	208	Luke 22:14	100
Matt 10:2	100	Luke 22:24–30	83
Matt 10:8–10	102	Luke 24:10	100
Matt 11:18	180	Luke 24:47	117
Matt 15:1–11	190		
Matt 20:20–28	228	Acts 1:2	100
Matt 28:19	117	Acts 1:8	117
		Acts 1:26	100
Mark 6:8–9	102	Acts 2:9–11	194
Mark 6:30	100	Acts 2:37	100
Mark 7:14–23	180	Acts 2:42	100
Mark 9:1	86	Acts 2:43	100
Mark 10:35–44	228	Acts 4:1–31	84
Mark 12:1–17	228	Acts 4:33	100
Mark 13:9	71	Acts 4:35	100
		Acts 4:36	100
Luke 6:13	100	Acts 4:37	100
Luke 9:3–4	102	Acts 5:2	100
Luke 9:10	100	Acts 5:12	100
Luke 10:25	225	Acts 5:17–42	84
Luke 10:26	225	Acts 5:18	100
Luke 10:27	225	Acts 5:27–42	70
Luke 10:28	225	Acts 5:29	100
Luke 11:49	100	Acts 5:34	100
Luke 17:5	100	Acts 5:40	100

INDEX OF ANCIENT SOURCES

Acts 6:6	100	Acts 24:14–21	66
Acts 6:8–8:4	77	Acts 26:4–23	66
Acts 6:9–12	78	Acts 26:9–12	76
Acts 6:12–14	75	Acts 26:9–11	69
Acts 6:12	84	Acts 26:14	71
Acts 7:54–8:3	70	Acts 26:30–32	236
Acts 8:1–3	84	Acts 28:21	236
Acts 8:3	78		
Acts 8:14	100	Rom 1:1	110, 166
Acts 8:18	100	Rom 1:2	117
Acts 9:1–2	69, 70	Rom 1:5	113, 120
Acts 9:7ff.	71	Rom 1:8–17	153
Acts 9:26–29	131	Rom 1:8–15	153
Acts 9:27	100	Rom 1:9–10	153, 155
Acts 11:1	100	Rom 1:10–11	160
Acts 11:17–18	93	Rom 1:10	155, 157
Acts 11:27–30	131	Rom 1:11–12	158
Acts 13:1–3	101, 106	Rom 1:11	159
Acts 14:4	100–102, 106	Rom 1:12	159, 163
Acts 14:14	100–102, 106	Rom 1:13	160–61
Acts 15	82, 85	Rom 1:16a	152
Acts 15:1–5	95, 108	Rom 1:16b–17	152
Acts 15:2	100, 112	Rom 1:17	225
Acts 15:4	100	Rom 2:13	220
Acts 15:6–29	102	Rom 2:14	220
Acts 15:6–21	102, 107	Rom 2:25	220
Acts 15:6	100	Rom 2:26	221
Acts 15:10	94	Rom 3–5	152
Acts 15:14–21	93	Rom 3:20	221
Acts 15:20	138	Rom 3:21	225
Acts 15:22–29	109	Rom 3:28	221
Acts 15:22	100	Rom 4:3	221
Acts 15:23–29	107	Rom 4:5	221
Acts 15:23	100	Rom 4:6	221
Acts 15:29	138	Rom 4:16–21	66
Acts 15:33	100	Rom 4:22	221
Acts 16:4	100	Rom 4:23	221
Acts 16:16–40	235	Rom 5:3–5	140
Acts 17:1–9	235	Rom 5:15–16	159
Acts 17:18	176	Rom 5:15	159, 225
Acts 18:1–18	115	Rom 5:16	159
Acts 18:12–17	236	Rom 6:23	159
Acts 18:27	121	Rom 7:12	190
Acts 21–28:16	236	Rom 7:22	190
Acts 21	78, 85, 163	Rom 8:18–25	192
Acts 21:18–25	75	Rom 9–11	152, 154–55, 162
Acts 21:21–26	76	Rom 9:3	65, 66
Acts 21:25	138	Rom 11:1	65, 66
Acts 21:26ff.	75	Rom 11:11–16	66
Acts 21:27–29	76	Rom 11:13	66, 113, 117, 119–20, 166
Acts 22–27	76		
Acts 22:3–5	76	Rom 11:14	65
Acts 23:6	66	Rom 11:25–26	66
Acts 24:11–20	76	Rom 11:25	160

Rom 11:26	162	1 Cor 1–4	14
Rom 11:28–29	66	1 Cor 1:1	110, 116, 166
Rom 11:29	159	1 Cor 1:2	224
Rom 12:1–15:33	160	1 Cor 1:4	225
Rom 12:3–8	160	1 Cor 1:7	159
Rom 12:3	66	1 Cor 1:10–13	116
Rom 12:6	159	1 Cor 1:12–13	116
Rom 13:1–7	232	1 Cor 1:12	13, 116
Rom 13:8	221	1 Cor 1:17	110, 117
Rom 14–15	152	1 Cor 2:6	177
Rom 14:1–15:13	154–56, 165	1 Cor 3:4–9	116
Rom 14	96, 140	1 Cor 3:5–4:5	14
Rom 14:1–23	180	1 Cor 3:5–15	120
Rom 14:2–3	180	1 Cor 3:6	115, 117, 120
Rom 14:3	165	1 Cor 3:10–15	143
Rom 14:5–6	180	1 Cor 3:10	117, 225
Rom 14:6	165, 180	1 Cor 3:12	120
Rom 14:10	165	1 Cor 3:22	116
Rom 14:14–17	180	1 Cor 4:6	116
Rom 14:14	165	1 Cor 4:9	117
Rom 14:15–17	165	1 Cor 5:1–5	141
Rom 14:17	165, 180	1 Cor 5:1	143
Rom 14:19–20	165	1 Cor 5:5	143
Rom 14:20–21	180	1 Cor 5:9–11	137
Rom 14:21	165, 180	1 Cor 5:9	116
Rom 14:23	180	1 Cor 6:1–8	233
Rom 15	137	1 Cor 6:13	189
Rom 15:1	154, 165	1 Cor 7:1	137
Rom 15:2	165	1 Cor 7:7	159
Rom 15:20	120, 122	1 Cor 7:17–24	92
Rom 15:22–23	160	1 Cor 7:29–31	192–93
Rom 15:22	161	1 Cor 8:1–11:1	116
Rom 15:23–25	161	1 Cor 8–10	96
Rom 15:23	161	1 Cor 8:4–6	234
Rom 15:25–32	78, 130	1 Cor 9:1–6	101, 117, 119, 121
Rom 15:25–27	162	1 Cor 9:1–5	105
Rom 15:26–27	166	1 Cor 9:1	106, 116–17
Rom 15:26	130	1 Cor 9:2	117, 120
Rom 15:28–29	166	1 Cor 9:5	103, 116
Rom 15:29	166	1 Cor 9:6	103
Rom 15:31	71	1 Cor 9:19–22	156
Rom 15:31b	142	1 Cor 10:1	160
Rom 16	143, 154	1 Cor 10:14–22	185
Rom 16:1	154	1 Cor 10:30	175
Rom 16:3–4	158	1 Cor 10:32	224
Rom 16:3	121, 154	1 Cor 11:3	160
Rom 16:7	103, 154	1 Cor 11:16	224
Rom 16:8	154	1 Cor 12	159–60
Rom 16:9	154	1 Cor 12:1	160
Rom 16:10	154	1 Cor 12:3	160
Rom 16:11	154	1 Cor 12:4	159
Rom 16:12	154	1 Cor 12:7	159
Rom 16:13	154	1 Cor 12:9	159

INDEX OF ANCIENT SOURCES

1 Cor 12:12–27	159	2 Cor 7:2–4	116
1 Cor 12:28	105, 117, 159	2 Cor 7:5–8:24	116
1 Cor 12:30	159	2 Cor 7:8–12	141
1 Cor 12:31	159	2 Cor 7:12	143
1 Cor 15	140	2 Cor 8–9	130, 141, 147
1 Cor 15:1–11	87	2 Cor 8	137, 148
1 Cor 15:1–8	106	2 Cor 8:1	160
1 Cor 15:1	160, 166	2 Cor 8:4	130
1 Cor 15:5	116	2 Cor 8:18–9:5	142
1 Cor 15:7–11	119	2 Cor 8:18	141–42
1 Cor 15:7	105, 117	2 Cor 8:20–21	142
1 Cor 15:8–9	117	2 Cor 8:20	142
1 Cor 15:8	117	2 Cor 8:22	141
1 Cor 15:9	224	2 Cor 8:23	100, 122, 141–42
1 Cor 15:10	225	2 Cor 9	137, 149
1 Cor 15:25–29	139	2 Cor 9:1–15	116
1 Cor 15:31	139	2 Cor 9:1	130
1 Cor 16	137	2 Cor 9:3	141–42
1 Cor 16:1–4	130	2 Cor 9:4	142
1 Cor 16:1	130, 139, 145	2 Cor 9:5	141–42
1 Cor 16:2	139	2 Cor 10–13	15, 118–19, 131, 140
1 Cor 16:3–4	137		
1 Cor 16:4	130	2 Cor 10:1–13:10	116
1 Cor 16:5	139	2 Cor 10:10	120
1 Cor 16:8	141	2 Cor 11:4	120
1 Cor 16:10–15	143	2 Cor 11:5	15, 118–19
		2 Cor 11:7–11	121
2 Cor 1–9	131, 134, 140–41	2 Cor 11:9	121
		2 Cor 11:12	119
2 Cor 1:1–2:13	116	2 Cor 11:13	118–20
2 Cor 1:1	110, 166, 224	2 Cor 11:14–15	120
2 Cor 1:8–11	141	2 Cor 11:15	119
2 Cor 1:8	160	2 Cor 11:20	121
2 Cor 1:11	159	2 Cor 11:21–22	66
2 Cor 1:12	225	2 Cor 11:22	119
2 Cor 2:1	119	2 Cor 11:23	131
2 Cor 2:3–4	141	2 Cor 11:24	66, 71
2 Cor 2:5–11	141, 143	2 Cor 12:11	15, 118–19
2 Cor 2:5–6	224	2 Cor 12:12	105, 120
2 Cor 2:12–13	141	2 Cor 12:13–18	121
2 Cor 2:14–6:13	116	2 Cor 12:14–13:13	15
2 Cor 2:14–3:3	15		
2 Cor 3	15, 53	Gal 1–2	23, 119
2 Cor 3–4	166	Gal 1:1–2	104
2 Cor 3:1–3	121	Gal 1:1	90, 106, 110, 145, 166
2 Cor 3:1	121		
2 Cor 3:6	225	Gal 1:4	97
2 Cor 4:16–18	192	Gal 1:6–9	107
2 Cor 5:12	86	Gal 1:6–8	120, 152
2 Cor 5:16	86, 106	Gal 1:6	64, 96, 120
2 Cor 6:1–10	120	Gal 1:9	92
2 Cor 6:4–10	140	Gal 1:10–11	90
2 Cor 6:14–7:1	116	Gal 1:11–2:14	104, 110

INDEX OF ANCIENT SOURCES

Gal 1:11–12	111, 166	Gal 2:12	109
Gal 1:11	160	Gal 2:14–3:14	108
Gal 1:13–2:14	85	Gal 2:14	90, 97, 144
Gal 1:13–14	69, 73, 76, 87	Gal 2:15	66
Gal 1:13	92, 224	Gal 2:16	201, 221
Gal 1:15–17	130	Gal 2:17	152
Gal 1:15	110	Gal 2:19	192
Gal 1:16–2:14	108	Gal 3:1–3	223
Gal 1:16	105–106, 110–11, 113, 117	Gal 3:1	97, 143, 152
		Gal 3:2	221
Gal 1:17–18	130	Gal 3:3	152
Gal 1:17	112	Gal 3:5	221
Gal 1:18–2:10	130	Gal 3:6	221, 223
Gal 1:18–21	130	Gal 3:8–9	93
Gal 1:18	90, 112, 131	Gal 3:8	66, 95
Gal 1:19	102, 112	Gal 3:10	221
Gal 1:22–24	73	Gal 3:14–18	107
Gal 2:1–14	81, 105	Gal 3:14	93
Gal 2:1–10	2, 59, 61–62, 77, 102, 107, 119, 130–31, 138, 145	Gal 4:1–11	196
		Gal 4:3	31, 192
		Gal 4:9	31, 192
Gal 2:1–5	86	Gal 4:10	107, 181–82, 198
Gal 2:1–2	87	Gal 4:12–20	92
Gal 2:1	62, 82, 112–13, 130–31	Gal 4:12–16	146
		Gal 4:12	97
Gal 2:2	62, 82, 85, 87, 106, 113	Gal 4:17	96
		Gal 4:20	107
Gal 2:3–7	86	Gal 4:21–31	107–108
Gal 2:3–5	108	Gal 5	96
Gal 2:3ff.	96	Gal 5:1–5	90
Gal 2:3	62, 81, 86–87, 144	Gal 5:2–18	46
		Gal 5:2–12	144
Gal 2:4–6	86–88	Gal 5:2–3	107–108
Gal 2:4–5	61	Gal 5:2ff.	96
Gal 2:4	86, 96	Gal 5:2	108, 198
Gal 2:4b	65	Gal 5:3	92, 108
Gal 2:5	84	Gal 5:6	108
Gal 2:6–8	113	Gal 5:8	96
Gal 2:6	86, 106, 113	Gal 5:10	107
Gal 2:6b	85	Gal 5:11	23, 109, 144, 146
Gal 2:6c	85–86	Gal 5:12	152
Gal 2:7–10	87, 89	Gal 5:13–26	108
Gal 2:7–9	90, 105	Gal 5:14–25	97
Gal 2:7	113, 115	Gal 5:19–23	47
Gal 2:8–9	120	Gal 5:24–6:10	47
Gal 2:8	102, 113	Gal 6:3	86
Gal 2:9	62, 85–86, 89–90, 113–14, 138, 143	Gal 6:10	146
		Gal 6:12–15	198
Gal 2:10	130, 137	Gal 6:12–13	144, 191
Gal 2:11–21	80, 85	Gal 6:12ff.	96
Gal 2:11–14	101, 107, 114	Gal 6:12f.	96
Gal 2:11ff.	82	Gal 6:12	51, 108, 109, 144
Gal 2:11	90, 152		

Gal 6:13	108, 145	Col 2:3	176
Gal 6:15	108	Col 2:4	173–76, 198
Gal 6:17	97	Col 2:5	174
		Col 2:6–19	173
Eph 1:1	166	Col 2:6–15	178
Eph 1:21	234	Col 2:6–7	173, 175–76
Eph 4:14	25	Col 2:8	31, 53, 173–77, 192–93, 195–96, 198–200
Eph 5	234		
Eph 6	234		
		Col 2:9–15	173, 175, 178
Phil 1:1	224	Col 2:10	188, 199
Phil 1:12	160	Col 2:11–15	178
Phil 1:15–18	28	Col 2:11	197
Phil 1:28	28	Col 2:13–15	198
Phil 2:25–30	141	Col 2:13	194, 197
Phil 2:25	100	Col 2:15	199
Phil 3	27–28, 50	Col 2:16–23	186
Phil 3:2–7	27	Col 2:16–17	173, 186, 190
Phil 3:2	28	Col 2:16–17a	173, 175, 179, 182, 189, 193
Phil 3:4–6	28, 66		
Phil 3:9	140	Col 2:16	174–75, 179–80, 182, 186, 188–90, 195, 198
Phil 3:10–11	140		
Phil 3:12–21	27		
Phil 3:18–19	26–27	Col 2:17–19	175
Phil 3:18	27	Col 2:17	174–75, 181, 190–91, 195
Phil 3:19	28		
Phil 3:20–21	140	Col 2:17a	190
Phil 4:8	191	Col 2:17b	173, 181
Phil 4:15–18	121	Col 2:18–19	173, 190
		Col 2:18–19a	193
Col 1:1	166, 169	Col 2:18	31, 32, 171, 173–76, 182–83, 186–92, 195–96, 198, 199
Col 1:3–3:4	173		
Col 1:3–8	174, 195		
Col 1:7	150		
Col 1:8	188	Col 2:18b	191
Col 1:9–10	198	Col 2:19	173, 175, 188, 193, 195–96, 199
Col 1:12–23	175, 198		
Col 1:12–14	173, 194, 198	Col 2:20–3:4	173–75, 189
Col 1:12	198	Col 2:20–23	173–74, 189–90, 193, 196
Col 1:14	198		
Col 1:15–20	169, 172	Col 2:20–21	189
Col 1:15–17	198	Col 2:20	31, 53, 174–76, 186, 189–90, 192, 195, 199
Col 1:15	199, 235		
Col 1:16	199		
Col 1:20–23	173	Col 2:21–22	52, 175
Col 1:20–22	198	Col 2:21	174, 180, 189
Col 1:21–23	198	Col 2:22	189–90, 195
Col 1:21	194	Col 2:22a	193
Col 1:24–2:5	173	Col 2:23	52, 174, 178, 183, 189–90, 192, 195–96
Col 1:24–26	140		
Col 1:27	194, 199		
Col 2:1	160	Col 3	235
Col 2:2–3	175, 198	Col 3:1–4	174–75

Col 3:1–3	192	2 Thess 2:17	159
Col 3:1–2	174	2 Thess 3:3	159
Col 3:1	173, 192		
Col 3:2	192	1 Tim 1:1	166
Col 3:3	174, 199	1 Tim 1:3–11	42
Col 3:4	174	1 Tim 4:1–7	42
Col 3:5	194	1 Tim 4:3	180
Col 3:7	194	1 Tim 4:14	159
Col 3:9	191	1 Tim 6:3–5	42
Col 3:10	199	1 Tim 6:20–21	42
Col 3:11	197		
Col 3:12	183, 188, 198	2 Tim 1:1	166
Col 3:13	198–99	2 Tim 2:16	159
Col 4:2–6	195	2 Tim 2:18	43
Col 4:7–10	143	2 Tim 3:1–9	42
Col 4:12	150		
Col 4:13	150	Titus 1:1	166
Col 4:18	169	Titus 1:10–16	42
		Titus 3:8–9	42
1 Thess 1:7–9	134		
1 Thess 1:8–9	131	Heb 8:5	181
1 Thess 2:1–13	35	Heb 10:1	181
1 Thess 2:1–12	34		
1 Thess 2:1–10	34	Jas 1:22	220
1 Thess 2:3	35	Jas 1:23	220
1 Thess 2:7	102, 110	Jas 1:25	220
1 Thess 2:8	34	Jas 4:4	231
1 Thess 2:9	121	Jas 4:11	220
1 Thess 2:11	119		
1 Thess 2:14–16	108–109, 140	1 Pet 1:1	100
1 Thess 2:14	224	1 Pet 2:9	231
1 Thess 2:17	134	1 Pet 2:13–17	231
1 Thess 2:18	134		
1 Thess 3:2	159	2 Pet 1:1	100
1 Thess 4:13–5:11	33	2 Pet 3:2	100
1 Thess 4:13–18	137, 140		
1 Thess 4:13	160	Jude 17	100
2 Thess 1:4	224	Rev 2:2	100
2 Thess 1:6–10	140	Rev 18:20	100
2 Thess 2:1–2	38	Rev 19:10	56
2 Thess 2:2	36	Rev 21:14	100
		Rev 22:9	56

PSEUDEPIGRAPHA

2 Bar. 9:2	183	*1 En.* 1–36	213
2 Bar. 12:5	183	*1 En.* 10:16–11:2	213
2 Bar. 21:1	183	*1 En.* 10:16	213
2 Bar. 47:2	183	*1 En.* 10:20–11:2	213
2 Bar. 54:6–7	52	*1 En.* 14	188
		1 En. 38:2	214
3 Bar. 4:13–15	52	*1 En.* 40:6	188

INDEX OF ANCIENT SOURCES 247

1 En. 41:1	214	*Jos. Asen.* 8:5	207
1 En. 46:7–8	188	*Jos. Asen.* 15:3–4	207
1 En. 61:8	214		
1 En. 81–108	213	*Jub.* 1:14	179
1 En. 100:7	214	*Jub.* 30:17	212
1 En. 100:9	214	*Jub.* 30:23	212
1 En. 102:6	214		
1 En. 102:11	215	*LAB* 64:7	222
1 En. 103:2–4	215	*LAB* 164:7	218
1 En. 108:7	183		
1 En. 108:9	183	*T. Ben.* 11:4	217
		T. Levi 13:5	216
3 En. 18	183	*T. Naph.* 8:4	217, 222
3 En. 35:6	183	*T. Reub.* 4:1	216
3 En. 39	183	*T. Reub.* 4:6	216
4 Ezra 5:13	52	*Sib. Or.* 3:233	215
4 Ezra 5:20	183		
4 Ezra 6:31	52	*Pss. Sol.* 9:3–5	208
4 Ezra 6:35	52, 183	*Pss. Sol.* 14:1–2	208
4 Ezra 7:77	217	*Pss. Sol.* 17–18	209
4 Ezra 7:125	183	*Pss. Sol.* 17:26	209
4 Ezra 8:33	217	*Pss. Sol.* 17:30	209
4 Ezra 9:23–28	52	*Pss. Sol.* 17:36	209
		Pss. Sol. 17:43	209
Hist. Rech. 12:8–9	218	*Pss. Sol.* 18:5	209
Hist. Rech. 12:9a	219	*Pss. Sol.* 18:8	209
Hist. Rech. 12:9e	219		
Hist. Rech. 12:9g	219		

QUMRAN

1QH 11[3]:19–23	186	1QS 10:25	225
1QH 14	86	1QS 11:12	225
1QH 19–20	86		
		1QpHab 2:3	225
1QM 4:10	225	1QpHab 7:10–12	219
		1QpHab 7:11	220
1QS 1:21	225	1QpHab 8:1–3	219
1QS 5:21	220	1QpHab 8:1	220
1QS 5:22	224	1QpHab 12:4–5	220
1QS 6:1	224		
1QS 6:7–9	224	1Q14 frgs. 8–10 lines 5–9	219
1QS 6:11–21	224	1Q28a 2:8–9	186
1QS 6:12	224	1Q34bis frg. 3 ii 6	225
1QS 6:18	220		
1QS 6:20	180, 224	4Q171 frgs. 1–2 ii 14	219–20
1QS 6:25	224	4Q174 frgs. 1–2 i 7	220
1QS 7:3	224	4Q174 frgs. 1–3 ii 2	219
1QS 7:20	180	4Q176 frg. 17 line 7	219
1QS 9:26–10:8	193	4Q204 5:3–4	213
1QS 10:23	225	4Q249g frg. 8 vii 1	225

4Q258 2:1	220	11Q19 25:11–12	183
4Q258 2:3	220	11Q19 27:7	183
4Q261 frg. 1a–b 203	220	11Q19 47:7	180
4Q265 frg. 4 ii 6	220	11Q19 49:7ff.	180
4Q284a frg. 1	180		
4Q394–399	221	CD 3:12–21	226
4Q398 frgs. 14–17 ii 1–8	221	CD 6:19	225
4Q399 frg. 1 i 9–11 + ii 1–5	221	CD 8:21	225
4Q400 2:2 = 14 i 8	184	CD 9:18–19	224
4Q403 1 i 10–29	184	CD 9:22	224
4Q403 1 i 30–33	184	CD 13:6–7	224
4Q470 frg. 1 line 4	219	CD 13:7	224
4Q509 frg. 97–98 i 8	225	CD 14:7	224
4Q511 10:11	186	CD 14:12	224
4QMMT C27	221–22	CD 15:8	224
4QMMT C31	221–22	CD 20:11–12	225
4QMMT C32–35	221		

Rabbinic Writings

Targums

Tg. Jer 12:5	203	*y. Ber.* 13a	184

Tosefta

Mishnah

		t. Hul. 2:18	185
m. 'Abot 2:16	206	*t. Sotah* 15:11–15	180
m. Hag. 2:21	191		

Other

Talmuds

		'Abot R. Nat. 23a	183
b. B. Metzia 59b	93		
b. Gitt. 59b	86		

Philo

Philo, *Contempl.* 37	180	Philo, *Migr.*	182

Josephus

Josephus, *Ant.* 12.147–153	194	Josephus, *Ant.* 20.197–203	65, 86
Josephus, *Ant.* 12.253	186	Josephus, *Ant.* 20.201	86
Josephus, *Ant.* 14.261	197	Josephus, *Ap.* 1.42	192

Christian Authors

Did. 11.6	102, 122	Herm., *Sim.* 5.3.7	183
Did. 11.12	102	Herm., *Vis.* 3.10.6	183
Did. 13.1–2	102	Ignatius, *Magn.* 8.1	197
Diogn. 4.1	195	Ignatius, *Magn.* 9.1–2	197
Diogn. 8.2	178, 195	Ignatius, *Magn.* 10.3	197
		Ignatius, *Phld.* 6.1–2	197

OTHER ANCIENT SOURCES

Appian, *Hist. rom.* 9	79	Polybius, *Hist.* 2.24.10	79
		Polybius, *Hist.* 3.95.8	79
Arist. 18	217	Polybius, *Hist.* 4.3.7	79
Arist. 30–31	177	Polybius, *Hist.* 10.20.2	79
		Polybius, *Hist.* 13.5.7	79
Cicero, *Pro Flacco* 28.68	194	Polybius, *Hist.* 14.3.7	79
		Polybius, *Hist.* 15.5.4–5	79
Eusebius, *Hist. Ecc.* 3.31.2–5	194	Polybius, *Hist.* 30.27.1–2	79
Plato, *Rep.* 2.361b–362a	85		

INDEX OF MODERN AUTHORS

Abbott, T. K.   30
Abegg, M. G., Jr.   213, 221–22
Abrams, D.   83
Achtemeier, P. J.   81
Ådna, J.   187
Aland, K.   179, 192
Aletti, J.-N.   162, 169
Allo, E.-B.   117, 124
Archer, G. L.   228
Argell, G.   36
Arndt, W.   134, 176
Arnold, C. E.   31, 51, 53–58, 153, 170–72, 176, 179, 184–87, 193
Attridge, H. W.   170
Aune, D. E.   105, 124, 153
Aus, R.   36, 89–90
Avery-Peck, A. J.   225

Bachmann, M.   221
Bammel, E.   71, 126
Bandstra, A. J.   32
Bar-Ilan, M.   56, 184–85
Barclay, J. M. G.   20, 48, 108–109, 120, 124, 157, 194, 196
Barnett, P. W.   153
Barrett, C. K.   10, 13, 15, 60, 85–87, 89, 99, 101, 108, 116–18, 121, 124
Baslez   132
Bassler, J. M.   21, 28
Bauckham, R.   71, 75, 95
Bauer, W.   11, 61, 83, 134, 176, 183, 186
Baumbach, G.   26–27
Baur, F. C.   1, 4, 7–13, 15, 59, 155
Baylor   106
Beer, G.   179
Beker, J. C.   21
Benoit, P.   25–26, 181
Berger, K.   44–45, 172
Berger, P. L.   83, 88, 96
Best, E.   24, 35, 37–38
Betz, H. D.   18–19, 34, 70, 77–78, 81, 84, 86–88, 91, 102, 106–108, 111–13, 124, 142–43
Betz, O.   151
Billerbeck, P.   180
Black, D. A.   118, 124
Black, M.   28, 179

Black. J. S.   211
Blass, F.   186
Bligh, J.   17
Blinzler, J.   192
Blommerde, A. C. M.   86
Böcher, O.   31
Boissevain, J.   61
Bonnard, P.   17
Borgen, P.   21, 107–108, 124
Bormann, L.   170
Bornkamm, G.   114, 118, 124
Boyarin, D.   106–107, 110, 124
Brewer, R.   29
Brinsmead, B. H.   104, 109, 124
Broekhoven, H. Van   172
Brown, F.   183
Brown, R. E.   60, 101, 106–107, 124, 169
Brox, N.   39–40
Bruce, F. F.   30, 36–37, 149, 156–57, 163, 179
Buck, C.   132, 134–35
Buckland, W. W.   100, 124
Bujard, W.   169
Bultmann, R.   118, 124
Burger, C.   178
Burkhardt, H.   180
Burkitt, F. C.   81
Burton, E. D. W.   17, 63–64, 78–79, 81, 83, 85–86, 96, 107–108, 124
Bush, P. G.   39
Buttrick, G. A.   18
Byrne, B.   19

Cadbury, H.   135
Caird, G. B.   28–29, 31
Campbell, W. S.   162
Campenhausen, H. F. von   112, 124
Cannon, G. E.   169
Carroll, J. T.   129
Carroll, M. D.   162
Carroll, R. P.   203
Carson, D. A.   152
Castelli, E. A.   106, 124
Chae, D. J.-S.   166
Charles, R. H.   212–13, 216–17
Charlesworth, J. H.   212, 218–19

Chilton, B.   203, 225
Chow, M. K.-M.   116, 121, 124
Church, F. F.   35
Cohen, S. J. D.   109, 124
Cole, H. R.   181
Collange, J.-F.   26, 28
Collins, R. F.   34–35, 106, 116–17
Conzelmann, H.   40, 124
Cook, J. I.   131
Cosgrove, C. H.   22, 45–46, 48, 129
Court, J. M.   15
Crafton, J. A.   118–21, 124
Cranfield, C. E. B.   155, 224
Cremer, H.   193
Crownfield, F. R.   19
Cullmann, O.   199

Dahl, N.   14, 44
Danby, H.   206
Danker, F.   134, 176
Das, A. A.   165
Davies, P. R.   162
Davies, W. D.   180
De Roo, J. C. R.   224
Deane, W. J.   207
Debrunner, A.   186
Delling, G.   176
DeMaris, R. E.   31, 171–72, 176, 178–79, 183, 194
Deming, W.   42
Denis, A.-M.   325
Denova, R.   94
Di Lella, A. A.   205–206
Dibelius, M.   30, 37, 40, 187
Dix, D. G.   77
Dobschütz, E. von   35, 37
Donfried, K. P.   34, 149, 152, 154, 158, 225
Doty, W. G.   153, 160
Drane, J. W.   149
Duncan, G. W.   17
Dunderberg, I.   224
Dunn, J. D. G.   20–21, 60–61, 64, 75, 78, 80, 99, 101–102, 104, 106–108, 110–15, 124, 137, 143, 169–70, 172, 174, 180, 182, 189, 191, 194, 196, 198–99, 221, 224

Ebeling, G.   20
Egger, W.   25
Ehrhardt, A. A. T.   100, 124
Ellicott, C. J.   18
Ellis, E. E.   7, 9, 19, 151
Endres, J. C.   224

Eriksson, A.   173
Ernst, J.   25, 27, 29
Esler, P. F.   81, 164
Evans, C. A.   5, 170, 183, 186–87
Everling, O.   199
Ewald, P.   176
Ezioni, A.   84

Fairweather, E.   136
Fairweather, W.   211
Farmer, W. R.   14, 135
Fee, G.   14, 41, 43, 116, 124
Fiebig, D.   179
Fischel, H. A.   211
Fischer, D. H.   48, 58
Fitzmyer, J.   132, 222, 225
Flint, P. W.   220–22
Foerster, W.   77
Fohrer, G.   28
Ford, D. F.   199
Fortna, R. T.   25–26, 29, 134
Fossum, J.   180
Frame, J. E.   33, 37
Francis, F. O.   30, 32, 77, 171, 182–84, 186–88, 191
Fredriksen, P.   59, 80, 96
Frerichs, E. S.   125
Friedrich, G.   33, 36, 38
Fuchs, E.   78
Fuller, R. H.   117, 124
Fung, R. Y. K.   78
Furnish, V. P.   118, 121, 124, 140, 142

Gager, J. G.   60
Gamble, H., Jr.   154
Gamson, W. A.   74
Gasque, W. W.   126, 163
Gaston, L.   109, 114, 117, 124
Gathercole, S. J.   222, 224
Gaventa, B. R.   18, 21, 25–26, 105, 125, 134
Gebauer, R.   170, 199
Gempf, C.   156
George, T.   35
Georgi, D.   12, 16, 53, 57, 61, 82, 99, 114, 116, 118–19, 121, 125, 163
Gesenius, W.   183
Gewiess, J.   30
Giblin, C. H.   36–37
Gill, D.   156
Gillman, F.   34
Gingrich, F.   134, 176
Gnilka, J.   25, 29
Goodman, M.   72–73, 93

INDEX OF MODERN AUTHORS

Goodrick, A. T. S. 207
Goodspeed, E. J. 131
Goranson, S. 220
Gorman, M. J. 165
Goulder, M. 4, 10–11, 24, 151, 171
Gouldner, A. W. 82
Green, W. S. 120, 125
Grenholm, C. 162
Gritz, S. H. 40
Gruchy, J. W. de 126
Gruenwald, I. 186
Grundmann, W. 183
Gundry, R. H. 36, 224
Gunther, J. J. 4, 15, 108, 116, 118, 125, 149, 170
Guthrie, D. 171

Haacker, K. 31, 163
Hafemann, S. 15, 187
Hagner, D. A. 60, 149
Hall, R. G. 18, 105, 108, 125
Hamerton-Kelly, R. 31
Hanson, A. T. 39, 100, 125
Hare, D. R. A. 129
Harnisch, W. 33–34
Harrington, D. 170–72, 180, 194–96, 218
Harris, M. J. 149
Hartin, P. J. 87
Harvey, A. E. 18
Haufe, G. 39–40
Haupt, E. 175–76, 181, 183, 186, 191
Hawthorne, G. F. 15, 151, 153, 186
Hay, D. M. 85–87, 91
Hedrick, C. 51
Hegel, C. 8
Heilgenthal, R. 21
Hengel, M. 106, 125, 151, 163, 177, 184, 187, 194
Hennecke, E. 185
Héring, J. 117, 125
Hester, J. D. 105, 125
Hickling, C. J. A. 44–45
Hill, C. C. 75, 95
Hock, R. 35, 121, 125
Hodgson, R., Jr. 51
Hoehner, H. W. 169
Hoffmann, E. G. 176, 178
Hofius, O. 112, 125, 187
Hogg, M. A. 83
Holladay, C. 16
Holladay, W. 203
Holmberg, B. 101–102, 106, 114, 116, 118, 121, 125

Holtzmann, O. 179
Hooker, M. 2, 21, 29, 45, 126, 150, 174–75, 199
Horbury, W. 33, 35
Horrell, D. G. 116, 121, 125
Horsley, R. A. 14
Houlden, J. L. 25–26, 29
Howard, G. 21, 107, 109, 112, 125, 201
Hughes, F. W. 34, 37–38
Hurd, J. C. 116, 124, 134

Isaac, E. 214–15

Jacobson, H. 218
James, M. R. 208
Jastrow, M. 185
Jeffers, J. S. 154
Jenkins, R. 79
Jervell, J. 163
Jervis, L. A. 13, 150
Jewett, R. 18–19, 27–28, 33–34, 37, 69, 99, 125, 133, 136, 201
Johanson, B. C. 35
Johnson, E. E. 129
Johnson, L. T. 39, 42–44, 51, 151
Johnson, M. D. 154
Jones, J. W. 100, 125
Joyce, P. 68

Käsemann, E. 1, 16–17, 118, 125
Karris, R. J. 42, 155
Kaye, B. N. 37–38
Kehl, N. 185
Kelly, J. N. D. 39
Kennedy, G. A. 104–105, 125
Keown, G. 203
Kern, P. J. 104, 125
Kertelge, K. 17, 39
Kertzer, D. I. 94
Kilpatrick, G. D. 28
Kim, S. 106, 110–11
King, D. 19
Kittel, G. 85, 192, 194
Klein, G. 100, 125, 158
Klijn, A. F. J. 26
Knight, G. W., III 40
Knox, J. 129–30, 132–35, 137–38, 146
Koch, D. 27
Koester, H. 25, 35, 108, 125
Koptak, P. E. 85, 95
Kraabel, A. T. 170–71
Kraft, R. A. 11
Krause, M. 51
Kretschmar, G. 180

Krodel, G.   11, 36
Kuck, D. W.   14
Kümmel, W. G.   107, 118, 125, 170

Lähnemann, J.   171
Lagrange, M.-J.   17
Lake, K.   81
Lambers-Petry, D.   195
Lambrecht, J.   34
Lampe, P.   154, 156
Lane, W. L.   42
Lang, F.   193
LaSor, W. S.   180
Lategan, B. C.   18, 22, 104, 125
Légasse, S.   71, 132
Leon, H.   156
Lévi, I.   206
Lewis, E.   30
Liddell, H. G.   178
Liertaert Peerbolte, L. J.   166
Lightfoot, J. B.   7, 11, 30, 81, 150, 170–71
Limburg, J.   204
Lindars, B.   2, 29, 150, 174
Linton, O.   20
Llewelyn, S. R.   156
Lock, W.   42–43
Logan, A. H. B.   9
Lohmeyer, E.   26
Lohse, E.   15, 29–30
Longenecker, B. W.   104, 125
Longenecker, R. N.   32, 64, 81, 84, 102, 105–108, 112–13, 125, 162, 201
Lovering, E.   11
Lüdemann, G.   4, 10, 13, 15, 60, 63, 99, 116, 118, 125, 149, 151, 162
Lührmann, D.   45, 172
Lütgert, W.   11, 15, 18
Lull, D.   19–20
Luther, M.   186
Lyons, G.   105, 125

MacDonald, D. R.   41
MacDonald, M. Y.   24
MacLennan, R. S.   170
Malherbe, A.   34–36
Malina, B. J.   74, 82–83, 110, 112, 125
Marshall, I. H.   33, 35, 169
Marshall, P.   116, 121, 125
Martin, R. P.   15, 24, 27, 31, 126, 153, 163, 186
Martin, S.   126

Martin, T.   31, 51–53, 57–58, 72, 178, 181–82
Martyn, J. L.   21, 25–26, 44–45, 107, 109, 126, 137, 143
Marxsen, W.   36, 38, 156
Masson, C.   34–35
Mattill, A. J., Jr.   163
Maurer, C.   170
Mayor, J. B.   151
McClelland, S. E.   118–19, 125
McDonald, L. M.   150, 153–55, 158, 160, 164
McEleney, N. J.   42
McLean, B. C.   102, 110, 113, 125
Mcnair, A. D.   100, 124
Meade, D.   150
Mearns, C. L.   25
Meecham, H. G.   218
Meeks, W. A.   30, 32, 67, 116, 126, 171
Meier, J. P.   60, 101, 106–107, 124
Meiser, M.   170
Melanchthon, P.   186
Mell, U.   187
Menge, H.   178
Menken, M. J. J.   37–38
Merk, O.   170
Meurer, S.   192
Meyer, P.   129
Michael, H.   27
Michaelis, W.   78
Michel, O.   177, 181
Millar, F.   179
Milligan, G.   35
Minear, P. S.   26, 155
Mitchell, M. M.   14, 117, 125
Moo, D.   13
Moore, A. L.   33
Moore, C. A.   210
Moray-Jones, C. R. A.   117, 126
Morgan, R.   165
Mosbech, H.   100, 126
Moses, A. D. A.   86, 89
Moule, C. F. D.   14, 126, 135, 150, 174, 183
Muddiman, J.   68
Müller, U.   41, 43
Mullins, T. Y.   160
Munck, J.   18, 35, 99–100, 109–10, 116–17, 126, 155
Murphy-O'Connor, J.   39, 41, 43, 65–66, 101, 104, 107–108, 112, 126, 131, 153
Mussner, F.   17

INDEX OF MODERN AUTHORS

Nanos, M.   2, 22–23, 46–48, 66–67, 69, 76–77, 80, 85, 151, 162, 165, 201
Neil, W.   33
Nestle, E.   179
Neumann, K. J.   169
Neusner, J.   7, 19, 124–25, 186, 225
Newsom, C.   184–86
Neyrey, J. H.   82–83, 110, 112, 125
Nickelsburg, G. W. E.   212–15
Nickle, K. F.   142, 163
Niebuhr, R. R.   14, 135
Nock, A. D.   227

Oberlinner, L.   39–40
O'Brien, P. T.   25, 29, 152–53, 186, 194
Oden, T. C.   42
Oepke, A.   36
Olbricht, T. H.   29, 173, 199
Ollrog, W.-H.   169
Oostendorp, D.   9, 15
Orchard, B.   86
Orton, D. E.   68
Overman, J. A.   170

Parsons, M. C.   135
Patte, D.   162
Paul, I.   169
Pearson, B. A.   14
Pearson, B. W. R.   150, 224
Percy, E.   32, 174, 176, 183
Peristiany, J. G.   83
Perkins, P.   23, 25, 27–28
Petzer, J. H.   87
Pitt-Rivers, J.   82
Pitts, J. R.   84
Plummer, A.   116–17, 126
Pogoloff, S. M.   14
Pokorny, P.   24
Poorthuis, M.   56, 184
Porter, S. E.   29, 68, 150, 153–55, 158, 160–64, 199, 224
Price, S. R. F.   227

Qimron, E.   221

Räisänen, H.   20, 224–25
Ramaroson   173
Rapa, R. K.   151
Rapske, B.   156
Reasoner, M.   165
Reed, J. T.   153
Reicke, B.   36, 108, 126
Reid, D. G.   153, 186

Rengstorf, K. H.   91, 100, 117, 126
Reumann, J.   25
Richards, E. R.   156
Richards, J. R.   136
Richardson, P.   77, 96, 124
Ridderbos, H. N.   64
Riddle, D. W.   132, 135
Riesner, R.   101, 106, 126, 133
Rigaux, B.   34–35, 38
Riggenbach, E.   182
Roberts, J. H.   171, 174, 186–88, 194–95, 198, 200
Robertson, A.   116–17, 126
Robinson, J. A. T.   237
Robinson, J. M.   125
Roetzel, C.   33
Roloff, J.   39–40
Ropes, J. H.   18
Rosenbaum, M. J.   68–69
Rowland, C. C.   32, 117, 126, 181, 183, 187, 190–91
Royalty, R. M.   170–72
Rusam, D.   192
Russell, R.   38
Ryle, H. E.   208

Sampley, J. P.   77, 115, 126
Sanders, E. P.   19, 80, 109, 126, 132, 222
Sandmel, S.   48
Sandnes, K. O.   110, 126
Sappington, T. J.   32, 52, 170–71, 173, 176, 179, 183, 188, 191
Saunders, R.   4–5
Scalise, P.   203
Schäfer, P.   184
Schenk, W.   26, 29, 39, 172
Schiffman, L. H.   225
Schlatter, A.   15, 77, 190
Schlier, H.   24, 35, 78
Schmithals, W.   4, 9–10, 13, 15–16, 18, 27, 57, 77, 100, 109–10, 112, 116–18, 126, 161, 163
Schnackenburg, R.   100, 117, 126
Schneemelcher, W.   185
Schnider, F.   153
Scholder, K.   1
Scholem, G.   184
Schubert, P.   153
Schürer, E.   179, 184
Schütz, J. H.   110, 112–14, 117, 126
Schulz, S.   181
Schwartz, J.   56, 184

Schweizer, E.   31, 169, 171, 192, 194
Schwemer, A.-M.   177, 184–85
Scott, D. F.   40
Scott, E. F.   31
Scott, R.   178
Scroggs, R.   31
Sederberg, P. C.   68–69, 91
Segal, A. F.   21–22, 110, 126
Segal, M.   205
Seifrid, M. A.   152
Seland, T.   69, 75
Sellin, G.   14, 116, 118, 126
Siebenthal, H. von   176, 178
Sievers, J.   162
Skehan, P. W.   205–206
Slee, M.   108, 126
Smalley, S. S.   2, 29, 150, 174
Smallwood, E. M.   156
Smit, J.   18, 104, 126
Smith, D. C.   24
Smith, T. V.   111, 126
Smothers, T. G.   203
Spicq, C.   40, 43
Stamm, R. T.   18
Standhartinger, A.   170, 176, 178, 181, 188
Stanton, G. N.   199
Stendahl, K.   106, 110, 126
Stenger, W.   153
Stettler, C.   3
Stirewalt, M. L., Jr.   152
Stökel Ben Ezra, D.   195
Strack, H.   180
Strecker, G.   15, 45, 172
Strobel, A.   182
Strugnell, J.   221
Stuhlmacher, P.   180
Sumney, J. L.   3, 11, 14, 17, 28, 34, 48, 116–18, 120, 126, 149–50, 153, 164, 172–74, 176, 178, 182–83, 188–89, 191–92, 198–99
Swartz, M. J.   84
Syreeni, K.   224

Talbert, C.   135
Talshir, Z.   211
Taylor, N. H.   2, 99, 101–104, 106–14, 116–17, 121, 126
Taylor, G.   132, 134
Tenney, M. C.   32, 228
Theissen, G.   116, 118, 120, 126
Thielman, F.   19
Thrall, M. E.   118–19, 126

Tomson, P. J.   195, 222
Tov, E.   225
Towner, P.   39–40
Toy, C. H.   205
Trafton, J. L.   208
Travis, S.   169
Trebilco, P. R.   194
Tredici, K. del   170
Trilling, W.   36
Tröger, K. W.   26, 39
Trudinger, L. P.   112, 127
Trummer, P.   39
Tuckett, C. M.   224
Tuden, A.   84
Turner, V. W.   84
Tyson, J. B.   44–45, 135

Übelacker, W.   173
Ulonska, H.   27

VanderKam, J. C.   220, 222, 225
Vanhoye, A.   23, 33–34
Vergeer, W. C.   181–82
Vermes, G.   179
Verner, D. C.   40
Vielhauer, P.   171

Wahlde, U. C. von   71–72
Walker, W. O., Jr.   86
Walter, N.   23
Walters, J. C.   154, 157
Wanamaker, C. A.   34, 38, 120, 126
Wasserberg, G.   162
Watson, D. F.   125
Watson, F. B.   20, 59, 108, 116, 118, 120–21, 126, 165
Wedderburn, A. J. M.   9, 150, 152, 161
Weiss, H.-F.   181–82
Wenham, D.   86, 89
Westerholm, S.   152
White, J. L.   153, 160
Whiteley, D. E. H.   33, 37
Wiefel, W.   154, 156
Wilckens, U.   89, 181
Wildberger, H.   202
Wiles, G. P.   154
Willis, W. L.   117, 126
Wilson, R. McL.   45, 118, 126
Wilson, S. G.   21, 45
Wink, W.   179
Winter, B. W.   87, 116, 126
Wintermute, O. S.   212

Wisse, F. 51
Wolter, M. 172
Wright, N.T. 2, 172, 174, 179, 196, 222
Wuellner, W. 34

Ysebaert, J. 183

Zahn, T. 74, 185–86, 193
Zetterholm, M. 108, 127

PAULINE STUDIES

ISSN 1572-4913

The name of "Paul" continues to stand at the heart of New Testament studies—as one of the first and most important interpreters and promulgators of Jesus Christ. Wherever he went as missionary, teacher, and preacher, or wherever his letters went in his stead, he rarely failed to cause a reaction. Paul continues to stand at the centre of theology and controversy, as scholars and laity alike continue to respond to him.

This series of volumes of essays by a variety of different scholars is edited by the well-known scholar Stanley Porter. The series offers an important contribution to New Testament scholarship in general, and particularly to Pauline scholarship, by uniquely focusing upon major areas of Pauline studies in order to throw new light on many different aspects of the man and his work. The scholars involved bring various interpretative methods to their task, depending upon their own approaches and the nature of the topic itself. The volumes progress logically through several of the issues of continuing importance in Pauline studies. As a result, the series is both broad in scope and focused and particular in approach.

1. PORTER, S.E. (ed.), *The Pauline Canon*. 2004
   ISBN 90 04 13891 9
2. PORTER, S.E. (ed.), *Paul and His Opponents*. 2005
   ISBN 90 04 14701 2

www.ingramcontent.com/pod-product-compliance
Lightning Source LLC
Chambersburg PA
CBHW030339240426
43661CB00052B/1684